The Turner Farm Fauna:
5000 Years of Hunting and Fishing
in Penobscot Bay, Maine

Arthur E. Spiess and Robert A. Lewis

Occasional Publications in Maine Archaeology
Number Eleven
2001

The Maine State Museum, The Maine Historic Preservation Commission
and the Maine Archaeological Society
Augusta

Occastional Publications in Maine Archaelology
Series Editor: Arthur E. Spiess

©2001 The Maine State Museum and The Maine Historic Preservation Commission
Augusta, Maine

ISBN 0–935447–14–8

Cover design by Donald Bassett
Maine State Museum

Contents

CHAPTER 1. Shell Midden Archaeology and the Turner Farm

CHAPTER 2. Analytical Methods

CHAPTER 4. Living Floors or Garbage Dump: Variability Within the Occupation 4 Levels

CHAPTER 5. Animal Behavior and Human Harvest Techniques:
Background for the Turner Farm Study

CHAPTER 6. The Turner Farm Fauna Synthesis:
Human Subsistence and Environmental Change

Preface

This volume is a monument to the exceptional talent and dogged persistence of two faunal analysts whose different interests and skills combined to produce the sophisticated and comprehensive analysis presented herein. Since 1978, day after day, year after year, I witnessed Arthur Spiess and Robert Lewis collaborate to solve a seemingly endless series of difficult analytical tasks and then to draft this synthesis of their efforts. Their feat is the more remarkable because of the ample distractions provided by their other professional responsibilities. In its size and complexity, the Turner Farm site faunal sample is probably unique among those from North American shell middens, and to Arthur Spiess goes credit for organizing and executing the basic plan of attack upon this daunting corpus. The sample is also highly diverse, fragmentary, and derived from numerous stratigraphically distinct deposits. Robert Lewis, who participated in most of the field work as my very able assistant, deserves credit for maintaining this huge collection in an analysis-ready state, analyzing it stratigraphically, handling the most difficult issues of identification and for carrying out so many of the microscopic and other close examinations that have shed some of the most important beams of light upon the ancient lives of those who created the midden. No one who reads this slim volume will doubt its highly analytical approach. But I hope that these readers will also see that its authors clearly understand the human story they have contributed to. As the initiator and organizer of the Turner Farm project, and the Fox Islands Project of which it is the crown jewel, I cannot express too strongly my appreciation for their selfless efforts.

Bruce J. Bourque
Director of the Fox Islands Project
Maine State Museum

Acknowledgments

Initial analysis of the Turner Farm site faunal sample was supported by National Science Foundation grant #13035 (Bourque and Spiess 1980). Subsequent analysis and the preparation of this monograph continued on a part-time basis with the support of the Maine Historic Preservation Commission for Spiess and the Maine State Museum for Lewis. Donald Bassett designed the cover, layout, charts and figures. Patricia Arey did the drawings of animal bones for chapter two. Ann Robinson provided indispensable and sensitive copy editing. We would like to thank Gary Stratton, Ethos Marketing & Design, of Portland, Maine, for his assistance with this project. We wish to offer special thanks to a group of Maine faunal analysts who provided extensive, thoughtful and helpful comments on a draft of the manuscript: Gerald Bigelow, Diana Crader, John Mosher, Kristin Sobolik, and Richard Will. We are blessed to have such competent and selfless peers.

Finally, we wish to acknowledge stimulating conversations about shell middens and Maine prehistory over many years with Bruce Bourque and Steven Cox, Nathan Hamilton, James B. Peterson, Brian Robinson, and David Sanger.

1
Shell Midden Archaeology and the Turner Farm

Introduction

The Turner Farm site (Figure 1–1) is a large stratified shell midden on the Island of North Haven in Penobscot Bay, Maine (Figure 1–2). Composed mainly of mollusk shell refuse, it is in many ways typical of the region's numerous coastal shell middens. It is unique in one respect, however: its cultural deposits span five millennia from about 5300 B.P. to the early contact period. With its bone-preserving shell-rich matrix, this makes it the longest and richest known surviving record of coastal occupation in the Gulf of Maine region.

The field work phase of the Turner Farm archaeological project spanned the decade of the 1970s. The corpus of data generated by that work is the largest from any site in New England and its analysis has been ongoing since fieldwork began. Much of this analysis was published in Bourque 1995. This volume presents in detail our analysis of the faunal remains, which Bourque summarized only briefly.

During this extended period, the field of zooarchaeology has developed rapidly. The large size and high quality of the Turner Farm site faunal sample has provided us with an opportunity to contribute to this development. Some of the innovations we introduced during our research include: a method for increasing the accuracy of standard faunal evidence measures such as minimum numbers of individuals; season of death determination from mollusk shell, fish bone and mammal teeth; the development of indexes of relative abundance for prey species; and the reconstruction of human diet from light stable isotopes in bone (reported in Bourque 1995:138–140).

HISTORY OF THE PROJECT

The Turner Farm project began in 1971 when Bourque directed a field school there under the auspices of the

State University of New York at Albany. Excavations continued each summer thereafter until 1975. In 1977, test excavations were made in a salt marsh adjacent to the midden and in the beach in front of it. A final brief excavation took place during the summer of 1980 (Bourque 1995). Lewis' involvement began in 1972 when Bourque joined the Maine State Museum staff. Thereafter, Lewis served as assistant project director and provided primary assistance to Spiess during the faunal analysis and report preparation. Spiess' involvement with the Turner Farm faunal analysis began in late 1977, when Bourque sought his experience in determining the seasons in which certain fauna died by sectioning and reading tooth cementum increments (Spiess 1976a; Bourque, Morris, and Spiess 1978). Bourque and Spiess (1980) subsequently obtained support from the National Science Foundation allowing Spiess to pursue the analysis, during which he and Lewis identified almost 15,000 vertebrate specimens. Faunal material from the first three seasons at the site had previously been analyzed by David Morse for a Master of Arts thesis (Morse 1975). Morse's analysis, however, did not produce the detail necessary for the types of questions that interested us. For this and other reasons, a complete reanalysis and identification was undertaken for this project.

Primary faunal analysis work continued part time through 1984 by Spiess and Lewis, with assistance from Mark Hedden on fish bone. Spiess took a position as Maine Historic Preservation Commission archaeologist in mid-1978, and soon thereafter produced a draft manuscript report (1979) on the Turner Farm site data. Subsequently, 15 years of experience with Maine archaeology and in interpreting archaeofaunas from New England and the eastern Arctic has led Spiess and Lewis to revise sections of the draft report pertaining to animal behavior, paleoethnography and data interpretation, and to include small amounts of new data generated since 1980. Revised drafts were prepared in early 1985, and again in 1988–1989. Bourque

(1995) summarizes the faunal information presented in the latter draft (cited as Spiess and Lewis 1993) describing the faunal contents of features, and the horizontal distribution patterns of the faunal remains.

ORGANIZATION OF THE VOLUME

Chapter 1 discusses the history and goals of the Turner Farm faunal identification project, some thoughts on shell midden formation and excavation, and a general discussion of quantification in faunal analysis. Chapter 2 presents a methodological discussion focusing on specific faunal analysis techniques used in the study. Chapter 3 presents the majority of the faunal attribute data grouped by taxon and subdivided by occupation units. Chapter 3 thus presents an overview of the faunal character of each major occupation and also allows diachronic (time-transgressive) comparisons that reveal change in any given taxon or attribute (e.g., age profile of a taxon) over the 5,000 year span of occupation at the site. Chapter 4 presents a detailed study of faunal attribute change within the Ceramic period strata (collectively labeled Occupation 4). Some faunal attributes indicate differences in the origins of the Occupation 4 deposits, as well as in the length of time during which they accumulated. Thus, Chapter 4

attempts a finer-scaled chronological resolution within the Ceramic period than has been attempted for the other occupations. Discussion of plow zone fauna is included in Chapter 4, where it adds perspective on temporal trends within Occupation 4. Chapter 5 summarizes relevant facts about the modern behavior of the animal species represented in the site, and presents ethnographic analogues that suggest how they may have been harvested. Chapter 6 applies these observations to the faunal attributes from Chapters 3 and 4 in an attempt to reconstruct seasonal rounds and activity patterning, and to suggest the hunting and gathering techniques that may have been used by the site's inhabitants. Finally, Chapter 6 puts the Turner Farm study in perspective with a critical review of other shell midden faunal studies in the region.

PURPOSE OF THE STUDY

When we began this project there were no comprehensive, published studies of archaeological fauna in the Northeast. We really had little understanding of the subsistence patterns practiced by Archaic coastal cultures north of Cape Cod and little quantitative information on those of the Ceramic period.

Table 1-1. Numbers of vertebrate faunal specimens (NISP) identified to genus or species from the Turner Farm site collection, grouped by taxon and occupation. This summary table provides a sense of the size and complexity of the collection. See Table 4-1 for definitions of abbreviations. The small sample from Occupation 1 is not included.

	Late Archaic		Occupation 4						
	OCC. 2	OCC. 3	B2GF	2GF	CCS	1GF	MCS	NGF	FCS
Deer	1023	1060	145	392	862	691	310	9	450
Moose	8	13	2	18	41	32	19	0	26
Seal	27	74	13	34	141	100	79	51	18
Bear	4	13	4	6	21	19	12	0	7
Mink	91	154	29	104	316	204	174	10	103
Beaver	37	104	14	57	165	134	62	3	84
Small Furbearers	35	29	1	7	18	21	10	0	28
Whale	0	0	0	1	1	0	0	0	0
Porpoise	0	0	0	0	5	0	0	0	0
Cod	169	104	15	13	72	23	19	2	20
Flounder	91	106	30	99	608	376	1139	17	296
Swordfish	127	24	3	8	9	8	0	0	1
Sculpin	14	19	14	24	87	120	216	2	69
Sturgeon	12	9	1	36	124	90	52	11	19
Other Fish	47	4	0	9	60	26	24	3	16
Birds	162	323	102	293	695	262	275	3	202
TOTAL	1847	2036	373	1101	3225	2106	2391	65	1439

Figure 1-1. Aerial view of the Turner Farm site under excavation in 1975. North is to the left. The sand and gravel beach, which fronts the site and continues to the west in front of an adjacent salt marsh/bog, is clearly visible to the right.

Our primary goal has been to explore evidence for the seasonality of faunal exploitation and human occupation at the site. Our method has been to rigorously quantify data on the Turner Farm site fauna and to examine them for evidence of change over time. The sample invited extensive analysis because, in addition to its uniquely long stratigraphic sequence, its size — nearly 15,000 vertebrate bones (Table 1–1) — makes it the largest well provenienced sample in New England.

The discovery of a Middle Archaic Stark point on the beach at the Turner Farm site suggests that humans first occupied it more than 6,000 years ago. However the earliest occupation to leave deposits, a series of pit features, dates from around 5,300 to 4,500 B.P. and pertains to the Small Stemmed Point tradition (Bourque 1995:34–35). No midden deposits survive however, apparently because they have been destroyed by bank face erosion. Occupation 2 pertains to the Moorehead phase, which dates from around 4,500 B.P. to 3,800 B.P. Although also reduced by erosion, Occupation 2 and all later deposits include extensive areas

of midden. The Moorehead phase is well known for its "Red Paint" cemeteries. Many of its salient attributes, including Red Paint mortuary ceremonialism, indicate descent from the Small Stemmed Point tradition (Bourque 1995:234–237). At the outset we were aware that the people of the Moorehead phase engaged in swordfish hunting, but we were unsure whether this activity extended back into Occupation 1 times or whether it was of major importance with respect to other marine and terrestrial fishing and hunting (Bourque 1975:36; 1976:25; 1992:119).

The succeeding Occupation 3 is a coastal manifestation of the Susquehanna tradition, a culture clearly intrusive from the south that brought radical changes in stone and bone material culture as well as mortuary behavior (Bourque 1995:7–10, 97–167). We wanted to learn whether the people of Occupation 3 exploited a range of animal resources different from those exploited by earlier occupants, and whether environmental change might have played a role in the transition from one population to the other.

Figure 1-2. Location of the Turner Farm site.

way or planned for the future (especially on other Maine shell middens). We present much of the data in greater detail than would be strictly necessary to draw conclusions about the Turner Farm itself. Archaeology, after all, is a cumulative science where much of the larger picture is derived from multisite comparison, often involving multiple archaeologists. Frankly, we hope that our detailed presentation of faunal analysis techniques may provide useful models for other researchers who are interested in similar questions, so that we can move toward some level of standardization in basic faunal analytical methodology for shell middens in the region.

Shell middens in the New England states and Maritime Provinces (as elsewhere) are cultural deposits, constructed by human discard behavior. When stratigraphically intact and well excavated these sites can reveal living (dwelling) floors, dumping episodes of shellfish and other debris resulting in low piles, and humus or soil development layers subsequently covered by later deposition (e.g., Bourque 1996, Spiess 1988).

An assumption of most shell midden faunal studies, and here as well, is that vertebrate faunal remains in shell middens are always cultural unless obvious and compelling evidence exists to the contrary. Such evidence might be the skeleton of a burrowing mammal found in anatomical position in a collapsed burrow. There is no regular source of vertebrate faunal deposition onto shell middens other than cultural deposition; there is no equivalent, for example, of owl pellet accumulation and mammal carnivore collection of bones in caves.

Cultural accumulation of vertebrate fauna in shell heaps admittedly includes processing and redeposition by dogs, which were probably an integral part of the life of all shell midden inhabitants (Kerber 1997a, 1997b); in fact, we infer a "dog yard" activity area in Occupation 2 of the Turner Farm site (Spiess and Lewis 1995:349). As well as moving and processing human discarded bone, dogs themselves may have contributed a light scatter of various vertebrate parts to many shell middens, perhaps pieces scavenged from the tide line on the adjacent beach. But the dogs were present because the humans were there, so their contribution is broadly cultural. In a similar vein, there might be multiple unintentional cultural contributions of vertebrate and invertebrate fauna to a shell midden by human behavior, such as small, less preferred shellfish species brought on site attached to

The upper strata at the site represent a series of occupations spanning the period from 3,000 B.P. to European contact and are collectively called Occupation 4 (Bourque 1995:10–11, 169–122). The first question concerning Occupation 4 was whether the Susquehanna tradition patterns of faunal exploitation had carried on into later periods. The second question was whether Occupation 4 had been a period of cultural stability, as was the common perception for the Ceramic period in Maine. More particularly, we wanted to learn whether subsistence practices had changed over time, and if so whether those changes were gradual or rapid. We also wanted to learn whether they were intensifications in the use of certain species or shifts to new species.

Regarding the concerns of faunal analysis as summarized in the late 1970s by Yesner (1978; also see Monks 1981), our work is an attempt at detailed data quantification, the primary purpose of which is the reconstruction and comparison of past human activity patterns. Demographic data (including skeletal measurements) of prey species are a prime data source. Taphonomic processes are addressed, but are of lesser concern.

One long range goal of this study is to provide sufficient data for comparison with other faunal studies in the region, published (reviewed in Chapter Six), unpublished (many cultural resource management reports), and under-

Photo: Maine State Museum.

Figure 1-3. Stemmed points from Occupation 1.

other shellfish, or smaller prey fish species brought onto the site inside the stomachs of larger predator fish, such as cod.

Taphonomy, which we define as the study of faunal assemblage formation processes, played only a small part in the analysis presented herein. We recorded some types of bone modification when it was visible and obvious on identifiable bone, but did little with tens of thousands (unquantified) of bone fragments that could not be identified to family, genus or species. This huge unidentifiable sample is dominated by small fragments of large mammal bone, probably mostly deer longbone judging from the frequencies in the identifiable portion of the collection. As the senior author has had the opportunity of examining dog-chewed seal bones among Labrador Inuit faunal samples, we recorded dog chewing when it was obvious, and it was especially visible on seal bones. Deer bone breakage for marrow extraction was

also noted, as were cut marks on some fur bearers indicative of purposeful pelt removal.

TURNER FARM SITE CULTURE HISTORY SUMMARY

Occupation 1 (Bourque 1995:33–39) consists of three submidden features and an associated scatter of stone tools at the midden base (Figure 1–3). Diagnostic artifacts include small stemmed points, a style commonly found in Late Archaic assemblages from coastal New Hampshire and Massachusetts and interior southern New England (Ritchie 1969). Radiocarbon dates on charcoal range from 4970±85 B.P. (SI 2392) to 5290±95 B.P. (SI 1925). Occupation 2 (Bourque 1995:41–95) was preserved in a large proportion of the excavated area of the site, and consisted of a dark, shell-free soil overlain by shell-rich refuse. Forty features were attributed to

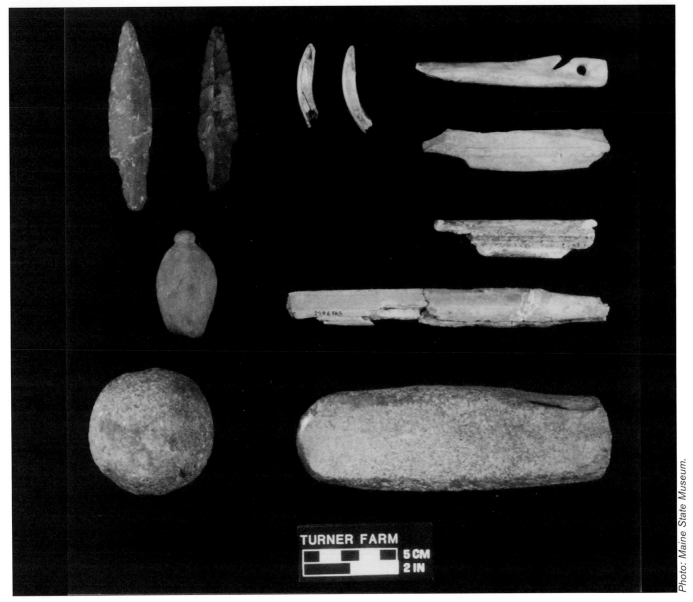

Figure 1-4. Projectile points, swordfish sword and bone tools, adze, pecking stone and plummet from Occupation 2.

Occupation 2. The tool inventory includes narrow stemmed points, pecked, polished and ground stone tools including plummets, and tools manufactured from bone, beaver incisors and swordfish sword (rostrum) (Figure 1–4). Acceptable radiocarbon dates on charcoal range from 4390±55 B.P. (SI 1921) to 4555±95 B.P. (SI 1923). Horizontal patterning of the faunal remains was highly nonrandom (Spiess and Lewis 1995:344–349). Burned rock features and artifacts revealed two shoreward areas with burned rocks and repetitive patterns of other material, probably two occupation "floors" or activity areas. Inland from, and associated with, each area was a more diffuse scatter of material and small, shallow pit features. These "backyard" activity areas probably included dog yards or tie-up areas. Five dog burials were

associated with Occupation 2. A full discussion of these skeletal remains is beyond the scope of this volume.

Occupation 3 (Bourque 1995:97–167) also consisted of a nearly shell-free occupation floor overlain by shell deposits which was extensively preserved across the excavated area. Associated with the habitation deposits are a series of burial features containing human remains, artifacts, and faunal remains. Radiocarbon dates on charcoal range from 3480±5 B.P. (SI 4248) to 4020±80 B.P. (SI 2393). Bifaces, including broad-bladed early Susquehanna tradition styles, and stone drills dominate the flaked stone artifact assemblage (Figures 1–5 and 1–6). Ground and pecked stone tools are markedly less common than in Occupation 2, as are bone and antler tools. Swordfish rostrum was not used at all. Occupation 3 artifacts and faunal remains are divided into several horizontal activity areas of large extent that may reflect a shift in the focus of occupation over time. Data from the burial area at the site support this inference.

The stratigraphy of Occupation 4 is more complex than that of the preceding Archaic occupations (see Table 4–1 and Bourque 1995:170–174 for details). It consists of a series of gravel floors that are more or less continuous across large areas of the site that alternate with massive shell midden deposits of varying thicknesses. The uppermost portion of the site has been incorporated into a (Euro-American farm) plow zone, and includes material from Archaic and earlier Ceramic occupations mixed upward by the plow and/or other disturbance, but is dominated by a late Ceramic period midden that includes thin collared ceramics of the fifteenth and sixteenth centuries A.D. date. The earliest dates from the lowest of the Occupation 4 strata (Below Second Gravel Floor) range from 2275±130 B.P. (GX 2463) to 3185±65 B.P. (SI 4244), associated with Vinette I ceramics. A broad range of Ceramic period artifacts (Figures 1–7 and 1–8) occur throughout the subsequent levels. Features include fire-cracked rock concentrations and pits. Horizontal distribution patterns appear to be much more complex (vertically) and localized (horizontally) than in the Archaic strata.

Figure 1-5. Stone tools from Occupation 3.

SHELL MIDDEN EXCAVATION CONSIDERATIONS

The Turner Farm excavations were carried out using trowels and other small hand tools. Point provenience was recorded for all artifacts. Within each five foot excavation unit, faunal elements were generally collected in situ by stratigraphic unit, although clusters of bone were often given point provenience. Bourque did not routinely screen the midden, fearing that small and delicate objects, such as flounder vertebrae, would be damaged or lost through a screen cluttered with the large shell fragments that comprised most of the midden (Bourque 1995:21–31). Recent experiments with fine screening of column samples in the laboratory suggest that, while screening shell midden through a standard ¼" mesh leads to the substantial under recovery of small bones, even the careful collection of bone in situ, as at the Turner Farm site, may still yield faunal samples that under represent the smallest fish.

Although the Turner Farm midden was clearly stratified, there remain sources of uncertainty concerning the proper cultural assignment of some specimens. The first source is excavator uncertainty or error regarding the association of artifacts and faunal remains found close to stratigraphic boundaries (Bourque 1995:25–26, Table 3–2). This situation is encountered in many excavations of stratified deposits and, while it has not generally been regarded as an important source of error, it has nevertheless probably caused incorrect assignments of some Turner Farm site specimens.

The second source concerns a small number of stratigraphic units encountered near the occupation boundaries that failed to produce culturally diagnostic material. This situation was most often encountered at the interface of Occupation 2 and 3 deposits. The modest amount of culturally ambiguous material arising from this problem is listed in Bourque 1995:25, Table 3–2.

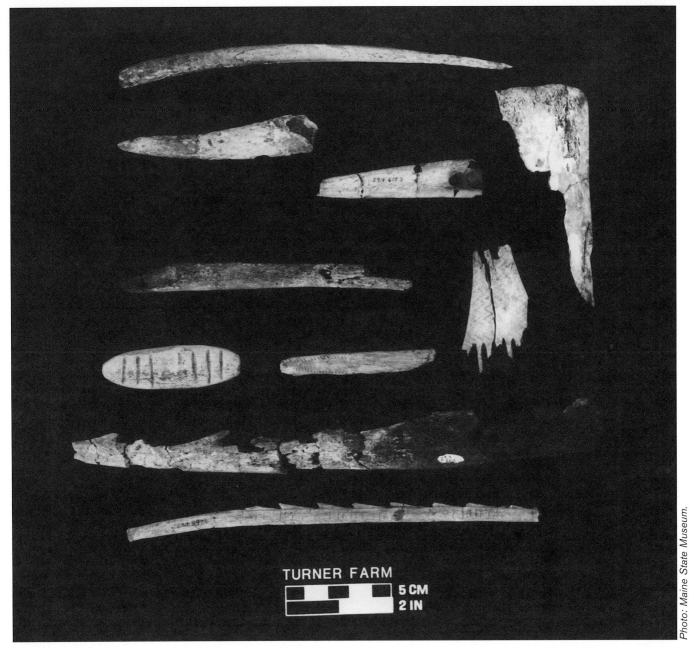

Photo: Maine State Museum.

Figure 1-6. Bone tools from Occupation 3 mortuary features (cremations), including a bone gouge or scraper blade (upper right) and bone comb (right).

Finally, both cultural and natural factors have clearly caused the movement of some specimens from their original context. In general, this movement has led to their redeposition in higher strata (Bourque 1995:25–26). As shell middens along the Maine coast tend to inhibit tree growth, whether because of high pH or excessive drainage, most effects of tree or root disturbance are absent. Fossorial animals such as rodents and foxes would produce highly localized upward and downward mixture, but under conditions that are easily spotted in shell midden. A special case of digging is the human excavation of pits and features

into existing midden, which also should be quite visible and produce a highly localized, upward mixture.

The importance of upward mixture between Occupation 2 and 3 is demonstrated by the distribution of plumb-bob-shaped stone implements called plummets. Known from several Moorehead phase and earlier Archaic contexts, they have never been reliably associated with the Susquehanna tradition or later cultures. Of the 67 plummets from the Turner Farm site, 55 were recovered from Occupation 2 deposits, while eight were recovered from strata otherwise unambiguously assignable to Occupation 3 (Bourque 1995:25). If we assume that those eight (12% of the total, 14% of those remaining behind) were mixed upward into Occupation 3 deposits, then we would expect that 12% of all Occupation 2 artifacts and faunal remains may have been mixed upward in a similar manner. In an attempt to correct for this upward mixture we subtracted 14% of the Occupation 2 bone counts from the Occupation 3 totals (see Chapter 3). By doing so, swordfish bone was removed from the Occupation 3 fauna and the relative proportion of cod was drastically reduced. This result suggests that all swordfish at the site originated in Occupation 2 (or earlier) deposits and that Occupation 3 people caught few cod. Both of these inferences are supported by stable isotope data from human skeletal remains, which indicate that the diet of the Occupation 3 population was much more terrestrially oriented than any other known prehistoric population on the Maine coast (Bourque 1995:138–140).

The implications of these three sources of stratigraphic ambiguity all tend to obscure time transgressive change in the faunal sample. Thus, any time transgressive changes that are still detectable in the data must be of magnitudes that are equal to or lesser than those originally deposited when the midden was forming. Consequently, the economic trends and changes reported in this volume, substantial as they sometimes seem, are conservative reflections of prehistoric subsistence and behavioral change. Economic differentiation between successive occupations could well have been greater than we report, but are unlikely to have been smaller.

MODEL OF SHELL MIDDEN FORMATION

The preceding discussion on mixture and the integrity of assemblages excavated from shell middens relates to an ongoing debate on shell midden formation in the Northeast (Bourque 1995, 1996; Dincauze 1996; Sanger 1981; Spiess 1988; Spiess and Hedden 1983). We have developed a model of shell midden formation that includes concepts of prehistoric occupation on an existing, usually vegetated surface often characterized by normal soil formation. Thus, deposition of shell on top of the soil will result in contemporary material culture being incorporated into two stratigraphic units, soil and overlying shell (Bourque 1995:27–29; Spiess 1988).

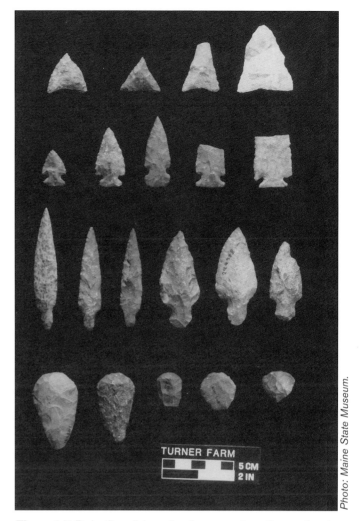

Photo: Maine State Museum.

Figure 1-7. Projectile points and end scrapers from Occupation 4.

Much recent research has augmented this model. Spiess (1988) has reviewed the discussion concerning varying interpretations of stratigraphic contexts by Sanger (1981), Spiess and Hedden (1983), McManamon (1984), and Barber (1982). By measuring amino acid racemization in shells, Skinas (1987) thought he could detect the amount of exposure to solar heat. Even in thick (50cm or thicker) shell deposits without visible living floors or buried humus, (sod) layers may contain surfaces that were exposed to the sun for some period of time (although the effect could have been produced by another source of heat such as boiling or roasting). Thus, stratigraphic integrity may be present even when there are no visible stratigraphic breaks in a massive shell layer. Black (1985, 1986, 1992) has examined shell midden formation in western New Brunswick using fine-grained stratigraphic analysis, and he too is fairly optimistic about the stratigraphic integrity of Gulf of Maine shell middens. Black has also contributed the

TURNER FARM
5 CM
2 IN

Figure 1-8. Ceramic period vessel rim sherds from Occupation 4.

hypothesis that different portions of a shell midden (front, near the shore versus back, near the inland margins of the site) were used preferentially at different seasons of the year. Belcher (1988) has contributed significant data on the effects of house construction on midden formation in one site.

Some aspects of our depositional model (Bourque 1995:29) may be helpful in understanding the Occupation 4 strata within the Turner Farm. Within Occupation 4 the relative proportion of flounder to other bone shows a general increasing trend with time (toward the present). However, there are dramatic differences in flounder bone concentration between the gravel floors (lower frequencies) and superimposed shell deposits (higher frequencies). We interpret this pattern (see Chapter 4) to indicate some functional and depositional differences between the two types of strata, with flounder bone being discarded preferentially with shellfish in midden deposits, not on "living floors" with other kinds

of debris. Such patterns of horizontal and vertical distribution within the Occupation 4 strata probably have multiple causes. One may be Black's hypothesis concerning seasonally differential use of areas of a large shell midden.

Where bone assemblages are generally similar between a living floor and a superimposed shell deposit, then the general model of their contemporaneity provides adequate explanation. Cases where bone distribution on a living floor is related to an underlying shell layer require a different explanation. The difficulty of excavating through an interface between two super-imposed stratigraphic units and recognizing the exact point of stratigraphic transition, coupled with the tendency to trample material downward a distance of some centimeters into substrate underlying an existing floor level, may cause some or all of the correlation in horizontal distribution patterns in such cases.

As shown by the trend of recent studies, microstratigraphic excavation techniques supported by column sampling and other intensive laboratory analysis are necessary to make progress within this paradigm. We suspect, however, that there will remain some inherent ambiguity in stratigraphic analysis. Moreover, such studies are expensive because they are labor intensive. Deep, extensive excavations such as at the Turner Farm site would be practically impossible to finance if painstaking micro-excavation methods were employed universally. Since shell middens all along the New England coast are disappearing due to coastal erosion and other causes, choices will have to be made regarding tradeoffs between intensive and extensive excavation. The Turner Farm essentially represents an attempt at compromise: careful stratigraphic control to recover high quality association data (Bourque 1995:24–29, 1996) and excavation of wide surface areas to reveal spatial patterning. The faunal sample size recovered, and the extent of horizontal distribution on living floors exposed, are not likely to be duplicated in any deeply stratified shell midden for decades to come. Our analysis focusses on maximizing return from these data.

The fauna of New England and Maritime Provinces shell middens has been reported with widely varying quality and detail, even in reports published within the last 20 years (reviewed in Chapter 6). Many reports make a brief effort to determine season-of-

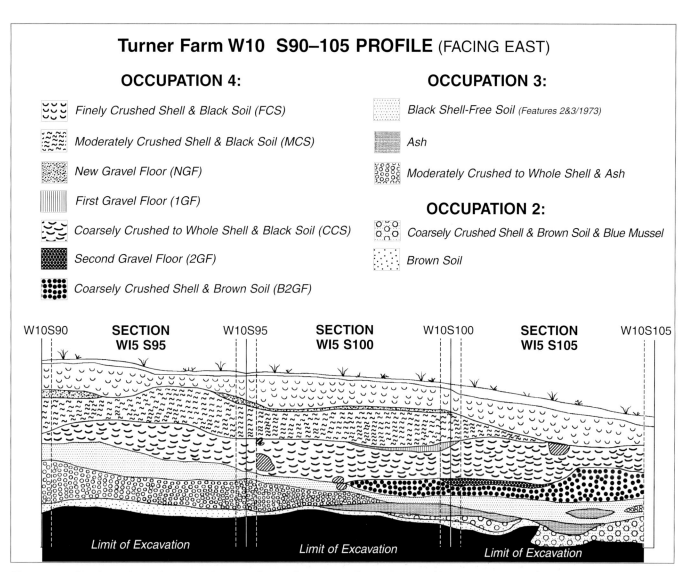

Turner Farm W10 S90–105 PROFILE (FACING EAST)

OCCUPATION 4:

- Finely Crushed Shell & Black Soil (FCS)
- Moderately Crushed Shell & Black Soil (MCS)
- New Gravel Floor (NGF)
- First Gravel Floor (1GF)
- Coarsely Crushed to Whole Shell & Black Soil (CCS)
- Second Gravel Floor (2GF)
- Coarsely Crushed Shell & Brown Soil (B2GF)

OCCUPATION 3:

- Black Shell-Free Soil (Features 2&3/1973)
- Ash
- Moderately Crushed to Whole Shell & Ash

OCCUPATION 2:

- Coarsely Crushed Shell & Brown Soil & Blue Mussel
- Brown Soil

W10S90   **SECTION WI5 S95**   W10S95   **SECTION WI5 S100**   W10S100   **SECTION WI5 S105**   W10S105

Limit of Excavation   Limit of Excavation   Limit of Excavation

Figure 1-9. Stratigraphic profile along W10 from S90 to S105 at the Turner Farm site (See also Figure 1-10). One notable stratigraphic element is the Coarse-Crushed shell (CCS) stratum which dominates the middle of the stratigraphic column. Another notable stratigraphic element is the Feature 2-3 (1973) complex of black shell-free soil toward the bottom third of the profile, which constitutes an Occupation 3 (Susquehanna tradition) hearth/house floor dated 3515±80 B.P. (Bourque 1995: 98).

occupation using species presence/absence or a few other attributes, and many report numbers of identified specimens. Techniques and standards of identification and reporting vary from investigator to investigator. The primary questions asked of faunal data are: What was most commonly eaten and during what season(s) was the site occupied? Unfortunately, the reliability of the answers to these questions is highly variable from study to study because the techniques used by different investigators has been variable. Whether or not the exact techniques we have used here are adopted by others, such detailed reporting will at least allow for more confident comparisons in the future.

QUANTIFICATION

The large quantity of faunal material from the Turner Farm project presents unique opportunities, but potential pitfalls as well. Our approach to quantification can be characterized as "detailed attribute analysis," which we define as recording a standard list of attributes observed for each taxon, and then inspecting the data for temporal and geographic (both intrasite and intersite) patterning.

For the purposes of inter-assemblage comparison we believe that the data should be transformed as little as possible. In practice this means that the basic comparative data set is a

Figure 1-10. Photograph of the W10 S95 to S105 stratigraphic profile shown in Figure 1-9.

count of the number of identified specimens (NISP) by species, age group, tooth wear category or other relevant data category. The use of minimum numbers of individuals (MNI) and other proportional or transformed data sets often violates some basic statistical rules, as well as being sample-size dependent (Grayson 1984). Moreover, Binford (1978) raises valid objections against the use of MNI for diet reconstruction when animals are field butchered, and subsequently used in "packages." In addition, MNI figures lose much of their meaning for comparison with large bone counts and multiple occupations. For example, we know that Occupation 3 involved the use of the site over a minimum of two to three centuries.

MNI does have its uses, however, most obviously in reconstructing food availability and attributes of prehistoric economy. (See Horton 1984 for a discussion of "minimum,", "original", "actual," and numbers measurements.) However, such use is practical only when analyzing the well preserved and entirely excavated contents of one feature, house floor, structure or component. For the Turner Farm sample, these data and conclusions are presented in Spiess and Lewis 1995.

The standard method (Grayson 1984) for computing MNI is to count a number of bones for each skeletal element of a certain taxon, usually including data on right versus left skeletal element, and then to pick the most abundant skeletal element to represent the minimum number of individuals of that taxon. Our approach begins in this way, but we further subdivide the skeletal element subsets by age where possible (e.g., epiphyseal closure state), and sometimes by size. For example, one may find that a count of five distal tibiae actually includes three juveniles and two adults, whereas a count of five distal radii includes three adults and two juveniles. The MNI represented is therefore six rather than five. When regression analysis of measurements is included, MNI calculation logic becomes more complicated. Often, especially when dealing with Cervid assemblages, one can produce an age demography based on teeth and another based on post-crania. A comparison of the two often identifies additional individuals. We refer to this computation as "maximal minimum numbers of individuals" (max MNI).

Likewise, we have not attempted to produce a definitive estimate of the total food supply available to each occupation or, therefore, to estimate human population. There are several reasons for our shyness in this regard: (1) we cannot control for differing lengths of occupation among the various occupation episodes; (2) we cannot control for differing age dependent effects of erosion of material from the front of the site; and (3), a related concern, we can hardly state that the main excavation recovered the comparable range of activity areas in each super-imposed occupation.

Given these limitations in comparability among occupations, we approach the faunal sample by searching for significant diachronic change in quantified fauna. The first step is to establish whether there exist statistically significant differences in one or more quantified faunal attributes from one occupation to the next. The null hypothesis is that of "no change" from occupation to occupation. Moreover, statistical significance does not necessarily imply significant change in cultural behavior. Taphonomic factors may be causal, such as the fragmentation caused by plowing. NISP and other simple counts of data (numbers of body parts, numbers of teeth exhibiting certain wear patterns, etc.) form the basic data set. Relying on raw counts and eschewing transformed and scaled data, such as MNI and various other indices for basic comparisons, allows us to use simple tests for statistical significance, specifically chi square and Fisher's Exact test.

The conclusions derived from this comparative approach are made more plausible by the elimination of several sources of variablity. First, all the occupations were at the same geographic locality. Second, all excavation was directed or directly supervised by one individual (Bourque), using a standardized set of procedures. Third, all laboratory processing of the faunal sample, and all identifications, were handled uniformly by Spiess and Lewis, assisted by Mark Hedden. Remaining sources of variability are therefore limited to (1) intrasite differences in activity, (2) taphonomic factors, (3) environmental change over time, and/or (4) human behavioral change over time.

As stated above, many of our conclusions derive from comparing bone element frequencies among taxa and between occupations. As we have not calculated MNI counts, however, we have no clear idea whether the approximately 1,000 identified deer bones in Occupations 2 and 3 represent 50 or 250 individual deer. Instead, everything is "relative" in this analysis. In comparing the quantities of various taxa recovered from each occupation, we picked an arbitrary baseline, most often the number of white-tailed deer (*Odocoileus virginianus*), the most commonly identified mammal in the sample. Judging by the numbers and ratios of body parts, deer seemingly were brought to the Turner Farm site as whole carcasses, and subsequent butchery and bone fragmentation does not seem to have varied substantially from occupation to occupation. Thus, summary data on the change in faunal exploitation over time are couched in counts of a given species relative to 100 identified deer bones (see Tables 3–39 to 3–41).

Our concluding chapter considers the nature of the faunal exploitation differences between occupations. There we couple faunal differences through time with examinations of other data, such as trends in other faunal attributes, paleoecological information, activity patterning reflected in horizontal distributions, material culture changes, and information from other sites. These examinations are then used to hypothesize cultural or ecological causes for observed changes.

NOTE ON NOMENCLATURE

Throughout most of Northeastern North America, archaeologists classify the cultures of later prehistory (after about 2800 B.P.) as part of an overarching typological pattern called the Woodland (variously called a pattern, tradition or period). In the late 1960's, however, Sanger (1987:112–113) and Bourque (1995:169–170) pointed out that because the Woodland concept derives from the Midwestern Taxonomic System (McKern 1939:309–310) and by convention has come to include horticulture and complex mortuary ceremonialism in addition to pottery making, it is not well suited to the latter prehistoric hunter-gatherer economies of Maine and the Maritime Provinces. Instead, they have used the term Ceramic period. We follow that convention here.

Analytical Methods

Introduction

In this chapter we discuss our methods of data recording and analysis. We then summarize the faunal data and discuss their implications for human subsistence ans settlement behavior. We are most interested in data relating to taxonomic identification, age, sex, relative size and season of death within the various taxa represented in the sample because these data categories are likely to yield important clues about hunting methods, social organization, seasonal cycles and technology. These data are also sensitive to changes in human behavior over time. In assessing the possibility of such changes we have assumed the null hypothesis of no change in faunal procurement patterns between successive occupations unless some statistically significant change was observed. Where we have detected differences we offer interpretations for them.

Faunal samples were collected by feature and stratum (or a subdivision thereof) within each excavation unit. We numbered and recorded these samples on manual-sort data forms, reproduced in Spiess and Hedden (1983:193, Figures 1a–1d). The sample tags were also color-coded to allow for easy stratigraphic reference. This procedure allowed us to associate faunal samples with other materials and information recovered with them. For the sample size involved (more than 10,000 identified bones), this methodology was only somewhat more labor-intensive or costly than (at the time) writing a customized computer program to handle the data, and then entering those data. It has subsequently been adapted for computerization, as the "need to systematize procedures for computerized banking of large amounts of faunal data through development of a universal coding system" (Yesner 1978:336; see also Gifford and Crader 1977) has emerged in the Gulf of Maine region.

WHITE-TAILED DEER

Analysis Methods

Our system for analyzing white-tailed deer *(Odocoileus virginianus)* bone (and, below, moose bone) is based on Spiess' (1979) method for caribou *(Rangifer tarandus)*, a closely related and similarly-sized cervid. It was adapted to deer by Spiess and Hedden (1983:187–195). We have modified it only slightly as noted below.

Tooth Eruption and Wear

Observation of tooth eruption and wear in deer is a classic wildlife management technique, allowing the investigator to place mandibles or isolated teeth in certain age-classes (Severinghaus 1949; see also Sauer 1984:89). Assignment of season-of-death to tooth-eruption age-groups is based on the fact that most Maine deer are born during early June, with a few born in May, late June and July.

The onset of rutting behavior in north temperate white-tailed deer populations is triggered by decreasing day length in the fall (Verme and Ullrey 1984: 93). Although climatic conditions in Maine have varied substantially through the Holocene, the astronomical parameter of day length variation with season has, for biological purposes, not varied. Thus, the timing of the peak of the rut probably has stayed the same. Since gestation is a near constant for the species, the birth frequency peak would also have remained the same. The climatic amelioration of the mid-Holocene may have allowed for greater survival rates of fawns born too early or too late. We expect that fawn survival rate changes would have had minor effects on deer demographic profiles. For the prehistoric period in question, we use a birth date of June 1st, but allow a one month variability around the modern date in our analysis.

We assigned mandibular fragments to seasonally-specific and age-specific wear classes according to tooth eruption stages (Table 2–1). When dealing with a multi-seasonal or year-round archaeological or biological sample, wear and eruption categories will intergrade. This effect occurs with both deciduous molars and the "adult" wear classes. Arbitrary but consistent decisions must be made for borderline cases. Further problems arise in interpreting isolated teeth because of the difficulty in separating first and second mandibular molars. Thus, these are recorded as M1/2, meaning either M1 or M2. Very light wear on such a molar either represents an M1 of less than 2 years of age, or an M2 of 2 years of age. It is thus recorded as "M1/2 ≤ 2 years." (See Figure 2–1 for deer dentition.)

As an incidental check on the tooth eruption seasonality estimates presented in Table 2–1, Spiess has examined in detail the dentition of a yearling female and several other deer taken during early November (Maine's legal hunting season). The doe was probably between 17 and 18 months of age. Its M3 was erupted, P2 and P3 were ½ erupted (deciduous premolars missing), and DP4 was just about to be pushed out of its last root-hold. The calendric age is thus in accord with the data in Table 2–1. Other deer in the same study examined personally by Spiess clearly fit the ½ and 1½-year tooth eruption states predicted by Severinghaus.

We have made no attempt to use dental crown height (Klein et al. 1981; Klein and Cruz-Uribe 1984) for age estimates, because work on numerous series of caribou mandibles (Spiess, unpublished) from Tukuto Lake, Alaska (see Spiess 1979 for an introduction to the site) have shown much individual variation in crown height differences between M1, M2 and M3, indicating different rates of wear. We suspect that Klein's dental crown height method is equivalent to visual wear pattern typology in accuracy of aging.

Incremental Growth in Teeth

Deer teeth record annual layers (increments) in the cementum pads around their roots much the way trees record growth rings. Benn (1974), Kay (1974), Spiess (1976a, 1979:68–69) and Bourque Morris and Spiess (1978) demonstrate the applicability of wildlife management techniques to reading these layers in archaeological samples. There are two basic methods of preparing tooth specimens: thin sectioning and staining with decalcified teeth, mostly applied to modern specimens, and mounting in epoxy followed by grinding a section for archaeological specimens (Bourque, Morris and Spiess 1978). The epoxy mounted specimens can be viewed either with reflected light as thick sections, or with transmitted light as thin sections. Both reflected and transmitted light were used in this study, but without use of polarizing light. The rest line or annulus, which is dark when thin-sectioned and stained, is

Table 2-1. Deer tooth eruption and wear classes, mandibular teeth only. After Severinghaus (1949). DM = deciduous molars (or milk premolars). End points of ranges of age and seasonality are inclusive. Subscripts indicate mandibular teeth following Hilson 1986.

ERUPTION CLASS	AGE	MAINE SEASONALITY	NOTES
DM < ½ erupted **DM ½ to fully erupted**	1-5 weeks 5-12 weeks	late May, June, early July July-September	deciduous molars beginning to erupt
M₁ erupting	2½-6 months	mid August-December	light wear on DM
M₂ erupting	6-10 months	December-April	wear on DM moderate
M₃ erupting	11-19 months	May-January	wear on DM heavy or extreme, roots may be resorbing
PM erupting	17-20 months	November-February	permanent premolars erupting
WEAR			
2 years	lingual cusps on M₁ sharp, wear on M₃ slight. Dentine layer on crests narrower than each of sandwiching enamel layers on molars and premolars (except M₁ toward 2½ years).		
3-4 years	lingual cusps of M₁ and M₂ blunt. Lingual cusps significantly higher than buccal cusps on PM and molars. Dentine layer on cusps wider than sandwiching enamel layers.		
5-7 years	lingual and buccal cusps of similar height, thus bucco-lingual relief of premolars and molar teeth gone, although they may still show some antero-posterior relief. Infundibulum a crescent or chevron-shaped design, or a shallow-narrow groove.		
8+ years	extreme wear on all teeth. Infundibulum gone on M₁ and M₂, disappearing after a few years on M₃. Leaves a scalloped dentine surface in top-view.		

narrow. The light-staining band or growth layer is wider in stained deer tooth thin sections. In the epoxy-mounted archaeological specimens, the thin annulus is usually more translucent than the intervening thicker growth layers which are opaque. In non-stained, epoxy mounted sections, dark versus light effects depend upon whether the sections are observed under transmitted (opaque = dark) or reflected (opaque = light) light. (See Lieberman 1993 for a discussion of the microstructural changes involved.) Caution and experience in making counts of layers is warranted (Rice 1980). Sauer (1973) reports the formation of the translucent (rest) line in February through June in Northeastern North America, or

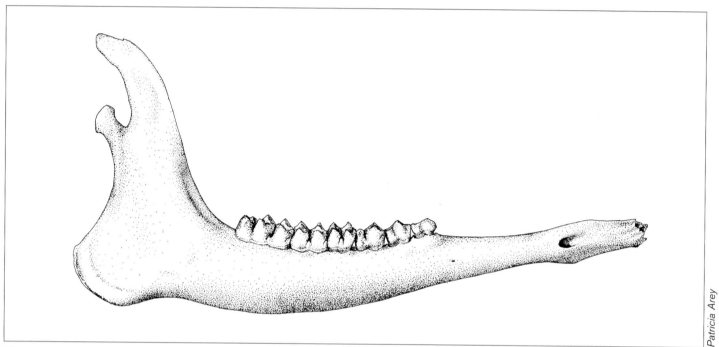

Patricia Arey

Figure 2-1. Schematic lateral view of the right jaw of deer, showing adult fully erupted and representing 3-4 year wear category. Incisors are missing. From right to left the teeth are P_2, P_3, P_4, M_1, M_2 and M_3.

Table 2-2. Deer tooth layer relative growth and age at death from a sample of 16 Maine deer with known month of death. A = annulus forming. % = relative growth of last layer compared with previous layer. Number of specimens given in parenthesis for a calculated relative amount of growth.

MONTH	RELATIVE GROWTH AND NUMBER OF SPECIMENS			
January	100%(1)			
February	A (1)			
March	A (3)			
April	A (5)			
May	A (5), 8%[1] (1)			
June	10% (1), 27%[2] (1)			
August	45% (1), 57%[3] (1), 60%[4] (1), 67% (1), 76% (1)			
November	56%[5] (1), 60%[3] (1), 65% (1), 66% (1), 73%[6] (1), 75%[6] (1), 76% (1), 79% (1), 80% (2), 83%[7] (2), 90% (1), 100% (2), 133%[6] (1), 143%[6] (1)	**Summary Statistics for November Sample**		
		for all specimens:	for 3 years and older:	
		n = 16	n = 8	
		$\bar{x}$ = 90%	$\bar{x}$ = 86%	
		σ = 25%	σ = 9½%	

NOTES: [1]Scarborough, southern Maine; [2]June mean = 18%, all from herd reduction at Ram Island Farm, Cape Elizabeth; [3]2 year-old; [4]August mean = 61%, s = 12%; [5]1½ years of age; [6]2½ years of age; [7]one is 2½ years of age.

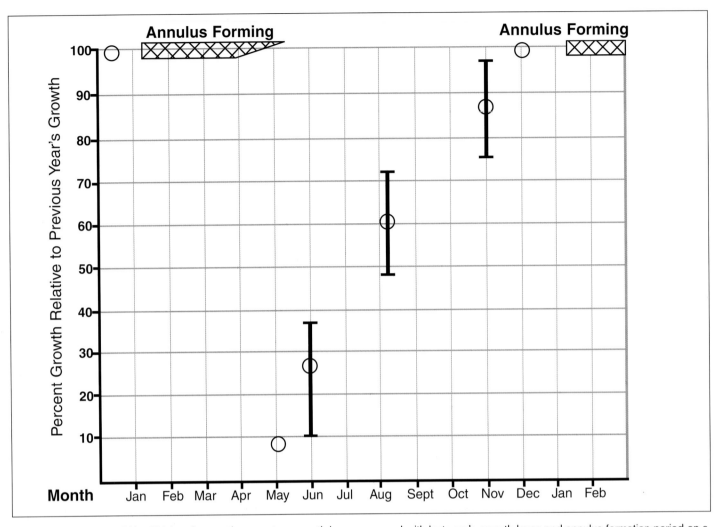

Figure 2-2. Relative width of Maine deer tooth cementum growth layer compared with last year's growth layer, and annulus formation period on a calendar year scale. Note that the calendar scale repeats January and February at the right hand margin.

"late winter-early spring" in the same area (Sauer 1984:89; see also Lockwood 1972).

In order to be as precise as possible as to the rates and dates of inception and cessation of rest line formation in Maine, Spiess (1990a) obtained a sample of 35 deer mandibles and inspected over 200 stained thin sections of incisor teeth from the Maine Department of Inland Fisheries and Wildlife. A section containing the roots of several molar teeth was cut from each mandible. Each section was then mounted in epoxy resin and ground on a lapidary wheel. These sections were observed under reflected light, analogous to the method used on the archaeological specimens. The stained thin sections were observed under transmitted light. The results of this study (Table 2–2), discussed below, are presented in more detail in Spiess (1990a).

The status of the last growth layer was determined at 100X magnification through a binocular microscope using an optical micrometer mounted in one ocular. If an annulus (rest line) was forming at time of death, "A" was recorded. Where a growth layer was forming at death, its width and the width of the preceding layer were measured The relative width of the last growth layer, compared to the preceding layer, was then calculated (measurement units are percentages).

Six of the mandibles and 32 of the teeth yielded observations in which the author had confidence. The largest sample (18) comes from the legal hunting season for Maine deer (November). The rest are scattered through winter, spring and early summer and were recovered from animals of known date of death including road kills, herd reductions, or recently killed animals found in the woods by wardens. The conclusions drawn are as follows (Figure 2–2): (1) Annulus (rest line) formation occurs beginning in early February and lasts into late May for most animals over most of the state. (2) In southern coastal Maine, where the effects of winter ameliorate earlier than in the rest of the state, a few individuals begin growth layer formation in mid-May or late May. (3) For the purposes of the Turner Farm analysis, we assumed that annulus formation occurred between February 1st and June 1st, a span of four months, leaving eight months for accretion of the growth layer. (4) In June, the first month of growth layer accretion, relative widths are less than or equal to ¼ of the growth layer width of the previous year. (5) By August, the third month of the eight-month growth season (3/8=37%), a sample from southern coastal Maine (Cape Elizabeth) showed average growth width of 60% compared with the previous year's growth layer width, with a standard error of 12%. And, (6) in the November sample, six months through the eight-month growth season (6/8=75%), relative growth width averages 90%.

At first inspection, these data seem to be reflect a wide range of relative growth layer widths (standard error=25%) in the November sample compared with the prior year's growth layer (56% to 143%), with two deer showing a marked increase in growth-layer width compared with the previous year. However, all eight of the teeth furthest from the mean value come from deer under three years of age. The older deer in the November sample have relative width averages similar to that of the entire deer sample (86% versus 90%), but they exhibit a much smaller standard error (9½% versus 25%). We suspect that this is because younger deer are more susceptible to physiological stress than are prime-age deer, and consequently that their growth rates might be more variable. We therefore gave them relatively less weight in estimating past seasonal hunting patterns than readings of older teeth.

In sum, deposition of the growth layer apparently does not proceed at constant rate, but is faster in the spring and early summer, slowing into the fall. Moreover, there is greater variability in younger deer than in older deer in growth layer width from year to year.

Because of the difficulty in using an optical micrometer to measure growth layer widths, and the 10% or greater standard error in mean relative growth layer widths in animals who died during one month, we recommend using estimates of relative growth that fall into discrete categories. For the Turner Farm site analysis, we estimated relative growth compared to the previous year's growth in the following categories: <¼, ¼, ⅓, ½, ⅔, ¾ and full growth. Annulus

forming was recorded if the outermost growth layer could be confirmed as such. Occasionally, even this level of precision could not be attained on marginally readable specimens, and we had to record a thin (< ½) or thick (½ to full thickness) relative width. In reconstructing deer kill patterns for the Turner Farm site, we used the following seasonality estimates: annulus forming, February-May; < ¼ growth, late May-June; ¼ growth, June-July; ⅓, growth, July; ½ growth, July-early August; ⅔ growth, August-September; ¾ growth, late August-October; between ¾ and full growth, late October-early December; and full growth, December-January.

There are several physiological adaptations related to growth layer formation in northern white-tailed deer that are important in interpreting archaeological specimens. In the late fall, deer in the northern end of the species range molt and grow heavy winter coats, at the same time decreasing their

Table 2-3. Epiphyseal closure sequence and timing; ages of fusion in deer, from *Lewall and Cowan 1963.

Epiphysis	Age Range of Fusion
Phalanges III, manus/pes	< 12 months
Vertebrae, laminae/pedicles	< 12 months
Sacrum, alar mass	< 12 months
Atlas, ventral/dorsal arch	< 12 months
Ribs, tubercles	< 12 months
Ox coxae, illium/isch./pubis	< 12 months
Vertebrae, transverse proces.	< 12 months
Scapula, coracoid base	< 12 months
Humerus, distal ep.*	14-17 months
Phalanges I, II, manus/pes*	14 months
Tibia, distal ep.*	14-15 months
Metacarpals, distal ep.*	29-35 months
Metatarsals, distal ep.*	29-35 months
Femur, head & greater tro.*	29-34 months
Femur, distal ep.*	35-52 months
Radius, distal ep.*	34-60 months
Tibia, proximal ep.*	24-60 months
Humerus, proximal ep.*	35-60 months
Vertebrae, ep.	> 48 months
Sacrum, component segments	> 48 months
Os coxae, growth stops	> 48 months
Sacro-illiac, ossifies	> 48 months
Scapula, vertebral border stops growing	> 48 months
(irregular: acromion, olecranon, calcanear epiphysis)	

metabolic rate, and restricting movement and feeding even when ample food is available (Verme and Ullrey 1984:110). By mid-winter they are in a relatively torpid state. To survive this winter period, deer must build up substantial fat reserves in late summer and early fall. Lipogenesis (fat formation) is under endocrine control triggered by decreasing day length, and is physiologically obligatory (Verme and Ullrey 1984:107). Young deer on mediocre late summer and fall range will still generate some fat reserves (Verme and Ullrey 1984:106) but will stop growing extra muscle or bone mass (Wood et al. 1962). As a result, in northern climates, poor diet or poor physical condition due to disease will cause a decrease in adult deer size from the genetic potential to build the necessary fat reserves.

The timing of the fall physiological change to obligate lipogenesis, however, is under photoperiod control. It would not be expected to vary substantially with past climatic change for a given latitude. Thus, the timing of inception of rest line formation probably was constant through time in one locality. Less is known about the cause of the spring physiological change, but our observation that growth line inception is earlier by a few weeks in southern Maine than elsewhere in the state indicates that access to the high protein content of new vegetation plants may be causal. Climatically induced variation in the timing of snow cover melt may thus have changed the date of growth line inception by a few weeks at any one location during the course of the Holocene.

Table 2-4. Definitions of caribou measurements from Spiess 1976, used in this study for deer. Spiess' numbers start with #101, followed in parentheses by any equivalent measurements from von den Driesch 1976.

Mandible and Maxilla	
101 (20)	maxillary tooth row, alveolar length, P^2-M^3
102 (22)	maxillary premolar tooth row length
103 (21)	maxillary molar tooth row length
104 (7)	mandibular alveolar tooth row length, P_2-M_3
105 (9)	mandibular premolar tooth row length
106 (8)	mandibular molar row alveolar length
107	length from posterior margin of mental foramen to posterior alveolar M_3 margin
108 (11)	diastema length, measured from canine lateral alveolar margin to alveolar margin of P_2
109 (2)	mandible length, infradentalli to posterior–most spot on mandibular articular head

Scapula	
110 (CL)	greatest diameter of glenoid cavity in plane of scapular blade
111 (SLC)	least width of neck behind glenoid

Humerus	
112 (Bp)	greatest proximal transverse width, from medial–most to lateral–most points on tubercles
113 (SD)	least diameter of diaphysis, ⅔'s shaft length distally
114 (BT)	distal transverse width of articular surface
115 (GLl)	total length

Radius	
116 (BFp)	proximal medio-lateral width of articulating surface
117 (BFd)	distal, medio-lateral width of articulating surface
118 (GL)	total length

Metacarpal/Metatarsal (second number)	
119, 12 (Dp)	proximal, antero-posterior width articular surface

120,126 (Bp)	proximal, transverse width articular surface
121,127 (Bd)	distal, medio-lateral width, inter-epicondylar
122,128	distal, transverse width of one condyle
123,129	distal, antero-posterior greatest diameter of ridge on condyle
124,130 (GL)	total length

Phalange I	(Forelimb/Hindlimb) No.'s for Ph II follow
131,134 (GL)	greatest length 137, 140
132,135 (Bp)	proximal width, transverse 138, 141
133,136 (Bd)	distal width, transverse 139, 142

Pelvis	
143	acetabular diameter

Femur	
144 (Bp)	proximal medio-lateral width including caput and trochanter
145 (DC)	greatest antero-posterior diameter of caput
146 (Bd)	distal width, biepicondylar
147 (GL)	greatest length

Tibia	
148 (Bp)	greatest medio-lateral proximal width
149 (Bd)	greatest medio-lateral distal width
150 (GL)	total length

Astragalus	
151 (GLl)	height
152 (DM)	medio-lateral

Calcaneus	
153 (GL)	greatest length
154	greatest width at midpoint

Epiphyseal Fusion

Epiphyseal fusion status (Table 2–3) can provide important data for constructing age-demographies of the kill. However, not all unfused long bone epiphyses represent sexually immature individuals. The distal humerus, for example, fuses at a little over one year of age (Lewall and Cowan 1963), while the proximal tibial epiphysis fuses at 3–4 years of age. Thus, by counting distal humeri and proximal tibiae, for example, we can estimate percentages of the kill aged under 14 months, under 4 years, and over 4 years.

Epiphyseal fusion is also helpful in estimating MNI, at least in small samples. For instance, first phalanges with unfused epiphyses cannot come from the same individual as a distal metacarpal with a fused epiphysis.

Antler Shedding

Male deer in Maine begin their annual antler growth in April or May, shedding their velvet in September. They shed their antlers after the breeding season, usually between December and February (Banasiak 1961). Antler shedding is under endocrine control, apparently triggered by photoperiodism (Verme and Ullrey 1984). The status of antler growth and shedding can be observed directly on archaeological male frontal bone fragments, which often preserve the base of the antler, or the bony pedicle from which it was shed.

Spiess has observed that the bone wall thickness (cortical bone) of some deer long bones varies considerably from specimen to specimen (e.g., several metapodials observed consistently at one portion of the broken shaft). We have yet to investigate the basis for this variability, but suspect that it is partly individual and partly seasonal, due to mobilization of mineral resources for antler formation. There is one report (Meister 1951:28) of enlarged Haversian canals in the cortical bone of male deer during antler growth. These enlarged Haversian canals apparently result from osteoblast mobilization of bone mineral for reuse in antler growth. Neither of these possible seasonal dating techniques has yet been applied systematically to an archaeological collection.

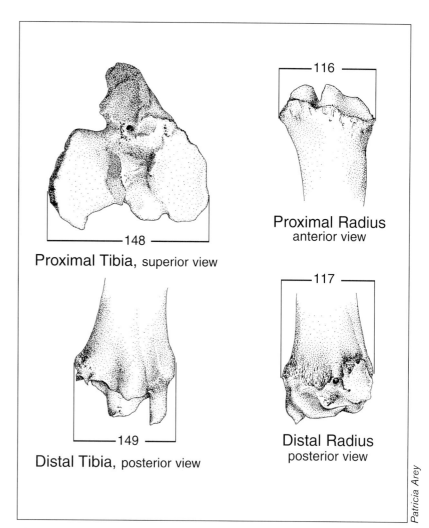

Figure 2-3. Selected views of deer postcrania and measurement definitions, tibia and radius.

Patricia Arey

Measurements

Bone measurements have a myriad of uses. Individual measurements can be compared between the same body part occurring in different samples as an indication of body size. Average sizes can be compared between geographic areas or over time (Purdue 1983, 1986). They also aid MNI reconstruction, since a large right bone element cannot come from the same individual as a small left element (see discussion of regression, below).

In immature animals the major determinant of size is age. For adults, sexual dimorphism is a major component of size variation. Bimodal distributions of adult bone measurements may thus help determine sex-ratio in a sample (Rasmussen et al. 1982). Conversely, change in average size of a sample over time, or between two sites, may be caused by either a change in the sex or age demography (possibly reflecting hunting technique) or change in the average size

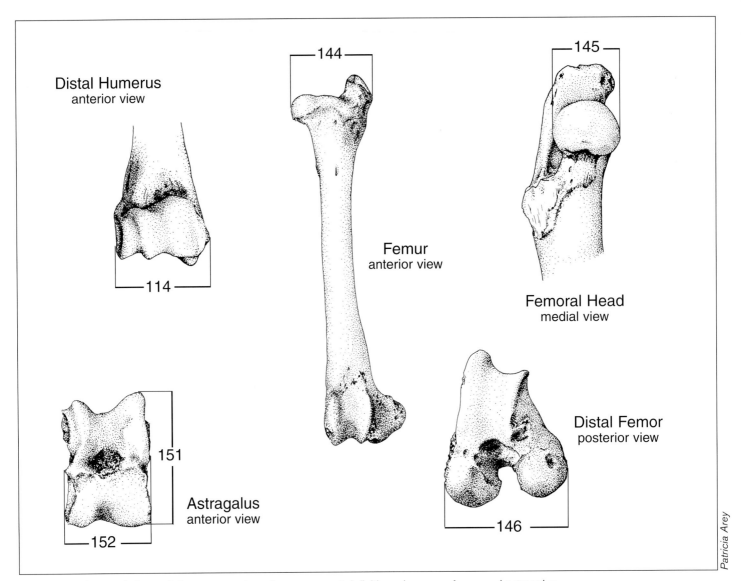

Distal Humerus
anterior view

— 144 —

Femur
anterior view

— 145 —

Femoral Head
medial view

— 114 —

Distal Femor
posterior view

151

Astragalus
anterior view

— 152 —

— 146 —

Patricia Arey

Figure 2-4. Selected views of deer postcrania and measurement definitions, humerus, femur and astragalus.

of the deer population overall (not necessarily due to climatic or environmental factors).

Table 2–4 presents definitions of 54 caribou skeleton measurements developed by Spiess (1979) which work well on other cervids, including deer (Figures 2–3 and 2–4). They have been designed to deal with archaeological samples containing broken bones. Table 2–5 presents measurements taken from museum specimens by Spiess. Collection data for these specimens (date and location) are presented in Spiess and Hedden (1983:194).

Regressions

Linear regression allows the prediction of the value of a dependent variable from one or more independent variables. Simple linear regression of form y=a + bx predicts much of

the size variability from bone to bone in our sample, where x and y are different bone measurements. The standard error of the estimate (Sy) is commonly used to set confidence intervals on the dependent variable (Blalock 1960). Regression equations are useful in MNI analysis. Given similar epiphyseal fusion states, we may want to know whether two long bone ends possibly belong to the same-sized individual or whether, with 96% confidence, they come from two individuals of different size (Figure 2–5). One then turns to the regression line and standard error of the estimate, calculating the plus-or-minus two standard error range. Such an analysis will be useful for faunal samples containing fragmentary remains of relatively few animals.

Regression analysis can also be used to compare average deer body size for different archaeological samples by

Table 2-5. Measurements of deer, in cm. Measurement definitions in Table 2.4. Museum catalogue number listed at the head of each column. USNM = Smithsonian Institution; MCZ = Museum of Comparative Zoology, Harvard; UMO-DoA = University of Maine at Orono, Department of Anthropology.

Meas#	USNM 256056	USNM 271871	USNM 256049	USNM 396283	USNM 251585	USNM 270960	USNM 254652	USNM 254653	USNM 238135	USNM 246055
110	2.8	3.0	2.5	2.9	2.8	2.2	–	–	3.1	2.5
111	2.2	2.3	2.0	2.2	2.0	2.0	–	–	2.2	2.1
112	4.6	5.1	4.0	4.4	4.1	4.5	5.2	4.1	4.9	4.2
113	1.6	2.0	1.8	1.8	1.5	1.6	2.0	1.7	1.8	1.7
114	3.9	3.7	3.4	3.3	3.3	2.9	3.7	3.2	3.7	3.3
115	18.9	20.1	18.8	19.4	17.5	19.5	20.9	17.4	19.4	18.0
116	3.5	3.8	3.3	3.4	3.4	2.8	3.7	3.2	3.7	3.3
117	3.4	3.5	3.1	3.0	3.2	2.8	3.6	2.9	3.5	3.2
118	20.9	21.3	20.7	20.3	18.3	17.3	22.1	18.9	20.6	17.9
119	1.9	2.2	1.7	1.9	1.8	1.5	2.1	1.6	1.9	1.7
120	2.7	3.1	2.4	2.7	2.6	2.1	3.0	2.5	2.7	2.4
121	2.8	3.0	2.5	2.7	2.7	2.2	3.1	2.5	–	2.1
122	1.3	1.4	1.2	1.3	1.3	1.0	1.4	1.1	1.4	1.7
123	1.9	2.1	1.8	1.9	1.8	1.4	2.0	1.6	2.0	1.7
124	18.7	20.1	18.5	18.8	17.7	15.1	20.7	17.5	19.1	17.0
125	2.7	2.7	2.5	2.6	2.6	2.1	2.9	2.4	2.6	2.4
126	2.6	3.0	2.5	2.6	2.5	2.1	2.6	2.3	2.5	2.4
127	2.8	3.3	2.7	2.9	2.8	2.3	3.0	2.7	–	2.5
128	1.3	1.5	1.2	1.3	1.2	1.0	1.4	1.2	–	1.1
129	2.1	2.2	2.0	2.1	2.1	1.6	2.1	1.8	–	1.8
130	22.6	27.1	22.3	22.4	20.8	18.1	24.1	21.3	–	20.4
131	–	4.5	–	3.9	3.9	–	–	–	4.5	–
132	–	1.5	–	1.4	1.3	–	–	–	1.5	–
133	–	1.3	–	1.2	1.1	–	–	–	1.2	–
134	–	5.1	–	4.3	4.1	–	–	–	4.7	–
135	–	1.7	–	1.4	1.4	–	–	–	1.5	–
136	–	1.5	–	1.2	1.2	–	–	–	1.3	–
137	–	3.5	–	2.9	2.9	–	–	–	3.6	–
138	–	1.6	–	1.4	1.2	–	–	–	1.4	–
139	–	1.3	–	1.0	1.0	–	–	–	1.0	–
140	–	3.5	–	3.5	3.3	–	–	–	3.6	–
141	–	1.6	–	1.5	1.2	–	–	–	1.4	–
142	–	1.3	–	1.1	1.0	–	–	–	1.0	–
143	2.6	2.8	2.5	2.9	2.7	2.5	–	–	2.8	2.2
144	5.7	5.8	5.2	5.6	5.3	5.1	5.8	5.2	–	4.8
145	2.3	2.4	2.2	2.5	2.3	2.1	2.6	2.3	–	2.0
146	5.2	4.7	5.0	5.1	4.9	4.5	5.7	4.7	5.2	4.5
147	24.0	23.2	23.4	24.1	21.3	22.8	25.7	21.3	–	20.8
148	5.2	5.6	5.0	5.3	5.0	4.5	5.5	4.6	5.3	4.8
149	3.3	3.6	3.3	3.3	3.2	2.7	3.7	3.0	3.4	3.2
150	27.2	29.1	27.1	26.9	24.8	24.7	28.7	25.9	28.4	24.4
151	3.9	4.1	5.6	3.9	3.7	3.0	3.5	3.5	3.9	–
152	2.4	2.7	2.4	2.5	2.4	2.0	2.3	2.2	2.6	–
153	8.3	10.9	–	8.5	7.9	7.3	9.1	7.9	8.6	–
154	1.1	1.0	–	1.1	1.9	0.9	1.0	1.0	1.1	–

Table 2-5. (continued)

Meas#	USNM 35139	MCZ 47478	USNM 254654	MSM Lab #7	MCZ 25377	UMO-DoA Mounted	UMO-DoA Lab #061	DoA Lab I	DoA Lab II	Oatway Deer Bowerbank,Me.
110	2.9	3.5	2.2	3.8	2.4	3.6	(2.7)	–	3.3	–
111	2.2	3.1	1.4	2.6	1.8	3.1	1.8	–	2.6	–
112	4.7	5.2	3.1	–	3.9	6.2	–	–	–	–
113	1.7	2.4	–	1.8	2.1	1.4	–	–	–	–
114	3.4	4.3	(1.3)	–	2.7	4.8	3.4	–	–	–
115	18.7	24.1	–	–	17.4	–	(14.2)	–	–	–
116	3.4	4.2	2.8	3.9	2.9	4.9	3.3	–	–	4.0
117	3.3	4.1	2.9	3.7	2.9	3.9	3.2	–	–	–
118	19.9	15.8	–	23.3	15.8	–	–	–	–	–
119	1.9	–	1.6	2.2	1.6	2.2	1.8	–	–	2.6
120	2.7	–	2.3	3.1	2.4	3.1	2.7	–	–	3.4
121	2.7	–	2.4	3.3	2.3	3.4	–	–	–	3.4
122	1.3	–	1.1	1.5	1.1	1.7	1.3	–	–	1.5
123	1.8	–	1.7	2.2	1.5	2.2	2.0	–	–	2.3
124	19.8	–	22.4	14.3	–	–	(16.1)	–	–	22.5
125	2.5	–	2.4	3.1	2.4	2.9	2.5	3.14	2.8	3.3
126	2.8	–	2.2	3.2	2.2	2.8	2.4	3.07	2.5	3.2
127	2.9	–	–	3.4	2.5	3.5	–	3.28	–	3.5
128	1.3	–	–	1.6	1.1	1.6	–	1.47	1.5	1.6
129	2.1	–	–	2.4	1.7	2.4	–	2.12	2.1	2.5
130	23.5	–	–	26.0	17.3	–	(10.3)	–	–	24.5
131	–	–	–	5.0	3.5	4.9	4.0	5.01	–	5.0
132	–	–	–	1.7	1.2	1.6	1.5	1.63	–	1.7
133	–	–	–	1.5	1.0	1.4	1.2	1.38	–	1.4
134	–	–	–	–	3.6	5.3	–	–	4.9	5.5
135	–	–	–	–	1.3	1.8	–	–	1.5	1.8
136	–	–	–	–	1.0	1.5	–	–	1.2	1.5
137	–	–	–	4.6	2.6	3.8	–	3.80	–	4.1
138	–	–	–	1.6	1.1	1.5	–	1.49	–	1.6
139	–	–	–	1.3	0.8	1.2	–	1.16	–	1.1
140	–	–	–	–	2.8	4.3	–	–	3.8	4.3
141	–	–	–	–	1.2	1.5	–	–	1.3	1.7
142	–	–	–	–	0.9	1.3	–	–	1.1	1.2
143	2.6	3.4	2.3	2.8	2.4	3.3	–	–	3.0	–
144	5.3	–	–	6.6	5.2	(6.8 est±.2)	–	–	–	–
145	2.3	–	2.1	2.8	2.2	2.8	2.4	–	2.6	–
146	4.9	–	4.0	5.4	4.3	6.2	4.6	–	4.9	–
147	23.8	–	–	28.0	22.9	–	(19.5)	–	–	–
148	5.1	–	4.3	6.3	4.6	6.4	5.2	–	–	–
149	3.1	3.9	3.0	3.9	3.3	4.1	3.3	–	–	4.0
150	26.8	34.6	–	32.7	24.1	–	–	–	–	–
151	–	–	–	–	3.4	(4.3est±.1)	3.9	4.21	4.2	4.6
152	–	–	–	–	2.2	2.9	2.5	2.58	2.6	3.1
153	–	–	6.6	9.9	7.6	10.6	(7.6)	9.64	(8.4)	10.1
154	–	–	1.1	2.5	1.0	2.5	1.8	2.50	2.1	2.2

Table 2-6. Regression statistics for deer postcranial measurements. For equations of formula y = a + bx. The upper set of regression data show regression lines on the distal breadth of the humerus (measurement #114). The lower set of regression data show regression lines on the distal breadth of the tibia (measurement #149).

	110 x on 114y	111 on 114	116 on 114	117 on 114	145 on 114	146 on 114	148 on 114	149 on 114	151 on 114	152 on 114
n	12	13	14	15	13	14	14	14	12	12
a	0.0004	0.924	-0.139	-0.783	-0.806	-0.837	-2.346	-0.666	-1.032	-0.961
b	1.249	1.178	1.048	1.306	1.823	0.870	0.937	1.250	1.218	1.843
r	0.90	0.88	0.93	0.91	0.76	0.87	0.92	0.81	0.78	0.83
x	2.851	2.232	3.419	3.309	2.344	4.969	5.153	3.321	3.727	3.425
y	3.563	3.553	3.446	3.539	3.468	3.485	3.485	3.485	3.508	3.508
s_x	0.423	0.422	0.358	0.370	0.219	0.507	0.499	0.329	0.350	0.245
s_y	0.587	0.484	0.403	0.531	0.523	0.506	0.506	0.506	0.457	0.547
s_b	0.246	0.255	0.140	0.253	0.325	0.240	0.187	0.097	0.324	0.295

	110 on 149	111 on 149	114 on 149	116 on 149	117 on 149	145 on 149	146 on 149	148 on 149	151 on 149	152 on 149
n	15	15	15	17	17	15	16	16	12	12
a	1.3994	1.911	1.393	1.199	0.447	0.317	0.839	0.464	0.583	0.515
b	0.691	0.665	0.555	0.624	0.885	1.279	0.506	0.556	0.742	1.169
r	0.90	0.82	0.84	0.91	0.89	0.86	0.78	0.92	0.75	0.82
x	2.86	3.354	3.354	3.482	3.305	2.359	4.938	5.169	3.727	2.425
y	3.375	3.359	3.359	3.372	3.372	3.335	3.339	3.339	3.349	3.349
s_x	0.489	0.531	0.531	0.537	0.371	0.246	0.547	0.589	0.350	0.245
s_y	0.372	0.350	0.350	0.369	0.369	0.366	0.354	0.354	0.348	0.348
s_b	0.185	0.182	0.182	0.157	0.163	0.181	0.214	0.128	0.221	0.179

regressing all measurements to a standard reference measurement. Bimodal distributions in a sample with fragmentary post-cranial bones, where multiple measurements from each original animal are unobtainable, may be used to estimate sex ratios, since mean values and ranges of some post-cranial measurements do differ between sexes. In samples where many bones may be extant from a few individuals, such as in the fill of a single trash pit, regression to one measurement should give multimodal distributions useful in detecting the minimum number of individuals that constitute the sample.

Table 2–6 presents regressions of 10 different independent variables (Table 2.4, measurements #110, #111, #116, #117, #145, #146, #148, #149, #151, and #152) on two dependent variables (measurements #114 and #149), based on data pairs from the nineteen measured museum specimens of deer presented above. These regressions are designed to provide comparison mainly between long bone epiphyseal end widths. Statistical parameters are presented for use in MNI and other analysis. Additional regressions can be run when necessary for use in answering specific questions, but these pairs have been selected to cover many foreseeable needs. Generally, correlation coefficients are greater than 0.80.

MOOSE

Analysis Methods

Because the moose *(Alces alces)* is a Cervid, the analysis of fragmentary moose bones follows very closely the procedure outlined above for white-tailed deer, and in Spiess (1979) for caribou.

Teeth

For moose the tooth eruption and wear sequence used in this analysis (Table 2–7) is derived from Peterson (1955:228–238). Tooth wear divisions are morphologically similar to those for white-tailed deer and caribou, but the wear progresses over an elongated time scale for this larger animal. The deciduous molars erupt at about one month of age, while we estimate that the total range of eruption may occur between two weeks and two months of age. In Maine today, most moose calves are born between very late May and mid-June. The deciduous molars erupt in June, July and early August.

In Peterson's sequence of jaws, M_1 is not erupted at one month, but is erupted at five months of age. From these dates we infer that M_1 erupts between 2 and 7 months of age, inclusive. Peterson's data show a jaw with M_2 erupted at 9 months of age. From this datum and by comparison with deer and caribou eruption sequences, we estimate that M_2 erupts in moose between 7 and 11 months of age. M_3 and the premolars are more erupted at 17 months of age in Peterson's data set, which leads us to conclude that eruption of these teeth occurs from 13 through 18 months of age in moose.

Moose tooth eruption timing has been little studied (Peterson et al. 1983), with all modern workers essentially reliant on Peterson 1955. Peterson's 1983 study compared the eruption of permanent I_1 and M_2 in two populations of moose: Isle Royale, Minnesota, and the Kenai Peninsula, Alaska. In the Isle Royale population permanent I_1 push out deciduous I_1 in late December or January, and are functional (fully erupted) by late January. The timing in the Kenai Peninsula population is approximately one month later than in the Isle Royale population, which was under some dietary stress. Perhaps because of that fact the Isle Royale population exhibited a wider range of M_2 eruption than the Kenai population. In the Kenai population eruption begins in a few individuals in December and is complete in nearly all by late April. A few individuals in the Isle Royale population exhibited continuing eruption into May or early June. For practical purposes we rely on the data from the Kenai population, where 90% or more of the

calves exhibit M_2 less than ½ erupted in December, January and February. Greater than ½ eruption is exhibited by more than 90% of the population in late February, March and April (data from Figure 1 in Peterson et al. 1983:886).

Tooth wear classes begin to be useful with the 2–3 year class, where the width of dentine exposure on the premolars, M_2 and M_3 is less than the width of the enamel layers. This condition is analogous to the 2-year classes in white-tailed deer and caribou. In moose, however, this youngest eruption class includes a few first molars in the 3-year age class where dentine exposure width may be as wide or just slightly wider than the enamel. The 4–7 year wear class morphologically corresponds with the 3–4 year wear class in deer and 3–5 year class in caribou. The lingual cusps of the premolars and molars are higher than the buccal cusps, and there is significant anterio-posterior and bucco-lingual relief preserved on the teeth. In moose, the 8–15 year class corresponds to the 5–7 year wear class in white-tailed deer and the 6–9 year class in caribou, where the occlusal surface of the molars is worn flat antero-posteriorly and bucco-lingually. Extreme wear in moose cheek teeth is classed in a 15-year-or-older year category, compared with 8-year-or-older in white-tailed deer and 10-year-or-older in caribou. In this oldest class, the wear on cheek teeth is extreme. M1 and other molars are so worn that only a small circle of enamel remains on a dentine basin.

Limited data suggest that the seasonal timing of tooth cementum growth in Maine moose is the same as in Maine deer. Since the forage quality improvement in late May/early June

Table 2-7. Moose tooth wear and eruption timing, after Peterson (1955).

	Known Data	Estimated Range
DM erupting	1 month	2 weeks - 6 weeks, June-early August
M_1 erupting	unerupted at 1 month, 3/4 erupted at 4 - 5 months	2 months - 6 months July-December
M_1 erupting	3/4 erupted at 9 months	6 months - 11 months, December-April
M_2 erupting	3/4 erupted at 17 months	13 months - 18 months, July-December
PM erupting 2 - 3 years	3/4 erupted at 17 months width of wear on PM, M_2, M_3 dentine narrower than enamel. M_1 may have slightly wider dentine than enamel.	13 months - 18 months
4 - 7 years	lingual cusps higher than buccal with significant antero-posterior relief.	
8 - 15 years	occlusal surface worn flat.	
15 + years	extreme wear, M_1 and/or other teeth with small circle of enamel left in shallow molar basin.	

is apparently what breaks the winter rest line formation in deer, the same would be expected for moose (Gerald Lavigne, Maine Department of Inland Fisheries and Wildlife, personal communication 1989). Spiess has examined two moose incisor thin sections from animals killed during the October hunting season. The last growth layer forming on both was about ⅔ thickness, just what it is for deer killed at that time.

Postcrania

The epiphyseal closure sequence in moose is identical to that of caribou and white-tailed deer. However, the sequence must be lengthened over several years, because moose take longer to mature. We assume that the correspondence of dental eruption and epiphyseal closure is such that a hypothetical epiphyseal closure time-table for moose can be based upon correspondence between tooth eruption and wear states in deer and caribou with epiphyseal closure events adjusted to the tooth eruption and wear time-table in moose. For an animal as large as moose, the epiphyseal closure sequence cannot be used to determine season-of-death because it occurs over too long a time span. Its utility to the faunal analyst is found solely in constructing demographic tables and in comparing isolated bone epiphyseal ends for relative age.

There is a quantum size difference between adult moose and adult white-tailed deer that helps differentiate bones of the two species. The differentiation of sub-adult bones that lack epiphyses (for example proximal metapodials, carpal, or tarsal bones) can be based upon size, as follows. For very young moose, lack of bone rugosity, lack of muscle attachment development and thin development of bone cortex indicates that a large cervid bone is in fact a juvenile or newborn moose, as compared with an adult white-tailed deer. Once the juvenile moose exceed adult male white-tailed deer in size, these subjective identification criteria are no longer necessary for species determination and measurements alone can be used. In this study we have taken extra care to differentiate exceptionally large deer bones from sub-adult moose bones. (When identification was not certain it was appropriately noted.)

SEALS

Analysis Methods

Our methods for analyzing seal (Phocid) bone are presented here in detail for two reasons. First, no such method has previously appeared in print. Second, we have encountered

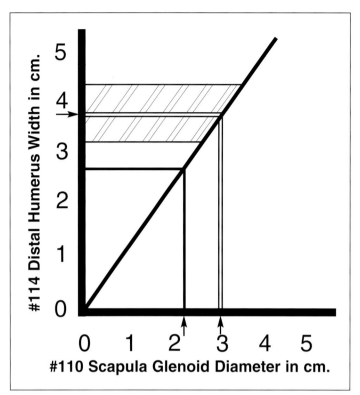

Figure 2-5. We use regressions to answer such questions as: Are either of two distal scapulae with measurements #110 of 2.2 cm and 3.0 cm likely to come from the same animal as a distal humerus (epiphysis fused) with measurement #114 of 3.8 cm? The methodology involved is to calculate the predicted y value for each measurement #110 and compare the results with the measurement of 3.8 cm. If the calculated values are more than two standard errors ($2\sigma = 2$ x $0.246 \approx 0.5$) from 3.8 cm, we assume (with 96% confidence) that the bones are from different-sized individuals. In this case a measurement #110 of 2.2 cm yields y = 2.74, well outside the 2 standard-error-range below 3.8 cm. Measurement #110 of 3.0 cm gives y = 3.75, within the 2 standard error range. Thus, we can say that the second measurement may have come from the same individual as measurement #114 of 3.8 cm, but that the first did not.

an unexpected diversity of Pinniped remains in Gulf of Maine shell middens. Most common are the grey seal (*Halichoerus grypus*) and the harbor seal (*Phoca vitulina*). Differentiating between bones of these two species is relatively easy, mostly based upon size. However, the harp seal (*Phoca groenlandica*) also occurs (infrequently) in the shell midden fauna, and differentiating it from *Phoca vitulina* is more difficult. Finally the walrus (*Odobenus rosmarus*) is definitely known from several Maine archaeological sites (see below).

Although infrequently encountered, harp seal is definitely identified on the basis of auditory bullae in several sites from the Gulf of Maine. The Grindle site (#42–10) in Blue Hill (excavated by Dean Snow of the University of Maine in the early 1970s, unpublished), has a right and left bulla preserved in the collection (specimens number 518 and 790).

The Loomis and Young collection at Amherst College, made before 1920 among the shell middens of Casco Bay, has at least one harp seal bulla. Faunal remains from the Seabrook site in New Hampshire includes a definite harp seal postcanine tooth (Robinson 1985, identified by Spiess). There is also a harp seal bulla from the Turner Farm site and another from the Todd site (Skinas 1987, identified by Spiess).

Walrus (*Odobenus rosmarus*) are also present, but rare, in the Gulf of Maine shell midden fauna. A small walrus tusk was recovered from Occupation 2 at the Turner Farm site (Bourque 1995:88). A worked ivory figurine has been recovered from probable Ceramic period context in site 9.12 on Great Diamond Island (Hamilton 1985, identified by Spiess), Casco Bay, and a walrus bulla is present in the Loomis and Young collection (Amherst College) from another Casco Bay site (identified by Spiess). Finally, a walrus femur comes from site 80.26 on Passamaquoddy Bay (R. S. Peabody Museum, site 126.26, labeled Minscher site).

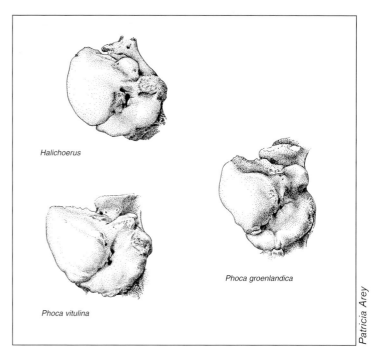

Halichoerus

Phoca groenlandica

Phoca vitulina

Patricia Arey

Figure 2-6. Seal auditory bullae, view of the left bulla, three different species.

Table 2-8. Some reliable morphological traits for taxonomic differentiation of Gulf of Maine Pinnepeds.

	Phoca vitulina	*Phoca groenlandica*	*Halichoerus grypus*
Dentition	Postcanine teeth close set, usually crowding each other. Alveoli angle across jaw. Postcanines have "plump" bases and short, rounded, multiple cusps.	Postcanine teeth well spaced, with multiple, distinctly sharp cusps. Base of tooth (above root) gracile, not "ballooned" as in *P. vitulina*.	Postcanines are generally canineform, with short, sharp cusps and a small ingual facet. Some incipiently bicuspid, and roots often incipiently bifucate. Well-spaced, roundish alveoli.
Mandible	Short symphysis, short and relatively thick body. Jaw height at 5th post-canine approximately 2½ times jaw width.	Jaw height at 5th postcanine approximately 4 times jaw width.	Rugose.
Bulla	Extension from bulla expansion to auditory meatus slopes evenly to a boney point.	Auditory meatus extension ends in a distinct, expanded boney hood bending anterad.	Resembles *P. vitulina* superficially, although more ruguse than Phoca. There is a distinct boney fold between the bulla expansion and the meatus extension, contrasting with the even slope in *P. vitulina*.
Scapula	Greater apparent growth of infraspinal area. Caudal (vertebral) border has appearance of great curvature.	Greater supraspinal growth.	Moderate supraspinous growth.

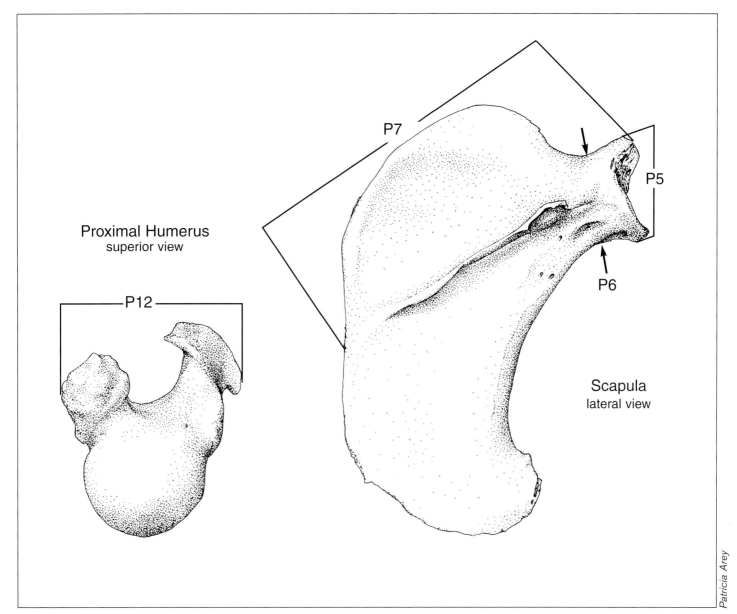

Proximal Humerus
superior view

P12

Scapula
lateral view

P7

P5

P6

Patricia Arey

Figure 2-7. Harbor seal bones, illustrating some of the measurements used in this study.

The Pinnipeds, and Phocids in particular, exhibit extreme postcranial morphological variability. It is rare that single postcranial morphological features by themselves can be used to separate closely sized species (harp and harbor seals, for example). Consequently, Spiess has developed a series of measurements and indices to be used in conjunction with morphological characteristics. However many bones, especially fragmentary bones, must be classified only as "Phocid sp."

Differentiation between *Phoca* and larger members of the Phocidae can be based upon size and rugosity, as well as simple morphological traits. Species differentiation within genus *Phoca* based on single morphological traits can only be accomplished on certain bones. One consequence of the great

individual variability in morphology is difficulty in assigning immature postcrania to species, or even to genus. Table 2–8 details the morphological traits that we used for taxonomic differentiation. They are mostly cranial, either related to the dentition or to the auditory meatus and bulla (Figure 2–6).

Measurements

Table 2–9 presents 48 mandibular and postcranial measurements, previously published (Spiess and Hedden 1983:198), that are specifically designed for applicability to archaeological specmens. Skeletons of harbor (Figures 2–7 and 2–8), harp, and grey seal, and of walrus in the Museum of Comparative Zoology at Harvard University (MCZ), the

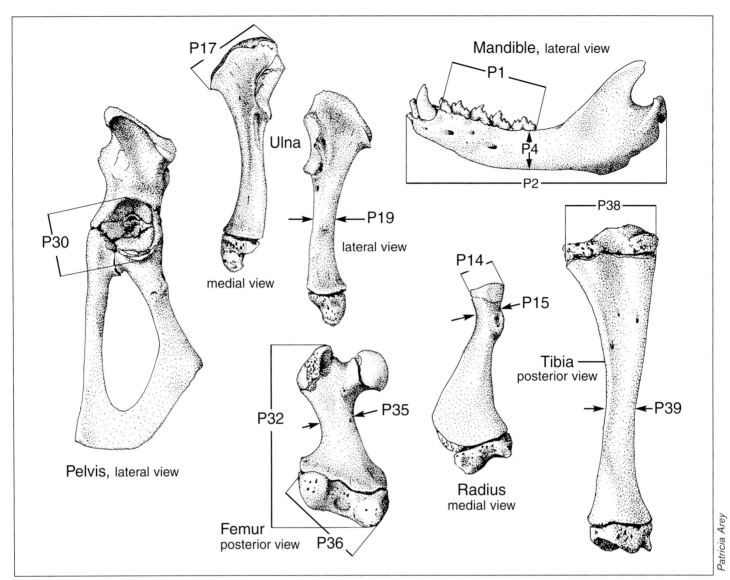

Figure 2-8. Harbor seal bones, illustrating some of the measurements used in this study. The long bones illustrated here are juvenile, with unfused epiphyseal ends.

National Museum of Natural History in Washington, D.C. (NMNH), and the Field Museum in Chicago (FM) were measured. These data provide the basis for taxonomic differentiation of adult bones and age estimation of sub-adults. In grey seal and walrus sexual size dimorphism can also aid in sex identification. Table 2–10 presents mean and observed measurement ranges for the four species that can possibly occur in Maine shell middens. (Few of the measured specimens were collected in the Gulf of Maine. An effort was made to obtain measurements from as many populations as were represented in the collections for each species.)

Use of multiple variables enables more accurate identification. Trivariate analysis of complete humeri, for example, increases the separation of similarly-sized harbor and harp seals. Index (e), defined as (P9) times (P10) divided by (P11),

for harbor seal an observed range from 8.7 to 12.7, while harp seal ranges from 10.5 to 14.2.

Measurements can be useful in aging, as well. For example, in harbor and harp seal measurement #11 (distal width) of 2.5 to 2.8 cm or less on a humerus with unfused epiphyses indicates a term foetus, newborn, or pup less than a few months old.

Epiphyseal Fusion

An epiphyseal fusion sequence for Phocids was constructed (Table 2–11) by seriating epiphyseal fusion states recorded in 29 sub-adult Phocid skeletons from the Museum of Comparative Zoology, National Museum of Natural History and Field Museum. Assigning ages to these specimens is extremely difficult since most are wild-shot and therefore of

Table 2-9. Phocid measurement definitions, after Pierard 1971.

Mandible	
P 1.	Length of postcanine tooth row, measured at alveolar margins.
P 2.	Length of ramus, gnathion to posterior point on condyle.
P 3.	Greatest thickness of ramus (bucco-lingual) under *5th* postcanine.
P 4.	Height (dorso-ventral) of ramus under *5th* postcanine.
Scapula	
P 5.	Maximum length across glenoid face including supraglenoid tubercle (i.e., not just articular surface).
P 6.	Width of scapular neck.
P 7.	Width of scapula, glenoid to vertebral border, in plane of scapular spine.
P 8.	Thickness of scapular border near midpoint of vertebral border.
Humerus	
P 9.	Total proximo-distal length.
P 10.	Distal-most point of deltoid tubercle to proximal border of epicondylar foramen.
P 11.	Distal width, just proximal to condyles or at epiphyseal line.
P 12.	Proximal width, tuberculum major to tuberculum minor, across anterior margin of humeral head.
Radius	
P 13.	Maximum proximo-distal length.
P 14.	Maximum width across proximal radial head.
P 15.	Least diameter of radial shaft between proximal radial head and the bicipital tuberosity.
Ulna	
P 16.	Maximum proximo-distal length.
P 17.	Length of olecranon border (straight line measurement).
P 18.	Least transverse width dorsally between olecranon expansion and trochlea.
P 19.	Narrowest shaft breadth (dorso-ventrally) distal of interosseous tendon tuberosity.
Manus	
P 20.	Length proximal bone of *1st* digit (which is ontogenetically the *1st* phalange rather than metacarpal).
Vertebrae	
P 21.	Medio-lateral width across atlanto-occipital articulation, from lateral margins.
P 22.	Body height of axis, including dens.
P 23.	Lower cervical vertebra, cranio-candal body length.

P 24.	Upper thorassic vertebra cranio-candal body length.
P 25.	Mid-thorassic vertebra carnio-candal body length.
P 26.	Lower thorassic vertebra, cranio-candal body length.
P 27.	Lower lumbar vertebra cranio-candal body length.
P 28.	Sacrum, width, measured from lateral borders of alar processes.
Ribs	
P 29.	Mid-shaft diameter.
Pelvis	
P 30.	Width of acetabulum, rim to rim, measured parallel to andon cranial side of the axis of the incisura acetabuli.
P 31.	Thickness of the illium, acetabular rim to medial margin.
Femur	
P 32.	Length, most distal point of medial condyle to most proximal point of trochanter major (i.e., not in direct proximi-distal axis).
P 33.	Minimum antero-posterior width of femoral neck.
P 34.	Minimum antero-posterior width of neck of trochanter major.
P 35.	Medio-lateral width at narrowest portion of femoral shaft.
P 36.	Distal condylar width, lateral to medialmost margins of femoral condyles.
Tibia	
P 37.	Greatest proximo-distal length.
P 38.	Medio-lateral width at proximal epiphyseal line (just below tibial plateau).
P 39.	Minimum medio-lateral width at mid- shaft.
Fibula	
P 40.	Greatest proximo-distal length, including fibular portion of proximal epiphysis, if fused.
P 41.	Minimum medio-lateral width at mid-shaft.
Pes	
P 42.	Talus, maximum length, heel to navicular articulation.
P 43.	Calcaneus, maximum length.
P 44.	Navicular, maximum medio-lateral width of proximal articular surface.
P 45.	Cuboid, maximum antero-posterior length.
P 46.	Hallux, proximal longbone, length
P 47.	Hallux (first digit), middle longbone, length.
P 48.	*5th* metatarsal (proximal bone, *5th* digit), length.

Table 2-10. Measurements for "adult" seal bones, in centimeters, (epiphyses fused or growth stopped). Only one grey seal and one walrus specimen were measured. A mean is given where three or more specimens were measured. These values are not meant to provide definitive statistical separation between the members of the genus *Phoca,* but to provide a metric guide for use with morphological characters.

Meas #	*P. vitulina* obs. range (mean)	*P. groenlandica* obs. range	*Halichoerus* (mean) one specimen	*Odobenus* one specimen
P1	3.1 - 4.3	4.1 - 4.9	5.4	28.9
P2	13.4 - 14.7	12.3 - 14.1	17.7	–
P3	0.9 - 1.2	0.7 - 0.8	1.7	4.0
P4	2.0 - 2.4	2.1 - 2.7	3.1	–
P5	3.2 - 4.0 (3.6)	3.3 - 3.8 (3.5)	4.5	11.3
P6	2.6 - 3.3 (3.0)	2.5 - 3.9 (3.02)	3.7	9.3
P7	10.2 - 13.7	12.5 - 14.7	17.2	42.0
P8	0.4 - 1.6	0.6 - 1.0	1.1	1.2
P9	10.6 - 12.0 (11.2)	10.75 - 13.0 (12.0)	15.3	36.0
P10	3.3 - 4.3 (4.0)	3.6 - 4.7 (4.0)	5.3	–
P11	3.8 - 4.4 (4.1)	3.6 - 4.3 (4.1)	5.5	14.0
P12	3.8 - 4.1 (4.0)	4.0 - 4.2	5.5	10.8
P13	9.85 - 11.7	10.7 - 13.3	14.7	about 28
P14	2.1	2.4 - 2.5	2.9	8.2
P15	0.9 - 1.2	1.0 - 1.4	1.5	3.0
P16	13.1 - 14.7 (13.9)	13.7 - 16.7 (15.2)	18.9	37.5
P17	5.0 - 6.0	4.3 - 5.2	7.2	11.5
P18	0.9 - 1.1	1.4 - 1.7	1.4	3.4
P19	1.2 - 1.7	1.3 - 2.0	2.2	5.0
P20	4.8	5.4	5.9	12.5
P21	5.6	4.3 - 5.2	6.8	–
P22	4.6	4.7 - 5.2	6.1	–
P23	2.5 - 3.5	2.9 - 3.3	3.7	4.0
P24	2.3 - 2.2	2.7 - 3.6	3.7	–
P25	2.6 - 4.1	3.9 - 3.5	3.7	6.5
P26	2.7 - 4.0	3.5 - 4.5	3.7	–
P27	4.1 - 4.5	4.4 - 5.2	5.2	7.0
P28	8.3 - 10.2	9.3 - 9.5	11.6	–
P29	0.7 - 1.0	0.85 - 0.9	1.1	2.5
P30	2.4 - 2.5	2.4 - 2.5	2.2	6.7
P31	1.6 - 2.3	1.6 - 2.0	3.5	5.0
P32	10.0 - 11.1	9.7 - 11.0	13.0	25.0
P33	1.0 - 1.2	1.2 - 1.5	1.5	3.3
P34	1.5 - 1.9	1.6 - 2.0	2.0	4.6
P35	1.9 - 2.8	2.5 - 3.3	3.4	5.6
P36	4.3 - 4.6	4.5	5.3	10.3
P37	19.0 - 22.1	25.9	26.7	38.0
P38	3.6 - 4.7	4.1 - 4.5	4.9	9.1
P39	1.9 - 2.7	1.9 - 2.0	2.6	3.6
P40	18.3 - 21.1	25.4	25.6	35.0
P41	1.0 - 1.3	1.2 - 1.4	1.9	2.1
P42	4.4 - 7.6	5.3 - 5.9	6.5	11.0
P43	4.9	5.1 - 5.4	6.8	–
P44	2.2	2.6	3.1	–
P45	2.1	2.6	3.1	–
P46	5.7 - 6.6	9.1 - 9.8	19.3	13.8
P47	5.5 - 6.4	8.1	9.3	11.8
P48	6.5 - 7.2	8.3 - 8.5	9.3	16.5

unknown age. A newborn harp seal from the Gulf of St. Lawrence (MCZ 28681) is helpful. Museum records indicate that it was killed in April, and since pupping in this population occurs in late February, the animal was one and one-half to two months old. Sumner-Smith et. al. (1972) have X-rayed harp seals of 1½ to 2 months of age, and 2½ years of age. These data provide the only absolute chronology for the epiphyseal fusion sequence, which, however, does not hinder its use for relative age determination.

Incremental Growth in Teeth

Phocid teeth deposit annual incremental growth both within the dentin cavity and in cementum around the tooth root (Smith 1973, 1987; Weber et al. 1993). The dentine layer is deposited from the tooth wall inward. Using various microscopic preparatory techniques, including either decalcification and staining after sectioning or cutting and polishing an undecalcified tooth, the rest lines appear as dark (stained) or translucent (dark in reflected light) while the growth lines appear as light (stained) or opaque (light in reflected light).

In several phocid species, it has been reported that the rest line forms during a span of a month or two, during the molting season, which overlaps and follows the breeding and pupping season. It is unclear whether rest line formation is controlled by the molt or by mating, but the evidence seems to favor the molt. For harbor seals in Maine, the molt period includes June and July.

Table 2-11. Preliminary epiphyseal closure sequence for genus *Phoca*.

Event	Timing in *Phoca*
1. Permanent dentition (erupts)	At birth or before.
2. Atlas midline suture	---?---
3. Distal phalanges	For events 3 through 6, 1½ to 2 months in sequential order.
4. Vertebral bodies fuse to later process.	
5. Humerus, distal, two ossification centers fuse to form one epiphysis.	
6. Illium, ischium and pubis fuse.	
7. Humerus, proximal, 3 ossification centers fuse to form one epiphysis.	Between 2 months and 2½ years for events 7, 8 and 9; order not confirmed, however.
8. Proximal tibial and fibular epiphyses fuse to form one epiphysis.	
9. Caudal epiphysis of axis fuses to body.	
10. Femus, head and trochanter major fuse to shaft.	Events 10-22 are listed in sequential order of occurrence. Absolute timing unknown but after 2½ years.
11. Humerus, distal epiphysis fuses to shaft.	
12. Radius, proximal epiphysis fuses to shaft.	
13. Humerus, proximal epiphysis fuses to shaft.	
14. Femur, distal epiphysis fuses to shaft.	
15. Tibia, proximal epiphysis fuses to shaft.	
16. Ribs, proximal epiphysis fuse.	
17. Vertebral epiphyses fuse to bodies, beginning to form cranial and caudal ends of vertebral column. Completion of this event overlaps following events.	
18. Radius, distal epiphysis fuses to shaft.	
19. Ulna, distal epiphysis fuses to shaft.	
20. Phalanges, metacarpals, and metatarsals: epiphysis fuse to shaft.	
21. Fibula, proximal epiphysis fuses to shaft.	
22. Tibia/fibula distal epiphyses fuse to shaft.	

We assume that the rest line forms during the molt in grey seal during February for females and February and March for males in Nova Scotian populations (Cameron 1970). This assumption regarding females is strengthened by Spiess' analysis of a canine from a female grey seal (MCZ 5 1488) with known date of death: February 6, 1964 (in Massachusetts?) which showed a rest line forming. As with deer, if a growth line is forming, seasonality can be estimated (with precision of 2 or 3 months) by the relative width of the line compared to previous annual layers. Some male grey seals live to over 30 years of age, and a female has been reported at 46 years of age (Bonner 1971). At these advanced ages the annual layers become indistinct, making old seal teeth unreadable for season-of-death.

BEAR

Analysis Methods

Bones of the black bear *(Ursus americanus)* were identified by comparison with other bear specimens. Measurements follow von den Driesch (1976). All the bones identifiable to species are *Ursus americanus*, the black bear. Although grizzly bear and polar bear are known from the eastern subarctic (Spiess 1976b, Spiess and Cox 1976), none of the specimens yet identified from Maine belong to either species. Epiphyseal closure status was recorded from longbones. Cementum annuli in bear canines form during their annual hibernation (Grue and Jensen 1979).

MINK

Analysis Methods

Mink *(Mustela Lutreola)* include two species, the common mink *(M. L. vison)* and the extinct sea mink *(M. L. macrodon)*. The sea mink has undergone a comprehensive taxonomic restudy by Mead et. al. (2000) which supports the taxonomic identification of sea mink as specifically distinct from common mink. Early studies describing the sea mink include Prentiss (1903) and Loomis (1911). The larger Turner Farm site sample supports this conclusion on the basis of: (1) minor differences in morphology, generally due to extreme rugosity in sea mink; (2) overall size difference between sea mink and common mink, including relatively little overlap between female sea mink and male common

mink; and (3) notable contemporaneity on North Haven Island of sea mink and a minority population of common mink since Occupation 2 at the Turner Farm site (about 4,500 years ago).

Hardy (1903) states that the sea mink became extinct about 1860. The only known mounted specimen in existence is described (Keene 1929) as being larger than the ordinary mink, with noticeably larger and stronger feet. "The hair is a light reddish-brown, and exceedingly coarse in comparison with that of the common mink."

Cut marks that have incised the bone were noted on several sea mink specimens. Loomis (1911:728) illustrates such a mark on a mandible from a Casco Bay shell midden. Several Turner Farm site skulls exhibit transverse marks across the maxillary-nasal bone, presumably for removing the pelt from the skull. These marks indicate that sea mink were being skinned, based on analogy with cuts made by modern mink trappers.

Measurements

Separation of sea mink (Figures 2–9 and 2–10) from other mustelids was based on a series of skeletal measurements, used in conjunction with reference specimens of pine martin *(Martes americana)*, fisher *(Martes pennanti)*, and common mink. In addition, Mead et. al. (2000) compare Turner Farm and other coastal Maine sea mink with five subspecies of common mink, including *M.v. nesolestes*, a large Northwest Coast subspecies. Martin is similar to the sea mink in overall body size. Cranially, the pine martin is easily distinguished from sea mink by premolar count (four in *Martes*, three in *Mustela*). Postcranially, individual bones of pine martin are slightly longer and significantly more gracile than those of sea mink.

Measurements used here follow a system developed by von den Driesch (1976) for *Canis*. Measurements for a male pine martin specimen in the Maine State Museum collection are presented in Table 2–12. Measurements for a modern Maine male and female common mink and for archaeological sea mink specimens (Table 2–16) from the Turner Farm and other Maine shell middens document size and proportion differences. Measurements (Figure 2–11) were taken to the nearest tenth of a millimeter. No complete skull of a sea mink was available, so skull measurements were rare. Mandibles are much more common; five measurements and a combined cross-section calculation describe the mandible (Figure 2–11, Table 2–13). Seven measurements were taken

Table 2-12. Marten. Selected measurements from a Maine State Museum specimen. Measurements in cm, following definitions or numbers for analagous measurements of *Canis* by von den Driesch 1976 or Leach 1977 (measurements A-H.)

Skull		Mandible		Femur		Tibia/Fibula		Radius and Ulna			Scapula	
1.	7.50	1.	4.95	Bp	1.31	A.	6.80	GL (radius)	A.	4.55	A.	3.22
2.	7.25	2.	4.80	Bd	1.21	B.	6.66	PL "	B.	4.44	B.	1.31
3.	6.84	4.	4.09	GL	6.21	C.	6.39	Bd "	C.	0.78	C.	1.11
9.	3.20	7.	2.70			Bp	1.20 (tibia)	Bp	0.54		D.	0.81 (SLC)
13a	3.50	8.	2.50			Bd	0.85 (tibia)	GL (ulna)	D.	5.59	E.	4.80
15.	2.13	10.	1.05					DPA (ulna)	0.74			
17.	1.80	12.	1.45									
18.	0.71	13.	0.78									
19.	0.66	14.	0.74									
22.	1.74	17.	0.38									
23.	3.44	18.	2.02									
27.	1.12	19.	0.78									

Skull		Atlas	Sacrum	Calcaneus	Humerus			Pelvis	
30.	4.27	GB. 2.49	GB. 1.47	GL 1.59	GL.	E.	5.73	A.	2.76
31.	1.29					F.	5.64	B.	1.55
32.	2.21				SD.	G.	0.38	C.	0.8
33.	1.70				Bd.	H.	1.22	D.	1.25
34.	2.31				Bp.	–	1.00	GL.	4.69
35.	1.38							LA.	0.66
36.	1.48								
38.	2.19								

M$_1$ bucco-lingual width: 0.70

Table 2-13. Descriptions of measurements of sea mink mandibles and postcrania. See Figure 2-11 for visual representations.

Mandible	
LTR	Length of the Tooth Row; anterior edge of canine alveolus to posterior edge of M$_2$ alveolus
HM	Height of Mandible; dorso-ventral height measured below middle portion of M$_1$, lingual side
WM	Width of Mandible; bucco-lingual, measured at greatest width below middle of M$_1$
LM$_1$	Length of M$_1$, greatest antero-posterior measurement (near the base of the enamel)
WM$_1$	Width of M$_1$, greatest bucco-lingual width measured at talonid

Postcrania (Humerus, Radius, Femur, Tibia)	
GL	Greatest Length
BP	Breadth of Proximal end
BD	Breadth of Distal end
LD	Least Diameter of the diaphysis, medial lateral, usually mid-shaft

Femur (additional measurements)	
LT	Total Length, greater trochater to distal condyles
BT	Breadth of Trochanters, medio-lateral
BH	Breadth of femoral Head, antero-posterior

on the femur, and four each were taken on the humerus, radius and tibia (Figure 2–11, Table 2–17).

The vast majority of small mustelids in the Turner Farm sample are specimens of sea mink. Based upon the few skulls available, the sea mink palate is wider between M1

Figure 2-9. Reconstructed sea mink partial skull and mandible, recovered from Allen's Island, Maine. Left lateral view; calvarium fragmentary and distorted. This is a large, rugose male.

and longer than any common mink. The external and internal nares of sea mink are larger, producing, in combination with the wider palate, a more robust-looking skull. The posterior teeth (P^4 and M^1) exhibit larger (crushing) surfaces than in common mink, apparently reflecting use of the larger muscle mass around the robust skull. The sea mink is relatively prognathic, exhibiting forward extension of the upper anterior teeth, and the junction of the anterior margin of the zygomatic with the cranium is farther posterior relative to placement of the tooth row. This juncture is over the P4 in sea mink, but is over the area between P3 and P4 in common mink.

Mandibles, the most abundant mink skeletal element recognized in the Turner Farm sample, exhibit a slight overlap in dimensions between sea and common mink (Table 2–14). Sea mink shows a distinct sexual size dimorphism, as has been noted in marten, fisher (Leach 1977; Boise 1975) and other mustelids. Table 2–15 shows the distribution of carnassial length measurements obtained from *Mustela* species mandibles in the Turner Farm sample. There is an evident bimodality in specimens of what we interpret as sea mink

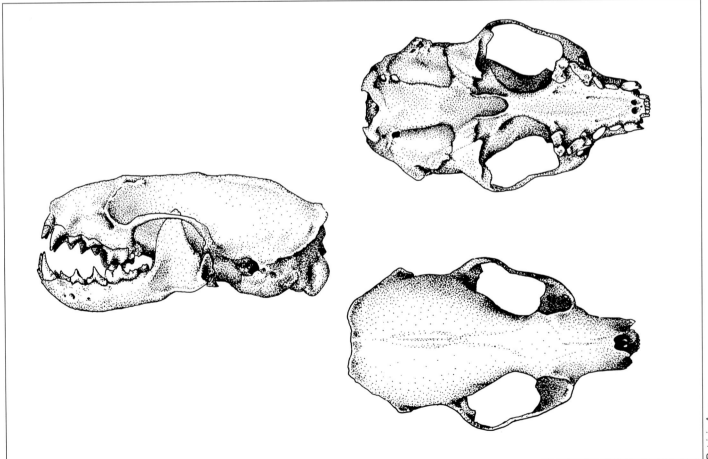

Patricia Arey

Figure 2-10. Three views of *Mustela vison* skull.

plus a very few (adult) mandibles of a size and rugosity similar to common mink. Thus, a small percentage of the sample from all occupation levels at the Turner Farm site exhibit a distinctly less rugose morphology and smaller size range, which fits the morphology of common mink.

Postcranial measurement ranges are presented in Table 2–16. Sea mink has a slightly longer and more robust forearm than the common mink, a pattern that appears in all other appendicular longbones. Radii and ulnae of sea mink exhibit greater development of the bony ridges for attach-

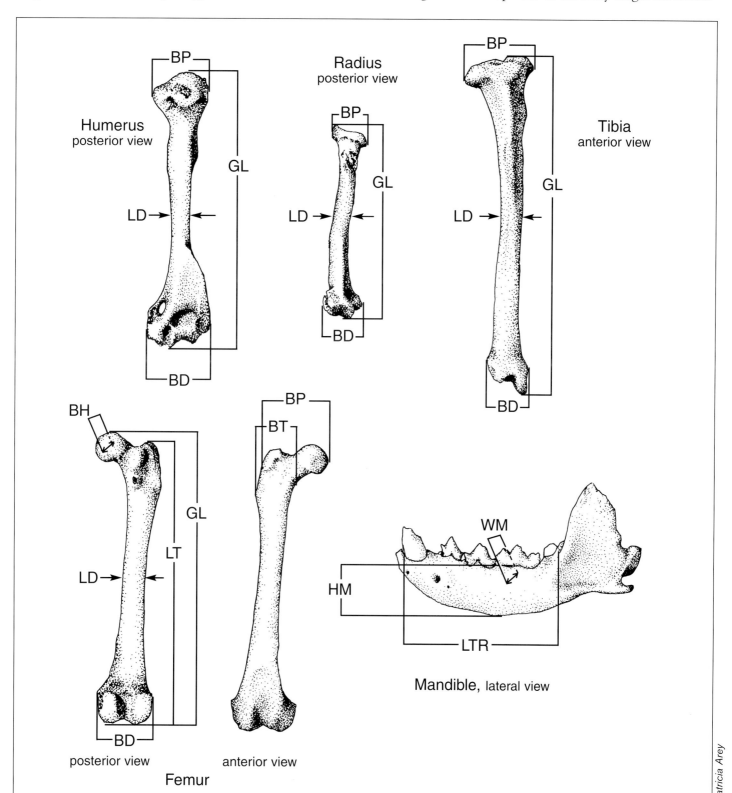

Figure 2-11. *Mustela macrodon* mandible and postcrania, showing Mustela measurement definitions.

Patricia Arey

ment of the interosseous ligament between these two bones. Distally on the radius, the tubercle for attachment of the hand flexor muscles is much more rugose in sea mink, and the bicipital tuberosity on the proximal radius is bilobate in form on many specimens but never on common mink, indicating greater power in the biceps. These morphological differences reflect much greater power in the forelimb and hands of sea mink. The femoral neck of sea mink is relatively elongate compared with common mink, lengthening the lever arm from the lateral surface of the greater trochanter to the acetabulum, which adds power to (and subtracts speed from) abduction of the femur. Distally, the lateral epicondyle of the femur is more strongly developed, indicating much more powerful muscles acting in certain hindlimb movements in sea mink. The tibial crest is also relatively more strongly developed, especially at its distal end, which indicates a larger extensor muscle mass on the tibia, in keeping with the general rugosity of the species. Based upon the comparison of sea mink to multiple subspecies of mink by Mead et. al. (2000), the measurements in Table 2–17 can be used definitely to identify the former. Because these measurements differentiate it from all subspecies of mink, and because the Northeastern subspecies is smaller than the largest subspecies, a large number of sea mink females will fall below these definitive identification measurements. Therefore, the identified ratio of sea mink to common mink might be less than the true ratio, given the difficulty of identifying the smaller females.

Incremental Growth in Teeth

Several score sea mink canines were sectioned during this study, and examined microscopically. Several provided clear readings, exhibiting alternating translucent and opaque zones in both dentin and cementum. We used canines because they

Table 2-15. Sea mink carnassial length measurements in mm from Turner Farm specimens. Number of specimens in each measurement range. Note the bimodality with modes at 8.6-8.7 and 10.0 -10.1, most visible in the Ceramic period sample, probably sea mink females and males, respectively. Some of specimens less than 0.76-7 are *M. vison*.

Length M1	Occ. 2 4200 B.P.	Occ. 3 3000 B.P.	Occ. 4
7.0-1	–	1	–
7.2-3	–	1	–
7.4-5	–	1	1
7.6-7	–	–	1
7.8-9	1	–	1
8.0-1	–	1	4
8.2-3	–	1	5
8.4-5	–	1	7
8.6-7	–	1	8
8.8-9	–	5	7
9.0-1	2	3	6
9.2-3	2	3	10
9.4-5	2	1	12
9.6-7	1	4	17
9.8-9	5	5	25
10.0-1	1	7	31
10.2-3	2	3	20
10.4-5	2	1	6
10.6-7	–	1	1

Table 2-14. Statistics for mandibular measurements of sea mink versus common mink from the Turner Farm site. N = number of specimens measured, $\bar{x}$ = mean, s = standard error, and OR = observed range. Measurements are defined in Table 2-14 and Figure 2-11. Measurement in mm.

	LTR	HM	WM	LM$_1$	WM$_1$
M. macrodon (Turner Farm)					
n	29	39	41	41	40
$\bar{x}$	23.1	9.1	5.1	9.7	4.6
s	1.7	0.5	0.4	1.4	0.2
OR	19.5–25.7	7.7–10.1	4.1–6.1	9.4–10.6	4.1–5.2
M. vison mink					
n	6	6	6	6	6
$\bar{x}$	18.7	6.5	3.5	7.3	3.2
s	1.2	0.9	0.3	0.3	0.1
OR	15.5–21.1	5.8–8.0	3.2–4.1	7.0–7.8	3.2–3.4

were by far the most common teeth in the sample assignable to this species. Strickland et. al. (1982) report that better sections are obtained in fisher premolars than in fisher canines, but the archaeological sample did not allow us that luxury of choice. These authors report good correspondence between the number of visible annuli and age in fisher. The annulus is apparently formed during winter and/or early spring, becoming clearly visible after the formation of a thin layer of contrastive growth forms by mid-June (Strickland et. al. 1982:92). Other studies (Kelly 1977 in Strickland et. al. 1982) report an annulus visible on the edge of fisher cementum during May. Thus, problems of seasonality interpretation

Table 2-17. Measurements for definitive separation of *M. macrodon* from all subspecies of *M. vison* (from Mead et. al. 2000). Measurements in mm.

Skull	Palate length > 36.0		
	Width between M^{1}s > 11.8		
	Length M^1 > 4.6 & breadth > 7.6		
Mandible	LTR > 22.5		HM > 8.0
	LM$_1$ > 9.2		WM$_1$ > 4.0
Humerus	GL > 55.0	DB > 15.8	LD > 4.7
Radius	GL > 38.5	BP > 6.5	LD > 3.0
Femur	GL > 58.0	BD > 6.5	LD > 5.0

Table 2-16. Statistics for postcranial measurements of sea mink from the Turner Farm site, and for two specimens from Maine of common mink. Specimens 027-2 (probably male) and 027-1 (probably female) are in the Univeristy of Maine, Orono, Department of Anthropology collection. For the Turner Farm specimens of sea mink: N = number of specimens measured, $\bar{x}$ = mean, s = standard error, and OR = observed range. The measurements of each of the common mink specimens are given individually (in mm). All epiphyses were fused on all specimens measured (where complete).

Humerus		GL	BP	BD	LD			
Sea mink	n	11	23	48	48			
(Turner Farm site)	$\bar{x}$	57.0	13.0	16.0	4.8			
	s	2.2	0.6	1.0	0.2			
	OR	54.0–60.7	12.0–14.7	13.3–18.4	4.1–5.6			
Common mink–027-2		45.6	9.2	6.1	–			
Common mink–027-1		38.1	7.9	5.2	–			
Radius	GL	BP	BD	LD				
Sea mink	n	13	32	16	33			
(Turner Farm site)	$\bar{x}$							
	s	0.8	0.3	0.4	0.3			
	OR	38.5–41.4	6.2–7.5	6.2–7.5	2.8–4.8			
Common mink-027-2		31.5	5.0	6.1	–			
Common mink-027-1		26.2	4.0	5.2	–			
Femur	LT	GL	BD	LD	BT	BP	BH	
Sea mink	n	17	17	19	30	35	34	35
(Turner Farm site)	$\bar{x}$	58.9	60.3	4.4	5.9	9.1	14.9	7.5
	s	2.1	2.2	0.6	0.4	0.5	2.7	0.4
	OR	55.0–62.7	56.1–63.6	13.4–15.7	5.1–6.9	8.1–10.6	13.0–19.4	6.7-8.5
Common mink-027-2		47.3	–	10.2	–	–	12.1	5.4
Common mink-027-1		39.7	–	8.7	–	–	9.4	4.4
Tibia	GL	BP	BD					
Sea mink	n	10	10	11				
(Turner Farm site)	$\bar{x}$	65.6	14.1	9.8				
	s	1.4	0.4	1.0				
	OR	63.3–68.3	13.4–14.8	–				
Common mink-027-2		52.2	10.7	7.3				
Common mink-027-1		44.0	8.6	6.1				

in sea mink revolve around the timing of annulus formation in an extinct species. Analogy with common mink (Grue and Jensen 1979) indicates annulus formation sometime during the period of November through March.

BEAVER

Analysis Methods

The beaver (*Castor canadensis*) postcranial sample was often fragmentary, and crania were never found complete. When possible, longbone total lengths and proximal or distal widths were obtained, and the state of epiphyseal fusion observed. In this species, distal tibial epiphyses fuse to the diaphysis during the third year of life (Robertson and Shadle 1954). The proximal tibial epiphysis fuses during the following year, and fibular ankylosis occurs in the fifth year. Other criteria of age, including skull measurements and incisor lengths, are not useful in fragmentary shell midden samples.

Tooth Eruption

Beaver kits are born in May and June, but not all of the litter may be born simultaneously (van Nostrand and Stephanson 1964). Consequently, developmental stages in very young animals make relatively poor seasonal indicators. The most useful demographic detail in such a fragmentary sample can be obtained from beaver cheek teeth (one premolar and three molars in each jaw). At 6 months of age all three molars are erupted, and the deciduous premolar is being forced from the jaw by an erupting premolar (van Nostrand and Stephanson 1964:431).The permanent premolar is fully erupted by 1 year of age. Little tooth development occurs between December and April, however.

Tooth Wear and Annual Layers

Van Nostrand and Stephanson (1964) use the status of cheek tooth root closure as a macroscopic visual aging criterion. Information on the status of cheek tooth root closure was collected for the Turner Farm site sample, and tabulated using an "open, closing, closed" typology. In animals less than 2 years of age, the molar root cavity is open to the bottom. Between 2½ and 4 years of age the basal cavity closes by growth of dentin and cementum. After 4 years of age, all cheek tooth roots are closed. Van Nostrand and Stephanson

(1964:433) also report successful microscopic reading of annual layers in cheek tooth cementum but we were unable to observe these layers in the Turner Farm site sample.

A similar series of tooth-based aging criteria have been developed for the *Marmota monax* (woodchuck or marmot) a large Sciurid rodent (Munson 1984). Cheek tooth eruption in this species occurs rapidly with deciduous molars and the first permanent molar erupted before the young leave their maternity burrow, allowing complete upper or lower cheek tooth rows for individuals less than 6 months old to be aged to a precision of ±20 days. Although these observations of tooth eruption produce less resolution in slower-growing beaver, Munsun (1984) introduces the technique of bucco-lingual incisor width measurement for woodchuck aging, which might be applicable to beaver. Munsun (402) points out that the curation of beaver incisors for tools among Northeastern prehistoric groups limits their use as seasonal indicators. We have therefore not attempted to do so.

MUSKRAT

Analysis Methods

Muskrat (*Ondatra zibethecus*) bones are uncommon in the Turner Farm site sample. However, because this small mammal species grows rapidly, means of differentiating between subadults and adults may allow season-of-death determinations. Eruption of the lower first molar tooth, specifically the appearance of the base of the anterior enamel fold on the lingual side of the tooth above the bone line, demarcates adulthood from subadulthood (Alexander 1960, wherein this enamel fold is called the "first proximal fluting"). Fusion of certain longbone epiphyses is also a marker of adulthood, which occurs late in the first season of growth. In Maine, the peak of muskrat breeding and birthing occurs in May and June, although there may be late litters into the fall. Approximately 90% of the muskrat births in an Iowa population occurred during the late spring (Errington 1963). A tentative epiphyseal fusion sequence (Munyer 1964), confirmed by several fall-trapped specimens in the Maine State Museum collection, indicates that the epiphyses on the proximal femur, proximal ulna, proximal radius, and distal tibia fuse by 4 to 7 months of age, or before early winter (December) in the vast majority of individuals (Table 2–18). Mature animals (>1 year) often

Table 2-18. Muskrat epiphyseal fusion state, as seen in two Maine specimens trapped in November. Epiphyseal bone ends are arranged in three apparently sequential fusion groups. Epiphyseal fusion status codes are as follows: "0" = epiphysis closed completely and bone remodeled to obliterate epiphyseal line; "-" = epiphysis fused but epiphyseal line present; "+" = epiphysis fusing, synostosis beginning or incomplete; "++" = epiphysis open.

Bone/epiphysis	Specimen 1	Specimen 2
Early Group		
Distal Humerus	0	0
Proximal Radius	0	0
Lesser Trochanter	0	0
Middle Group		
Distal Tibia	–	0
Calcanear Tuberosity	–	0
Femoral Head (prox)	– / 0	–
Greater Trochanter	–	0
Olecranon (ulna)	–	0
Late Group		
Distal Femur	++	+
Proximal Tibia	++	++
Distal Radius	++	++
Humeral Head (prox)	++	++

lack epiphyseal fusion on the distal radius, distal ulna, distal femur, proximal humerus and proximal tibia. One of us (Lewis 1990, see also Cox 1991) has been particularly successful in using postcrania bone fusion in muskrats to determine season of occupation in a sample of calcined bone from a Maine Archaic nonshell midden site. A high proportion of unfused epiphyses on the distal humerus, distal tibia and femoral head indicate late spring, summer or early fall harvesting of this species.

SMALL CANIDS

Analysis Methods

Most small furbearing species were identified by comparison with a skeletal specimen, supplemented if necessary with notes or photographs. We made a concerted effort to determine whether the faunal sample included bones from grey fox (*Urocyon*). There is historic evidence for the occurrence of the species in southwestern Maine since the seventeenth century, and some question about previous archaeological identifications (Palmer 1956:62–70). There

are marked differences in postcranial rugosity, red fox (*Vulpes*) being more gracile. There are also marked differences in skull morphology and dental proportions and morphology, grey fox exhibiting greater emphasis on molar chewing surfaces, red fox exhibiting greater cutting edge emphasis. Eight of the 23 fox bones in the Turner Farm sample have been identified to genus (7 jaw parts and 1 humerus). All are unequivocally *Vulpes*. Canid bones recovered from the midden context are included in this section for convenience. All Canid specimens identified to species are *C. familiaris*.

BIRDS

Analysis Methods

Bird bones were identified by direct comparison with osteological collections, where possible. In the case of the great auk (*Pinguinus impennis*) comparison was made with unpublished photographs of a mounted skeleton (Knight 1908, facing p. 38), drawings, and other alcid skeletal elements (Olsen 1974; see also Meldgaard 1988). Fragmentation of the sample reduced bird bone identifiability, and often precluded identification to genus/species. A bone was recorded only if the bone element could be identified, which is a necessary first step in approaching taxonomic identification.

There were many fragments, especially of longbones, that were clearly bird bone structurally that could not be identified as a particular skeletal element. This group of several thousand fragments was left uncounted and unrecorded. Highly fragmented bird ribs were present in moderate quantity. However, they were left in the unrecorded sample because of degree of fragmentation and difficulty of identification. Similarly, unidentifiable bone fragments that were probably mammal, and a group of probable fish unidentifiable fragments were left uncounted and unsorted. In dealing with smaller faunal collections in subsequent years (e.g., Spiess 1984a, 1984b, 1992) we have attempted to quantify this material by counting and weighing it.

Other bird bones also presented special difficulty in taxonomic and element identification. Foot phalanges were grouped into two categories: the "claw", or terminal phalanges, of the foot (Phalange III), and other foot phalanges (recorded simply as "phalange"). The fused proximal phalanges of the carpus (wing) are recorded as "PhI/II carpus." These phalange categories, and several other bones (vertebrae, sacrum, radius, furcula) were identified only by size, and divided in to those that were duck-sized, larger-than-duck-sized, and smaller-than-duck-sized. In addition, it was noticed that humerus fragments of large birds were more often identifiable to taxon than medium-sized humerus fragments. To correct for this bias, a category of "medium sized bird" was created for humerus fragments not otherwise identifiable.

The coracoid seemed to provide the most taxonomic information within the sample due to morphological variability between genera and species, coupled with limited postdepositional breakage. For this bone element only did we attempt to subdivide the ducks (Anatidae) into finer divisions, each containing one to a few species. This goal was approached by sorting the archaeological sample into three groups based upon perceived differences in morphological detail. It was then possible to further subdivide each group into several distinct size categories. Comparative specimens of known species showed that these categories, while valid for this archaeological sample, did not correspond with sub-family taxonomic subdivisions. For example, one group included one or more species of the surface-feeding ducks (Anatinae) and the diving ducks (Aythyinae). Still, based upon this sorting process it is possible to divide Turner Farm site duck coracoids into the following identifiable groups: (1) an eider, probably common eider (Somateria mollissima); (2) the white-winged scoter (Melanitta fusca); (3) a group containing the greater and lesser scaup (Aythya marila and Aythya affinis); (4) a group containing possibly several species of the genus Anas of similar size to the black duck (Anas rubripes); (5) a group containing several species significantly smaller than the black duck, including Anas and species of Aythyinae, possibly including the teals, the bufflehead (Glaucionetta albeola) and relatives, and the harlequin duck (Histrionicus histrionicus), among others; and (6) the American merganser (Mergus merganser). Leach (1979) has shown that consideration of relative representation of bird skeletal parts in New Zealand midden samples occasionally has cultural significance. He ascribed anomalous frequencies of various skeletal parts to prehistoric use of special groups of feathers associated with those parts. While frequency variation in most skeletal parts is probably a result of breakage and identifiability at the Turner Farm site, skeletal parts frequencies are nevertheless presented in an effort to search for cultural significance.

Seasonality

The seasonality of bird death can be reconstructed from three sources, although not all techniques may be applicable to each specimen or taxon. For some species, simple presence is a seasonal indicator, assuming behavior roughly similar to that of today. The majority of all individuals of some species are present seasonally along the Maine coast. The old squaw (Clangula hyemalis), bufflehead (Glaucionetta albeola) and goldeneye (Glaucionetta clangula) are present in great numbers along the coast during the late fall and winter. Any formal assemblage with a large number of these ducks must represent winter hunting, even though an isolated individual could conceivably be killed at any time of year. Some species, such as the red-throated loon (Gavia stellata), are uncommon but most likely present during spring and fall migrations (Palmer 1949). Some species only migrate locally. Because the common loon (Gavia immer) breeds on inland lakes, few individuals are found along the seacoast during the season when Maine inland lakes are free of ice (roughly late April through early December).

Secondly, immature bird bones were identified on the basis of cartilaginous ends that had not calcified and diaphysis that were poorly calcified. It is assumed that these birds are of fledgling age or younger. In mammals, both ends of the long-bone diaphysis grow with a cartilaginous cap. In most (but not all) mammal longbones, diaphysis growth is accompanied by growth of a cartilaginous and bony end-cap, the epiphysis. In birds, these epiphyses are missing, but the longbones grow with cartilage on either end. Before growth cessation, the end of a bird longbone is characterized by a particularly rough or pitted surface. Moreover, the bone cortex near the end of the diaphysis, and sometimes elsewhere on the shaft, is thin, friable and incompletely hardened compared with the adult. Based upon observations of a few wild-shot specimens of ducks (Anatidae) and gulls (Lariidae), this recognizably immature cortical pattern persists until the bird is a mature fledgling, nearly ready for independent flight. Different species fledge at different times during summer and fall. Moreover, much basic research has yet to be done to correlate longbone diaphysis lengths and bone cortex states with age in young birds. In the absence of this research base, recognition of this immature state in bird longbones represents merely the presence of a juvenile or fledgling bird.

Thirdly, there are transitory macroscopic and microscopic histological changes in bird longbones that can be used for

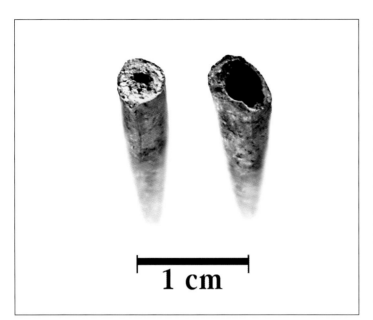

Figure 2-12. Presence (left) and absence (right) of bird medullary bone in the shafts of two cormorant tibiotarsi, viewed from proximal toward distal. (Samples are from the Kidder Point site, catalogue 41.40.231b; see Spiess and Hedden 1983 for a site report.)

aging, for seasonality determinations in female birds during the breeding season, and to a lesser degree during the molt and feather formation in both sexes. Annual microscopic layers form in the periosteum of some portions of longbones of some bird species (van Soest and Utrecht 1971). Other histological changes are related to the storage and mobilization of calcium for the production of eggshell. Enlargement in the diameter of Haversian canals in bird bone cortex has been reported during the molt in taxa that molt "precipitously" (e.g., *Anatidae, Accipiteridae*). In species from these families, in both male and female birds, the height of the molt is accompanied by enlargement of the Haversian canals in longbone cortex, sometimes to the point of apparent extreme osteoporosis. These histological changes can be observed in thin sections of bird longbone. We have not yet applied this technique systematically to the Turner Farm fauna, but we have observed a related calcium-metabolism feature, the deposition of medullary bone.

An examination was made of broken tibiotarsi from the Turner Farm sample for the macroscopic presence of medullary bone, a calcium reserve noticeable in female birds before and during egg-laying (Taylor 1970; Rick 1975). It can be observed as a slightly porous deposit on the inside of the long-bone diaphysis wall, and constriction of the bone cavity (Figure 2–12). Unfortunately, the exact timing of formation and disappearance of medullary bone has only been studied in

domestic pigeons and in ducks (Bloom et al. 1941). The female pigeon will lay her first egg within seven days of successful mating, and a second egg about 40 hours afterward. Medullary bone appears in the "marrow" cavity of the female pigeon's longbones approximately 60 hours before the first ovulation, which occurs shortly before the egg is laid. By 10 days after the second egg has been laid, all signs of medullary bone have disappeared, and the inside of the longbone marrow cavity has returned to normal. Thus, the presence of medullary bone marks a roughly two-week segment of time beginning after mating (and hence after nesting). Its presence in Turner Farm site specimens is taken as prima facie evidence of local breeding of the species in which it is identified.

TURTLES

Analysis Methods

Turtle bone (carapace and plastron, or the bone portions of turtle "shell") was identified with the help of a reference collection in the possession of Dr. Kristin Sobolik, Department of Anthropology, University of Maine, Orono. Bone names were assigned following the usage in Sobolik and Steele (1996).

FISH

Analysis Methods

Fish bone identification was based mainly upon comparison to specimens in the Maine State Museum collection. Nomenclature was adopted from Cannon 1987. Several identification problems unique to fish are discussed below.

Sample Recovery

Approximately 300 soil samples, totaling 83 liters, were sieved through fine mesh following the removal of large shell particles. These samples yielded approximately 200 fish bones, mostly from flounder. The midden volume processed in this way amounted to 0.25% of the total volume excavated from the site, yet it produced roughly 7% of all small fish bone from the site. These data suggest that hand recovery in the field yielded roughly two orders of magnitude fewer small fish bones that were actually present. They also confirm recent quantitative work on fish bone from other shell middens by Casteel (1972a), Payne (1972), Carlson (1986:98–101, Appendix B) and Spiess (n.d.) that indicates an increase in small fish bone recovery with the use of small screens to process the matrix.

We have not included fish bone data from these sieved samples in our relative counts presented in chapters 3 and 4. No radical shift in species frequencies was evident, and only one additional species, herring *(Culpea harengus)*, was identified. However, we have included these data in our analysis of seasonality from vertebral readings to increase our sample size for this relatively scarce data type.

Identification

Fish species identifications were based on direct comparison with prepared skeletons. The flounder family is represented by at least five species: winter flounder *(Pseudopleuronectes americanus)*, sand flounder *(Lophopsetta maculata)*, American

Table 2-19. Cod mean thoracic vertebral diameter compared with live length, in cm. (From Carlson 1986:123).

Thoracic Vertebra	Diameter (cm)	Live Length (cm)
Specimen 1	1.0	58
Specimen 2	1.1	70
Specimen 3	1.2	81
Specimen 4	1.8	112

NOTE: Rojo (1987:215) gives much more detailed data, including linear regression coefficients for vertical and horizontal diameter of several thoracic and caudal vertebrae on total length and weight of cod.

Table 2-20. Cod mean length in cm compared with age in years (after Bigelow and Schroeder 1953:189).

Age	Live Length (cm)
1	15
2	37
3	52
4	68
5	83
6	95
7	102
8	117
9	125

dab *(Hippoglossoides plattesoides)*, halibut *(H. hippoglossus)*, and yellowtail *(Limanda ferrogina)* and/or smooth flounder *(Liopsetta putnami)* (the latter two being difficult to distinguish). No complete skeletan was available for some species, and some specimens are therefore identified as "flounder: species indeterminate." Moreover, fragmentation and poor archaeological preservation of the sample contributed more significantly to species indeterminate identifications.

Because of their asymmetric body structure, each flounder family specimen contains a single bone, the first interhaemal bone, whose fragments are easily recognized. For first interhaemal bones we recorded the recovered portion (proximal or distal end, or medial fragment) and if possible some measurement (length or diameter). Because each fish has one of these bones, which preserves well in archaeological sites and yields measurement information, they usually provide the most reliable MNI and the most metric information as well.

Cranial bones for all species were identified to bone element and as right or left if applicable. Vertebrae were identified as atlas, axis, thorassic (pre-caudal), or caudal. For some species, such as striped bass, fin-ray fragments were counted as well. For the smallest species most fin-rays are unidentifiable.

Swordfish are the largest fish species in the sample, which, coupled with a distinctive fin ray structure, allowed us to identify much swordfish postcranial material. In addition, swordfish rostrum (sword) has a distinctive, easily identified structure (large voids or air spaces, matte exterior surface). Some cod family skeletal elements are distinctive to species, which make it evident that the vast majority of cod family bones in the sample are cod *(Gadus morhua)*. Dogfish, a shark, have mostly cartilaginous skeletons, but their dorsal spines ossify and provide identification. Likewise, sturgeon have cartilaginous skeletons and are represented solely by large, thick, well calcified dermal scutes, which are difficult to compare quantitatively with other fish species. For this study, sturgeon scutes are quantified by weight and by occurrence, which was defined as a group of scutes not demonstrably from more than one individual from one excavation unit. Given uniform factors of preservation, comparative weights may give the best relative frequencies for this species (Table 3–51).

Measurements

Fish cranial bones were rarely recovered whole at the Turner Farm. The absence of a large sample of complete cod cranial

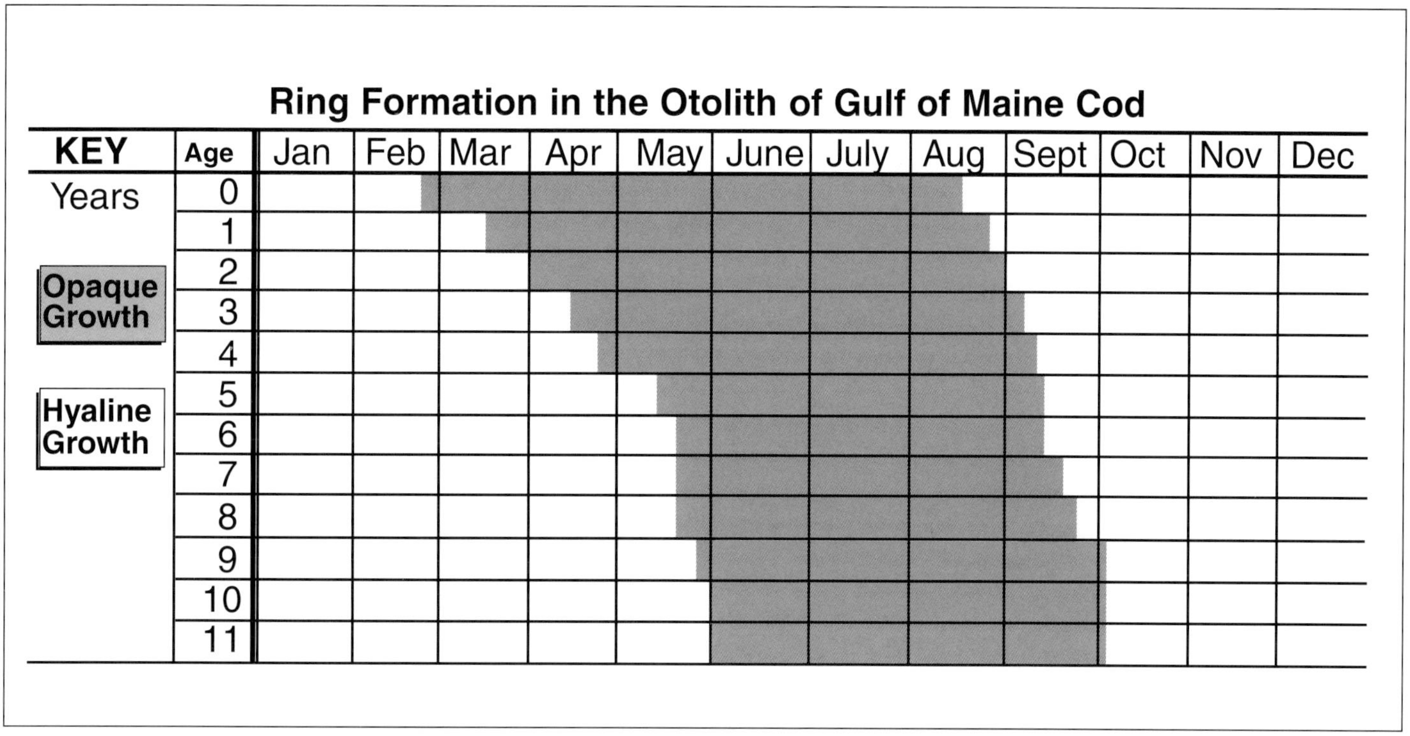

Ring Formation in the Otolith of Gulf of Maine Cod

KEY	Age	Jan	Feb	Mar	Apr	May	June	July	Aug	Sept	Oct	Nov	Dec
Years	0			▓	▓	▓	▓	▓	▓	▓	▓		
	1			▓	▓	▓	▓	▓	▓	▓			
Opaque Growth	2				▓	▓	▓	▓	▓	▓			
	3				▓	▓	▓	▓	▓	▓			
	4					▓	▓	▓	▓	▓			
Hyaline Growth	5					▓	▓	▓	▓				
	6					▓	▓	▓	▓				
	7						▓	▓	▓				
	8						▓	▓	▓				
	9						▓	▓					
	10						▓	▓					
	11						▓	▓					

Figure 2-13. Cod dates of inception and cessation of annual "rapid growth" layer, depending on age. Based on information from Williams and Bedford (1974:119) and Judy Pentilla (personal communication, to Mark Hedden, 1981, Woods Hole Marine Laboratories). Dark bar indicates rapid growth (redraw from Carlson 1986).

bones forced us to rely on the much more common vertebral centra for size data. Two metric attributes are recorded for fish vertebrae: largest vertebral diameter and growth ring status. The vertebral diameter was recorded from either the cranial or caudal articular surface. Caudal vertebrae vary in size within one fish, decreasing in diameter toward the tail, which lowers the utility of caudal vertebrae in determining fish size. However, for thorassic vertebrae and many cranial and shoulder girdle bones, there is a clear relationship between vertebral diameter, fish size, and fish age (Tables 2–19 and 2–20) (Bigelow and Schroeder 1953; Carlson 1986; Casteel 1974; Rojo 1986, 1987). Carlson (1986:120–122) shows that cod size, as measured by thorassic vertebral diameter, is correlated with seasonal presence inshore, in estuary mouths, on the central Maine coast under modern conditions. Small cod are present, or can be present, year-round in the estuaries. Adult cod, defined as 4 years of age or older, come inshore in November through June, frequently spawning in water as shallow as three to five fathoms in February to May. Carlson (1986: 167) also cites records of a peak in spawning activity in the Sheepscot estuary from late April through at least July in 1978–1982. A thorassic vertebral diameter of 1.1cm is used by Carlson to separate juvenile cod, which might be available year-round, from adult specimens, which have a more limited inshore seasonal availability.

Annual Layers

Analysis of annual and subannual layering in fish skeletons for age is an old technique (Marion 1949; Appelget and Smith 1950; Galtsoff 1952; Bardack 1955; Casteel 1972b; Marzoff 1955). More recent studies (Panella 1971; Bagenal 1974) have focussed on attempts to use incremental growth for analysis of partial-year or seasonal growth. In particular, Casselman (1974) demonstrated by tetracycline labeling that in pike (*Esox lucius*) growth was highly seasonal, and even non-linear within the rapid growth season.

The most common technique is to cut a section through an otolith, but many of these references refer to visible structure on skull and shoulder girdle bones, or on the articular surface of vertebrae. In the Turner Farm site study, we have found that the concentric rings on vertebral articular surfaces are particularly useful because of the large numbers available for analysis and the ease with which these data can be correlated with vertebral diameters and other independent estimates of fish age or size. Counting the rings on vertebral surfaces provides an age estimate of the fish. If a marginal portion of the vertebral articular surface is well preserved, it is usually possible to observe the status of the last stage of growth before the fish was caught. If the last layer forming at the time of death is a growth layer then its relative width compared with the preceding growth layer is recorded as < ¼, ¼, ½, ¾, or fully formed. If the annulus or growth arrest layer is the last layer forming then that fact is recorded. Unfortunately, the exact seasonal timing of growth arrest layer formation in Gulf of Maine fish species is poorly known at present, so seasonality deductions from these data must be tentative. However, these data can be used for comparisons between assemblages to detect shifts in fishing strategy even if the exact seasonality is not understood.

According to Bigelow and Schroeder (1953), the seasonal timing of maximal growth rates differ among species of fish. Williams and Bedford (1974) state that most North Sea demersal species begin to grow the wide growth zone in late winter or spring, but that growth begins much earlier in plaice than in sole. Growth of the wide growth zone begins earlier in the southern extremes of a given species range and becomes progressively later further north. Moreover, "within each stock the younger fish, in which wide opaque zones are growing, begin to lay down the opaque zone before older fish (Williams and Bradford 1974:119–120)." For all species except cod we simply compiled the growth ring data according to a simple summer/fall/winter/spring typology and searched for patterning, while being cognizant that the exact dates of annulus formation vary between species and between age groups within species.

A major complication with the reading of annual layers from vertebral surfaces arises when dealing with cod and its relatives. The articular surfaces of cod family vertebrae exhibit concentric ridge and valley relief which obscures the growth and growth-arrest layers. On fresh cod specimens the annual growth layers are more easily recognized by a pattern of translucent (or hyaline) and opaque bone alternation than by the relief of the vertebral articular surface, although even in fresh vertebrae the pattern can be confusing.

Carlson (1988) reports pessimistically on an experimental reading of cod family vertebral articular surfaces. Spiess participated in these experiments, during which he concluded that ridge-and-groove relief on the articular surface was non-congruent with and did obscure the alternating layers of translucent and opaque bone that actually constitute the annual increments. When preserved archaeologically in shell middens, this translucent/opaque contrast disappears as the bone degrades. In our experience, only under uncommon conditions of preservation are annual layers readable on cod vertebrae from shell middens. These examples are cases of very poor preservation where concentric cracks have begun. These concentric cracks appear to form in the translucent bone layer, because they can be seen there on desiccated modern specimens, and because the cracks are not congruent with the ridge and groove series. Only a very small proportion of the Gadid vertebra sample were in this state of preservation.

Table 2-21. Flounder size and seasonality data. The smooth founder and first winter flounder specimens are in the Department of Anthropology, University of Maine, Orono collection. The other winter flounder specimens were obtained by Spiess. Age is the count of completed growth arrest layers.

	Smooth flounder,					
1.	Passamaquoddy Bay, February 1, Translucent layer just finished forming					
	Winter flounder					
	Date	**Length**	**Weight**	**Age**	**Vert. Diameters**	**Annulus state, notes**
2.	mid-June	?	?	?	?	< ¼ growth
3.	June 24	30cm	0.55kg	6	4.7 x 5.3mm thoracic 5.5 x 5.3mm anterior caudal	annulus fully formed –
4.	July 4	34cm	?	9 or 10	6.1 x 6.0mm thoracic 5.4 x 5.2mm caudal	annulus forming –
5.	July 18	38.1cm	?	> 5	6.4 x 6.9mm anterior caudal	annulus forming, female with roe
	NOTE: interhaemal bone of specimen 3, greatest length 5.71cm interhaemal bone of specimen 4, greatest length 6.26cm					

One-year-old and 10-year-old Gulf of Maine cod show a 3-month difference in inception of rapid summer growth in otoliths, and a 2-month difference in cessation of growth (Williams and Bedford 1974:119–120). We assume the same variability in growth timing in cod vertebral annulae as in the otoliths and can correct for it by knowing the age of the fish. Only in cod has an attempt been made to correct for age variation in inception and cessation of annual growth rings. We have used the age-dependent growth patterns produced by Williams and Bedford, coupled with data derived from eight years analysis of Gulf of Maine cod otoliths (Judy Pentilla, personal communication, 1981), to produce the growth zone/rest zone timing chart reproduced as Figure 2–13.

We have information on the season of vertebral translucent (growth arrest) line formation for several flounder specimens, as well as size, age and weight data (Table 2–21). The data indicate that different species of flounder form the growth arrest line at different times of the year. Winter flounder (*Pseudopleronectes americanus*) in inshore waters, at least in Casco Bay, exhibits growth arrest line formation in late spring and early summer (late May into early July) in conjunction with spawning. Fish otoliths exhibit perhaps daily, fortnightly, monthly, and seasonal (basically summer-winter) growth patterning (Panella 1971). The Turner Farm site preserved few otoliths, so our sample is basically limited to vertebrae, whose state of preservation is not always excellent. Only for one species, the tomcod (*Microgadus*), were enough otoliths recovered and sectioned to demonstrate a season-of-catch pattern.

SHELLFISH

Analysis Methods

Two types of questions were asked of our shellfish data: those pertaining to quantification and to seasonality. Quantification involves evaluating relative species composition, amount of shell deposited in the site, number of individuals and their size distribution, and estimating total meat weight for comparison with the vertebrate remains. Since the soft-shelled clam (*Mya arenaria*) represents more than 97% of the bulk of the shellfish in the site, most of our work focussed on that species. Seasonality of harvest was investigated for both *Mya arenaria* and the hard-shelled clam or quahog (*Mercenaria*). Unfortunately all the quahog were too old, with their annual layers too closely spaced, to provide season-of-death readings (Beth Turner, personal communication, 1983).

Two types of shellfish samples were saved from the site. Exceptionally well-preserved individual valves were saved sporadically. They proved useful in increasing the number of specimens available for seasonality readings. Bulk midden samples of known volume were systematically collected from balks at the site. These soil samples were analyzed in the laboratory to provide the quantitative information we desired.

Quantitative Analysis Methods

Treganza and Cook (1947–8) may have been the first to attempt a carefully measured estimate of the amount of shell in a single midden deposit. The logic and methodology of the Turner Farm study parallels their method.

For each midden sample, an initial dry weight and volume estimate (hand-packed into a graduated beaker) were taken. The sample was sieved through 4 mm mesh. Shell fragments retained on the screen were sorted by species, and a weight obtained for each species' fraction. Sectionable and measurable chondrophores (the hinge on the left valve) were removed from the sample for further processing. The shell, dirt and soil passing through the mesh were saved and weighed. For selected samples, this mixture was treated with acid until effervescence ceased. It was then washed, dried and weighed. The difference between this weight and the pre-acid wash weight, i.e., the weight of the shell fragments that had passed through the screen, was added to the weight of shell retained on the mesh to determine the total shell weight for the sample (Table 2–23). As expected, the highest average and highest absolute values for shell fragments passing through the mesh came from the plow zone.

The following shellfish species were found in the soil samples: soft-shelled clam (*Mya arenaria*), quahog (*Mercenaria mercenaria*), blue mussel (*Mytilus edulis*), deep-sea scallop (*Placopecten magellicanus*), sea urchin (*Strongylocentrotus*), surf clam (*Spisula solidissima*), northern moonshell (*Lunatia heros*), and waved whelk (*Baccinum undatum*). Only in rare cases does the weight of non-clam shell exceed 1% (see Table 2–22).

The most precise step was to estimate the volume of a stratum in an excavation unit. The problem was approached on a unit-to-unit basis by estimating the area of each stratum using stratigraphic profiles and floor plans. Profiles of all four walls for each excavation unit were also used to estimate the average depth, which was multiplied by the area to produce a volume estimate.

The total weight of shell recovered from each stratum was then estimated by the following logic. We knew the total weight of shell and the volume of each of several hundred soil samples. (n=301 totaling 83.1 liters). We assumed that the shell fraction in the soil sample from any stratum in any excavation unit was representative of the shell fraction from that unit/stratum. Estimated shell weights for each unit/stratum were summed for all excavation units to produce an estimated shell weight for each stratum over the whole excavation. This method is more precise than one derived by simply multiplying the average shell weight per liter by total occupation volume because it reflects local variability in midden composition within each stratum.

These estimates are not precisely comparable throughout the stratigraphic column, however. Because midden soil acids are neutralized by the slow dissolution of calcium carbonate from the shells, we would expect midden shell to have lost some of its calcium carbonate and to be slightly less dense than fresh shell as a result. Moreover, this loss in shell density should be age-dependant. To correct for this density loss, we obtained specific gravities from samples of broken archaeological and modern shell by taking their dry weight, placing them in a graduated beaker and measuring (from a graduated cylinder) the volume of water necessary to make up 1,000 ml. The average modern clam shell specific gravity is 1.2 (gr/ml), with archaeological samples having specific gravities 5–15% lighter (Table 2–24). As expected, the oldest shells measured (from Occupation 2) have the lowest specific gravity.

Estimates of total meat yield from clams can be derived directly from estimates of total shell weight. The method is simply to buy or harvest a "mess" of clams, boil them, remove and weigh the meat (wet) and dry and weigh the shell (air dry weight). Spiess and Hedden (1983:202) report a ratio of 100:65 for dry clam shell weight to wet meat weight for two modest batches of clams harvested in June, 1982. Their analyses of blue mussels yielded a shell : meat ratio of 100:16.

A useful attribute to estimate harvesting pressure and other ecological factors affecting a clam population is some measurement of clam size. Nelson (n.d.) used chondrophore width on a sample of very young (small) clams from Boston Harbor, attempting to correlate chondrophore width with shell weight and meat yield. Spiess and Hedden (1983:201–202) found Nelson's correlation equations inapplicable to larger, more mature Maine clams. They therefore measured and weighted a sample of several hundred Maine clams (Table 2–25) and produced a regression equation from these data.

Spiess and Hedden weighed only left valves. However, since the right valve weighs almost the same as the left, doubling the left valve weight allows us to estimate total clam shell weight. Thus, we have a method of converting chondrophore width distributions, multiplied by the number of clams, into total clamshell weight. Direct interassemblage comparisons of chondrophore widths, without conversion to weights, are also useful in detecting shifts in size distribution of harvested clams.

Table 2-22. Examples of shellfish weights retained on 4-mm mesh screen from soil sample analysis.

Sample Number	S-004	S-014	S-045	S-202
Occupation	2	2	3	4-CCS
Provenience	W30S70 14-16"	W35S80 14-20"	W50S80 19-23"	E15S75 20"
Volume of Sample	250ml	325ml	400ml	300ml
Weight *Mya*	86.7gr	156.0gr	181.6gr	137.6gr
Weight *Mercenaria*	–	0.5gr	–	–
Weight *Mytilus*	0.3gr	0.3gr	0.3gr	6.9gr
Weight *Lunatia*	–	–	0.2gr	–

Clam Seasonality

Mya seasonality reading and interpretation methods were adopted by Spiess and Bourque from techniques published elsewhere and applied simultaneously to the Kidder Point (Spiess and Hedden 1983) and Turner Farm site samples. This section essentially repeats the methodology reported by Spiess and Hedden (1983: 203–206) with the addition of some new comparative data.

The periodicity of growth layers in bivalves has been investigated extensively (see Lutz and Rhoads 1980 for a review; Kent 1988; Claasen 1988). Koike (1980) first applied detailed work on molluscan periodic growth patterns to an analysis of prehistoric shell midden formation, in this case in coastal Jomon-period Japan. The most obvious internal patterning in *Mya arenaria* has been proven to be annual (MacDonald and Thomas, 1980).

Table 2-23. Weights of shell in various soil samples, per volume (grams/milliliter). Shell fragment weight passing through 4mm mesh, determined by acid treatment until effervescence ceased.

Occupation	Soil Sample	Weight of Shell Lost	Volume of Sample Original	Loss gr/ml	Average Loss for Occupation
I	S-164	38.5gr	350ml	0.11	0.11gr/ml
2 (Shell-Bearing Portion)	S-001	23.3gr	250ml	0.09	0.15gr/ml
	S-004	45.0gr	250ml	0.18	
	S-091	73.4gr	425ml	0.17	
3 (Shell-Bearing Portion)	S-011	27.6gr	225ml	0.12	
	S-228	72.9gr	400ml	0.18	
	S-043	86.9gr	275ml	0.32	0.21gr/ml
4 Coarse-Crushed Shell	S-002	24.9gr	175ml	0.14	0.11gr/ml
	S-005	22.7gr	250ml	0.09	
	S-164	38.5gr	350ml	0.11	
4 Medium-Crushed Shell	S-156	35.5gr	400ml	0.09	0.13gr/ml
	S-279	60.6gr	450ml	0.13	
	S-145	77.0gr	450ml	0.17	
Plow zone	S-299	103.2gr	350ml	0.29	
	S-300	106.3gr	250ml	0.43	
	S-301	64.1gr	250ml	0.26	0.32gr/ml

Table 2-24. Weights of shell in various soil samples, per volume (grams/milliliter). Shell fragment weight passing through 4mm mesh, determined by acid treatment until effervescence ceased.

	Number samples (n)	Average specific gravity	Standard error	Correction factor
Occupation 2	7	1.58	0.06	1.132
Occupation 3	5	1.72	0.08	1.055
Occupation 4	8	1.73	0.09	1.049
Modern Clamshell	3	1.82	0.03	1.000

Claassen (1990: Table 7) makes two errors in interpreting Spiess and Hedden's (1983: Appendix Table 14) modern comparative clam incremental growth samples, and thus in questioning their archaeological data interpretation. First, she combines all clams exhibiting a growth zone into her fast growth category. But since clam growth appears to slow down during the growth season, Claassen is lumping fast-growing clams, clams with slow growth, and clams with no growth. Secondly, Spiess and Hedden (1983) and Spiess and Lewis (herein), reject growth increment measurement series with an irregular growth mode from further statistical analysis, which Claassen apparently does not. For example, Spiess and Hedden (1983) reject 2 out of 6 clams in the 1/24/82 sample exhibiting irregular growth patterns as useful for any predictive statistics, while Claassen includes these specimens in her statistics (n = 6 in Table 7).

Bourque, Spiess and Lewis have been developing clam harvest seasonality techniques for application to Penobscot Bay shell midden samples since 1980. Our method involves the following: placement of a *Mya* chondrophore on edge in a small, disposable capsule, sealing it against epoxy penetration (which might alter its optical properties) with polyvinyl alcohol, and pouring epoxy resin to surround the specimen. A plane is then ground or sawn and polished on a lapidary wheel to expose a section through the middle of the chondrophore (Figure 2–14). The epoxy-embedded specimen is etched with dilute

Table 2-25. Chondrophore length versus left valve weight. For widths of 5 mm to 13 mm, these values were determined from a sample of several hundred clams harvested on North Haven, Maine. For 14 mm to 17mm, chondrophore width, valve weights are estimated from very rare, nearly complete archaeological specimens.

Chondrophore Width	Mean Valve Weight	Standard Error
5mm	0.9 gr	0.26gr
6mm	1.8 gr	0.20gr
	2.6gr	0.72gr
8mm	3.2 gr	0.88gr
9mm	4.7 gr	1.20gr
10mm	5.8 gr	1.50gr
11mm	7.3 gr	1.60gr
12mm	9.7 gr	2.70gr
13mm	16.2 gr	0.14gr
14mm	est. 22.0 gr	
15mm	est. 25.5 gr	
16mm	est. 37.0 gr	
17mm	est. 45.0 gr	

HCl for at least 30 seconds, washed to stop etching, and dried. Acetate peels are produced by placing the specimen on a sheet of clear acetate with a drop of acetone, weighted until dried. The resulting acetate peel is mounted between two glass slides and viewed with transmitted light at 50 magnifications.

The peels reproduce microscopic detail (see Figure 2–15). In the region where the chondrophore joins the main shell, annual growth-arrest lines appear as hair-thin dark lines. The period of growth is represented by wide, lighter bands containing some further detail. We "read" the concave shell margin by noting the presence of an annulus forming (as in the specimen in Figure 2–15), or by measuring the thickness of the last growth layer and its antecedent growth layers, using an optical micrometer of 100 gradations mounted in one ocular of the microscope. Each graduation measures 0.033 mm at the magnification used. Annual increments in our *Mya* samples range from 2–20 units (0.07 to 0.7 mm) in width. Measurements are taken by aligning micrometer gradations across the area of tightest curvature in the periodic growth structure at the chondrophore-shell juncture. The practical resolution limit is ½ reticule unit, as observed by repeated measurement series.

Readings of the several years growth prior to harvest are reported, as in the following example, in micrometer units: x/8/8/7/8/. Time (growth), as represented by these numbers, proceeds from left to right (see Table 2–26). The right-hand-most number or symbol represents the layer growing at time of death. Forward slashes (/) represent a growth arrest line (annulus). X represents previous, unmeasured growth, which may be represented further by a number of years or annuli. Although the thin annual growth-stoppage lines are clear on well-preserved specimens, the rate of growth-layer accretion is neither constant through the year nor completely consistent from year to year. These factors complicate estimation of season of harvesting, as will be explained below.

The timing of annual *Mya* growth arrest line formation from the central Maine coast is well understood (Newell 1983). Newell prepared acetate peels from a wild population with 30% tidal exposure at Lows' Cove, Damariscotta River estuary. This sampling effort concentrated on the periods of rest line formation (February to April). Newell found that by mid-February, over half the clams in his sample had begun annulus formation, with higher rates of inception at lower elevations (with less tidal exposure). By March 4th, at 30% tidal exposure, 82% of the clam popu-

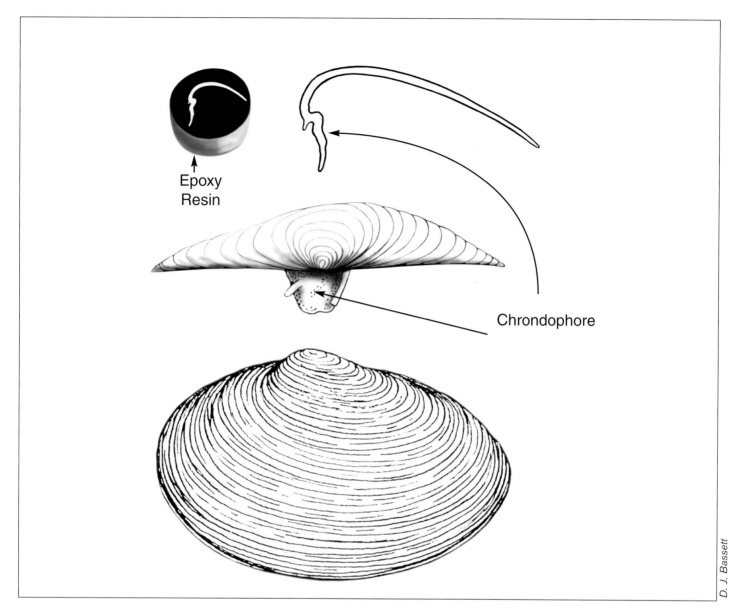

Figure 2-14. Clam shell chondrophore preparation for acetate peel preparation. The chondrophore is the "hinge" on one of the two valves of the soft-shelled clam. The chondrophore is removed and mounted on edge in epoxy resin, then a transverse section is ground through the middle. On the specimen in the left of the figure, the chondrophore is to the right, and the remaining portion of the main part of the clam shell is to the left.

lation had initiated annulus formation; and by March 23rd, 100% of the population had initiated annulus formation. By April 8th, 10% of the population had new growth outside the annulus, a figure increasing to 33% by April 22nd. By May 6th, 100% of the population had new growth (annulus completed).

We have supplemented Newell's data with samples collected from Kidder Point in Searsport, Rockport and North Haven Island in Penobscot Bay, Allens Island in the St. George estuary, and Cobscook Bay (Table 2–26).

In our Penobscot Bay samples, 1 of 6 specimens had begun annulus formation by late February (compare 50% in Newell's sample). By May 20th, 2 of 7 had completed annulus formation (compare 100% by May 6th in Newall's sample). Thus, it appears that modern Penobscot Bay clams, from the areas of the archaeological sites under consideration, exhibit an annulus formation delay of about one month compared with Newell's Damariscotta River sample. We will use the following attributes as rough criteria for characterizing the month of collection of clam samples: late January-early February, 10% or less with annulus forming; late February-early March, 10–50% annulus forming; late March-early April, 50–99%

Figure 2-15. Photomicrograph of an acetate peel of a clam chondrophore section from Occupation 2. The image is of the junction between the chondrophore and the main body of the shell: the chondrophore is to the left and the main portion of the shell is to the right. The growth layers accreted sequentially toward the bottom of the figure (long directional arrow), with the last layer (of eight or more, short arrows indicating rest lines) being a rest line forming.

annulus forming; late April-early May, 100% annulus formed or forming, 10–30% new growth initiated; late May-early June, 25–90% new growth initiated; late June, 100% new growth initiated; and June-October, increasing growth width.

Inspection of the May-October samples (Table 2–26) shows a generally increasing amount of growth relative to previous growth layers as the season progresses. On an inspection (non-statistical) basis, the modern sample and a sample of several hundred archaeological specimens exhibit either near-constant growth on a year-to-year basis, or increasing or decreasing growth rates over periods of 3 to 4 years. A small percentage are irregular. Thus, we define four modes of growth for the last 3–4 years preceding death: (C) constant, year-to-year variability being less than 15%; (I) monotonic increasing; (D) monotonic decreasing; and (Irr) irregular.

The causes of these growth patterns do not seem to be exclusively age-dependent, although the older clams (North Haven 7/30/1981 and 8/5/1981 samples) do exhibit higher proportions of constant growth. The relative width of the last layer is easily estimated on constant-growth specimens except for a small, unascertained percentage of this sample that may have just switched to irregular growth in the year of death. Irregular-growth specimens are useful only for "annulus forming/not forming" determinations. For increasing or decreasing growth, the thickness of the last layer must be compared with a projection based on the assumption of regular change in growth rate. Obviously, specimens in constant-growth mode will yield more reliable estimates of relative growth, but those in increasing-growth or decreasing-growth modes are valuable in augmenting small samples.

April/May samples include a majority of clams with annuli forming, and a few with growth layers of 10% or less rela-

Table 2-26. Clam annular growth data, from measurements of annual growth increments visible on chondrophor acetate peels. Each individual specimen is listed by a sequential letter under groups by date of harvest. X stands for unmeasured previous annuli. Annular width measurements are in microscope optical micrometer units, not reported for exact metric equivalent. Each slash (/) represents one growth arrest layer. Annual layers are read from left (younger) to right (older), with status of last growth layer shown by presence or absence of growth arrest layer (/) or not. Growth mode, projected full growth width, and percentage of last year's growth attained are also given. Percent of last year's growth can either be a numerical figure, "annulus forming" (= annulus forming) or 100% if growth width is not different from completed prior year's growth width. Growth mode is C = constant, I = increasing, D = decreasing, or Irr = irregular.

	Growth Mode	Proj. Full Growth	% Growth
Allen's Island 7/22/84			
NOTE: Mature clams recovered from near 50% tidal exposure.			
A. X/14/15/15/4	C	(15)	27%
B. X/4.5/5.5/6.5/7/1.5	I	(7.5)	20%
C. X/4/6/5.5/4/4/1	C	(4)	25%
Whiting/Cobscook Bay 9/25/84			
NOTE: 33-67% tidal flat exposure in an area heavily harvested. 21 clams sectioned, most showed multiple or irregular (trauma) lines.			
A. X/11.5/12/9/4.5	D	(6.5)	69%
B. X/3/2/1	D	(1.3)	75%
C. X/6/4.5/7/4.5/2I	----	----	
D. X/6.5/3/2	I	----	----
E. X/2/2/1.5	C	(2)	75%
Kidder Point 1/24/83			
A. X/X/X/6.5/8/3	Irr	----	Irr
B. X/6/8/12/8/2	Irr	----	Irr
D. X/X/8/9/7	C	----	F
E. X/8.5/8.5/8/8/	C	----	Annulus
F. X/X/5/5.5/6/10	I	----	F
G. X/7/6/9/8	? I	----	F
Rockport 4/12/82			
A. 6/5/5/0.5	? D	(4)	13%
B. X/5.5/6/	C	----	Annulus
C. X/7.5/6.5/	D	----	Annulus
D. X/6/6/	C	----	Annulus
E. X/16/13/6/	D	----	Annulus
H. X/10.5/9	D	----	Annulus
I. X/9.5/8.5/4.5/	D	----	Annulus
J. X/12/8/	D	----	Annulus
Kidder Point 5/20/82			
C. X/4/5.5/6.5/0.5	I	(7.5)	7%
D. X/5/6/7/I		(8)	Annulus
E. X/4.5/4.5/10/0.5	? Irr	----	3%-10%
F. X/6.5/4.5/5.5/	C	----	Annulus
H. X/6/5.5/6/	C	----	Annulus
I. X/X/11/10/10.5/	C	----	Annulus
J. X/5.5/5/5/3.5/	D	----	Annulus
Kidder Point 6/27/82			
A. X/X/3/3.5/7/1	I	(14?)	7%
B. X/X/5.5/5.5/6/1	C	----	17%
C. X/X/5/8/1	I	(12)	8%
D. X/X/5/6/7/1.5	I	(8)	19%
E. X/5/6.5/13.5/3		(27??)	11%

	Growth Mode	Proj. Full Growth	% Growth
Kidder Point 6/27/82 *continued...*			
G. X/3/2/6.5/1.5	? I	----	?%
H. X/4/5/10/1.5	? I	----	?%
I. X/X/4.5/5/1	? C	----	20%
J. X/5/5/10.5/2	? Irr	----	10-40%
North Haven 7/11/81			
B. X/X/6/5.5/3.5/1.5	D	(2.5)	60%
C. X/X/8/8/2.5	C	----	31%
D. X/X/11.5/7.5/2.5	D	(5)	50%
E. X/X/X/8.5/7.5/4	D	(6.5)	62%
F. X/X/X/7/2	?	----	----
H. /X/X/10/9/7/2	D	(5.5)	36%
North Haven 7/30/81			
A. X/6.5/3.5/1.5	D	(2)	75%
B. X/6.5/5/5/5/3/3/1	C	----	33%
D. X/5/4/1.5	D	(3)	50%
E. X/X/13.5/9/4	D	(6)	67%
H. X/7/4.5/4.5/3	C	----	67%
I. X/7/10.5/10.5/3.5	C	----	33%
North Haven 8/5/81			
C. X/6/6/5/8/5	I	(12.5)	40%
E. X/2/2.5/2.5/1	C	----	40%
G. X/3.5/2.5/4/2	? Irr	----	? 50-100%
I. X/3.5/2.5/2.5/3/2.5/1.5	C	----	60%
John's Bay, Pemaquid 9/5/93, clam bake			
A. 15/14/7	D	(13)	54%
B. 18/18/12	C	(18)	66%
C. 20/18/10	D	(16)	62%
D. X/14/8	unknown	----	----
Commercial Purchase 9/29/82			
Unknown date and place of harvest.			
A. X/X/15/13/3	D	(11)	34%
B. X/X/9/12/6	I	(16)	38%
E. X/10/9.5/9/6.5	D	(8.5)	75%
F. X/X/5.5/5/3	D	(4.5)	67%
Kidder Point 10/20/82			
A. X/5.5/7/16/11	? Irr	----	----
B. X/X/3/5.5/6	? I	(10)	60%
C. X/X/4/9/9	? C	----	F
D. X/6.5/6.5/7/3/2	D	(2)	F
F. X/X/X/5/4.5/3	D	(4)	75%
I. X/X/3.5/3.5/10/9	? Irr	----	----

tive thickness. By late June all clams exhibit growth layers, most in the 10–20% relative thickness range. Mid-July through August samples exhibit 25% to 67% relative thickness. In some locations or at some tidal exposures growth initiation is later, or slower, so that 20–25% growth clams can be found at some places in late July. By late September most clams show growth thickness of 66–75%. By mid-October the samples contain a significant number of clams with growth indistinguishable from full-thickness growth, with some still in the 67–75% relative growth range. Presumably, samples from late October, November, December, January, and early February would be indistinguishable, all with full-thickness growth.

CONCLUSION

A number of excellent season-of-death indicators are to be found among the faunal analysis techniques presented here. The eruption state of all white-tailed deer teeth (and presumably moose teeth), except for the third molar, are useful seasonal indicators, with a precision of 2 to 5 months. However, because this technique requires teeth embedded in jaw fragments to gauge the relative amount of eruption, its utility declines in highly broken assemblages. Tooth sectioning and reading annual growth layers has a comparable precision: 2 months at best and 5 or 6 months for the annulus forming state. Epiphyseal fusion in deer and moose is a poor season-of-death indicator since many of the epiphyses fuse over spans of time approaching a year or more. It is a mistake, for example, to assume that an unfused deer epiphysis indicates a fawn and therefore a summer or fall kill, because some epiphyses fuse in the third or fourth year.

Seal season-of-death is most easily determined from tooth sectioning, and seal tooth sections from the Turner Farm site were often readable for an approximate age of the individual (number of annuli) as well. Foetal or newborn seal bones are recognizable by measurements and provide a firm spring–early summer seasonal estimate. However, as in deer and moose, epiphyseal fusion of some bones requires many years and it is thus unwise to assume that a seal bone with an unfused epiphysis is a newborn absent appropriate measurements.

Season-of-death in bear seemingly must be estimated from tooth sections. Beaver teeth do not yield easily readable sections. Beaver cheek teeth exhibit gradual closure around the root canal. However, since the canal begins to close around 2½ years of age, recording root closure state is a technique for assessing beaver demographics, not season-of-death. For small fur bearers, including mink, the best season-of-death observations are those on sections of their incisors. However, the amount of baseline information available for interpreting these readings is limited, and absent for the extinct sea mink for whom we must make the assumption of similarity to modern mink. The fusion of certain muskrat postcranial bone epiphyses is a useful season-of-death indicator. The percentage of certain muskrat epiphyses exhibiting fusion or lack of fusion is useful demographic and seasonal information, but requires a muskrat bone sample larger than that recovered from the Turner Farm site.

A fragmented bird bone assemblage contains distinct types of season-of-death indicators: medullary bone, and fledgling bone, as well as spiecies seasonally present. Since many of the bones carrying this information can be identified to species, especially for the larger birds, this information carries highly specific information about local bird nesting and breeding.

Fish season-of-death and age reconstructions at the Turner Farm site are based primarily upon annulae visible on vertebrae. Annulae on cod vertebrae are especially hard to read, and require a moderately-advanced stage of disintegration. Flounder vertebrae are much more easily read, but baseline modern data for interpreting the seasonal significance of their growth layers remains inadequate. Fish otoliths, rare at the Turner Farm Site but more common in other shell middens, can be sectioned and read microscopically to provide season-of-death and age information of relatively high resolution.

Soft-shell clam season-of-death and age can be easily read from acetate peels made from sections through the chondrophore. A large sample (20 or more) should be sectioned for each archaeological provenience (feature, level) requiring a season-of-death estimate. Interpretation of season-of-death is dependent upon assessing the regularity of growth mode in the preceding few years in each individual, and discarding clams whose growth is highly irregular. Even then, there is a high percentage (20% or more) of random noise in the data generated. Estimates of season-of-death as precise as one month can be made if all clams in a sample were collected during a season of rapid growth, but in late fall and winter precision to a 5 or 6 month span of time is all that can be obtained.

3

Faunal Attributes
And Change Over Time

Introduction

This chapter compares the fauna of the five major stratigraphic divisions on a taxon-by-taxon basis. Our main interest is to explore long-term trends in the faunal data. These data are also relevant to the reconstruction of faunal procurement techniques, which are addressed in a later chapter. The roughly 14% of identifiable vertebrate fauna from mixed or uncertain contexts (Table 3–1) are not further considered.

Some domestic animal bone was recovered in the plow zone. These specimens either result from admixture of Euro-American farm debris, or from a post-contact Amerindian occupation for which there is little other evidence. We assume that the former is more likely, and provides evidence for historic plow turbation of this uppermost stratum. A total of 12 domestic cattle (*Bos*) and 30 Ovicaprid (sheep-goat) bones were identified from the plow zone, roughly 6% of the over 700 mammal bones recovered there.

WHITE-TAILED DEER

Total Number of Bones, and Skeletal Element Frequency

There are two identified white-tailed deer (*Odocoileus virginianus*) bones from Occupation 1. The identified sample from later occupations is much larger (Table 3–2). The total numbers of identified deer bone fragments in Occupations 2 and 3 are roughly equivalent, while the total number is substantially greater for the Occupation 4 and the plow zone. However, conclusions concerning the relative intensity of deer utilization must be tempered by some consideration of archaeological deposit volume, total number of bone and lithic artifacts, areal extent of the occupations (within the area excavated), and the relative importance of taxa (see below).

Theoretically, shifts in either butchery and discard practices or in the bone preservation and depositional environment between occupations would cause a shift in the relative frequency of deer parts. Visual comparison of skeletal element frequency between occupations (Table 3–3) is made easiest by comparing the relative total bone counts. For example, Occupation 2 and 3 skeletal elements should be approximately equal for each category because the total deer bone counts are nearly equal. Likewise, all Occupation 4 body-part counts should be nearly twice as great as those in Occupations 2 and 3, and the plow zone skeletal element counts should be ¼ as large as other Occupation 4. Comparison of observed with expected skeletal element frequencies shows that there were in fact no drastic shifts in deer carcass utility over time. However, there are four interesting changes in detailed skeletal element representation.

In Occupation 2, vertebrae are consistently over-represented compared with the frequency of other skeletal elements (Table 3–4), while they are under-represented in Occupation 4 and the plow zone. This effect may be due to vertebral fragility. The relative frequencies of the first cervical vertebra (Table 3–3), which is the most solidly constructed, are approximately 2½ times greater in the Occupation 4 than in Occupations 2 and 3, as we would expect if some destructive force had been acting more intensively on the more fragile deer vertebrae in Occupations 3 and 4 than in Occupation 2. Human traffic and dog scavenging are possible contributing factors. There is clear visual evidence of dog chewing on some deer bone elements in the sample. However, we did not record dog chewing in a consistent fashion. Such taphonomic questions are topics for future research.

Skull and antler fragments show a pattern similar to that of the more fragile vertebra. In Occupation 4, skull fragment counts are lower than those expected from total deer bone counts (Table 3–5). However, teeth (e.g., upper molars) are represented as expected compared with total bone count in all Occupation 4 subdivisions (and the plow zone). The presence of the expected number of teeth indicates that the entire head was probably treated the same during all occupations. Thus, under-representation of skull and antler fragments in Occupation 4 probably was not caused by an anomalous pattern of field butchery of the carcass, but rather by some taphonomic factor, most probably reduction to unidentifiable fragment size by plow turbation.

Forelimb bones proximal to the metacarpals show no anomalous patterns. Samples of hind limb bone proximal to the metatarsals are too small for conclusions, except for the distal tibia. Metapodials and phalanges, however, do show changes in relative frequency over time (Table 3–6). In Occupations 2 and 3, the metapodial proximal ends (Figure 3–1) are relatively over-represented while metapodial diaphysis fragments, metapodial distal ends and phalanges are relatively under-

Table 3-1. Count of identified bone with mixed provenience compared with bone counts of secure provenience for various taxa. Mixed provenience includes bone from stratigraphic units that are not clearly assignable to one of the major occupation units. Number of bones (NISP).

Taxon	Mixed Provenience	Secure Provenience	% Mixed of Total
Deer	157	4,997	3.2%
Moose	7	163	4.1%
Seal	19	604	3.0%
Bear	7	681	0.3%
Mink	30	996	3.0%
Beaver	33	580	5.7%
Small Furbearer	6	102	5.9%
Bird	109	2,354	4.6%
Fish	192	4,432	4.3%
TOTAL	560	14,278	3.9%

Table 3-2. White-tailed deer

Occupation	Total Bone Count
Occupation 1	2
Occupation 2	1,023
Occupation 3	1,060
Occupation 4	2,461
Plow zone	450

represented. Among Occupation 4 metapodial shaft fragments, distal metapodial fragments, and phalanges are relatively over-represented. (This pattern does not continue into the plow zone, again possibly due to plow breakage.) Since each metapodial is a single bone, disparity in number of proximal and distal metapodial parts indicates that breakage of the metapodials themselves probably explains these differences. Much metapodial breakage was achieved by striking the proximal articular surface in order to split the bone longitudinally. Such breakage patterns are clearly related to human processing, not dog chewing. Perhaps this breakage was part of the final butchery processing of the carcass, or processing for marrow extraction, and these behaviors varied from occupation to occupation.

The distal tibia does not follow the proximal metatarsal pattern of being over-represented in Occupations 2 and 3 and under-represented in Occupation 4 and the plow zone. The frequency pattern of the astragalus (Figure 3–2) parallels that of the distal tibia, except for the plow zone, where we expect extreme breakage of longbone elements due to plowing. The most resistant postcranial element in the deer skeleton, the astragalus is highly recognizable. It is attached to the distal tibia by tough ligaments, making it difficult to separate even during butchery. Yet astragalus frequency does not follow the pattern of the distal metapodials, which showed relative under-representation in Occupations 2 and 3 and over-representation in the Occupation 4 and plow zone, but rather parallels the frequency pattern of the distal tibia.

Binford (1978) has clearly demonstrated that butchery of caribou carcasses by Nunamiut Eskimo proceeds through disassembly of a variety of body part units. White-tailed deer are similar in construction to caribou, but slightly smaller in size. Although our evidence indicates that whole deer carcasses were being habitually brought to the site, the butchery process must have included breakage into body part units. Distal tibia and astragalus frequency patterns are uniform throughout the stratigraphic sequence. In contrast, metapodial shafts, distal metapodial ends and phalanges show anomalous frequency variation in Occupations 2, 3 and 4, as discussed above. Thus, we deduce that there was some change in the treatment of a body part unit distal to the astragalus on the hind limb during the site's sequence of occupations. Since separation of the carpal/tarsal metapodial joint is difficult, we suggest that this change in body part processing involved the relative frequency of smashing the metapodial shaft versus separation of the intercarpal/tarsal joint. There is a lower-than-expected frequency of recognizable proxi-

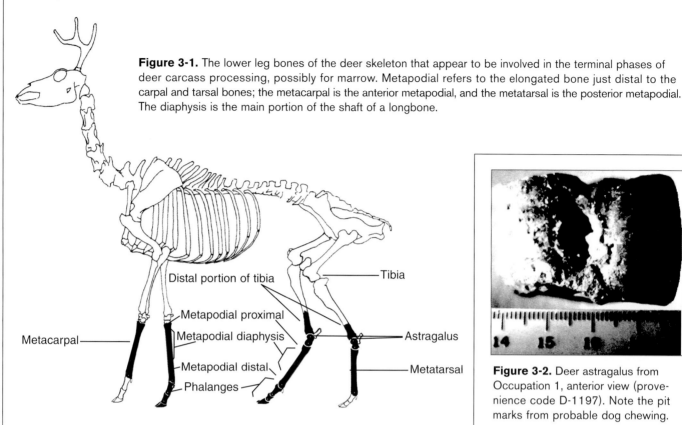

Figure 3-1. The lower leg bones of the deer skeleton that appear to be involved in the terminal phases of deer carcass processing, possibly for marrow. Metapodial refers to the elongated bone just distal to the carpal and tarsal bones; the metacarpal is the anterior metapodial, and the metatarsal is the posterior metapodial. The diaphysis is the main portion of the shaft of a longbone.

Distal portion of tibia
Tibia
Metapodial proximal
Metacarpal
Metapodial diaphysis
Astragalus
Metapodial distal
Metatarsal
Phalanges

Figure 3-2. Deer astragalus from Occupation 1, anterior view (provenience code D-1197). Note the pit marks from probable dog chewing.

Illustration: JPM

mal metatarsals during Occupation 4. Therefore, during Occupation 4 there must have been more instances of separation at the tarsal joint and subsequent smashing of the whole metatarsal as a separate bone. During Occupations 2 and 3, more often than during the Occupation 4, butchery of the lower leg seems to have involved smashing the metapodials at mid-shaft while they were still attached to the leg.

An analog to the Occupation 2 and 3 pattern may be that documented for the Beothuck of Newfoundland, who are known to have stored marrow for later use in a variety of ways, including binding groups of caribou metapodials and hanging them off the ground on a pole or structural support (Howley 1915:69–79). We suspect that variability in some similar form of behavior is causing the astragalus, tibia, metapodial, and phalange frequency shifts.

In sum, variation from occupation to occupation in deer skeletal element recovery (and identifiability) is apparently related to differences in the terminal phases of carcass processing, including breakage for marrow access, dog chewing (see Figure 3–2), and human trampling. Variability in butchery before deer carcasses were delivered to the site appears to be minimal.

Seasonality Based on Tooth Eruption and Sectioning

As stated in Chapter 2, molar series were examined for tooth eruption seasonality information, and relatively well-preserved incisors and molars were selected for sectioning. We regard all of these specimens as derived from deer killed for food and brought back to the site, and thus reflecting the seasonality of hunting.

OCCUPATION 1

There was only one deer tooth recovered that was definitely associated with Occupation 1. It is a P_2, which represents a 5–7 year old individual. It does not contribute seasonality information.

OCCUPATION 2

Twenty-nine specimens from 19 deer provided seasonality data for Occupation 2. Twelve jaw fragments with erupting teeth document kills from October or November through the following spring. Out of 40 teeth sectioned, eight teeth from seven individuals yielded high resolution data on season-of-death (Table 3–7, Figure 3–3). These data augment the winter, late-

Table 3-3. Deer skeletal element counts. Numbers of identified bone elements.

DEER ELEMENT	Number in Deer Body	Occupation 2	Occupation 3	Occupation 4	Plow zone
Axial Skeleton					
scapula, distal	2	39	43	131	9
scapula, other	–	22	26	32	5
pelvis, including acetabulum	2	9	9	28	6
pelvis, other	–	1	2	3	–
vertebra: C1	1	6	5	16	–
C2	1	7	7	7	–
other cervical	5	6	5	8	–
thorassic	13	15	11	18	2
lumbar	6	2	0	2	–
sacrum	1	1	2	2	–
caudal	18	–	1	1	–
fragments	–	2	2	–	–
skull and antler frags.	–	80	82	121	31
OTHER					
sesamoid, sternum, rib, etc.	–	4	11	9	1
Teeth and Jaws					
mandible body fragments	–	8	10	14	2
condyle	2	32	33	61	8
coronoid process	2	3	3	7	–
mandible	–	6	13	16	5
maxilla frags. with	–	–	–	–	–
teeth (free teeth)	–	9	13	15	1
upper deciduous molars	6	4	6	16	–
lower deciduous molars	6	4	4	15	1
incisors and canines	8	13	14	25	7
lower premolars	6	23	17	55	8
$M_{1/2}$	4	41	35	127	22
lower M_3	2	19	14	40	12
upper premolars	6	21	22	51	9
mandible frags. with teeth	–	66	56	63	6
upper molars	6	69	6	167	24
Forelimb					
humerus, proximal	2	1	–	1	–
humerus, distal	2	19	15	43	5
ulna, proximal	2	13	12	38	4
radius, proximal	2	19	29	37	7
radius, distal	2	8	12	16	7
radius, shaft fragment	–	2	4	3	–

(continued on facing page)

Table 3-3. Continued.

DEER ELEMENT	Number in Deer Body	Occupation 2	Occupation 3	Occupation 4	Plow zone
Hindlimb					
femur, proximal	2	2	4	19	2
femur, distal	2	4	2	4	1
tibia, proximal	2	3	6	2	–
tibia, distal	2	31	17	55	4
patella	2	4	1	3	–
fibula (distal)	2	2	4	–	–
patella	2	4	1	3	–
Carpals/Tarsals					
carpus ulnare	2	4	2	8	3
carpus intermediate	2	9	7	11	3
carpus radiale	2	7	9	13	3
carpus accessorium	2	1	1	3	1
carpus 2/3	2	4	10	13	9
carpus 4	2	8	3	13	1
astragalus	2	52	38	103	44
calcaneus, incl. articular surf.	2	25	28	83	13
calcaneus, other, frag.	–	14	11	13	6
distal tarsal	2	9	17	33	6
Metapodials/Phalanges					
metacarpal, proximal	2	30	29	40	7
metatarsal, proximal	2	37	44	57	12
MC/MT, distal	4	43	39	140	38
MC/MT, diaphysis frag.	–	60	72	291	40
phalange 1	>8*	43	65	178	35
phalange 2	>8	28	33	107	24
phalange 3	>8	19	23	62	6
auxiliary MC, Ph (dew claw)	16	10	12	22	10
TOTALS Inventoried *includes proximal epiphyses, fragments, etc.		1,023	1,060	2,461	450

NOTE: The two deer bones for Occupation 1 are a distal metapodial condyle fragment with a fused epiphyses, and a right P_2 with a 5-7 year old wear pattern.

Table 3-4. Deer vertebrae versus other deer bones, chi-square comparison. Expected frequencies are shown in parentheses.

	Occupation 2	Occupation 3	Occupation 4	Plow zone
Vertebrae	39 (26.22)	33 (27.19)	54 (63.06)	2 (11.53)
Other Bones	984 (996.78)	1,028 (1,033.81)	2,407 (2,397.94)	44 (438.47)
TOTAL BONES	1,023	1,061	2,461	450

$X^2 = 17.21$ df = 3 $p < 0.001$

winter and early-spring kill totals derived from eruption data. The greater resolution of the eruption data confirm continuing deer kills through the late fall and winter into spring.

Of these 19 deer deaths, none fall definitely in the period between late June and late September, which should be readily detectable by both methods. Only one jaw fragment is a possible late June–July kill. These data also demonstrate that adults (tooth sectioning), calves and yearlings (tooth eruption) were hunted in the same general seasonal pattern. We conclude that deer hunting by Occupation 2 hunters began sometime in October or November, continued heavily through the fall, winter, and early spring, and ended sometime in late May or June.

OCCUPATION 3

Occupation 3 provided a total of 20 specimens which yielded seasonality information. Nine teeth from eight deer (of approximately 25) sectioned gave high resolution readings for season of death. Six of these teeth document kills in the February–June period (Table 3–8 and Figure 3–4), while two others document summer or early fall kills. Tooth eruption data allowed assignment of season-of-death to 11 specimens. One falls in spring, two in later summer-early fall, and two in spring or early summer. The rest document fall or winter hunting. Thus in Occupation 3 there is defin-

itive evidence from 19 individuals of deer hunting during all seasons of the year. Note, however, that these data do not allow us to differentiate between continuous year-round

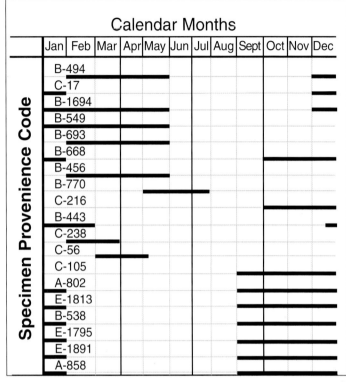

Figure 3-3. Possible seasons of deer hunting based on tooth eruption and sectioning, Occ. 2.

Table 3-5. Chi-square comparison: skull and antler fragments versus other deer bone. Expected frequencies are shown in parentheses.

	Occupation 2	Occupation 3	Occupation 4	Plow zone
Skull & antler fragments	80 (64.31)	82 (66.70)	121 (154.71)	31 (28.29)
Other deer bone	943 (958.69)	979 (994.30)	2,339 (2,306.29)	419 (421.71)
TOTAL BONES	1,023	1,061	2,460	450

$x^2 = 15.95$ df = 3 $0.001 < p < 0.01$

Table 3-6. Deer metapodials and phalanges, chi-square comparison. Expected frequencies are shown in parentheses.

	Occupation 2	Occupation 3	Occupation 4	Plow zone
metapodial, proximal	67 (42.23)	78 (50.35)	97 (142.11)	9 (26.31)
metapodial, diaphysis	60 (74.91)	72 (89.32)	291 (252.10)	40 (46.67)
metapodial, distal	43 (42.07)	39 (50.16)	140 (141.57)	38 (26.21)
phalanges	90 (100.80)	121 (120.18)	347 (339.22)	65 (62.80)
TOTAL BONES	260	310	875	162

$x^2 = 68.59$ df = 9 $p \leq 0.001$

deer hunting and the existence of multiple hunting seasons, perhaps a half-dozen, scattered around the calendar.

COMPARISON OF OCCUPATIONS 2 AND 3

All 19 of the Occupation 2 deer of known season-of-death are from fall, winter, or spring (if we include B–770 which could have been killed between May and July). None fall with certainty in the summer period of late June, July, August, or September. In contrast, at least two and as many as six of the 19 kills of known season from Occupation 3 were killed in late June, July, August, or September. During Occupation 2 times, deer hunters delivered their game to the site during seven or eight months of the year; during perhaps June and October, and definitely during July, August and September, deer were not delivered to this location. The pattern in Occupation 3 contrasts strongly with deer hunters actively hunting and returning carcasses to the site during all seasons, including the summer.

Table 3-7. Seasonality of Occupation 2 deer hunting from tooth sectioning and tooth eruption. Specimen numbers are revised slightly based upon original laboratory notes compared with those published in Spiess 1990a. The specimen numbers in this table are correct.

Tooth Sectioning Specimen # Provenience Code	Tooth wear state and microscopic observation
13 B-494	Right P^3, wear state: 3-4 years. Last layer forming is the third translucent (annulus). February-May kill.
16 C-17	Left $M_{1/2}$, wear state 5-6 years. Last layer forming is a wide opaque layer, full width. (More than 3 translucent layers formed.) December-January kill.
21 E-1694	Left $M_{1/2}$, wear state: 3-4 years of age. Last layer forming probably a translucent line (annulus) but because of indistinct edge, it could be a full thickness opaque band. December-May possible kill.
22 B-549	Upper molar, wear state: 3-4 years. Last layer forming is either a full thickness opaque layer, or a translucent line forming (annulus). December-May possible kill.
27 B-693	Left $P_{3/4}$, wear state: 3-4 years. Third translucent line (annulus) forming. February-May kill.
34 B-456	Left $M_{1/2}$, 2 or 3 years old from wear state (depending on whether tooth is M_1 or M_2). First translucent (annulus) forming. February-May kill.
38 B-668	Right M_1, wear state: 3-4 years. Last layer forming is a ¾ to full thickness opaque band. (Four translucent bands formed previously.) Late October-January kill.
39 B-668	Right M_2, same individual as #38 (same jaw). Three translucent layers formed. Last layer forming is definitely 4th opaque layer close to full thickness. September-November kill; four year old deer.
Tooth Eruption (from samples of jaws with teeth or alveoli)	**Tooth wear state and microscopic observation**
B-770	A symphysis and diastema fragment with incisor and DP2 alveolar margins present. A term foetus or calf. Late May-July kill .
C-216	M_1 erupted, M_2 not erupting yet. Late October-November-December kill.
B-443	M_2, ½ erupted. Late December-January-February kill.
C-238	M_2, ¾ erupted. February-March kill.
C-56	M_2, just in occlusion. March-April kill.
C-105	M_3, < ¾ erupted, not fully in occlusion. November-December kill.
E-1813	PM, ¼ erupted, October-January kill.
B-538	PM, ¾ erupted, October-January kill.
E-1795	PM, ¼ erupted, October-January kill.
E-1891	PM, ¾ erupted, October-January kill.
A-858	P_2, ½ erupted, October-January kill.

Table 3-8. Seasonality of Occupation 3 deer hunting from tooth sectioning and tooth eruption.

Tooth Sectioning Specimen # Provenience Code	Tooth wear state and microscopic observation
42 C-213	Left incisor, lightly worn. First translucent line (annulus) forming. February-May possible kill.
45 E-1561	Right M_3, 3-4 years of age by wear pattern. Second translucent line forming. February-May possible kill.
48 C-68	Left M_1 from mandible of 2½-3 year old. Second translucent line forming. February-May possible kill.
52 B-665	Right $M_{1/2}$, 2 or 3 years old by wear pattern. First translucent line forming. February-May kill.
53 B-409	Right M_1, 3-4 years of age. Three translucent lines formed, last layer forming at time of death is a thin opaque line about ¼ width. June-July kill. (from Feature 19.)
56 B-723	Left M_2 from a mandible 5-7 years of age. Unknown age more than 4 annuli. Last layer forming is a translucent line. February-May kill.
57 B-723	Left M_3 from same mandible as #56. By wear, 5-7 years of age. Seven translucent lines formed (i.e., actual age 8 years). Last layer forming is a translucent layer. February-May kill.
64 D-1008	Right $M_{1/2}$, 5-7 years of age by wear. Four or five translucent lines formed. Last layer forming is a thin opaque band definitely less than ½ thickness, about ¼ to ⅓ thickness. June-early August kill.
no# S-082	$M_{1/2}$, 3-4 years of age by wear. Three translucent lines formed. Last layer is an opaque growth layer of unknown width but greater than ¼ thickness. Late July-January kill.

Tooth Eruption	Tooth wear state and microscopic observation
C-255	Right mandible ascending ramus and condyle, small and poorly ossified. Probably term foetus. April-June kill.
C-29	DP with light wear. Equivalent of 3-4 month wear pattern in Severinghaus. September-October kill.
D-1148	M_1, ¾ erupted. September-October kill.
B-553	M_2, ¾ erupted. January-February kill.
E-1719	M_2, just in occlusion and wear beginning. March-April kill.
B-409	M_1, in and worn, M_2 erupting unknown amount. November-March kill.
B-589	M_1, in and wearing, M_2 unerupted or in early stages of eruption (alveolus only). November-January kill.
D-1021	M_2, erupted, M_3 erupting $<$ ½, moderately heavy wear on DP, premolar grids present but not near eruption. 11-15 months of age. April-August kill.
D-1012	M_3, ¼ to ½ erupted. 12-15 months. May-August kill.
D-1110	M_3, between ¾ and fully erupted, barely beginning to come into occlusion. October-December kill.
D-1001	Premolars ¼ to 1½ erupted. October-December.

(NOTE in proof: Tooth 57 was read in thick section under reflected light, Tooth 56 was read several weeks later in thin section with transmitted light, and without realizing that specimens were from the same jaw. This circumstance represents a double-blind test. It also indicates that tooth wear state may be slightly underestimating age in the Occupation 3 sample.)

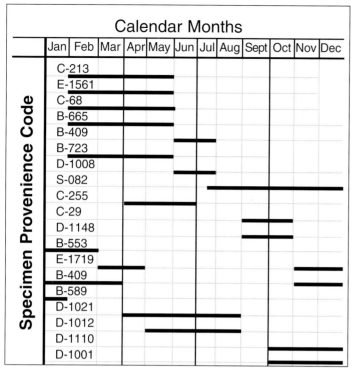

Figure 3-4. Possible range of deer hunting seasons based on tooth eruption and sectioning, Occupation 3.

OCCUPATION 4 AND THE PLOW ZONE

Table 3–9 and Figure 3–5 present deer kill seasonality data for Occupation 4. The pattern is similar to that of Occupation 3, with probable hunting during all seasons of the year. Again, the majority of the data indicate fall or winter hunting, but spring and summer are also represented. There is a slim chance that April and May saw no deer hunting. No teeth were preserved well enough to allow successful reading of thin sections. From the plow zone, two jaw fragments preserved evidence of hunting during late summer or fall (Table 3–10 and Figure 3–6).

Age Demography of the Kill

In comparing demographic distributions derived from tooth wear, the problem is to combine isolated teeth and mandibular categories that do not overlap. For example, we cannot combine "M1/2—2, 3 years" with either "M3—2 years" or "M3—3-4 years" in the same statistical comparison because the age categories overlap. The most reasonable solution is to count the age-wear categories of all third molars (M3) (whether isolated teeth or still in their jaws), since this tooth can be placed in discrete, easily read, and non-overlapping wear categories. The only additional tooth used to construct datum summary Table 3–12 is the "third deciduous molar

with light or moderate wear", to include a category for animals of 11 months or less in age (before M3 erupts). The small sample size of 5–7 and 8+ year-old categories necessitates their combination for chi-square comparison (Table 3–14).

A crude demographic record of the deer kill in the four major temporal subdivisions of the site is presented in Tables 3–11 and 3–12. Table 3–11 presents data derived from preserved mandibular fragments. Table 3–12 presents the data derived from isolated teeth.

Epiphyseal fusion data (Table 3–15) indicate that the proportion of very young deer (less than 14–17 months of age) does not change from Occupation 2 through 4. The tooth eruption data (Table 3–13) agree; the proportion of calves and yearlings in the death assemblage ranges from 21% to 27%. (The sample from the plow zone is too small for reliability and, because of plow disturbance, may under-report delicate younger deer bones.) However, there is a clear increase in the number of skeletally immature animals aged 29 to 60 months between Occupation 2 and Occupation 3. Moreover, the tooth-wear-based demography (Table 3–14) reflects a dramatic drop in the proportion of older individuals between Occupation 2 and Occupation 3, continuing to drop into Occupation 4. The plow zone pattern is enigmatic and, again, the probable explanation is the postdepositional destruction of more fragile bone. An alternative hypothesis is that the demographics of the deer kill during the latest occupations reverted to an Occupation 2-like pattern. We cannot differentiate these two hypotheses with existing data.

In sum, the demographic data show that the proportion of aged individual deer (5–7 years, 8+ years) in the kill drops between Occupation 2 and 3, and again between Occupations 3 and 4. The proportion of very young deer remains relatively constant, but the proportion of skeletally immature (29 to 65 month) animals increases between Occupation 2 and 4.

Postcranial Measurements

As stated in Chapter 2, we have based size estimates on the most common postcranial bone widths or regressions from other bones to those measurements. Distal tibiae provide the largest sample of postcranial measurements (measurement #149, Table 3–16, Figure 3–7). They show a slight decrease in average size between Occupation 3 and 4. As the distal tibial epiphysis fuses between 14 and 17 months of age, some growth in width must occur after fusion, possibly making measurement #149 sensitive to age-frequency change in the sample as well as to change in the average body size of adult deer. However, the drop in deer size between Occupation 3 and 4 does not correspond with the major demographic change of decrease in the proportion of older deer, which occurs between Occupation 2 and Occupation 3. Thus, we feel that this measurement is probably accurately reflecting a decrease in the average size of the deer killed.

Table 3-9. Seasonality of *Occupation 4* deer hunting from tooth sectioning and tooth eruption.

Tooth Sectioning Specimen # Provenience Code	Tooth wear state and microscopic observation
E-1556	Right M$_{1/2}$. Opaque layer forming, between ½ and full thickness. July-December kill.
D-1242	Left M$_{1/2}$. Last layer forming is thin opaque layer of ¼ to ½ thickness. June-early August kill.
E-1901	M$_3$. Very thin opaque layer just beginning to form. Late May-June kill.
E-1809	Right M$_2$, 3-4 years of age by tooth wear. Last layer forming is ½ to ¾ thick opaque layer. July-Oct. kill.
E-1672	Left M$_3$. Last layer forming is a ½ thickness opaque layer. July-early August kill.
D-1454	Right M$_{1/2}$. Second translucent line forming. February-May kill.
D-1233	Left M$_{1/2}$. Second translucent line forming. February-May possible kill.
C-253	Left incisor. Full thickness opaque layer forming. December-January kill.
B-434	Left M$_2$ from 2½ year old, based on tooth wear pattern. Full thickness opaque layer forming at time of death, with one translucent layer formed. December-January kill.
Tooth Eruption	
E-1539	DP ½ erupted. June-July kill.
D-1216	M$_1$ erupting, light wear on DP. Mid-August-November kill.
D-1009	DP (deciduous premolar) wear light, but all in occlusion. September-November kill.
D-1237	M$_1$ in occlusion with very light wear. November-January kill.
D-1311	M$_2$ in eruption or < ¼ erupted, M$_1$ in. Late October-December kill.
E-1524	M$_2$ erupting. November-March kill.
C-139 (Feature 8)	M$_2$ just beginning eruption.< ¼, or about to begin eruption. October-December kill.
D-1216	M$_2$ erupting. November-March kill.
D-1216	M$_2$ ¼ erupted. December-January kill.
E-1772	M$_3$, ¾ to fully erupted. October-December kill.
D-1440	M$_3$ erupting. April-December kill.
D-1454	M$_3$, ¾ erupted. October-early December kill.
B-707	M$_3$, ¾ erupted. October-early December kill.
C-24	Premolars erupting. October-January kill.
C-200	Premolars less than ¼ erupted. October-November kill.

Table 3-10. Deer hunting seasonality in the plow zone.

Tooth Eruption	
E-1793	DP$_3$ with very light wear (i.e., erupted, just in occlusion). Late August-early October kill.
D-1407	Deciduous premolar wear very heavy, premolars almost ready to begin eruption. August-November kill.

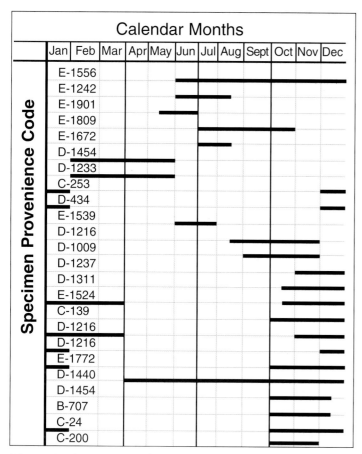

	Calendar Months											
Specimen Provenience Code	Jan	Feb	Mar	Apr	May	Jun	Jul	Aug	Sept	Oct	Nov	Dec
E-1556												
E-1242												
E-1901												
E-1809												
E-1672												
D-1454												
D-1233												
C-253												
D-434												
E-1539												
D-1216												
D-1009												
D-1237												
D-1311												
E-1524												
C-139												
D-1216												
D-1216												
E-1772												
D-1440												
D-1454												
B-707												
C-24												
C-200												

Figure 3-5. Possible range of deer hunting seasons based on tooth eruption and sectioning, Occupation 4.

	Calendar Months											
	Jan	Feb	Mar	Apr	May	Jun	Jul	Aug	Sept	Oct	Nov	Dec
E-1793												
D-1407												

Figure 3-6. Possible range of deer hunting seasons based on tooth eruption and sectioning, plow zone.

There is a slight difference (0.26 cm) between the mean size of Occupation 2 distal tibia (3.81 cm) and those of Occupation 4 (3.55 cm). In this case, the difference between the means is nearly 3 times the standard error, which indicates the difference is significant with a confidence level of about 99%. Based on a few comparative specimens examined by Spiess, a distal tibial width of between 4.0 and 4.2 cm is likely to have come from a deer in the 260 lb to 300 lb live weight class (almost certainly a buck). Anything over 4.2 cm is likely to have represented an extremely large deer, with live weight over 300 lbs. Using the 4.0 cm measurement to define "large adult bucks", Occupation 2 yielded three of 18 individual deer (17%) large adult bucks, Occupation 3 yielded four of 10 (40%), and Occupation 4 and the plow zone yielded two of 24 (8%) large adult bucks. Thus, there appears to be a decrease in frequency of large bucks in the kill from the Late Archaic (Occupation 3 at least) to Occupation 4. We would expect such a pattern in parallel with the drop in frequency of older individuals in the population.

Skull Fragments with Antler or Pedicles

It is comparatively easy to recognize male deer frontal bones with shed, shedding, or still-attached antlers. There is a marked shift from a majority of frontals with shed antlers in Occupation 2 to a majority of attached antlers in Occupations 3, 4 and the plow zone (Table 3–13). Male deer shed their antlers in mid-winter (December–February) and begin growth again in spring. Thus, the majority of male deer killed by Occupation 2 hunters were taken between roughly January and April. In later times (Occupations 3, 4 and the plow zone), the vast majority of male deer were killed between May and January. This shift correlates well with the summer hiatus in deer hunting in

Table 3-11. Deer age demography based on ageable mandibular fragments count (with 2 or more teeth). These are a number of identified specimens, ignoring left versus right, separated by occupation and age class.)

	Occupation 2	Occupation 3	Occupation 4	Plow zone
Newborn and calves, < 11 mo.	11	9	9	1
Yearlings (11-22 months) (M$_3$ erupting, PM erupting)	8	3	7	–
2 years (23 months and older)	11	9	18	1
3-4 years	20	25	21	4
5-7 years	12	8	8	–
8+ years	4	2	0*	–
TOTAL	66	56	63	6

*Note: a few upper molars exhibit this wear pattern, so this age group is not absent from the Occupation 4 sample.

Table 3-12. Deer age demography based on ageable isolated teeth. These are individual tooth (NISP) counts, so minimal MNI can be calculated by dividing by 2 for most categories and by and dividing by 4 for $M_{1/2}$ or M_1 or M_2. Subscripts indicate mandibular teeth following Hilson 1986.

	Occupation 2	Occupation 3	Occupation 4	Plow zone
DM$_3$ wear light or moderate	–	2	2	1
DM$_3$ wear moderate-heavy or heavy	–	1	2	–
M$_1$ or M$_2$ erupting	–	2	6	–
M$_3$ erupting	1	3	9	–
M$_{1/2}$ ≤ 2 years	6	6	36	2
M$_{1/2}$ = 2 and 2, 3 years	9	4	22	5
M$_3$ = 2 years	7	4	12	2
M$_{1/2}$ = 3-4 years	25	19	44	9
M$_3$ = 3-4 years	9	8	18	9
M$_{1/2}$ = 5-7 years	6	8	14	1
M$_3$ = 5-7 years	3	1	1	2
M$_{1/2}$ = 8+ years	1	1	–	1
M$_3$ = 8+ years	1	–	–	–
Total	68	59	166	32

Table 3-13. Number of male parietal bones exhibiting antlers attached, shedding, or shed. Percent within occupation, total 100% for each occupation. NISP, not accounting for right *versus* left.

	Attached	Shedding	Shed
Occupation 2	9 (28%)	4 (13%)	19 (59%)
Occupation 3	25 (78%)	1 (3%)	6 (19%)
Occupation 4	47 (84%)	1 (2%)	8 (14%)
Plow zone	0	0	0

Table 3-14. Summary MNI age demographics of white-tailed deer from Tables 3-11 and 3-12. Expected frequencies in parentheses, followed by percentages for each category, occupation totals 100%.

	Occupation 2		Occupation 3		Occupation 4		Plow zone	
Calves (DM$_3$ with light or moderate wear)	7 (5.98)	16%	6 (4.73)	18%	8 (10.29)	11%	1	7%
Yearlings (M$_3$ erupting or just in occlusion)	2 (4.84)	5%	3 (3.83)	9%	12 (8.33)	16%	–	0%
M$_3$ = 2 years	8 (10.54)	19%	8 (8.33)	24%	21 (18.13)	28%	2	13%
M$_3$ = 3-4 years	15 (16.23)	35%	13 (12.83)	38%	29 (27.93)	39%	10	67%
M$_3$ = 5-7 and 8+ years	11 (5.41)	25%	4 (4.28)	11%	4 (9.31)	6%	2	13%

df = 8, x^2 = 14.52, 0.05 < p < 0.10

Table 3-15. Deer epiphyseal fusion states.

	Fusion at 14–17 months (distal humerus, phalanges 1 and 2, distal tibia)		
	Unfused (++) or Fusing (+)	**Fused (– or 0)**	
Occupation 2	6 (14%)	37 (86%)	100%
Occupation 3	11 (15%)	62 (85%)	100%
Occupation 4	27 (13%)	184 (87%)	100%
Plow zone	3 (9%)	31 (91%)	100%
	Fusion between 29 and 60 months (distal metapodials, femoral head, distal femur, distal radius, proximal tibia, proximal humerus)		
	Unfused (++) or Fusing (+)	**Fused (- or 0)**	
Occupation 2	15 (33%)	31 (67%)	100%
Occupation 3	30 (53%)	27 (47%)	100%
Occupation 4	66 (50%)	67 (50%)	100%
Plow zone	15 (37%)	26 (63%)	100%

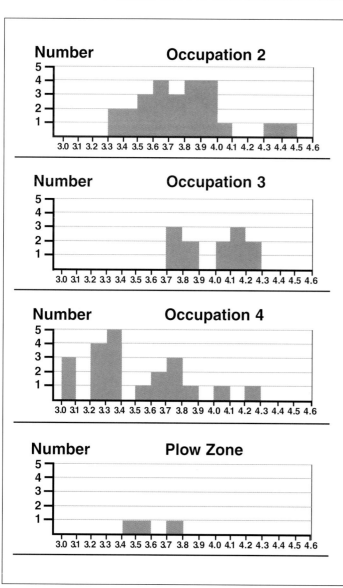

Figure 3-7. Frequency of distal tibial width (measurement #149).

Table 3-16. Deer postcranial measurement #149, distal tibial width. All measurements reported are from bone with fused distal epiphyses. In centimeters.

	N	$\overline{X}$	S	Obs. Range
Occupation 2	20	3.81	0.25	3.37 – 4.49 cm.
Occupation 3	10	3.83	0.18	3.63 – 4.11 cm.
Occupation 4	24	3.55	0.34	3.11 – 4.36 cm.
Plow zone	3	3.56	0.19	3.41 – 3.78 cm.

Occupation 2 inferred from tooth eruption and tooth sectioning data. There are also in Occupation 2 a significant number of kills recorded for fall/early winter, before the mid-winter shedding.

Summary of Skeletal Patterns

Throughout the site's occupations, deer complete carcasses were habitually delivered to the site. Variation in skeletal element recovery between occupations is related to factors of breakage during or after burial, and to terminal-stage butchery, probably related to processing for marrow cavity access.

Deer tooth sectioning, tooth eruption, and antler shedding data are all consistent with a shift from a season of no deer hunting in the summer during Occupation 2 to year-round hunting of deer thereafter, although sparse data from the plow zone may indicate a focussed fall hunting season. Various demographic measures indicate a decrease in the average age of deer being killed after Occupation 2, concomitant with a decrease in average size, most of it due to a reduction in the number of very large males killed. These data suggest increased hunting pressure on the deer herd, although in fact they may reflect merely lower survivorship rates between deer age cohorts with ecological change, or some combination of these factors.

MOOSE

The moose (*Alces alces*)) sample consists of eight bones from Occupation 2, 13 bones from Occupation 3, 115 bones from Occupation 4, and 26 bones from the plow zone. The Occupation 2 sample consists of a molar or premolar fragment, a distal metapodial condyle, two metapodial shaft fragments, a pelvis fragment, a second phalange from the dew

Table 3-17. Comparison of moose and deer skeletal parts frequency for the Occupation 4 levels. Number of bones.

Bone element	# Deer bones	# Moose bones
AXIAL SKELETON		
scapula, distal	131	4
scapula, other	32	1
pelvis, incl.	28	1
pelvis, other	3	–
vertebra: C1	16	–
vertebra: C2	7	1
other cervical	8	–
thorassic	18	–
lumbar	2	2
sacrum	2	–
caudal	1	–
fragments	–	–
skull and antler frags.	121	–
TEETH AND JAWS		
mandible body frags.	14	1
condyle	61	1
coronoid process	7	–
mand. symphysis and dia.	16	–
mand. frags. with teeth	62	–
max. with teeth	15	–
upper deciduous molars	16	–
lower deciduous molars	15	–
incisors and canines	25	4
lower premolars	55	–
lower $M_{1/2}$	127	–
lower M_3	41	–
upper premolars	51	2
upper molars	167	–
FORELIMB		
humerus, proximal	1	1
humerus distal	43	2
ulna, proximal	38	1
radius, proximal	37	1
radius distal	16	1
radius shaft	3	1

Bone element	# Deer bones	# Moose bones
HINDLIMB		
femur, proximal	19	3
femur, distal	4	–
tibia, distal	55	2
tibia, proximal	2	–
patella	3	–
fibula, distal	–	–
CARPALS/TARSALS		
carpus ulnare	8	1
carpus, intermediate	11	–
carpus, radial	13	3
carpus, accessorium	3	–
carpus, 2/3	13	2
carpus, 4	13	–
astragalus	103	3
calcaneus, w. arctic. surf.	83	1
calcaneus, other, frag.	13	–
distal tarsal	33	4
METAPODIALS/PHALANGES		
metacarpal, proximal	40	6
metatarsal, proximal	57	4
MC/MT, distal	140	5
MC/MT, diaphysis frag.	291	2
phalange	178	19
phalange II	107	23
phalange III	62	2
auxiliary MC, Ph	22	7
OTHER		
sesamoid, sternum, rib, etc.	9	4
TOTAL	2,461	115

claw, a distal tarsal bone with the greatest breadth of 6.15 cm, and a distal second phalange. The Occupation 3 sample consists of an incisor, two calcanei, one astragalus, two proximal phalanges, two second phalanges, one distal phalange, one distal metapodial fragment, one distal tarsal bone, a pelvis fragment, and a rib fragment.

The list of moose skeletal elements present in Occupation 4 is presented in Table 3-17, which includes a comparison with Occupation 4 deer skeletal counts. The plow zone moose sample contains 15 phalanges or dew claw parts, four teeth, one mandibular condyle, four metapodial fragments, and two carpal or tarsal bones from an MNI of three.

Species of grossly dissimilar size, even though closely related taxonomically, require different butchering strategies (Binford 1978). Transportation of an intact 45 kg (100 lb) deer can be attempted by one man, but a 450 kg (1,000 lb) moose must be butchered in the field, which probably has resulted in some bones being discarded there, thus introducing some bias into the sample delivered to the site. Furthermore, as bones are broken for marrow and/or smashed for bone-grease extraction, recognizability of the same bone from various sized species will be affected differently.

The sum total of these effects in the moose bone sample can be seen in Table 3–17. Moose jaws and teeth are present at only 1.2% of the frequency of the same deer parts. Moose axial skeletal bones are present at 2.5% of the frequency of the same deer parts. Longbones, metapodial fragments, and carpals and tarsals are represented at 5.2%, 6.3% and 4.9% of the deer count, respectively. Relatively most common are moose phalanges and dew claw parts (13.9%) which together comprise the distal-most portion of the hoof.

Moose bone, and especially teeth, are resistant to destruction in Maine shell middens. Therefore, the low proportion of teeth and other head parts is most likely due to a practice of leaving the moose head at the kill site, or in a field-camp. We conclude that the high relative frequency of phalanges and dew-claw parts is due to their resistance to breakage coupled with the frequent delivery of these bones to camp (possibly used as toggles to strip bundles of meat from the legs). Intermediate recovery of other bones reflects varying effects of field butchery and bone breakage for marrow extraction. For the above reasons the relative number of moose and deer phalanges and dew-claw parts must reflect a truer picture of the relative number of moose and deer individuals killed than do the total bone counts. (See Tables 3–18 and 3–19.)

To calculate the relative contribution of moose to the diet on a gross scale, we need only multiply the figures in Table 3–19 by an average live weight correction: roughly 80 kg (150 lbs) for deer and 400 kg (900 lbs) for moose. This exercise demonstrates, suprisingly, that moose were as important or slightly more important in gross diet contribution than were deer during Occupation 4 (Table 3–20), even though their total skeletal relative representation by bone count is only 4–6% of deer.

Table 3-18. Summary moose and deer bone count comparison.

Occupation	# Deer	# Moose	Relative Frequency of Moose
Occupation 2	1,023	8	0.7%
Occupation 3	1,060	13	1.2%
Occupation 4	2,461	115	4.7%
Plow zone	450	26	5.8%

Table 3-19. Calculated numbers of moose based upon phalange and dew-claw counts.

Occupation	Number of Moose per 100 Deer
Occupation 2	2
Occupation 3	4.5
Occupation 4	14
Plow zone	21

Table 3-20. Live weight, relative contribution to total diet, deer *versus* moose, per 100 deer. Weight in pounds.

Occupation	Deer	Moose
Occupation 2	15,000	1,800
Occupation 3	15,000	4,000
Occupation 4	15,000	12,600
Plow zone	15,000	18,900

SEALS

All parts of the seal skeleton are represented (Table 3–21). Many postcrania exhibit large Canid-sized punctures and knawed ends, as with the deer bone sample. The dense auditory bulla is the most abundant Phocid bone in this sample, as it is in many others. The bulla would not have been attractive to the Canids since it lacks adhering meat. With its attached boney auditory canal, the bulla is the most species-diagnostic bone in a Phocid collection, and there are only two per individual. Thus, this bone is most useful for making inter-specific frequency comparisons, and is an excellent basis for MNI estimates. Twenty-two of 74 teeth were sectioned to provide demographic and/or season-of-kill data. The humerus is the most commonly preserved postcranial element, again probably due to its compact, heavy structure. It carries demographic data in epiphyseal closure states and in measurements.

Table 3-21. Number of seal bones in the four major occupation subdivisions at the Turner Farm site.

Element	Occ. 2	Occ. 3	Occ. 4	Plow zone
Mandible or max. frags.	1	5	20	10
Isolated teeth	3	17	80	30
Bullae	12	22	88	28
Other skull parts	–	–	5	3
Vertebrae	3	3	38	3
Scapulae	–	2	10	–
Inominate	1	2	13	2
Ribs	(Present, not counted.)			
Humerus	2	7	41	11
Radius	–	1	9	2
Ulna	2	2	8	4
Carpals/tarsals	–	–	5	2
Phalanges/ metapodials	1	9	47	13
Femur	2	3	14	7
Tibia	–	2	–	–
Fibula shaft/ distal	–	–	2	–
Other	–	–	3	–
TOTAL	27	74	387	118

Table 3-22. Seal bones identified to genus.

Occupation	Grey Seal	Harbor Seal
Occupation 2	8	9
Occupation 3	15	16
Occupation 4	78	95
Plow zone	18	33
Total	119	153

Species Frequency

There are three species of Phocidae represented in the faunal sample: grey seal (*Halichoerus grypus*), harbor seal (*Phoca vitulina*), and harp seal (*P. groenlandica*, one specimen only). Table 3–22 presents the relative count of *Halichoerus* versus *Phoca* bones for the whole site. The relative proportion of *Halichoerus* remains constant (around 33–45% of the total Phocid kill) throughout the sequence. Using bulla counts (Table 3–23), the relative proportion is 33% to 46%, comparable with the total bone counts. We conclude from these data that approximately 1½ to 2 times more harbor than grey seals were taken. Because there is a disparity in size between grey and harbor seals, however, the grey seals would have provided more total gross food weight than the harbor seals.

Seasonality of the Hunt

Only one tooth from Occupation 2 was successfully sectioned (Figure 3–8). It confirms grey seal hunting at the time of the molt in January–March (annulus formation). Seasonality of harbor seal hunting during Occupation 2 is

Table 3-23. Counts of identified seal bullae and bullae fragments.

Occupation	Grey Seal	Harbor Seal	Harp Seal	Phocid *sp. indet.*
Occupation 2	4	6	1	1
Occupation 3	3	6	–	11
Occupation 4	13	26	–	49
Plow zone	5	6	–	16

Table 3-24. The relative frequency of seal compared with the deer bone at the Turner Farm site. Statistical comparison with a chi-square test. Expected frequencies in parentheses.

Occ.	Number Deer Bones	Number Seal Bones	Total	Relative Frequency
Occ. 2	1,023 (936.38)	27 (113.63)	1,050	2.6%
Occ. 3	1,060 (1,011.29)	74 (122.72)	1,134	7.0%
Occ. 4	2,461 (2,539.81)	387 (308.19)	2,848	15.7%
Plow zone	450 (506.53)	118 (61.47)	568	26.0%
Totals	4,994	606	5,600	

$X^2 = 176.64$, d.f. = 3, $p \geq 0.001$

problematical as no well-preserved teeth were read from this small sample. However, none of the Occupation 2 seal postcrania are of the small size associated with foetal or newborn seals (May–July), while bones of this size do occur commonly in later samples.

The only harp seal bone to be identified came from the small Occupation 2 sample. Spiess has successfully sectioned a harp seal postcanine tooth from the Late Archaic Seabrook Marsh in coastal New Hampshire (Robinson 1985), which proved to be a juvenile killed in late fall or early winter. The great harp seal herds of the northwest Atlantic move northward into the Arctic in spring and summer, and congregate on the ice off Newfoundland for pupping and mating in late winter (March). The species is rare in the Gulf of Maine today, and we conclude that stragglers would most likely have been young or adolescent seals who appeared in the Gulf of Maine during the fall and winter. The Occupation 2 population paid less attention to seals than did any later occupants.

There is a marked increase in the frequency of seal bones relative to deer in Occupation 3 (Table 3–24). Three teeth from grey seals and two from harbor seals confirm seal hunting during Occupation 3 during the pupping/mating or molt season of each species (Figure 3–9): January–March for the grey seal, and May–June for the harbor seal.

Occupation 4 levels yielded teeth that produced data from grey seals and five harbor seasl. These data (Figure 3–10) indicate that grey seal hunting centered on both the January–March pupping/mating season as well as during April–May. The harbor seal data also show a concentration on hunting during the pupping and hauling-out season (May–June for this species), but clear-

ly preceding and possibly following that period as well. The plow zone seasonality data (Figure 3–11) again demonstrate a relative increase in seal usage.

Demography of the Kill

An age demography of the kill based upon humeral epiphyseal fusion and measurements is presented in Table 3–25. These data show an increased proportion of immature seals in the kill in Occupation 4 and the plow zone compared with Occupation 3.

PORPOISE AND WHALES

A group of four porpoise (*Phocaena*) vertebrae were recovered from Occupation 4. The sample consisted of three thorassic and one lumbar vertebrae, all with an epiphyseal line visible between the vertebral body and epiphysis. This epiphyseal state lasts for only a short period of time (one or several years) after epiphyseal fusion. Thus we feel that these four bones represent a single adult individual. One additional porpoise vertebral fragment was recovered from the plow zone.

Two whale bones were recovered from Occupation 4. Both exhibit chopping marks that have modified the bone beyond any simple needs of carcass butchery. One is a rib or jaw fragment of about 14x9x2 cm dimension. The curvature indicates that it can only have come from a very large cetacean. The other fragment is a modified 31cm-long proximal end portion of a left, anterior rib of a very large Balaenid whale, either bowhead (*Balaena*) or right whale (*Eubalaena*). (This identification was made by comparison with specimens in Harvard's MCZ.) We specifically exclude the possibility that this piece is from a hump-back (*Megaptera*) or one of the fin whale family (*Balaenopteridae*), again based on comparision with MCZ specimens. These two fragments were recovered from two different stratigraphic subdivisions within the Occupation 4 deposits, probably indicating that two different individual whales were involved.

Whales represent the ultimate butchering logistics problem, and their bones are subject to an extreme negative bias in being carried onto an archaeological site. Only in some high arctic whale-hunting Eskimo sites where wood is scarce (e.g., Labrador Inuit, Spiess 1978) is whale bone incorporated into habitation sites, mainly for architectural use as roof supports, furniture such as

Table 3-25. *Phoca* or Phocid age demography based upon humeral fusion and measurement. Foetal or newborn humeri exhibit measurement #11 < 2.8 cm and un-fused epiphyses. Immature humeri exhibit #11 between 2.9 and 3.9 cm. Subadults and adults exhibit #11 > 4.0 or fused epiphyses.

Occupation	Foetal and/ or Newborn	Immature	Subadult and Adult
Occupation 2	0	1	0
Occupation 3	3	0	2
Occupation 4	13	12	6
Plow zone	2	6	2

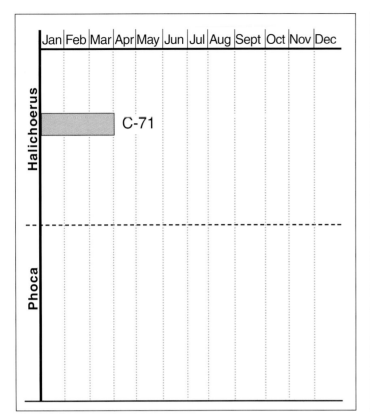

Figure 3-8. Occupation 2, seasonality of seal kill.

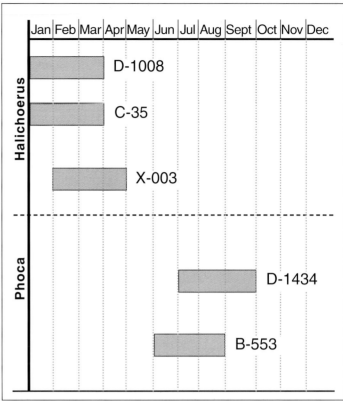

Figure 3-9. Occupation 3, seasonality of seal kill.

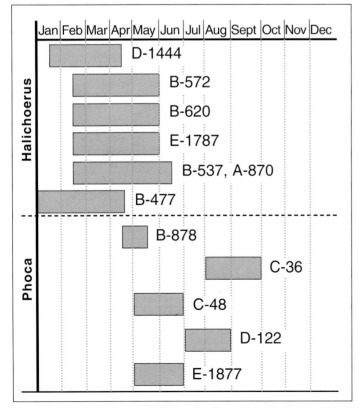

Figure 3-10. Occupation 4, seasonality of seal kill.

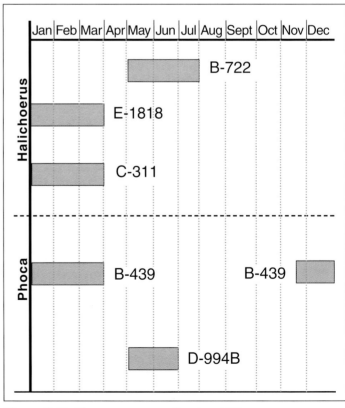

Figure 3-11. Plow zone, seasonality of seal kill.

stools, or for tool manufacture (McCartney and Savelle 1985). A whale carcass must usually be butchered on a beach (lacking European ships, tackle and iron tools). There is very little incentive to carry vertebrae, ribs and jaw parts weighing hundreds of pounds uphill onto an associated habitation site. Thus, whalebone counts drastically under-represent the relative contribution of whales to the economy. The extraction of these two bones from a beached carcass certainly cannot be ruled out, but if they record the consumption of two whales, they represent between 30 and 40 tons of live-weight animal mass.

BEAR

The count of identified bear (*Ursus americanus*) bones for the major stratigraphic divisions of the site, and their comparison with deer post-cranial counts (expressed as a percentage) is presented in Table 3–26. As with other large mammal species, the identified bone frequency (and the assumed economic importance) of black bear versus deer increases with time after the Occupation 2. There is a noticeable increase in relative frequency of bear between Occupations 2 and 4. The plow zone did not produce evidence of further bear hunting intensification (in contrast to the intensification of seal hunting).

Mandibles, maxillae and skull parts (Table 3–27) demonstrate that bear skulls frequently found their way into the midden deposits. Postcrania are also well represented. The paucity of identified longbones is ascribed to fragmentation of the sample, and our lack of confidence in identifying small scraps of longbone diaphysis.

Table 3-26. Bear, number of bones by occupation.

Occupation	Numbers of Bones	Frequency Relative to Deer Bone Count
Occupation 2	4	0.5%
Occupation 3	13	1.2%
Occupation 4	62	2.5%
Plow zone	7	1.7%

Teeth and Seasonality

Five bear canines were successfully sectioned and read. Three originate in Occupation 4, and two were recovered from the plow zone. The results (Table 3–28) indicate that most bear were taken between late fall or early winter (just before dormancy) and early spring. There was no single bear hunting season, and no concentration on any particular age group. Hunting can be characterized as opportunistic.

MINK

Mink frequency relative to seal and deer increases markedly from Occupation 2 deposits through the plow zone (Table 3–29). One sea mink radius originated in Occupation 1. In Occupation 2, the mink bone count is nearly 9% of the seal and deer bone count, increasing to nearly 14% in Occupation 3 and to 20% in Occupation 4. A drastic increase occurs in the plow zone. Where observed,

Table 3-27. Bear, catalogue of bones by occupation.

Occupation 2. 4 bones
1 M_1, fractured crown; 1 proximal metacarpal or metatarsal fragment; 1 navicular; 1 phalange
Occupation 3. 13 bones
2 left mandibles with teeth, wear state light. M_2 at cingulum: 1.91, 1.78 cm; 1 canine; 2 metacarpal/ metatarsal fragments; 1 distal femur, epiphysis fused, distal breadth 7.3 cm; 1 cuboid; 1 ulna; 1 talus; 1 calcaneus; 3 phalanges
Occupation 4. 62 bones
1 left 3 right maxillae; 3 other skull portions 13 canines or fragments thereof; 6 isolated teeth; 1 distal radius, epiphysis closed, distal breadth: 2.93 cm; 1 right pelvis; 1 patella; 15 metacarpal or metatarsal fragments; 13 phalanges; 3 tali; 1 rib fragment; 1 femoral fragment
Plow zone. 7 bones
1 right mandible, M_2 length at cingulum 2.03 cm; 2 canine fragments; 1 incisor; 2 femoral heads; 1 tarsal or carpal fragment

Table 3-28. Bear, tooth sectioning results.

C-254 (Occupation 4)	Probably 8-10 translucent rest lines formed. Last five lines in dentin clearly readable. Definite translucent (rest) line formed, and it appears to be wide (completely formed). Conclusion: late winter kill.
E-1546 (Occupation 4)	Last four rest lines visible in internal dentin. Last layer forming is a translucent (rest) line. Killed during winter.
A-841 (Occupation 4)	Over 13 rest lines formed. Last layer forming is a translucent (rest) line. Killed during winter.
E-1818 (Plow zone)	Nineth translucent (rest) line has just finished forming, there being the slight beginnings of an opaque (growth) layer on the inside edge of the pulp cavity. Killed in spring, after dormancy.
E-1545 (Plow zone) (incisor)	First translucent (rest) line has formed. Last layer forming is a full thickness growth (opaque) layer. Killed in fall or early winter. Animal was 1½ or 2½ years of age, depending on whether incisor forms first annulus during first or second year.

butchery marks on bone indicate special attention to removing pelts, although such marks were not common enough to have been quantified. We infer that mink were being sought at least partially for their pelts during the whole sequence of occupation, and that interest in them peaked in the late Ceramic period.

Table 3–30 presents the distribution of mandibular carnassial alveolar length, providing a relative count of the two species in the sample. There is a scattering of specimens that match common mink (*M. L. vison*) in size and rugosity (carnassial length less than 0.78 cm.). The sea mink (*M. L. macrodon*) sample is strongly bimodal, which we interpret as a result of male/female sexual size dimorphism. Males predominate in the sample, and the modal size of the sample does not seem to change over time. Only between 2% and 6% of the bone sample is identifiable as common mink or a mink of borderline size between common and sea mink (Table 3–31). There is no time trend in the data, nor is there any difference in the relative proportion of the two species between the Late Archaic and Ceramic period strata. We therefore infer that common mink was a consistent, small percentage of the mink population in lower Penobscot Bay during the past 5,200 years, and that sea mink was numerically dominant until its recent extinction.

The right and left mandibles of mink do not fuse tightly, and never remain paired in archaeological context in our experience. Thus, as with paired postcrania, we would expect no differential preservation of left versus right mandibles if

Table 3-29. Mink skeletal element frequency and bone counts. Most of the specimens are sea mink. Hindlimb/forelimb ratio is calculated by dividing counts of femur + tibia by humerus + radius + ulna.

Element	Occ.1	Occ. 2	Occ. 3	Occ. 4	Plow zone
Skull/maxilla		5	4	30	3
Mandible		24	40	181	31
Isolated teeth		6	14	42	23
Vertebra		3	11	34	4
Scapula		0	1	8	0
Pelvis		0	5	22	2
Humerus		10	17	83	10
Radius	1	5	7	34	7
Ulna		8	10	36	4
Femur		11	20	84	4
Tibia		8	18	58	8
Metapodials/ phlanges		6	6	24	6
Calcaneus		1	0	7	1
Talus		1	1	3	0
Other		0	0	2	0
TOTAL	1	91	154	655	103
Hindlimb/ forelimb		0.83	1.09	0.93	0.42
Deer and seal count		1,050	1,134	2,848	568
Relative frequency of *Mustela*		8.7%	13.6%	23.0%	18.1%

Table 3-30. Common mink and sea mink carnassial length measurements. Note bimodality, with modes at 0.86–0.87 and 1.00–1.01 cm. In addtion, about 2% of specimens have length measurements less than 0.79 cm, which are common mink.

Length cm	Occupation 2	Occupation 3	Occupation 4
0.70-1	–	1	–
0.72-3	–	–	–
0.74-5	–	1	1
0.76-7	–	–	1?
0.78-9	1?	–	–
0.80-1	–	1	4
0.82-3	–	1	5
0.84-5	4	1	7
0.86-7	1	1	8
0.88-9	–	5	7
0.90-1	2	3	6
0.92-3	2	3	10
0.94-5	2	1	12
0.96-7	1	4	17
0.98-9	5	5	25
1.00-1	1	7	31
1.02-3	2	3	20
1.04-5	2	1	6
1.06-7	–	1	1

each side received similar cultural treatment. In fact, however, there is a strong left-right assymetry in the Occupation 2 mandible sample. (Table 3–32, probability of chance <5%). The small sample from the New Gravel Floor, a subunit of Occupation 4, also approaches 95% confidence of being non-random (<5% probability of a chance distribution). These data suggest some sort of differential human treatment of right versus left mandibles of sea mink during some periods of occupation. Perhaps one side was preferentially curated as a trophy by certain hunters at certain times and places. For example, Spiess has personally observed that some Labrador Eskimo hunters retain caribou mandibles of one side only as a casual count of hunting success. The effect may also be somehow related to the handedness of the person skinning the carcass.

Bone elements from all parts of the body (Table 3–29) are well represented in the sample. There is little change in hindlimb-forelimb ratio over time except in the plow zone. Where we suspect that bone fracturing due to mechanical disturbance is a likely cause of the aberrant ratio. We interpret these data as evidence that whole mink carcasses were delivered to the site, and their skeletons incorporated into the middens.

Table 3-31. Proportion of the mink sample possibly identifiable as common mink, including *Mustela* sp. indet.

Occupation	Total *Mustela*	Number *M. vison*	Number sp. indet.	% Non-*macrodon*
Occupation 2	91	2	3	5.5%
Occupation 3	154	1	3	2.6%
Occupation 4	655	7	17	3.7%
Plow zone	103	0	4	3.9%

Table 3-32. Sea mink, left versus right mandible counts. The finer stratigraphic subdivisions of Occupation 4 (see Chapter 4) are used. p = probability of being due to chance alone.

Occupation	Left	Right	p = chance
Occupation 2	8	15	0.047
Occupation 3	16	17	> 0.1
Occupation 4			
B2GF	2	2	> 0.1
2GF	10	11	> 0.1
CCS	36	30	> 0.1
1GF	23	25	> 0.1
MCS	23	17	> 0.1
NGF	0	4	0.064
Plow zone	14	16	> 0.1

Seasonality

Apparently, sea mink hunting or trapping was highly seasonal throughout the site's history. Occupations 2 and 3 each yielded a single readable canine, with a thin growth layer forming. Ten canines from Occupation 4 yielded similar results. Assuming that canines from sea mink, like common mink, accumulated a cementum rest line between November and March, the beginning of growth layer formation occurred in late winter or early spring (March – April). Therefore, the trapping/hunting season must have focussed on late winter/early spring.

BEAVER

The exploitation of beaver *(Castor canadensis)* evidently increased markedly in relation to large mammal usage at several times during the deposition of the Turner Farm sequence. Table 3–33 presents bone and tooth counts, as incisors, cheek tooth and skull fragments, and postcrania.

Beaver incisor tools have been analyzed with the artifact sample (Bourque 1995:186–190) and are excluded from the faunal sample because they may have been curated over multiple seasons or years and discarded long after death.

A comparison between beaver bone counts and deer and seal bone counts (Table 3–36) shows that relative beaver abundance increased three-fold between the Occupations 2 and 3 samples and continued to increase in the Occupation 4 and the plow zone samples (see next chapter). We have attempted to detect whether beaver carcass useage was partially for meat. Postcranial counts (Table 3–33) have been tabulated as either "forelimb," "hind limb," or "other nonlimb." There is much disparity in the relative size of beaver fore and hind limbs; the forelimbs being diminutive and the hindlimbs rugose, carrying much more meat. Thus, change in the proportion of forelimb to hind limb might reflect either changes in the importance of beaver meat hunting versus pelts, or perhaps a change in the spatial distribution of processed carcass parts. There is a trend toward a decreasing ratio of

Table 3-33. Beaver, bone counts. *Note:* worked beaver tooth incisors are excluded. The lower half of the table includes various ratios discussed in the text.

Element	Occ. 2	Occ. 3	Occupation 4	Plow zone
Incisors/fragments	12	30	121	34
Cheek teeth and jaw fragments	7	41	113	35
Forelimb elements	3	14	63	8
Hindlimb elements	5	6	25	2
Other postcrania	10	13	39	5
TOTAL POSTCRANIA	18	33	127	15
Hindlimb/forelimb ratio	1.67	0.43	0.40	0.25
Incisor/postcrania ratio	0.67	0.91	0.94	2.27
TOTAL BEAVER BONE	37	104	361	84
Beaver to deer + seal proportion	3.5%	9.2%	12.7%	14.8%

Table 3-34. Number of teeth observed with various beaver cheek tooth root closure states and equivalent age in years.

Occupation	Roots Open (< 2 years)	Roots Closing (2½-4 years)	Roots Closed (>4 years)
Occupation 2	4	2	1
Occupation 3	7	6	7
Occupation 4	27	24	19
Plow zone	10	16	4

hindlimb to forelimb elements in the Turner Farm sequence from Occupation 2 on. This trend may indicate that beaver carcasses were increasingly left in the field. If so, this would contradict the notion that beaver meat became more important with time and support the inference that pelts became more imporant with time.

Demographics and Seasonality

Of the three beaver molars that were successfully sectioned and read, one lower left molar from Occupation 3 indicated hunting from December through March. The two others were from Occupation 4. One indicated an adult killed between December and March inclusive, the other a late fall or winter kill. Thus, beaver were apparently hunted during winter or late winter, when beaver pelts were in prime condition.

There do not appear to be any consistent changes over time in beaver demography as represented by tooth root closure (Table 3–34). Apparently the increase in beaver hunting during Occupation 4 did not change the demographic structure of the beaver population. Whatever techniques were used, hunters took beaver of a wide age and demographic distribution.

SMALL FURBEARERS

Here we consider 10 species of small furbearers whose remains are not abundant in the sample (Table 3–35), but, some of their furs may have had special value as decorative trim, use for special purpose clothing, and/or some use as food (the porcupine and the dog, for example). The taxa included are fisher *(Martes pennanti)*, muskrat *(Ondatra zibethecus)*, river otter *(Lutra canadensis)*, porcupine *(Erethizon dorsatum)*, genus *Lynx* (probably Bobcat, *L. rufus*), racoon *(Procyon lotor)*, skunk *(Mephitis)*, rabbit *(Sylvilagus)*, red fox *(Vulpes)*, and dog or wolf *(Canis)*.

Aside from sea mink and beaver, the taking of small furbearers was confined to otter, muskrat, fox, and porcupine. The relative frequency of small fur bearers' bones to large mammal bones doubles in Occupation 4, and species diversity increases as well. Compared to mink and beaver, however, these other species remained quantitatively unimportant.

All of these minor furbearing species could easily have maintained populations on the large islands of Penobscot Bay. It is possible that the trapping of these species in the Ceramic period was an adjunct to beaver trapping, for the more common species are wetland oriented. There was no heavy reliance on boreal species (e.g., fisher, marten, lynx), indicating that inland winter-based traplines were unimportant or unused.

The dog bones recorded here are those that appeared in the midden debris, outside of any burial feature. The high proportion of dog bones in the Occupation 2 sample may perhaps be due to a series of dog burials dating to that period (Bourque 1995:42–43) disturbed by subsequent occupations, although we did not analyze the overall distribution of the dog bone or skeletal element counts. No butchery marks were noticed on dog bones. We leave the analysis of the dogs for future research, acknowledging the range of functions that dogs played in the region (Kerber 1997b).

Table 3-35. The total number of identified specimens (NISP) of small furbearers. Isolated teeth are counted as one specimen. The number of poscranial bones is shown in parentheses.

Species	Occ. 2	Occ. 3	Occ. 4	Plow zone
Porcupine	–	3 (1)	13 (3)	–
Muskrat	1 (0)	1 (0)	7 (0)	1 (0)
Otter	10 (6)	6 (6)	21 (10)	10 (5)
Fisher	–	–	1 (1)	–
Lynx **sp.**	–	–	1 (1)	1 (1)
Racoon	–	–	3 (2)	–
Skunk	–	–	1 (1)	–
Rabbit	–	–	1 (1)	–
Red fox	2 (1)	1 (1)	13 (2)	7 (0)
Canis cf. *familiaris*	22 (17)	18 (12)	35 (5)	9 (4)
TOTAL	35	29	96	28

THE RELATIVE IMPORTANCE
OF VARIOUS MAMMAL TAXA

The following trends in the faunal data suggest an increasing intensity and diversity in mammal exploitation toward the present. The trend is manifest in the deer demographics and in dramatic increases in usage of large mammal food species other than deer (moose, seals and bear). A monotonic increase in relative usage of moose versus deer is documented, with the largest quantitative change coming between Occupations 3 and 4. Data presented in this discussion (Table 3–36, Figure 3–12) document the increased relative use of seals and bear compared with deer. Moreover, the ratio of moose to seal changes as well. If the ratio of deer to the other species changed, but the ratio of seal, bear and moose to each other remained constant, then the effect might simply be a shift away from deer. But this is not the case; the relative importance of these other species, to say nothing of fish, birds and shellfish, do not remain constant. Therefore, the trend is not a shift away from deer, but a complex interaction of choice and availability among these major mammalian species.

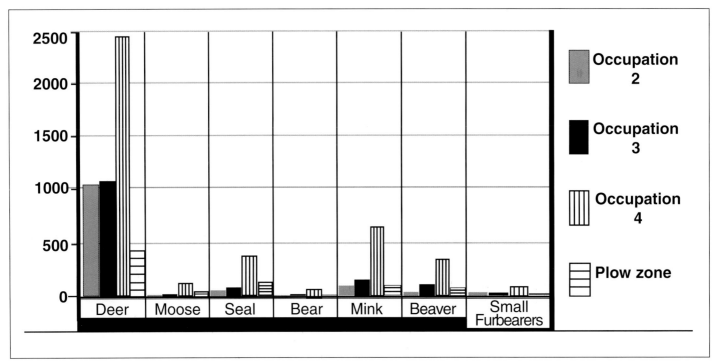

Figure 3-12. Graphic representation of the number of identified specimens (NISP) for the more common mammal taxa. Graph based on Table 3-36.

Table 3-36. Summary of mammal total bone counts.

Species	Occ.1	Occ. 2	Occ. 3	Occ. 4	Plow zone
Deer	2	1,023	1,060	2,461	450
Moose	0	8	13	115	26
Seal	0	27	74	387	118
Porpoise	0	0	0	4	0
Bear	0	4	13	62	7
Total large mammal	3	1,062	1,160	3,029	601
Mink	1	91	154	650	103
Beaver	0	37	104	359	84
Small furbearers	0	35	29	96	28

COMPARISON OF MAJOR EXPLOITED LARGE MAMMAL SPECIES

The relative frequency of seals to deer increases ten-fold between Occupation 2 (2.6%) and the plow zone (26.0%). This change is highly significant (chi-square = 177, 3 d. f.). Relative bone counts do not reflect the relative numbers of seals and deer killed, however, because Phocid and Cervid skeletons are constructed differently and contain different numbers of bones. Phocid longbones exhibit a thick cortex and their marrow cavities contain little fat, which is deposited subcutaneously in this family. (The major destructive agent of Phocid bones at the site is apparently chewing by domestic Canids: the epiphyseal ends are often ragged and exhibit canine puncture marks.) Therefore, to obtain an order-of-magnitude estimate of relative frequency of carcass delivery to the site, we must compare sets of the bones from each species that are most resistant to destruction (Table 3–37). These bones are the first and second lower molar in deer, and the auditory bulla in Phocids. We make the assumption that the number of first and second molars divided by 2 (since two teeth are involved) can be compared with the number of seal bullae. (Although similar in concept, these numbers are in fact only crude Minimum Numbers of Individuals counts, not taking age and size into account.)

Many fewer seal individuals were killed than deer individuals during Occupation 2 (one seal for every four deer), with grey seals comprising 40% of the total. In Occupation 3 strata the seal to deer ratio rose, with about half as many seal individuals killed as deer. In Occupation 4 strata, seals approach deer in frequency of kill (still with grey seals com-

prising 40% of the total). This increase over Occupation 3 corresponds with intensification of the harbor seal hunt to include all seasons. Finally, in the plow zone, we estimate that seals were killed about 2½ times as often as deer, and that seal hunting was multiseasonal.

A marked increase in the frequency of moose hunting relative to deer hunting occurred between Occupations 3 and 4, followed by another that is apparent in the plow zone. Neither were coincident with the primary relative increase in moose, again suggesting a complex pattern of human choices about which resources to hunt, tempered by environmental or social factors.

Comparing the relative numbers of bears represented with the other large mammal taxa (Table 3–38) is conceptually difficult. Bears are terrestrial omnivores whose long bones are thinner-walled and longer than those of seals and therefore fracture more easily. Bears possess five digits on each hand or foot, like seals and unlike Cervids, so there are many more foot/paw bones per individual bear or seal. Their tooth and mandibular structure is more rugose than either Cervids or Phocids, so bear mandibles and teeth would better survive breaking forces. Again the best means of comparison may be to use the most resistant bones for each taxon: the mandible and maxillary fragments in the case of bear. From the very small samples available, we conclude that

Table 3-37. The frequency of seal versus deer, based upon best-preserved element. The first column is the number of deer lower 1st and 2nd molars. The second column represents a relative measure of the number of deer, dividing the first column by 2. The third column is a relative measure of the number of seals. The percentage figure in the last column is column three divided by column two.

Occupation	# Deer Teeth	÷ 2	Seals	Seals: Deer
Occupation 2	105	52	12	23%
Occupation 3	83	42	20	48%
Occupation 4	189	94	88	94%
Plow zone	28	14	27	193%

Table 3-38. Relative number of seal and bear kills, based upon most resistant skeletal parts.

Occupation	Seal Bullae ÷ 2	Bear Max./ Mandibular
Occupation 2	6	Trace
Occupation 3	11	2
Occupation 4	44	3
Plow zone	14	1

Table 3-39. Estimated relative frequency of kill, nomalized for a hypothetical kill of 100 deer for each occupation.

Occupation	Dear	Moose	Seal	Bear
Occupation 2	100	2	24	1
Occupation 3	100	4.5	46	6
Occupation 4	100	14	92	9
Plow zone	100	21	225	15

bear numerically represent roughly 10% (±5%) of the seal kill. No matter what the exact relative representation of bear, it peaked in Occupation 4 strata and declined in the plow zone.

The data discussed in the preceding paragraphs are used to prepare an estimate of relative frequency of kill for large mammal species (Table 3–39) by calculating the number of each species killed for every 100 deer killed. A gross estimate of their food value can be had by multiplying relative frequency data by a live weight factor. The relative amounts of food (Table 3–40) derived from the large mammals for each major stratigraphic subdivision can then be calculated by taking estimated total live weights per 100 deer killed (Table 3–41) and multiplying those figures by the relative number of deer in each level (number deer bones/1,000). These figures are not estimates of actual available food because minimum numbers of individuals are not involved in the calculations. They may, however, reflect intensity and length of occupation, as well as differing degrees of reliance on mammals for food. Length of occupation cannot at present be independently controlled either by radiocarbon dating or stratigraphic information.

The degree of reliance on mammals for food, compared with other souces of protein and fat, can be assessed by comparison with the amount of fish bone and clam shell (see below). It must be emphasized, however, that fat and protein content will vary between species for a given weight of animal, and within a species on the basis of age, season and sex. For purposes of estimating live weight we use a deer weight of 70 kg (150 lbs).

BIRDS

Bird bone identifications to specific species or genera were often not straightforward due to much overlap in size between species of economic importance, and to multiple species within important subfamlies. In many cases it was therefore necessary to group several species into one identifiable faunal group (Table 3–42). Among the ducks, for example, only the coracoid was consistently identified to a low taxonomic level.

Skeletal Elements

Bird skeletal element counts for Occupation 2, Occupation 3, and the plow zone are presented in Tables 3–43 through 3–45. Although there is great variability within taxa in fragmentation and identifiability for various skeletal parts, there is little evidence that any particular skeletal part has been given preferential treatment. One exception may be

Table 3-40. Estimated relative live weight of kill per 100 deer killed (rounded to nearest 100kg).

Occupation	Deer	Moose	Seal	Bear	Sum /100 deer
Occupation 2	7,000	900	3,400	70	11,370
Occupation 3	7,000	1,900	6,400	400	15,700
Occupation 4	7,000	5,900	12,900	600	26,400
Plow zone	7,000	8,900	31,500	1,000	48,400

Table 3-41. Relative total estimated live weight of large mammals per 100 deer times relative number of deer.

Occupation	Live weight/ relative 100 deer	Relative number of deer (# bones divided by 1,000)	Est. large mammal live weight (kg based)
Occupation 2	12,400	1.02	12,600
Occupation 3	15,700	1.06	16,600
Occupation 4	26,400	2.43	64,200
Plow zone	48,400	0.45	21,800

Table 3-42. Taxa assigned to bird bones.

1	**Canada Goose** Goose bones of a size that match *Branta canadensis*.	**9**	**Small alcids** Small alcid bones. Possibilities include: dovekie (*Plautus alle*), black guillemot (*Cepphus grylle*), and/or Atlantic puffin (*Fratercula arctia*). Only dovekie and guillemot have been positively identified.
2	**Other geese** Goose bones of species smaller than *Branta canadensis*. None were positively identified to species. Possibilities include: white-fronted goose *(Anser albifrons)*, brant *(Branta berniculala)*, snow goose *(Chen hyperborea)*, and blue goose *(Chen coerulescens)*.	**10**	**Ducks** See Table 3-60.
		11	**Grebes** This group contains at least two species of the family Podicipedidae. Smaller bones may represent the pied-billed grebe (*Podilymbus podiceps)* or the horned grebe (*Podiceps auritus*). Larger bones represent the red-necked grebe (*Podiceps grisegena).*
3	**Loons** Bones mostly identifiable as common loon *(Gavia immer)*, although several are identifiable as red-throated loon *(Gavia stellata)*.		
4	**Cormorants** Larger comorant bones are assigned to European cormorant (*Phalacrocorax carbo*). Smaller comorant bones are assigned to double-crested cormorant (*P. auritus*). A noticable size range occurs in the comorant sample, indicating that both species are present. Unfortunately, the range of overlap makes specific identification difficult.	**12**	**Hawks** Bones of the genus *Buteo*. Bones of the osprey (*Pandion haliaetus*), and the eagles (golden and bald) are easily separable from *Buteo*, and so are noted in miscellaneous identifications.
		13	**Shearwaters** One bone of the family Procellariidae was found in the Second Gravel Floor of Occupation 4. Based on size, it is probably sooty shearwater (*Puffinus griseus*).
5	**Large herons** Heron bones identified as northern great blue heron (*Ardea herodias)*. It is unlikely that other species are present in the sample.		
		14	**Swans** Several Anatid bones were found in Occupation 4. Much larger than *Branta canadensis*, they are identified as whistling swan (*Cygnus columbianus*).
6	**Medium-sized herons** Ardeid bones smaller than northern great blue heron. Possibilities include: American egret (*Ardea alba*), snowy egret (*Egretta thula*), little blue heron (*Egretta coerulea*), American bittern (*Nycticorax nycticorax*).		
		15	**Rails, sandpipers, etc.** A single humerus attributable to a large member of the families Rallidae or Scolopacidae was found in the Medium-Crushed Shell of Occupation 4. The specimen could be king rail (*Rallus elegans*), clapper rail (*Rallus longirostris*), coot (*Fulica americana*), or Eskimo curlew (*Numenius borealis*).
7	**Great auk** Bones of *Pinguinnis impennis*, now extinct. This species was the largest Alcid. Many of its bones are easily distinguished by anatomical changes associated with flightlessness.		
8	**Medium alcids** Medium-sized alcid bones. More than one species seems to be represented. Possibilities include: razor-billed auk (*Alca torda*), Atlantic murre (*Uria aalge*), and/or Brunnich's murre (*Uria lomvia*).		

Table 3-43. Number of specific bird skeletal elements in Occupation 2. "Other" includes vertebrae, sacrum, phalanges.

Species	Skull Parts	Sternum-Furcula	Scapula	Coracoid	Humerus	Ulna	Carpo-Metacarpus	Femur	Tibio-Tarsus	Tarso-Metatarsus	Radius	Other
Canada goose	–	–	–	–	2	4	1	–	1	–	–	–
Other goose	–	–	–	–	–	–	–	–	–	–	–	–
Cormorant	–	–	–	2	1	–	–	–	1	–	–	–
Adreid, larger	–	–	–	1	–	–	–	–	–	2	–	–
Adreid, medium	–	–	–	–	–	–	–	–	–	–	–	–
Loon, common	–	–	–	3	1	–	2	1	5	2	–	–
Loon, red throated	–	–	–	–	–	–	–	–	–	1	–	–
Great Auk	–	–	1	1	5	2	1	1	–	–	–	–
Alcid/Medium	–	–	–	–	–	1	–	–	1	1	–	–
Alcid/Small	–	1	–	–	1	–	–	2	–	–	–	–
Duck	–	2	4	14	7	14	4	–	–	2	–	–
Podicipedidae	–	–	–	–	–	–	–	–	–	1	–	–
Buteo	–	–	–	–	–	–	–	–	–	–	1	–
Eagle species	–	–	–	–	–	1	–	–	–	–	–	–
Small wading	–	–	–	–	–	–	–	–	–	–	–	–
Larger-than-duck	–	–	–	–	–	6	–	–	–	1	3	7
Duck-sized	5	1	–	–	18	–	1	–	1	4	6	6
Smaller-than-duck	–	3	–	–	–	1	–	–	–	–	1	–

Table 3-44. Number of specific bird skeletal elements in Occupation 3. "Other" includes vertebrae, sacrum, phalanges.

Species	Skull Parts	Sternum-Furcula	Scapula	Coracoid	Humerus	Ulna	Carpo-Metacarpus	Femur	Tibio-Tarsus	Tarso-Metatarsus	Radius	Other
Canada goose	–	1	–	8	4	1	–	–	1	–	–	–
Other goose	–	–	–	–	–	1	–	–	1	–	–	–
Cormorant	–	–	–	1	4	1	–	–	1	–	–	–
Adreid, larger	–	–	–	–	–	1	1	1	1	–	–	–
Adreid, medium	–	–	–	–	–	–	–	–	2	–	–	–
Loon, common	1	–	–	2	3	1	2	9	7	5	–	–
Loon, red throated	–	–	–	–	–	–	–	–	2	4	–	–
Great Auk	–	1	–	3	4	1	1	–	–	1	–	–
Alcid/Medium	–	–	–	–	–	2	–	–	3	–	–	–
Alcid/Small	–	1	–	2	3	2	–	2	3	–	–	–
Duck	–	7	6	51	10	11	9	8	8	3	–	–
Podicipedidae	–	–	–	–	–	1	–	–	–	1	–	–
Buteo	–	–	–	–	–	–	–	1	–	–	–	–
Small wading	–	–	–	–	–	–	–	–	1	–	–	–
Larger-than-duck	–	2	–	–	–	5	–	–	5	–	1	1
Duck-sized	–	8	–	–	41	–	–	1	9	–	8	20
Smaller-than-duck	–	4	–	–	–	1	–	–	–	–	–	1

Table 3-45. Number of specific bird skeletal elements in the plow zone. "Other" includes vertebrae, sacrum, phalanges.

Species	Skull Parts	Sternum-Furcula	Scapula	Coracoid	Humerus	Ulna	Carpo-Metacarpus	Femur	Tibio-Tarsus	Tarso-Metatarsus	Radius	Other
Canada goose			2	1	1	–	–	–	1	1		
Other goose						1						
Cormorant		1	–	–	2	–	1	–	1			
Adreid, large				1								
Adreid, medium								1				
Loon, common				11	2	2	–	2	2	3		
Loon, red throated									1	3		
Great Auk		1	1	3	5	1	–	–	–	2		
Alcid/Medium						1	–		4			
Alcid/Small					6	–	–	1	–			
Duck	1	5	1	26	8	5	1	2	3	3		
Podicipedidae	1	–	1						–	–		
Buteo									1	1		
Rallidae							1		–			
Larger-than-duck	2	–	–	–	1				1	–	1	9
Duck-size		2	–	–	25				1	–	7	27
Smaller-than-duck								1				

Table 3-46. Bird bone counts and percentages within each Occupation.

Species	Occupation 2		Occupation 3		Occupation 4		Plow zone	
Canada goose	8	8%	15	7%	40	4%	6	5%
Other goose	–	–	2	1%	2	1%	1	1%
Cormorant	4	4%	7	3%	44	4%	5	4%
Adreid, large	3	3%	4	2%	13	1%	1	1%
Adreid, medium	–	–	2	1%	15	1%	1	1%
Loon, common	14	15%	30	14%	169	16%	22	18%
Loon, red throated	1	1%	6	3%	25	2%	4	3%
Great Auk	11	11%	11	6%	47	5%	13	10%
Alcid/Medium	3	3%	5	2%	24	2%	5	4%
Alcid/Small	4	4%	13	6%	76	8%	7	6%
Duck	47	48%	113	53%	539	51%	55	44%
Podicipedidae	1	1%	2	1%	18	2%	2	1%
Buteo	1	1%	1	0.5%	2	5%	2	1%
Other	1	1%	1	0.5%	9	1%	1	1%
IDENTIFIED TOTALS	98	100%	212	100%	1,023	100%	125	100%
Larger-than-duck	17		14		112		14	
Duck-size	42		87		516		62	
Smaller-than-duck	5		6		42		1	
TOTAL BIRD BONE	162		319		1,693		202	

the selective retention of eagle and hawk hind limb bones. Of the five bird-of-prey bones identified, all are hind limb longbones. Axial skeleton elements of eagles and hawks would be tallied in the "larger than duck" category. However, the birds-of-prey sample seems to be lacking the most identifiable bones, the coracoid and humerus. It is possible that this phenomenon is somehow associated with use of the primary (and secondary) wing feathers, and deposit of the wing bones off-site, perhaps associated with curation of heirloom artifacts.

General Frequency Change of Birds

Curiously, there is no drastic change in species proportions within the bird sample over time. However, there is change in the magnitude of the sample (Tables 3–46 and 3–47). The relative proportion of ducks (as a group) stays approximately constant, as do all other taxa except the great auk. Great auk *(Pinguinnis impennis)* bones are about twice as abundant in the Occupation 2 sample as in later samples. Bird hunting in general, however, was less important in Occupation 2, as reflected in lower bird bone counts in comparison to mammal bone counts. The higher incidence of

great auk during Occupation 2 may reflect the importance of maritime pursuits during summer.

While the proportion of ducks to other birds does not change throughout the sequence, duck species proportions do change (Table 3–47). There is a strong increase in the frequency of the scaups compared with all other duck taxa between the Late Archaic (2 and 3 combined) and Occupation 4 samples (chi-square = 4.24, d.f.=1, probability between 0.01 and 0.05 of being due to chance). Scaups *(Aythya)* are present in significant numbers only between October and April in Maine, and are noted for their tendency to form rafts or concentrations of individuals. We suspect that the increase in scaup abundance reflects increased fall/winter hunting that relied on finding such rafts of birds in inshore concentrations. This increased reliance on scaups would probably have been accompanied by less active hunting of other duck species, as the total reliance on ducks compared with other birds apparently did not increase.

The relative abundance of bird bone doubles between the Occupation 2 and 3 samples, and doubles again in the Occupation 4 sample, which we attribute to an increase in the importance of bird hunting (Table 3–48). The trend does not

Table 3-47. Taxonomic separation of the coracoid in the duck sample. Number and proportion of identified taxonomic groups. A chi-square comparison for the proportion of scaups in the sample is presented at the bottom of the table. Eider is probably common eider (*Somateria mollissima*). "Scaup" includes both greater (*Aythya marila*) and lesser scaup (*Aythya affinis*). "*Anas*, or black-duck sized" contains several species, probably of genus Anas, similar in size and build to *Anas rubripes*. "Small *Anas*" includes small ducks, both of genus *Anas* and *Aythinae*, among which bufflehead (*Glaucionetta albeola*) is definitively identified; others possible include teals, and harlequen duck.

Species	Occupation 2		Occupation 3		Occupation 4		Plow zone	
Eider	1	10%	4	13.5%	12	10%	1	12.5%
White-winged scoter	0		3	10%	5	4%	1	12.5%
Scaups	3	35%	7	23%	51	43%	5	62.5%
Anas or black-duck sized	1	10%	4	13.5%	7	6%		
Small *Anas*	4	45%	12	40%	42	35%	1	12.5%
Common Merganser					2	2%		
TOTAL	9		30		119		8	
Duck, not further identified	5		21		85		18	

X^2 Analysis, Scaups *versus* other ducks, Ceramic (Occupation 4 and plow zone) *versus* Archaic (Occupation 2 and 3)

	Archaic		Ceramic		Total	
Scaups	10	(15.51)	56	(50.49)	66	
Other	29	(23.49)	71	(76.51)	100	
TOTAL	39		127		166	$X^2 = 4.24$, d.f. = 1, $0.05 < p < 0.01$

continue into the plow zone, which may or may not be a function of bone destruction and identifiability of fragments.

Seasonality

All major occupations at the site practiced both warm and cold season bird hunting, with perhaps an increasing concentration on winter species during the Ceramic period as mentioned above. Immature long bones of several species have been identified, indicating the hunting of young or fledglings in the summer or early fall, indicating warm-season hunting during Occupation 4 of Canada goose (*Branta canadensis*), a medium-sized Ardeid (probably black-crowned night heron), one or more locally-breeding ducks, and a grebe (*Podilymbus* or *Podiceps*) (Table 3–49). Two bones of immature great auks were

Table 3-48. Relative frequency of bird bones compared to large mammal bones.

Occupation	# Large # Bird	Relative Mammal	% Bird
Occupation 2	162	1,062	15.3%
Occupation 3	319	1,160	27.5%
Occupation 4	1,693	3,029	57.1%
Plow zone	202	601	33.6%

Table 3-49. List of immature bird bones identified at the Turner Farm site.

1	**Canada goose** Two longbones approaching adult size. Probable early fall kills. From Occupation 4: Second Gravel Floor and Coarse-Crushed- Shell.
2	**Small Alcid** Incompletely calcified longbone. Occupation 4: First Gravel Floor.
3	**Medium-sized Ardeid** Immature longbone. Occupation 4: First Gravel Floor.
4	**Ducks** Several immature longbones in Occupation 4.
5	**Podicipedidae** Two very immature individuals. Occupation 4: Coarse-Crushed Shell. One immature individual, First Gravel Floor. One immature individual, Occupation 2.
6	**Great Auk** Two tibiotarsi from Occupation 4 (First Gravel Floor, Coarse Crushed Shell) with incompletely hardened cortical bone. One of these specimens (C-10, First Gravel Floor) is the distal half of a tibiotarsus with an unfused distal epiphysis, indicating a fledgling individual.

Table 3-50. Spring killed female birds, as indicated by medullary bone deposits, # tibiotarsi column is the number of bones examined.

Species	# Tibiotarsi	# with Medullary Bone	Comment
Ducks	53	7	
Great Auk	27	0	
Canada Goose	2	0	
Loon	18	3	As expected, most loons breed inland.
Medium-sized Alcid	12	0	Mostly winter visitors.
Small Alcid	25	5	Local breeding colonies.
Cormorant	2	0	
Great Blue Heron	1	1	Local breeding colonies.
Medium-sized Heron	7	2	Raids on heron rookery.
Buteo	2	0	
Eagle	2	0	

Table 3-51. Number of bird tibiotarsi with medullary bone deposits, arranged by stratigraphic provenience.

Occupation	Ducks	Small Alcids	Ardeidae	Loon
Occupation 2	–	–	–	1
Occupation 2 or 3	–	1	–	–
Occupation 3	–	1	–	–
Occupation 3 or 4	–	–	–	1
Occupation 4	6	3	3	1
Plow zone	1	–	–	–

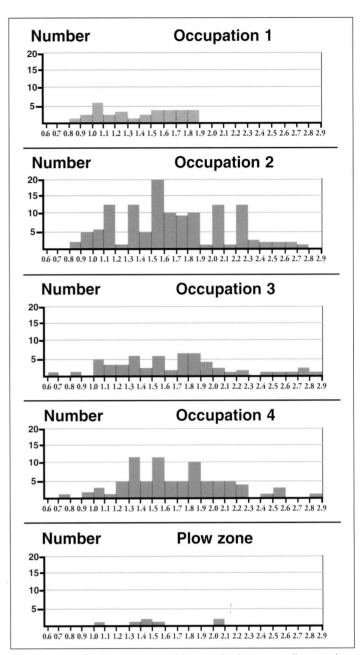

Figure 3-13. Cod size measured by vertebral centrum diameter in centimeters.

recovered. Whether or not these bones indicate summer or fall seasonality or proximity of a breeding colony to the site is unknown, because maturation rates of this large Alcid species are unknown, and there is some evidence of migration by immature birds (Meldgaard 1988:163).

Examination of tibiotarsi for medullary bone deposits confirmed spring-early summer bird hunting for at least five taxa (Table 3–50): ducks (sp. indet.), common loon, small Alcid (probably black guillemot), great blue heron, and medium-sized Ardeid (possibly black-crowned night heron). The sample was not large enough to detect change over time in the frequency of spring/early summer bird hunting. Thus, none of 11 duck tibiotarsi of Late Archaic age contained medullary bone deposits, while six of 41 of Ceramic period age did. This distribution is probably not significant (by Fisher's Exact Test, $p = 0.27$ of being due to chance alone). However, Occupation 4 spring bird hunting at small Alcid colonies is confirmed (Table 3–51), as are raids on duck and loon nesting areas and heron rookeries.

TURTLES

Identifiable turtle bone in the Turner Farm midden sample is comprised of carapace (top "shell") fragments (Table 3–52). Two species of relatively large turtle, snapping turtle (*Chelydra*), and Blanding's turtle (*Emydoidea blandingii*) dominate the identifiable sample, with a single piece of probably spotted turtle (*Clemys*) (Spiess and Sobolik 1997). Both the snapping turtle and Blanding's turtle are present throughout the sequence (Occupation 2 and 4), and the snapping turtle seems to represent about twice as many individuals as Blanding's turtle in both samples.

FISH

It is difficult to estimate the relative contribution of fish versus mammal to the diet of the site's inhabitants. However, we assume that the ratio of fish individuals to mammal individuals that were consumed varies proportionately to the identified bone count, given consistent excavation and identification techniques. Thus a ratio of one identified fishbone to one identified mammal bone does not necessarily represent equivalence in subsistence importance. But if the ratio changes from one to two fish bones per one mammal bone, then fish

Table 3-52. Turner Farm turtles by occupation. Identifications by Spiess and Sobilik. *Chelydra* is the snapping turtle; *Emydoidea blandingii* is Blanding's turtle, and *Clemys* is the genus including *C. insculpta,* the wood turtle. Letter and number combination is provenience code. Occupation 4 abbreviation (see Chapter 4) given after provenience code for turtle bones from Occupation 4.

Occupation 2	
D-1156	*Chelydra*, small to medium individual, plural frag, 1.8 gr
E-1564	*Chelydra*, medium individual, plural frag. 2.6 gr
D-1158	*Emydoidea blandingii.* Nuchal bone, 1st right and left peripherals, right 2nd through 6 peripherals, left 2nd peripheral, and 3 plural fragments. All conjoin. 34.0 gr. Medial-lateral width of the nuchal at scute scar line is 31.7 mm. A very large individual for family Emydidae. *Note:* 2nd left peripheral was recovered from provenience C-252 (plow zone) but definitely conjoins this specimen from Occupation 2.
B-742	Unidentified plural frag.
Occupation 3	
B-742	*Chelydra*, small to medium individual, plural frag. 0.6 gr
B-650	*Chelydra*, medium individual, peripheral frag. 2.1 gr
Occupation 4	
C-48	(CCS) *Chelydra*, small to medium individual, plural frag. medial, 1.4 gr
C-258A	(CCS) *Chelydra*, large individual, plural, proximal frag 6.4 gr *Chelydra*, medium individual, two peripherals conjoin, 4.5 gr
E-1739	(1GF) *Chelydra*, small to medium individual, plural frag. 2.9 gr
A-818	(CCS) *Chelydra*, medium individual, peripheral (posterior one) 3.4 gr
C-73	(MCS) *Chelydra*, large individual, 2 plural frag. 9.0 gr
C-141	(B2GF) *Chelydra,* medium individual (all same sized individual), est. 30 cm carapace length 7th and 8th right peripheral, conjoined 8.4 gr 11th peripheral, left, 4.5 gr ?th peripehral, 5.4 gr 3 plurals, 15 gr 5 plural fragments, 8 gr
E-1803	(2GF) Emydid family, probably *Clemys.* Nuchal fragment. Estimated length of turtle carapace: 15-20 cm.
C-373	(MCS) *Emydoidea blandingii*, left 1st peripheral. Identical in shape to D-1158 specimen, but the C-373 specimen is 20-25% larger.
B-635	(B2GF) *Emydoidea blandingii*, right 1st peripheral, fragmentary. 3.7 gr. Slightly smaller than specimen C-373.
D-1115	(2GF) *Emydoidea blandingii*, nuchal, 1.3 gr. Medial-lateral width at scute scar margin is 19.8 mm. (Approximately ⅔ the size of D-1158 specimen.)
Plow zone	
B-640	*Chelydra*, small to medium individual, 2 plural frag. 2.2 gr
Mixed or disturbed provenience	
B-647	*Chelydra*, medium to large individual, peripheral (7 or 8th, right) 5.7 gr
D-1432	*Chelydra*, large individual, 2 peripherals 19.7 gr, est. carapace length 50 cm +/- 10% *(see note on C-252 under D-1158 in Occupation 2 above)*

economic importance (measured as bone counts, NISP) has doubled.

Cod

Cod (*Gadus*) are the most common fish in the Archaic faunal samples (Table 3–53). Relative to the mammal bone count, cod bone frequency decreases drastically toward the present. Because of the vicissitudes of preservation and recovery, we cannot tell whether cod provided more total protein than did mammals during Occupations 1 and 2. Occupation 3 people placed less relative reliance (by a factor of 3) on cod than did those of Occupation 2. Beginning with Occupation 4 cod dropped to a resource of moderate or low importance. (We return to a discussion of primary, secondary, and tertiary resources in Chapter 6.)

The few cod vertebrae that yielded season-of-death data are presented in Table 3–54. Cod fishing during Occupation 2 was clearly a summer activity. Although the sample is small (n=2), the seasonality of cod fishing during Occupation 3 occurred later in the year, perhaps early fall. The mean size of the cod caught throughout the occupation of the Turner Farm site remained roughly constant (Table 3–55 and Figure 3–13).

Flounder

The relative frequency of the flounder species, of which 86% were identified as winter flounder (*Pseudopleuronectes americanus*), increases through time, from about 9% of the

Table 3-53. Number of cod bones and relative count versus mammal bones.

Occupation	Number of vertebrae	Total Cod bones	Cod bone/ large mammal bone
Occupation 1	53	58	–
Occupation 2	141	169	15.9%
Occupation 3	71	104	9.0%
Occupation 4	97	144	4.8%
Plow zone	13	20	3.3%

Table 3-54. Seasonality of cod fishing from vertebral growth ring analysis. All specimens are precaudal vertebrae.

Provenience Codes	Number Annuli	Vertebral Diameter	Last Growth Layer	Seasonality
Occupation 1				
B750	7	1.48cm	¼-½ thickness	June-August
B750	8	1.56cm	¼ thickness	June-July
B750	6	1.68cm	½ thickness	July-earlyAugust
B750	6	1.68cm	< ¼ thickness	June
B750	6	1.76cm	¼-½ thickness	June-July
B750	6	1.80cm	¼ thickness	June-July
Occupation 2				
C68	11	2.87cm	½-¾ thickness	August-early September
C69	5 or 6	1.65cm	¼ thickness	June
C267	6	0.94cm	½ thickness	June-July
C63	8	1.48cm	< ¼ thickness	June
C216	7	1.58cm	½ thickness	July-August
Occupation 3				
D1032	6	1.7	Full Thickness	September-October
E1719	?? < 6	2.4	Full Thickness	September-October

Note: Seasonality estimates are based upon the assumption that rapid growth in cod vertebral rings is simultaneous with rapid growth in cod otoliths. For adult cod (6-11 years) rapid growth begins in late May or about June 1st and continues through September.

larger mammal bone count in Occupations 2 and 3 to an average of about 83% in Occupation 4 and the plow zone (Table 3–56, Figure 3–14). There is no detectable difference in vertebral growth pattern between winter flounder, sand flounder and the unidentified flounder sample. Winter flounder show a growth-arrest line in June and July (Table 2–21). Overall, flounder fishing seasonality does change with time, however (Table 3–57). The middle of the growth period is missing from the Occupation 2 sample, while that period is predominant in that of Occupation 3. During

Table 3-55. Cod vertebral size distributions, number of specimens for each 1mm increment in vertebral centrum diameters, diameters given in centimeters.

Vertebral Diameter	Occupation I	Occupation 2	Occupation 3	Occupation 4	Plow zone
0.6	–	–	1	–	–
0.7	–	–	–	1	–
0.8	1	2	1	–	–
0.9	2	5	–	2	–
1.0	6	6	5	3	1
1.1	2	13	4	1	–
1.2	3	1	4	5	–
1.3	1	13	6	12	1
1.4	2	5	3	6	2
1.5	4	20	6	12	1
1.6	4	10	2	5	–
1.7	4	8	7	6	–
1.8	4	10	7	10	–
1.9	–	1	4	5	–
2.0	–	7	3	5	2
2.1	–	1	1	5	–
2.2	–	7	2	4	–
2.3	–	3	–	–	–
2.4	–	–	1	1	–
2.5	–	2	1	3	–
2.6	–	2	1	–	–
2.7	–	1	2	–	–
2.8	–	–	1	1	0
2.9	–	–	–	–	–
TOTAL	29	117	62	87	7
Mode	1.0 cm	1.5 cm	1.7, 1.8 cm	1.3, 1.5 cm	1.4, 2.0 cm
Mean	1.55cm	1.56 cm	1.61 cm	1.64 cm	.52 cm

Table 3-56. Flounder family total bones counts and comparison with large mammal bone frequency.

Occupation	Species Indet.	Winter Flounder	Sand Flounder	American Dab	Halibut	Yellowtail &/or Smooth	Flounder Total	% Relative to Mammal
Occupation 1	10	0	0	0	0	0	10	—
Occupation 2	38	50	0	0	0	3	91	8.6%
Occupation 3	36	59	1	2	0	8	106	9.1%
Occupation 4	1,348	981	1	31	19	124	2,504	82.7%
Plow zone	110	164	1	7	2	12	296	49.3%
Total	1,542	1,254	3	40	21	147	3,007	

Occupation 4, flounder fishing became much more important and the activity occurred year-round, including the growth-arrest (summer?) period. The plow zone material indicates a continuation of the year-round orientation.

Swordfish

Swordfish *(Xiphias gladius)* were taken in large numbers during Occupation 2, as measured by relative frequency of swordfish bone (see Table 3–58). Evidence of swordfishing is present in Occupation 1, but the small sample size does not allow an estimate of relative importance. There is a dra-matic decrease in the abundance of swordfish bone following Occupation 2 (Table 3–58). Specific refits between fragments from different occupations, and the horizontal pattern of swordfish bone distribution, demonstrate that probably all of the swordfish material in later occupations is derived from Occupation 2 by various types of disturbance (mostly house and feature construction by later inhabitants). There is a marked difference in swordfish body part representation between Occupation 2 and later occupations. The Occupation 2 sample is dominated by swordfish sword, a material which was used to make tools at the time.

Table 3-57. Vertebral annulus states at time of death, all flounder species.

Annulus State	Occupation 2	Occupation 3	Occupation 4	Plow zone
Ann. Forming	l	0	65	4
Growth < ¼	4	1	15	1
Growth ¼	0	3	63	9
Growth ½	0	5	75	9
Growth ¾	0	5	16	4
Full Growth Layer	1	2	69	1

Table 3-58. Counts of swordfish bone in number of discoveries, where fragments from one blade are counted as one unit. Weights are in grams. (An occurrence is defined as one large piece, or a group, of smaller pieces of swordfish blade in one excavation unit.)

Occupation	Sword	Spine, ribs, etc.	Vertebrae	Total	Frequency Relative to Deer Bone
Occupation 1	0	2 (24.7 gr)	0	2	–
Occupation 2	61 (3,027 gr)	61 (422.9 gr)	5 (52.6 gr)	127	12.4%
Occupation 3	5 (152.1 gr)	15 (84.5 gr)	5 (69.3 gr)	24	2.3%
Occupation 4	8 (116.9 gr)	15 (111.5 gr)	5 (22.4 gr)	28	1.1%
Plow zone	1 (24.0 gr)	0	0	1	–

Table 3-59. Sculpin bone counts.

Occupation 2	14
Occupation 3	19
Occupation 4	505
Plow zone	69

Table 3-60. Striped bass vertebrae, annulus state at death for specimens in the Ceramic levels.

Annulus State	# Specimens
Growth ¼	2
Growth ½	13
Growth ¾	2
Full Growth Layer	1

The later samples reflect radically different sword-to-post-cranial bone proportions, coincident with the absence of sword tools. Episodes of upward mixture by later house construction and other digging activity (e.g. graves) were certainly not randomly distributed across the site. The low proportion of swordfish sword in Occupation 3 and 4 samples compared with swordfish postcrania reflects a low frequency of swordfish sword in the underlying Occuaption 2 deposits in the portion of the site where most of the upward mixture occurred.

Sculpin Family

Table 3–59 presents data on species of the sculpin family, including longhorn sculpin (*Myoxocephalus octodecimspinous*), shorthorn sculpin (*Myoxocephalus scorpius*), and unidentified sculpin. Sculpin was a minor resource during Occupations 2 and 3. Usage increased dramatically during the Occupation 4 in the plow zone (in parallel with flounder). Probably sculpin were taken with lesser frequency using the same method as flounder fishing.

Striped Bass

Striped Bass (*Morone saxatilis*) appear as a modest resource only in the Occupation 4: 88 of 90 striped bass bones from the site come from that sample, while one each are recorded

for Occupation 2 and the plow zone. Eighteen striped bass vertebrae were "read" for season-of-death (Table 3–60). Ages of the fish range from 8 to 13 years. The fishing season appears to have covered the last ¾ of the growth season, with heaviest fishing half-way through the growth season (probably July–August).

Table 3-62. Occurrence of miscellaneous fish species, number of identified bones. *Carcharodon* is the great white shark, represented by a tooth. P = present in soil sample processed in laboratory.

Species	Occ. 2	Occ. 3	Occ. 4	Plow zone
Carcharodon	–	–	–	1
Alewife	1	–	–	–
Pollock	3	–	1	–
Wolf-fish	–	–	–	3
Mackerel	–	–	2	–
Bluefish	–	–	1	–
Cusk	–	–	3	–
Tomcod	32	P	1	2
Haddock	3	–	3	1
Salmonid (large)	2	–	–	–
Cunner	–	4	4	–
Dogfish (Spine)	1	–	15	9
Herring	5	–	P	–
American Eel	–	P	P	–

Table 3-61. Sturgeon occurrence by occupation.

Occupation	Scutes (#)	Weight (gr)
Occupation 2	12	46.2
Occupation 3	9	31.8
Occupation 4	77	352.9
Plow zone	19	26.9

Table 3-63. Tomcod vertebral annual ring growth states.

Annulus State	Occ. 2	Occ. 3	Occ.4
Annulus Forming	1	0	0
Growth < ¼	0	0	6
Growth ¼	6	3	6
Growth ½	4	0	2
Growth ¾	0	0	0
Full Growth Layer	17	9	17

Table 3-64. Turner Farm fish otolith readings. Only 10 specimens from two species were recovered and sectioned.

Species	# Annuli	Growth Status
Occupation 2		
Tomcod	2	1/4 (note 1)
Tomcod	2	Full Thickness
Tomcod	3	1/4
Cod	8?	< 1/4
Occupation 3		
Tomcod	1	Full Thickness
Tomcod	2	Full Thickness
Cod	4	1/4 to1/2 Thickness
Occupation 4		
Tomcod	3	Full Thickness
Tomcod	3	Full Thickness
Cod	8	Full Thickness

[1]Measured 8/35 optical micrometer units, or 23% of previous growth width.

Sturgeon

The comparative weights of sturgeon (*Acipenser*) scute are given in Table 3–61. Few sturgeon were taken during Occupation 2, however, with only 12 occurrences (46 gr), indicating that sturgeon fishing was a secondary activity. Nevertheless, sturgeon seems more important than flounder or the other minor fish species during Occupation 2. As with all other fish, sturgeon drops in relative frequency during Occupation 3, but becomes much more important economically during the whole of Occupation 4 (with a possible slight drop in the plow zone).

Fish Species of Minor Economic Importance

Table 3–62 presents bone counts for fish species of minor economic importance. The overall pattern is one of an explosion in the diversity of fish species being utilized as minor resources during the Ceramic period, (Occupation 4) and the plow zone.

The only alewife (*Pomolobus pseudoharengus*) and salmon (*Salmo salar*) vertebrae identified at the site, and most herring (*Clupea harengus*) as well, came from Occupation 2 deposits. Thus, these species may represent spring anadramous fish runs harvested from some other location, and later delivered to the site. Other species identified in the Occupation 2 sample are pollock (*Pollachius virens*), haddock (*Melanogrammus aeglefinus*), spiny dogfish (*Squalus acanthias*),

and tomcod (*Microgadus tomcod*). Occupation 3 deposits yielded bones of only three of these minor fish species: cunner (*Tautogolabrus adspersus*), tomcod and eel (*Anguilla rostrata*). Those of Occupation 4 yielded a modest sample of spiney dogfish, plus single bones or small samples of pollock, haddock, bluefish (*Pomatomus saltatrix*), cusk (*Brosme brosme*), tomcod, mackerel, cunner, herring, and eel.

The seasonality of these minor catches can be inferred from some vertebral growth state readings. During Occupation 2 the herring were spring catches. The haddock (½ to ¾ growth thickness increments) is probably a summer catch. The tomcod catch (Table 3–63) exhibits frequency peaks at ¼ to ½ growth (late spring/early summer), and a major peak at full growth (late fall or winter?). Tomcod fishing seasonality is similar in the Occupation 3 sample. In the Occupation 4 sample there is again a spring peak and a late fall or winter peak, but the spring peak begins earlier. Fish otolith readings (Table 3–64), which are much less numerous than vertebral readings because fewer otoliths were recovered, agree with those from the vertebrae.

SHELLFISH

Soft-shelled clam (*Mya*) shell clearly dominates shell weight totals from the soil samples (Table 3–65). In the Occupation 4 sample, *Mya* shell proportion of total shell weight never falls below 99.5% (Table 3–66). In the Occupation 2 and 3 samples,

Table 3-65. Turner Farm shellfish representation obtained from samples retained on 4 mm. mesh from soil sample processing. Total weight in grams.

Occupation	Clam	Quahog	Blue Mussel	Sea Urchin	Waved Whelk
Occupation 2					
"shell"	3,557.6	0.5	67.7	0.2	
"shell-free"	490.5		2.9		1.1
Occupation 3					
"shell"	2,382.3		36.6		
"shell-free"	575.2		0.7		
Occupation 4					
B2GF	381.0				
2GF	497.5		1.4	1.0	
CCS	4,633.3		13.1		
1GF	804.8		0.1		
MCS	686.5				
NGF	97.2				
Plow zone	573.3				

Table 3-66. Turner Farm shellfish representation obtained from samples retained on 4 mm mesh from soil sample processing. Percentages of each level.

Occupation	Clam	Quahog	Blue Mussel	Sea Urchin	Waved Whelk
Occupation 2					
"shell"	98.1 %	< 0.1%	1.9%	< 0.1%	
"shell-free"	99.2 %		0.5%		0.2%
Occupation 3					
"shell"	98.5 %		1.5%		
"shell-free"	99.8 %		0.1%		
Occupation 4					
B2GF	100　%				
2GF	99　%		0.3%		
CCS	99.5 %		0.3%	0.2%	
1GF	100　%		< 0.1%		
MCS	100　%				
NGF	100　%				
Plow zone	100　%				

Table 3-67. Estimate of total clam shell weight as deposited at Turner Farm site. Total wt = total weight of shell in kilograms, Corr = correction factor for shell specific gravity, Total dep. = total weight of shell when deposited, meat weight = estimated clam meat weight (wet) represented by shell weight.

Occupation	Total wt.	% Clam	Corr.	Total dep.	Meat weight
Occupation 1	223.9	?	?	Est. 250-300	130-190
Occupation 2					
Shell	12,747.5	98.1 %	1.132	14,150	9,200
Shell-Free	778.6	99.2 %	1.132	870	560
Total				15,020	9,760
Occupation 3					
Shell	11,423.7	98.5 %	1.055	11,870	7,720
Shell-Free	829.5	99.8 %	1.055	870	560
Total				12,740	8,280
Occupation 4					
B2GF	5,096.5	100 %	1.049	5,350	3,480
2GF	949.0	99.5 %	1.049	990	640
CCS	29,292.1	99 %	1.049	23,150	15,050
1GF	1,111.3	100 %	1.049	1,160	750
MCS	7,928.8	100 %	1.049	8,320	5,400
NGF	42.2	100 %	1.049	44	30
Total				39,010	25,350
Plow zone	52,435.7	100 %	1.049	55,000	35,750

Mya shell weight tends to range from 98% to 99% of total shell weight. Thus, we can safely regard other shellfish species as unimportant to the total food supply.

Total Clam Shell

We calculate the clam shell weight originally deposited in an excavation level (Table 3–67) by multiplying the estimated shell weight recovered by the percentage that is clam, then correcting for the specific gravity of the archaeological shell (see detailed discussion in Chapter 2). Inhabitants of Occupations 2 and 3 deposited 13,000 to 15,000 kg of shell in the excavated area of the site. Occupation 4 (combined) represent about three times (39,000 kg) more clam weight that do those of either Occupation 2 or 3. When we consider that the bulk of the shell in the plow zone (55,000 kg) also derives from Occupation 4, then the total Occupation 4 shell deposition represents perhaps six times the amount in Occcupations 2 or 3. Such a comparison is complicated by the probability that Occupations 1, 2 and 3 must have been relatively brief compared with the long sequence represented by the Occupation 4

Clam Size

The average size (mean and mode) of clam shell, as measured by their chondrophores, remains remarkably constant from Occupation 2 onward (Table 3–68). (No data are available for Occupation 1.) The only exception is a small sample from the relatively shell-free strata in Occupation 3, which are slightly smaller because they lack the largest clams in the 1.2 mm to 1.5 mm chondrophore width range. With this exception, we see no change at all in size over 4,000 years. Thus we see no evidence for adverse impacts upon size that might be expected from environmental change or a sustained increase in harvesting pressure.

Total Number of Clams Harvested and Estimated Meat Yield

Unchanging chondrophore size indicates that the number of clams harvested to produce one kilogram of clamshell remained relatively constant at roughly 60 to 75 clams per kilogram from Occupation 2 onward (Table 3–68). Therefore, a rough measure of the number of clams harvested by each occupation and

Table 3-68. *Mya* chondrophore width distribution: number of chondrophores and summary statistics. Each column represents a different stratigraphic/excavation unit sample. Estimated total shell weight for a left clam valve with a given chondrophore width presented in the right-hand column.

Chondrophore Width (cm)	Shell size distributions in individual shell samples											Shell weight
0.5	–	–	–	–	1	–	–	–	–	–	–	0.9
0.6	–	–	–	1	2	–	–	–	2	–	1	1.8
0.7	–	–	2	5	15	1	–	2	4	4	6	2.6
0.8	–	1	1	7	31	–	5	2	13	5	26	3.2
0.9	4	1	5	14	51	4	3	8	34	10	35	4.7
1.0	2	1	10	16	72	14	14	9	42	14	47	5.8
1.1	7	2	7	14	60	6	3	3	26	12	40	7.3
1.2	4	2	7	11	47	4	6	5	21	4	39	9.7
1.3	–	–	–	1	21	1	1	5	9	–	8	16.2
1.4	–	–	–	2	10	1	–	1	9	1	5	22.0
1.5	1	–	–	1	3	–	–	1	3	–	1	25.5
1.6	–	–	–	–	–	–	–	–	–	–	–	37.0
1.7	–	–	1	–	1	–	–	–	–	–	–	45.0
Mode	1.1	1.1, 1.2	1.0	1.0	1.0	1.0	1.0	1.0	1.0	1.0	1.0	
Mean	1.07	1.04	1.04	1.01	1.03	1.05	1.02	1.05	1.04	0.98	1.03	
n	19	7	33	72	314	31	32	36	163	50	208	
#clams/kg (both valves)	60	70	64	73	66	70	76	60	64	93	70	

Table 3-69. Clam shell sectioning results. Growth layers (annulae) are read from left (younger) to right (older), with X recording multiple prior annuli. / = rest lines. The last layer forming is recorded on the right, either as a number (measureable width of growth layer, or as a (/) rest line. Growth mode is either constant (C), decreasing (D), increasing (I), or irregular (Irr.) and is based upon the relationship among the prior 3 growth layers. Projected full width growth (Proj. width) is an estimate of full growth that could have been attained (or was obtained) by the clam based upon the ratio of the 3rd-from-last and next-to-last growth layers, multiplied by the next-to-last growth layer (i.e., a simple regression). "% growth" records the % of projected full growth obtained if the last layer is a growth layer, or the growth is recorded as "annulus" or F (= full) for 100%+-.

SPECIMEN #	ANNULUS READINGS	AGE (YRS)	GROWTH MODE	PROJ. WIDTH	% GROWTH
Occupation1					
I 45	/X/12.5/10/8/5.5/	5	D		Annulus
Occupation 2					
I 1	X/15/12/9/	7	D		Annulus
I 2	X/2.5/2.5	9+	?C		F
I 3		21	(Oldest in Sample)		
I 5	X/9/9/7/5/5/	12	?C		Annulus
I 6	X/9.5/7.5/3.5/4/	9	?C		Annulus
I 8	X/7/5/0.5	8+	D	3.5	14%
I 10	X/5/4/3.5/6/	14	I		Annulus
I 46	X/10/10/8/5	7	D		77%
I 47	/X16/6.5/7	3	C?		F?
I 48	X/9/10/7.5/6.5	9	D	5.5	F
I 50	X/10/8/10/8/	9	Irr.		Annulus
I 51	X/8/7/8.5/	13+	Irr.		Annulus
I 53	X/7.5/6/5.5	6	D		F
I 61	X/9/6/6	5	C	6	F
I 63	X/1.5/1.5/	16	C		Annulus
I 66	X/4.5/2.5/3/	12	Irr.		Annulus
Occupation 3					
I 11	X/12.5/12/	3			Annulus
I 13	X/12/8.5/5	5	D	6	83%
I 14		21	(Oldest in Sample)		
I 19	X/11.5/9/9.5/	6	C		Annulus
I 52	X/5/4.5/3/4/	8+			Annulus
I 74	X/5.5/6/6/5.5/6.5/5/	11	C		Annulus
I 76	X/4.5/4/3	9	D	3	F
Occupation 4 - Below Second Gravel Floor					
I 43	X/8/7/7/	5			Annulus
Occupation 4 - Second Gravel Floor					
I 110	X/11/9.5/10/	5	C		Annulus
Occupation 4 - Coarse-Crushed Shell					
I 31	X/11/6/2.5/	7	D		Annulus
I 34	X/5.5/5/3.5/5/4.5/	19	Irr.		Annulus
I 37	X/3.5/2.5/4.5/3/	12+	Irr.		Annulus
I 40	/X/16/9/4.5	4	D	5	90%
I 93	/13/14/6	3	C?	13	45%
I 95	X/5/6.5/4.5/5/	10			Annulus
I 96	X/8/10.5/7/7/	8			Annulus
I 97	X/8/4.5/4.5/5/5	11	C	5	F
I 99	/X/10.5/10	3	C	10	F
Occupation 4 - First Gravel Floor					
I 102	X/4.5/5/4.5/3/	9	D		Annulus
I 103	X/10/11/8/	4	?		Annulus
Occupation 4 - Medium-Crushed Shell					
I 23	17/13/5/7	3	D	10.5	67%
I 24	X/5.5/5.5/5/4.5/	15	C		Annulus
I 27	X/12/7/7/4/	8+	D		Anulus
I 30	X/7/6/5.5/6	10	C	6	F
I 83	X/13/9/9.5	8	C	9	F
I 84	X/4/2.5/4.5/2	9	Irr.		
I 85	X/3.5/4/4.5	10	I	4.5	F
I 106	X/11/10/	3	D		Annulus
Occupation 4 - New Gravel Floor					
I 112	X/9.5/6.5/5/4.5/	9	D		Annulus
I 114	X/3.5/2/3.5/2/3	13	C?	3	F

deposited within the excavated area can be had by multiplying the total kilogram figures in Table 3–67 by 65. Thus Occupation 2 inhabitants left the shells of nearly one million clams on the excavated portion of the site, Occupation 3 inhabitants left roughly 800,000 clams, and the Occupation 4 inhabitants left roughly six million clams (including the plow zone).

At the Kidder Point site (Spiess and Hedden 1983:103) the remains of 32,000 clams were recovered in what may be a single-component seasonal occupation in the N176–194 area of that site (a 20 cm or less level over about 85 m2). Using the Kidder Point N176–194 occupation as a least common denominator (at 30,000 clams), and ignoring erosion, the Occupation 2 sample included 30 times as many clams, that of Occupation 3 about 27 times as many, and those of Occupation 4 and the plow zone 200 times as many. Clam meat yield (wet weight) can be estimated by multiplying total shell weight by 0.65. The total clam shell weights are converted to wet meat weights, so the shell weights reflect some proportionate changes in clam contributions to overall food supply.

Seasonality

The only chondrophore read for Occupation 1 exhibited annulus formation, a growth state that may occur in an individual clam from February-early April. The sample from Occupation 2 is dominated by annulus formation (8 of 15, 53%). Five of 13 (33%) are interpreted as full thickness growth, one was measured at 77% of full growth and another was measured at 14%. Full growth may occur on individuals from late October through early February. The small Occupation 3 sample had 4 of 6 shells with annulae formed. Samples from Occupation 4 and the plow zone wree even more dominated by annulus formation (13 of 22, 59%) than Occupation 2. Full growth occurred on 6 of 22 speci-

mens (27%). Only three specimens (14%) exhibited growth layers of less than 100% formed. As explained in Chapter 2, clams switch growth mode often enough to cause 20% noise in any sample, and it is therefore possible that these clams were in fact in a full growth state and had just switched growth mode.

As none of these samples can be differentiated from a winter-early spring harvest pattern, the seasonality of clam usage (like clam size) does not change detectably from the earliest occupation to the latest. Perhaps all of the clam harvest occurred in one long season, from late February through early April.

The Relative Importance of Clam

We have no direct means of comparing the total meat contribution of mammal, fish and bird taxa with clam meat weight, since we have only relative live meat weight estimates and no sure way of knowing the total meat consumed. Table 3–70, however, compares the relative live weight contributions of large mammal taxa (derived from Table 3–41) with the total clam shell weight in each occupation as a ratio (see also Figure 3–14). The dietary contribution of clams relative to large mammals decreased by a factor of two between Occupations 2 and 4, with Occupation 3 being intermediate. However, a sharp reversal of this trend is evident in the plow zone sample, where the clam-to-large-mammal ratio increased dramatically (four-fold) over the Occupation 4 sample. We suspect that some, but perhaps not all, of this increase is a result of breakage of identifiable mammal bone in the plow zone.

Excluding the plow zone, Occupation 2 was more reliant on clam (by a factor of two) than were the Ceramic period occupations. This difference becomes even more

Table 3-70. Comparison of change in contribution to diet of clam verses mammal. Each unit is number of kilograms live weight of total mammal kill per 100 deer bones divided by 1,000 (Table 3-41.). A direct measure of the amount of meat would depend on an accurate Minimum Number of Individuals count.

Occupation	Large Mammal Relative Live Weight Factor	Total Mya Shell Weight	Ratio Col. 2 / Col. 1
Occupation 2	12,600 Units	15,020kg	1.19
Occupation 3	16,600 Units	12,740kg	0.77
Occupation 4	64,200 Units	39,010kg	0.61
Plow zone	21,800 Units	55,000kg	2.52

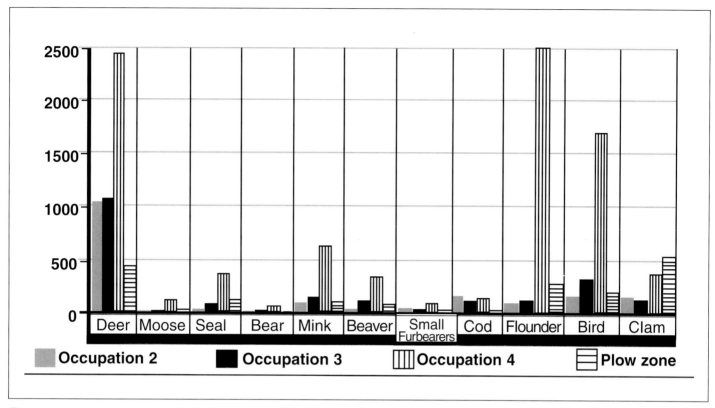

Figure 3-14. Graphic representation of the number of identified specimens for the most common mammal and fish taxa, plus birds (all bird taxa combined) and clam shell weight. *Note*: the clam bar graphs are clam shell weight divided by 100. Graphic representation based on Tables 3-36, 3-48, 3-53, 3-56, and 3-70.

pronounced when we consider that birds and fish seem to have contributed more to the Ceramic period diet than to those of earlier occupations. Unfortunately we must leave unresolved the relative contribution of clam to the site's latest occupants because of the disturbance caused by plowing.

These results are surprising. This relative decrease in economic importance of shellfish directly contradicts the conventional wisdom that shellfish harvesting along the coasts of the New England region increases steadily (Aikens, Ames and Sanger. 1986:13) over several millennia beginning in the Late Archaic. In part this presumed increase in shellfish use is probably based upon the sheer number of surviving later shell middens, which is actually merely artifact of relative sea level rise.

SUMMARY

The data presented in this chapter reveal significant changes in patterns of faunal exploitation throughout the Turner Farm site sequence. We have interpreted these patterns as evi-

dence for changes in subsistence and other kinds of behavior. Herein we summarize the most obvious trends, beginning with Occupation 2.

Changes between Occupations 2 and 3 include:
1) a change in deer hunting seasonality, from an absence of summer deer hunting to a year-round emphasis on deer hunting;
2) an increase in the proportion of skeletally immature deer, and a decrease in the proportion of very old deer, possibly reflecting an increase in hunting pressure on the deer herd;
3) a slight increase in moose numbers relative to deer, perhaps reflecting climatic cooling;
4) a slight increase in relative reliance on seal, and seasonal patterns indicating hunting during haul-out seasons of both harbor and grey seals;
5) disappearance of the summer swordfishery, and a drastic decline in cod fishing;
6) a decrease in the proportion of great auk among all birds taken, probably because of a decrease in emphasis on maritime exploitation during the summer;

7) a doubling of relative emphasis on bird fauna; including cold-season hunting of inshore birds;

8) a relative decrease in the emphasis on clams compared to all other fauna, with Occupation 2 being relatively most heavily reliant of all occupations.

Changes between Occupations 3 and 4 include:

1) minor changes in butchering and use of distal limb bones in deer;

2) a further increase in the proportion of skeletally immature deer, and a decrease in the proportion of very old deer, possibly reflecting a further hunting pressure on the deer herd;

3) a marked increase in the number of moose relative to deer killed;

4) a marked increase in proportional reliance on seals, and broadening seasonality of hunting, including openwater hunting;

5) increased emphasis and breadth of fur bearing species;

6) increased reliance on a taxonomically broad group of inshore fish species, including sturgeon, flounder and sculpin, and a dramatic increase in the number of minor fish taxa taken;

7) another doubling of emphasis on bird fauna, including cold-season hunting of inshore birds;

8) a further relative decrease in reliance on clams.

4

Living Floors or Garbage Dumps: Variability Within The Occupation 4 Levels

Introduction

The Occupation 4 levels were subdivided into six stratigraphic units (Bourque 1995:21–31; Table 4–1). This chapter continues the pattern established in Chapter 3 of discussion by major taxonomic groups. In this case, however, we are looking for variability in faunal use patterns over finer time scales. The First and Second Gravel Floors of Occupation 4 can be traced across most of the excavated area. Other levels, such as the New Gravel Floor for example, are more limited in extent. Thus, the size of the faunal samples available for analysis can be affected by the horizontal extent of the deposit as well as its thickness and intensity of use. Basically, however, these strata record a detailed time sequence within Occupation 4 (3000 B.P. to 500 B.P.).

The strata of Occupation 4 alternate from shell-rich to darker relatively shell-free "floors". We assume that the floors represent living surfaces, and that the shell-rich levels primarily represent dumping areas. Thus, faunal variability within the Occupation 4 levels can be examined as a dichotomy between these two types of archaeological deposit. As we shall see, the combination of these factors accounts for much of the variability in the faunal sample.

In some cases the Occupation 4 levels continue trends in faunal use begun in the Late Archaic period, so we may refer to Late Archaic data from Chapter 3 as a base-line in this discussion. Moreover, a small proportion of bone from excavated areas noncontiguous with the main excavation is not referable with certainty to any one of the six Occupation 4 subdivisions. In Chapter 3 this material was reported in the Occupation 4 data, but it cannot be further assigned to the stratigraphic subdivisions used in this chapter. Therefore, the total faunal specimen counts reported in this chapter are usually less than the ones reported for Occupation 4 in Chapter 3.

FAUNAL PATTERNING

White-tailed deer

First we examine body parts frequencies for White-tailed deer (*Odocoileus virginianus*).

The only unexpected frequency figure in the data (Table 4–2) is the number of metapodial diaphysis fragments relative to the rest of the deer skeleton. With the exception of lower leg bones (metapodials), no other skeletal element shows any effect of activity patterning (shell-rich levels versus floors) or changes in relative frequency over time.

Though not meat-bearing bones, metapodials do contain a significant amount of fatty marrow. Consequently, modern-day Inuit caribou-hunters curate and process them specifically for that marrow (Binford 1978:146–148). Metapodial diaphysis fragments from the Turner Farm site appear to be the by-products of similar processing. These bone fragments are longitudinal slivers, created by striking the flat metapodial proximal surface with a sharp blow from an edged or blunt instrument.

We assume that the rate of recovery of metapodial fragments parallels their rate of production. Thus the greatest attention to extracting their marrow occurred in the earlier portion of the Occupation 4 (2GF). The relative frequency of metapodial diaphysis fragments (Table 4–3) peaks in the Second Gravel Floor at almost 14% of the total deer bone count, and falls to 8.7% in the Medium Crushed Shell. Within the Occupation 4 strata, this distribution is of marginal statistical significance (comparison of diaphysis fragments versus all other deer bone, chi-square = 8.57, 5 d. f., probability between 0.20 and 0.10). However, the trend toward higher frequency of metapodial diaphysis fragments began earlier, in Occupation 2 (5.8%) and Occupation 3 (7.9%), so Occupation 4 up to 2GF continues a long-term trend. In other words, as the proportion of deer to other fauna falls over time from Occupation 2 to 2GF, the intensity of breakage of deer metapodials increases.

Three other deer bone groups, all lower leg bones, show activity patterning differences in Occupation 4. Carpal/tarsal bones (which occur just proximal to the metapodial in an articulated limb), and distal metapodial fragments are present in slightly higher frequencies on the floors than in the shell-rich levels. Conversely, the phalanges and dew claw parts (which occur just distal to the metapodial) are much less frequent on the floors than in the shell-rich levels.

Table 4-1. The six subdivisions of Occupation 4 of the Turner Farm site, listed from the upper-most downward. Stratigraphic labels are shown in italics. From Bourque 1995:170-174.

Stratigraphic Unit	Dates (B.P.)	Occupation 4 Subdivisions
Below Second Gravel Floor (B2GF)	2275±130 to 3280±50	Terminal Archaic, Early Ceramic
Second Gravel Floor (2GF)	1955± 50 and 2105±75	Early Middle Ceramic
Coarse-Crushed Shell Level (CCS)	1200±100	Middle Ceramic
First Gravel Floor (1GF)	875± 70	Late Middle Ceramic
Medium-Crushed Shell Level (MCS)	–	Late Ceramic
New Gravel Floor (NGF)	–	Late Ceramic

Table 4-2. Deer body part count from Occupation 4 strata. Expected frequencies appear in parenthesis below observed frequencies. The New Gravel Floor (NGF) sample is too small to include in the chi-square analysis, so it is shown to the right. Other level abbreviations are as in Table 4-1. Row and column totals are shown. Numbers in parentheses are the expected values for each cell.

	B2GF	2GF	CCS	1GF	MCS	Row Total	NGF
Axial skeleton, postcranial	19 (14.14)	46 (38.14)	76 (84.08)	66 (67.40)	27 (30.24)	234	0
Skull and antler frags.	2 (7.68)	24 (20.70)	38 (45.63)	35 (36.58)	28 (16.41)	127	2
Jaw parts	13 (8.82)	21 (23.80)	64 (52.46)	32 (42.05)	6 (18.87)	146	0
Teeth (isolated)	26 (29.68)	71 (80.03)	170 (176.42)	167 (141.43)	57 (63.45)	491	5
Longbones (ex. metapodials)	14 (12.57)	36 (33.90)	74 (74.74)	54 (59.91)	30 (26.88)	208	0
Metapodial proximal	7 (5.80)	18 (15.65)	37 (34.49)	21 (27.65)	13 (12.41)	96	0
Metapodial distal	10 (8.64)	26 (23.31)	47 (51.38)	49 (41.19)	11 (18.48)	143	0
Metapodial diaphysis	12 (16.44)	53 (44.33)	105 (97.73)	75 (78.35)	27 (35.15)	272	0
Carpals, Tarsals	20 (18.80)	49 (50.69)	101 (111.75)	109 (89.58)	32 (40.19)	311	1
Phalanges and dew claws	22 (22.42)	47 (60.47)	150 (133.31)	83 (106.86)	69 (47.94)	371	1
Column Total	145	391	862	691	310	2,399	9
Other	0	1	4	4	3	12	0

These differential distributions, which must be related to disposal patterns, pertain to the distal portion of the deer leg while the rest of the skeleton is not affected. Binford's Nunamiut analysis (1978:145–149) offers a likely explanation for these effects. Nunamiut women remove the bones from the lower legs of caribou (carpals/tarsals, metapodials, and phalanges) and do not make them regularly available for consumption during daily meals. Often, the metapodial is separated from the carpals/tarsals and phalanges, leaving the carpal/tarsals and phalanges all attached by the main foot flexor ligament. The metapodials are then processed separately from the carpals/tarsals and phalanges if marrow is scarce. In any case, at the Turner Farm site, the carpals/tarsals and distal metapodials remained preferentially on the living floors after metapodial marrow processing, and the feet (phalanges and dew claws) were most often being discarded onto the shell-rich midden without processing for their small marrow content.

Moose

The proportion of moose to deer bones (Table 4–4) increases from about 1% in the Late Archaic levels to between 4½% and 5% in 2GF, CCS, and 1GF of Occupation 4. A slight relative increase to 6% occurs again in the MCS, and in the plow zone. These data indicate a major increase in moose usage relative to deer between Occupation 3 and early Occupation 4, and a slight increase again in the MCS (after 875±70 B.P.).

Seals

Seals show a pattern similar to moose when compared with deer bone frequency (Table 4–5). The early Occupation 4 levels begin with a drastic (2–3 fold) relative increase of seal frequency over the Occupation 2 and 3. The relative seal bone frequency (9–16%, Table 4–5) holds roughly steady through the 2GF, CCS, and 1GF. Then it increases again, dramatically, in the MCS (to 25%), and maintains that relatively high level through the NGF and into the plow zone (27%). There are no functional/depositional patterns of seal skeletal body parts observable in the data. Nor are there any consistent functional or temporal trends in relative proportions of grey versus harbor seal (Table 4–6), with only the CCS having a slightly higher proportion of grey seal than other Occupation 4 strata.

Porpoise and Whales

Large and small cetacean remains occur early in the Occupation 4 sequence, in the 2GF and CCS (Table 4–7). While the exploitation of these species by hunting or scavenging does not seem to parallel the late Occupation 4 increase in seal hunting, the cetacean faunal sample is too small to be statistically significant.

Bear

Bear bones (Table 4–8) occur at about a 1% frequency relative to deer bones in Occupation 3. In the B2GF, bear frequency begins a modest increase, which peaks at about 4% in the MCS. But it is not statistically significant due to small sample size.

Mink

Mink skulls in this sample sometimes show distinctive cut marks related to pelt removal. Occupation 4 strata exhibit a trend (Table 4–9) toward increased mink relative to deer bone frequency, although the 1GF has a slightly lower fre-

Table 4-3. Deer metapodial diaphysis fragments versus all other deer bone: expected frequencies in parentheses. The New Gravel Floor (NGF) sample is small, but only one cell value falls below 5, making inclusion in the chi-square computation valid.

Stratigraphic Unit	# Metapodial Diaphysis Fr.	Other Deer Bone	Metapodials % of Total
B2GF	12 (17.65)	145 (139.35)	7.6%
2GF	53 (43.90)	339 (343.10)	13.5%
CCS	105 (97.68)	761 (763.32)	12.1%
1GF	75 (78.62)	620 (614.38)	10.8%
MCS	27 (35.51)	286 (277.49)	8.6%
NGF	0 (1.02)	9 (7.98)	0%

Table 4-4. Number of moose bones recovered from Occupation 4.

Element	B2GF	2GF	CCS	1GF	MCS	NGF
Phalanges and dew claw parts	1	9	15	13	13	0
All other	1	9	26	19	6	0
Total moose	2	18	41	32	19	0
% relative to # deer	1.3%	4.6%	4.7%	4.6%	6.1%	0%

Table 4-5. Seal body parts and total bone count from Occupation 4 .

Element	B2GF	2GF	CCS	1GF	MCS	NGF
Bullae	1	10	22	28	26	1
Axial skeleton incl. teeth	3	13	62	36	27	3
Appendicular skeleton	9	11	57	36	26	1
Total	13	34	141	100	79	5
% relative to # deer	9.07%	8.7%	16.3%	14.4%	25.2%	55.6% (±20%

Table 4-6. Relative representation of grey seal and harbor seal from Occupation 4, based upon counts of identifiable bones. Many seal body parts are not identifiable to species, which creates the disparity between bone counts in Tables 4-5 and 4-6. *Phoca* is mostly or all harbor seal.

	B2GF	2GF	CCS	1GF	MCS	NGF
Grey seal	2	7	38	15	14	2
Harbor seal	3	11	35	36	23	1
% Grey seal	40%	39%	52%	42%	38%	66%±

Table 4-7. Porpoise and whale remains from Occupation 4 levels.

Second Gravel Floor (2GF)	Large whale	1 piece worked rib
Coarse Crushed Shell (CCS)	Large whale	1 piece worked rib or jaw
	Porpoise	4 vertebrae of one individual

quency than this trend would predict. There is a parallel increase in the relative proportion of jaw parts in the total mink bone sample through the Occupation 4 sequence. Possible explanations include increased retention of skulls or mandibles as trophies, an increased trend toward skinning the mink bodies elsewhere and returning the capes and skulls to camp, or differential discard over time of the bodies, perhaps to the dogs. None of these explanations is entirely satisfactory, and none can be tested against the small existing data sample.

Beaver

There is a steady increase in the relative count of beaver versus deer bone in the Occupation 4 sequence (Table 4–10). This increase does not seem to be due to an increase in use of beaver incisor or jaw parts as tools. Therefore, we conclude that the pattern of beaver exploitation is yet another indication of increasing hunting pressure on a wider range of resources available to Occupation 4 occupants of the site as time went on. (See discussion in Chapter 6).

Table 4-8. Bear bone frequency in Occupation 4.

Element	B2GF	2GF	CCS	1GF	MCS	NGF
Skull mandible and teeth	2	1	5	11	6	0
Postcrania	2	5	16	8	6	0
TOTAL	4	6	21	19	12	0
% relative to # deer	2.8%	1.5%	2.4%	2.7%	3.8%	0%

Table 4-9. Sea and common mink body parts and bone counts in Occupation 4. The ± after the % relative count in the New Gravel Floor indicates a small sample size and a probable large confidence margin on the proportion.

Element	B2GF	2GF	CCS	1GF	MCS	NGF
Mandible maxilla	5	22	72	53	46	4
Teeth isolated	2	–	12	13	9	1
Other	22	82	232	138	119	5
TOTAL	29	104	316	204	174	10
% postcrania	76%	79%	73%	68%	68%	50%
% mandible and maxilla	17%	21%	23%	26%	26%	40%
% relative to #deer bone	20%	27%	36%	29%	56%	111%±3

Table 4-10. Beaver body parts and total bone counts in Occupation 4 strata. The ± after the % relative count in the New Gravel Floor indicates a small sample size and a probable large confidence margin on the proportion.

	B2GF	2GF	CCS	1GF	MCS	NGF
Cheek teeth and jaw frag.	4	22	78	63	28	0
Postcrania	7	19	47	38	9	1
Incisors	1	16	40	33	25	2
TOTAL	12	57	165	134	12	3
% relative to # deer	9.7%	14.5%	19.1%	19.3%	19.9%	±33%

Small Furbearers

Small furbearer bone counts are listed in Table 4–11. Relative rates of recovery compared with large mammal bone counts do not change appreciably within the Occupation 4 sequence. The identification of rabbit (*Sylvilagus*), generically distinct from the hare (*Lepus*) in the Medium Crushed Shell is noteworthy. Rabbits are rare in central Maine both archaeologically and at present, and are more common in Southern New England.

Birds

There are no noticeable shifts in bird species emphasis within the Occupation 4 sequence (Tables 4–12 and 4–13). A comparison of total bird with mammal bone frequencies

Table 4-11. Small furbearer bone counts from Occupation 4 strata.

	B2GF	2GF	CCS	1GF	MCS	NGF	Taxon Total
Vulpes/fox	–	2	3	1	5	–	11
Procyon	1	–	1	1	–	–	3
Lynx	–	–	1	–	–	–	1
Mephitis	–	–	1	–	–	–	1
Martes	–	–	1	–	–	–	1
Ondatra	–	2	4	1	–	–	7
Erethizon	–	2	3	5	2	–	12
Lutra	–	1	4	13	2	–	20
Sylvilagus	–	–	–	–	1	–	1
TOTAL	1	7	18	21	10	–	57

Table 4-12. Number of bird bones in Occupation 4 identified to species or family level, and to size for those bones not further identifiable.

Species	B2GF	2GF	CCS	1GF	MCS	NGF
Branta canadensis	3	8	11	11	7	–
Other goose	–	–	1	–	1	–
Cormorant	2	6	21	6	9	–
Ardeid, larger	–	4	3	4	1	–
Ardeid, medium	–	–	6	6	2	–
Loon, common	1	31	75	38	24	–
Loon, red throated	1	3	9	5	7	–
Great auk	–	10	17	9	11	–
Alcid/medium	–	5	7	4	8	–
Alcid/small	4	8	37	14	13	–
Duck	46	92	237	51	79	1
Podicipedae	–	4	7	4	3	–
Buteo	–	1	1	–	–	–
Eagle	–	–	–	2	–	–
Other	–	1	4	–	1	–
Bird– larger than duck	5	24	53	13	17	–
Bird– duck sized	29	79	168	83	83	2
Bird– smaller than duck	6	5	14	5	5	–
TOTAL	97	281	671	255	271	3

(Table 4–14) shows some variability in bird-to-mammal relative representation, however. Birds are higher in proportion compared with mammals in B2GF, 2GF, CCS, and MCS (about 64%). Bird proportions are relatively low (21% to 31% compared to mammal frequencies) in 1GF and NGF samples. This low frequency is matched by Occupation 3 and the plow zone. We note that this variation in relative frequency is not based upon a dichotomy between shell-rich midden and gravel floor levels, nor on a trend through time.

Fish

Fish bone relative frequencies change in a complex manner within the Occupation 4 levels. The importance of flounder increases dramatically between Late Archaic Occupation 3 and the early Occupation 4 (Table 4–15). It increases dramatically again in the Medium Crushed Shell and New Gravel Floor strata, then drops slightly in the plow zone. Throughout the sequence, however, the proportion of flounder is always much higher in the shell-rich midden levels than it is on the shell-poor floors (Table 4–16). Moreover, there is no special selectivity for or against flounder cranial bones or vertebrae in either shell-rich strata or shell-free floors. The seasonal pattern of catching flounder does not vary within the Occupation 4 sequence (Table 4–17). Neither is there a significant difference in growth state of the flounder bones that were discarded in the shell-rich levels or on the shell-poor floors (chi-square = 1.9 for 4 d. f., p > 0.50 of being due to chance). Behavioral models that might explain these data include discard of flounder bones in the dregs of soups and stews, picking the flesh off roasted fish and discarding the skeleton, or fillet removal and skeleton discard. Garbage such as boiled fishbone or fish "racks" was preferentially discarded with shell refuse, and only rarely incorporated into the living floors.

Sculpin proportions (relative to total mammal bone count) show a slow rise within the early Occupation 4 sequence, then a dramatic increase at the MCS level. This pattern parallels the overall increase in flounder bone frequency, but the differential

Table 4-13. Taxonomic separation of the coracoid within the ducks in Occupation 4. The coracoid is the bone that most easily separates the groups of ducks recognized here.

Species	B2GF	2GF	CCS	1GF	MCS	NGF
Eider[1]	–	1	6	3	2	–
Melanitta fusca	–	1	2	–	2	–
Scaups[2]	6	7	22	11	5	–
Anas[3], black-duck size	–	4	2	1	–	–
Small *Anas*[4] or small Aythinae	5	6	22	3	6	–
Duck, not further identifiable	22	8	23	19	13	–
Common merganser	–	1	1	–	–	–

[1] Probably common eider, Somateria mollissima.
[2] Contains both greater and lesser scaup (*Aythya marila* and *Aythya affinis*).
[3] Contains several species, probably of genus *Anas*, similar in size and build to *Anas rubripes*.
[4] Small ducks, both of genus *Anas* and sub-family Aythinae. Bufflehead (*Glaucionetta albeola*) definitely identified. Other possible identifications include teals and harlequin ducks among others

Table 4-14. Mammal/bird bone frequency comparison of Occupation 4 subdivisions.

	B2GF	2GF	CCS	1GF	MCS	NGF
Large mammal	164	436	1,058	835	422	14
# of bird	97	281	671	255	271	3
Bird/mammal	0.59	0.64	0.63	0.31	0.64	0.21

Table 4-15. Fish bone counts from Occupation 4 strata.

	B2GF	2GF	CCS	1GF	MCS	NGF
Flounder	30	99	608	376	1,139	17
Sculpin	14	24	87	120	216	2
Cod	15	13	72	23	19	2
Sturgeon	1	36	124	90	52	11
Striped bass	–	4	48	22	10	–
Swordfish	3	8	9	8	–	–
Spiney dogfish	–	1	5	1	6	1
Mackerel	–	–	–	–	–	2
Pollock	–	–	–	–	1	–
Tomcod	–	2	5	1	1	–
Cusk	–	–	–	–	4	–
Bluefish	–	1	–	–	–	–
Haddock	–	–	2	–	2	–
Cunner	–	1	–	2	–	–

Table 4-16. Number of mammal bones and Flounder bone from Occupation 4.

	B2GF	2GF	CCS	1GF	MCS	NGF
Total mammal	208	619	1,573	1,210	669	27
Flounder	45	99	608	376	1,139	17
Flounder/Mammal	.22	.16	.39	.31	1.71	.63

Table 4-17. Flounder seasonality, relative growth readings from vertebrae growth layers, status of last layer. There are no readings from B2GF.

Annulus State	2GF	CCS	1GF	MCS	NGF
Annulus forming	1	14	9	40	–
Growth < ⅛	–	6	4	3	–
Growth < ¼	1	11	12	38	1
Growth < ½	1	25	13	40	–
Growth < ¾	1	7	1	10	–
Full Growth	1	16	9	20	–
Full growth or annulus	–	–	1	6	–

discard pattern into shell-rich midden versus shell-poor floor levels which characterizes flounder bone is not evident. We might expect parallel increases in capture rate, since sculpin and flounder will both take bottom-set baited hooks in inshore water. Both species could also be speared in the same shoal water. However, there was some apparent difference in discard or processing behavior between the two families of fish.

Cod seem to become less important after the initial Ceramic period occupation at the site. Cod bone frequency (relative to mammal bone) is 8% in Occupation 3 and about the same level (11%) below the Second Gravel Floor. Cod frequency drops to 2–5% compared with mammal bone for the rest of the Occupation 4 sequence (Table 4–13), and in the plow zone. Cod thus become a tertiary fish resource behind flounder, sculpin and sturgeon in importance.

Sturgeon relative bone frequencies (Table 4–13) are not easily comparable with the rest of the fish sample because few calcified sturgeon remains preserve archaeologically (primarily the dermal scutes). However, based upon scute occurrence counts, sturgeon become important during deposition of 2GF, and maintain a roughly constant level of importance through the rest of Occupation 4 (except for a possible concentration in the small New Gravel Floor sample).

SUMMARY

There are major changes between Occupation 3 and the Below Second Gravel unit, and between the latter and 2GF. These changes predate 2000 B.P. A second major change in Occupation 4 subsistence patterns occurs at the time of deposition of MCS, postdating 875±70 B.P. Some of the trends continue into the plow zone, while others are reversed. A review of mammalian tooth sectioning data, fish seasonality and bird seasonality data reveals that all Occupation 4 subdivisions maintain a "year-round" focus without obvious seasonal specialization. Thus, seasonal specialization is not an obvious cause of these patterns.

Changes between B2GF and 2GF include the following:
(1) a noticeable increase in the frequency of deer metapodials being exploited for marrow;
(2) a dramatic increase in relative reliance on moose;
(3) a doubling of reliance on beaver;
(4) a strong increase in flounder usage and modest sturgeon increase;
(5) a drop in the use of cod; and

(6) the first high peak in bird hunting frequency.

Changes occurring between 2GF and 1GF are relatively minor:

(1) a gradual increase in proportion of mink mandibles and relative frequency, possibly indicating increased trapping.

Dramatic changes occurring at MCS (postdating 875±70 B.P.) include:

(1) another noticeable increase in moose frequency;
(2) a dramatic increase in seal frequency;
(3) a dramatic increase in flounder and sculpin frequency;
(4) a second high in bird hunting frequency; and
(5) a low point in deer metapodial shaft recovery.

We will explore the ethnographic and paleoenvironmental implications of these data in subsequent chapters. In general, however, they seem to reflect an increasing intensity and breadth of vertebrate faunal exploitation over time.

5
Animal Behavior and Human Harvest Techniques: Background for the Turner Farm Study

Introduction

This chapter presents information on modern animal behavior useful in interpreting the faunal data presented in previous chapters. In addition we summarize what may be relevant accounts of aboriginal hunting, fishing, trapping, and collecting methods from the Northeast and elsewhere. The discussion is organized by sections focusing on a single animal taxon or group of taxa of economic importance. In each section one sub-section discusses modern animal behavior and another the aboriginal methods of procurement.

WHITE-TAILED DEER

Behavior and Physiology

Seasonal Cycle

Most white-tailed deer in Maine are born in late May or early June, but a few births occur in July or even early August. Along the northern margin of white-tail range, including Maine, local variation in the timing of the rut is minimal (Marchinton and Hirth 1984:147) and seems to be under endocrine control induced by changes in day length (Verme and Ullrey 1984). In northern regions, reproductive success depends especially on the timing of snow melt and initiation of green plant growth in the spring (Mattfield 1984:313). Thus during possibly warmer climatic conditions of the Archaic period (e.g., CHOMAP 1988) modal birth timing may not have been affected; but the reproductive success of does bearing fawns earlier and later in the birth season may have been slightly higher, allowing greater survival of fawns born at the margins of seasonal variability.

Healthy deer shed their winter coats of thick guard hair and underfur in June, and grow the thin reddish summer coat.

Antler growth in bucks and nursing by does requires the highest caloric and protein intake of the year at this season. The growing shoots and new leaves of grasses and browse species provide abundant food. Young deer grow and mature deer put on weight, in the form of fat, until the rut occurs in late October and November. During spring, summer, and fall optimal deer habitat includes a "patchy environment" of mixed food source areas and dense growth cover to provide shelter. Fall fat production is physiologically obligatory, even on marginal diets, so some fat storage will occur for the winter. On marginal diets (poor warm-season ranges), growth in body size may suffer so that fat storage can occur.

In Maine, rutting begins in October and peaks in mid-November. Bucks actively seek receptive does. In contrast, does are receptive only during a short heat period of about 24 hours. If conception does not occur, heat re-occurs in 28 days. Sometimes conception occurs only during the third heat period, accounting for late fawn births. The timing of the rut is controlled by hormonal changes triggered by decreasing day length (Verme and Ullrey 1984:93) and so is primarily latitude-dependent (not climate-dependent). Thus, the peak of the rut regularly occurs in Maine in mid-November without influence by the weather (Behrend 1967–68). This fact, and the known gestation period, support the hypothesis that the peak of the birth season would have occurred in early June several thousand years ago, just as it does today.

During the rut, a buck tracks a single doe, and may stay with her for a few days. Bucks often lose 20–25% of their live weight (mostly stored fat) during the rut. Deer do not form large bands at any time of the year, which would make game drives in the interior less effective among deer hunters than among caribou hunters (see Spiess 1979). Drives on islands, however, using a combination of pedestrian and boat-based hunters, might work well for even isolated deer.

In the late fall, deer molt again and grow a thick insulating coat. Coincidentally there is a dramatic decrease in heat production (drop in basal metabolism rate) which brings about a semi-torpid state of reduced feeding and activity (Verme and Ullrey 1984:110). After the rut, deep snow and winter cold gradually force Maine deer to leave open hardwood forest and seek shelter from the wind in cedar swamps and dense stands of spruce or fir. While providing necessary cover, these stands are low in available browse, often causing intense competition for what food is available. This "yarding" behavior (Marchinton and Hirth 1984:134–5) occurs earlier and with more intensity in northern Maine than in southern or coastal Maine. In southern Maine, and elsewhere in the state during mild winters with low snowfall, deer roam a larger area (Banasiak 1961:37). A dominance hierarchy develops in yarding situations with adult males dominating adult females, who in turn dominate sub-adults. Often the smaller/younger/weaker deer are driven out of the yard area (Gilbert 1969). Deer at the northern margin of their range often starve to death in late winter.

During winter yarding Maine deer require 5 lbs of browse per day. When the temperature drops well below freezing, they may lose between 3% and 12% of their live body weight per week, regardless of quality or quantity of browse. Femoral and mandibular marrow are the last fat deposits to suffer depletion during starvation (Verme and Ullrey, 1984:107).

Mattfield (1984:313–4) summarizes the annual diet of deer in the Northeastern hardwood and spruce/fir forests as follows. In early spring (mid-March through mid-May) 67% of foraging is on herbaceous plants, 10% on woody browse. From mid-May through mid-June, 46% of foraging is on leaves of woody plants (vigorously growing), while 17% of foraging concentrates on herbs. In August and September new growth of woody species is the primary food source. Mast (nut crop) and the persistent green leaves of Rubus (blackberry and raspberry) are also important in fall. Northern white cedar is the principal winter food, so much so that its regeneration is controlled by deer population levels. Growing grass shoots are high in protein, water and mineral content, and low in fiber. Grass is a preferred spring food, but it loses much of its forage value after setting seed. Deer consumption of grass peaks shortly after the onset of its active spring growth after which legumes (like clover and beach peas in Maine) and other herbs become the principal food source (Dasmann 1971). But these too lose much of their nutrient value as they dry out. Deer browse more than they graze, except during spring and early summer. Late summer and autumn food is primarily browse: leaves of hardwood trees and bushes. It is necessary to know the detailed species and age composition of successional plant cover in an area to predict deer herd size (Gerald LaVigne, personal communication 1988). An important fall food is mast: acorns, beechnuts and hazelnuts, which are high in fat and starch content. Mast is avidly sought, and helps provide nutrients for the fall fat accumulation necessary for successful over-wintering.

Movement and Migration

White-tailed deer are generally non-migratory and may have seasonal ranges of less than 1 mile in diameter (Marchinton and Hirth 1984:129–130). The summer and winter range may be overlapping, usually within 10 miles. Studies in Wisconsin (Dasmann 1971:15) showed that 91% of deer moved less than 7½ miles between home and winter range, while the average distance was 3½ miles. Studies of deer movement along the Maine coast (Schemnitz 1975) indicate seasonal movement to exposed, seaward islands by mature individuals in May or June. A retreat to larger and more protected islands, or the mainland, occurs after September and before January. As shown in the following quotation, adult deer may swim long distances during these coastal movements:

> The maximum movement of deer documented during our coastal deer studies involved a 6.5 year old adult female deer, tagged on September 25, 1966 at Isle au Haut, Knox County, Maine, and observed 40 times between the time of release and 20 September, 1968. This deer was found dead as a bleached carcass at Vinalhaven Island at Coombs Hill 15 January, 1973, on a wooded bluff well above the high tide line. The minimum straight line distance traveled across open water was 10.9 km. (6.8 miles) (Schemnitz 1975:536).

Apparently the deer of the islands and peninsulas of any one section of coastal Maine form one population because of these movements of adult deer. Thus, over-harvesting on one island may be quickly ameliorated by immigration during the succeeding summer.

Drolet (1976) has studied the movements of deer in a mixed hardwood and softwood area of national forest 24 km east of Fredericton, New Brunswick. Mean annual snowfall there is 2.8 meters. In winters with little snowfall, individual deer winter range sizes were greater than in summer (probably due to the search for forage). Winters with heavy snowfall restricted deer movement and caused yarding in dense conifer stands. When snowfall reached 30 cm, deer travel became reduced. In excess of 55 cm, deer travel was drastically curtailed.

The largest groupings of deer in Crab Orchard National Wildlife Refuge in southern Illinois were feeding groups of 25–30 during late winter and early spring (Hawkins and Klimstra 1970). Such groups did not move and bed together as a herd, however. They can be compared with deer yarding in northern Maine. Adult bucks were gregarious (associating with each other) from February through August. Eighty percent of the groups located contained two, three, or four animals. Females and young deer (bucks less than 1 year old) also formed small groups, which tended to be family groups. The most common group was a doe, her yearling daughter and her two fawns. Most of these groups were matriarchal, with three or four generations represented, each with their own territory. During the fawning season adult does separated themselves from these family groups. The fawns rejoined the groups in September.

Size and Demographics

Newborn deer weigh between 2 and 4kg (4 and 9 lbs). Fawns of 5–6 months of age average 30kg (70 lbs) live weight in Maine. Adult Maine females average around 60kg (140 lbs) live weight. Table 5–1 presents Maine deer weights, and shows that the average Maine buck weighs 100–120kg (225–240 lbs). Among the largest in the United States, Maine bucks often exceed 135kg (300 lbs), and occasionally 180kg (400 lbs). The largest deer ever recorded in Maine had a dressed weight of 160 kg (355 lbs) on state-certified beam scales (Hinckley 1969). This deer's live weight may have exceeded 220 kg (480 lbs).

The extremely large Hinckley deer is a legend among Maine hunters. However, the 1972 hunting season yielded 15 bucks with live weights calculated over 300 lbs. In the 1960s and 1970s, the kill of deer weighing over 260 lbs (live weight) ranged from 380 to over 700 individuals per year (Shoener 1973). During the same period, deer registrations numbered between 25,000 and 35,000. The 1979 season produced 500 bucks over 260 lbs live weight in a total harvest of close to 25,000. Thus, deer of over 260 lbs live weight form 1–3% of the modern kill. These live weights are for deer taken during the hunting season, which

occurs during the rut. However, most of the kills are made just before the rutting peak in mid-November. Thus, it is probable that these high live weights of 260–400 lbs include about 20% fat by weight which is usually lost by a rutting buck. Lean live weights of these large deer probably range between 200 and 300 lbs.

Measurements of deer distal tibia widths from the Turner Farm site (Table 3–16) show that bucks over 260 lbs (live weight) were more commonly killed than during the modern hunting season (based upon a measurement of 4.0 cm from the skeleton of a 260 lb live weight buck, the "Oatway" specimen; see Table 2–5 and Figure 2–3). Prehistoric large buck kill rates (10–30%) are approximately an order-of-magnitude greater than today's large buck returns.

Stanton (1963:8) asserts that Native American population levels were too low to affect the deer herd. However, our data do show a change in deer demographics that is at least consistent with increasing pressure on the deer herd. At present the idea of human population growth in Maine from the Late Archaic through the Ceramic period is an intuitive interpretation of the archaeological record based upon the number, size and distribution of archaeological sites. However, we have not explicitly tested population growth as an hypothesis. Thus, we conclude merely that central coastal Maine was good deer habitat aboriginally, and that the Native Americans made significant use of that resource.

Table 5-1. Average Maine deer weights (from Banasiak 1961:31). Data were collected as dressed weights for several hundred deer for each age class between 1948 and 1957. Live weights are calculated by adding 30% to dressed weight.

Age	Sex	Dressed Weight (lbs)	Est. Average Live Weight (lbs)
Fawn (½ yr)	Male	60	80
	Female	59	80
1 ½ years	Male	105	135
	Female	92	120
2 ½ years	Male	145	190
	Female	105	135
3 ½ years	Male	173	225
	Female	111	145
4 ½ years	Male	185	240
	Female	110	145

Carrying Capacity

A study of deer carrying capacity in upstate New York (Jackson 1974) concluded that population was limited by insufficient winter range in deep snow years. About 20 deer per square mile of conifer subclimax and conifer-mixed hardwood forest cover was found to be a reasonable population estimate. We estimate a deer population density on this order of magnitude for coastal Maine west of the Mt. Desert region, where the hardwood (mast-producing) content of the forest is higher than farther east in Hancock and Washington counties.

Modern Maine deer hunting returns peaked in 1974–75 with a statewide kill approaching 35,000 deer. The 1988 post-hunting statewide deer herd is estimated at 250,000 deer, while estimates suggest that Maine's 30,000 square miles can support a healthy deer herd of 300,000 individuals (Maine Department of Inland Fisheries and Wildlife 1990).

Isle au Haut, an island roughly the size of North Haven, today supports over 25 deer (Cole 1993). The four central coastal counties of Knox, Lincoln, Waldo, and Sagadahoc yielded harvest figures of 2.74, 2.94, 3.61, and 2.46 deer per square mile of deer habitat respectively. The 1978–82 harvests statewide yielded an average of about 1.2 to 1.5 deer per square mile (0.36–0.52 per km^2; Mattfield 1984:322). We would expect similar rates of return (1–3 deer per square mile) for prehistoric hunters. Banasiak (1961: 42–43) estimates an annual increment of 42% for the modern Maine deer herd, with an allowable female cull rate to all mortality of 29%. We can see no reason why the prehistoric rate should have deviated significantly from this figure. (Annual cull rates of 30% of 20 deer per square mile is six deer per square mile per year to all sources of mortality, hunters and predators included.) In prehistoric Maine, wolves would have accounted for much of the annual deer herd reduction now caused by hunting and coyotes.

In one modern study area, reducing deer over-population to carrying capacity reduced winter starvation mortality rates from 25% of population to 1% (Mattfield 1984:316). Thus, in the Northern mixed forest environment deer fecundity that is not controlled by predators is controlled closely by winter weather and food availability.

Ethnography of Deer Hunting

Aboriginal deer hunting techniques in the Northeast, as reported by Europeans, include deer drives, snaring and a range of stalking or individual hunting techniques. Unfortunately, none of these reports is from Maine. Some of the techniques, such as drives on the mainland, required very large numbers of hunters. Whether Maine's prehistoric populations could have marshalled such forces is unclear.

The most detailed account of a deer drive is that of Samuel de Champlain, who witnessed a massive one by Hurons near Rice Lake, Ontario in 1615 (Webster 1979:817; see also Trigger 1981:420; Webster, 1981:421–22; Armstrong 1987:173). The operation occupied 38 days, mainly through October, and may have involved between 250 and 500 Hurons (men returning from an unsuccessful raid into Iroquois territory). For 10 days preceding the hunt, a huge V-shaped drive fence was constructed of stakes 2½ to 3 meters in height, closely interwoven with brush and branches. Each arm of the V is described as 1,500 paces long (roughly 1.3 kilometers). Drives were repeated every second day for about 38 days, commencing at dawn. Hunters placed themselves "about a half a league (or 2½ km)" from the opening of the trap, driving deer toward the trap by striking sticks and bones together. The narrow end of the trap formed a triangular corral where deer were killed by hunters armed with bows or spears. Net proceeds of the hunt were 120 deer. Webster (1979) calculates that the drive covered 9 km^2. Assuming that 90% of the deer in the area were killed, he calculates an original density of 14 deer per km^2 at about 40 per square mile. In so doing, he assumes that each drive started as a semi-circular area with 2½ km radius from the mouth of the V. Including the area inside the drive-fence itself, we calculate that between 9 and 20 km^2 may actually have been included in the drive.

In Champlain's account, Huron labor expenditure was between 7,500 and 15,000 hunter-days for a return of 120 deer (about 75 to 125 hunter-days per deer). Such a large labor investment indicates that deer were economically of extreme import, or that some other motivation was involved. The Huron were a horticultural people living in large villages, able to marshall a huge labor force when necessary. Gramly (1977) hypothesizes that deer hides, not deer meat per se, were the commodity that caused such an investment of labor. In discussing Gramly's hypothesis, McCabe and McCabe (1984:31) estimate a minimum need for each Huron for clothing of 3½ deer hides per year.

Early accounts of New England also mention a variety of deer driving techniques. Roger Williams stated that in Massachusetts and Rhode Island driving parties included up to "two or three hundred in a company." Writing of

Massachusetts, Wood (1865:98) mentions deer being driven through a very narrow opening at the end of a series of ever-narrowing hedges "a mile or two miles long, being a mile wide at one end." Thus, agricultural southern New England may have seen deer drives on scales similar to those of the Huron. In nonagricultural central Maine the use of fire may have compensated for smaller human populations. One early account (quoted below) describes the use of fire in driving moose into the sea, a technique that would have worked as well for deer. Another (Quinn and Quinn 1983:472) notes that on the Penobscot River "the Inhabitants doe burne once a yeere to haue fresh feed for their deer."

Spiess (1979) has reviewed literature concerning the construction of game fences and corrals for taking caribou in the sub-Arctic. The size of the drive-fence increases with the size of the available human population, and to some degree with the importance of caribou to the food supply. The largest drive fences appear to have been those constructed in southeast Alaska, which reached 5–10 miles in length, so Champlain's account sounds feasible. Spiess also reviewed caribou-hunting techniques and found that the principal of a game-drive can be applied on a variety of scales ranging from simple human surrounds to fences of various lengths and solidity of construction. If deer-corrals were used at all in coastal Maine prehistory, we expect them to have been small and quickly constructed, primarily because human population concentration was less than in Huronia. Interviews with modern hunters suggest that small island environments like North Haven and Vinalhaven provide especially effective terrain for driving big game with only a few drivers. As the game was driven to the shore, it was forced either to halt and be killed or to swim, where boat-based hunters awaited.

Spring-pole snares are mentioned in many early accounts of New England, including Wood (1865:98), Williams (1827:143), and William Bradford (1953:202). These snares are "made up of their own making (Bradford)," and strong enough "to tosse a horse (Wood)". Apparently these snares were set in conjunction with drive fences (10–20 hunters setting as many as 50 snares apiece), or set and checked as a trap-line by one hunter along game trails. Stalking deer is mentioned by several of these writers, without further details.

Nicholas Denys (1908:430–431), in his classic account of early seventeenth century aboriginal life on in what is now Nova Scotia, New Brunswick, and Maine, describes the use of dogs by Nova Scotia Indians to run moose. The

hunter followed the noise of the chase and killed the exhausted moose with spear or bow and arrow. This method could also have been applied to deer in winter. There is, in fact, an historic reference to Wisconsin Indians running down deer in deep snow (McCabe and McCabe 1984:48).

As with caribou (Spiess 1979), the archaeological record for deer hunting can be examined in hopes of assessing which techniques were used. Complete excavation of intact features or living floors, for example, can allow an assessment of the number of deer killed. Thus, one rubbish pit containing the remains of a dozen deer with the same season-of-death would be strong evidence for a modest game drive of some sort. Examination of kill demography reveals whether hunting was selective by age and/or sex, or whether deer were killed more-or-less at random. There is one hint in the ethnographic record of possible differential use of deer body parts that could show up as horizontal patterning on an archaeologically recovered surface. In the Journal of the English Plantation Settled at Plimoth (Anonymous 1622:12) the English explored two deserted Indian houses and noted two or three "deers heads ... also a company of deeres feete stuck up in the houses." Perhaps the feet contained stored marrow bones such as the metapodials and phalanges. Ancillary archaeological data, such as presence of dogs and evidence of special esteem for them, can also be interpreted as evidence for their use in hunting.

Interpretation of Deer Kill Demographies

The principal uses of faunal data to reconstruct deer hunting patterns have, to date, revolved around interpretations of the demographics of the death assemblage (Elder 1965; Waselkov 1978). Cleland (in Waselkov 1978) was the first to argue that selective hunting might over-represent certain age-classes in a death assemblage. Cleland reasoned that if deer were hunted by stalking, the very young and very old would be successfully killed more often than the prime-aged adult because they would be less successful in escaping or avoiding the hunter. Elder describes deer kill assemblages from the Lilbourn site in Missouri characterized by an under-representation of fawns, compared with modern kill data. He concludes that modern hunters shoot the first animal they see, often a fawn, while the Indians did not. The Indian, he says, was "practicing a voluntary and effective conservation measure sparing the fawns to grow into better hides and more meat." Elder does not consider whether non-selective drive methods were contributing to the kill, or whether all deer were taken by single-hunter techniques that allowed selectivity. Waselkov (1978) follows Cleland's reasoning in interpreting his archaeological data that hunters would have been more successful taking the very young and old deer individuals. In contrast we assume that stalking hunting, especially during winter or early spring when fat resources would have been in short supply, would have caused the human hunters to concentrate on taking prime-aged adult females, the fattest members of the herd at that time. Our assumption is that the hunters were capable of selecting whichever age group they wanted, and were not forced more often to take the "aged and infirm" as a non-human predator might be.

The demography of a wild deer herd, and consequently a random sample from such a herd, responds to hunting pressure more than to any other factor. A "mature" deer herd undergoing little hunting pressure, and little population contraction or expansion because of environmental change, exhibits low fawn production (Gerald LaVigne, personal communication, December 1982). Various physiological mechanisms minimize fawn production to roughly balance a low mortality rate when the herd is limited by total food supply during the growth season. In this case, fawns and young form a relatively small cohort and the demographic curve exhibits a bulge in the 3–4 year group and a long and strong "tail" of slowly decreasing frequency with many deer in the 5–7 and 8+ year old categories. When the deer herd is limited by winter-imposed starvation but with plentiful food during the growth season, or when predation increases, the herd responds with increased calf production. The demographic mode shifts toward the younger end, the 3–4 year old bulge flattens, and the long "tail" of aged deer shrinks. Relatively light hunting pressure, coupled with random sampling of the population (driving or non-preference individual hunting) could therefore account for the demographic curves of Elder, Waselkov's Lilbourn site, and at least the Occupation 2 deer sample at the Turner Farm site, where the number of prime-aged adult and aged deer is large.

Demographic changes in archaeological samples of Japanese Jomon-age Sika deer (*Cervus nippon*) are interpreted (Koike and Ohtaishi 1985, 1987) similarly to our Turner Farm site data interpretations. The continuous shift toward younger deer as time passes is interpreted as a steady increase in hunting pressure with the expansion of Japanese Jomon population. We add that the Turner Farm site deer population may have seen a demographic shift as absolute hunting pressure increased, but that general climatic change (CHOMAP 1988) over the last 5,000 years may also have increased winter severity and the degree to which winter food availability controls the deer population through winter-related mortality. Both human hunting pressure increase and climatic change toward more severe winters would increase the deer birth rate, and drive the demographic curve toward a younger mean.

MOOSE

Behavior and Biology

Moose calves are usually born in late May or early June (Peterson 1955), weighing 11–16 kg (25–35 lbs) at birth. Young moose continue to follow their mothers past one year of age, making a threesome (mother, yearling and calf) a common group in spring and early summer. Calf mortality is high. Peterson estimates long-term average calf crop survival (or the "annual increment") at 10% of herd size. Moose calves add ½–1kg (1–2 lbs) daily for the first month, and 1½–2 kg (3–5 lbs) daily during the second month. By 4½ months of age calves weigh 140–180 kg (310–400 lbs). Adult weights of 340–400 kg (750–880 lbs) are common. 540kg (1,200 lbs) is a rare live weight in Maine for an adult moose. The mean dressed weights of 5-year and older moose in the 1988 Maine moose season was 275 kg (605 lbs) for cows and 345 kg (760 lbs) for bulls (Maine Department of Inland Fisheries and Wildlife 1990). The carcass yield of moose older than 1½ years of age is 47–55% of live weight. Therefore, one average adult moose yields between 180 and 270kg (400 and 600 lbs) of meat. The sex ratio of moose herds without selective hunting is close to 50:50.

Moose in eastern North America do not migrate seasonally, instead exhibiting "rather indiscriminant shifts" (Peterson 1955:110) in response to seasonal availability of food. Although there are no modern studies from the Maine coast because of modern localized extinctions, until very recently moose must have been able to move among the islands as easily as deer. Their swimming ability is extraordinary, being able to match a well-paddled canoe in speed in many travelers' and hunters' accounts.

Moose browse woody twigs in winter, browse leafy deciduous trees in summer, and feed on aquatic plant growth during spring and summer when available. In eastern Canada and Maine, important winter woody browse species include balsam fir, white birch, and raspberry, (Peek 1974:202). In Maine's Baxter State Park, the most important herbaceous browse species are balsam fir, mountain maple, mountain ash, white birch, and fire cherry. Summer diet in Maine can include grass, sedge, and aquatic vegetation as well as browse. DeVos (1958) documents an increase in numbers of solitary individuals in areas of aquatic vegetation during summer, thereby creating a local population concentration. During winter several (2 to 4) animals of any age or sex may form loose bands. Up to six or eight animals will yard together in the worst weather.

There is some altitudinal separation of wintering moose and deer caused by snow conditions in Fundy National Park, New Brunswick (Kelsall and Prescott 1971). Moose tend to be found regularly above 190 meters altitude, while deer are rare above 260 meters altitude. Deer movements are inhibited with 20 cm of snow cover on the ground, and severely restricted with 40 cm snowcover. Moose are severely restricted only where snowcover reaches 70 cm, so that they are free to utilize a range of territory not accessible to deer where snow cover is between 20 and 70 cm depth.

Denys (1908:109) specifically states that there were "a great many moose" around Penobscot Bay in the early seventeenth century. However, moose populations in Maine were low during the late nineteenth century (Dodds 1974). By 1900 the species was found only in northern Maine, with a population low of several thousand animals in the 1940s (Peterson 1955:24). Since that time the population has recovered to 13,000 in 1971 (Dodds 1974), and more than 20,000 by 1988. Population density was estimated in 1965 at one moose per square mile in Nova Scotia (Peterson 1955:200). The Maine moose herd is approaching or has exceeded this density (25,000 head on 33,000 square miles), with locally higher figures in northern Maine. Peterson (1955) figures an annual average sustainable population yield of 10%. Thus, if moose population density was similar to present figures, Maine's aboriginal inhabitants statewide could have killed up to several thousand moose annually.

It should be noted that deer co-existed with moose in the North Haven fauna at least as early as 4500 B.P. even though moose are susceptible to infection and death by the meningeal worm *Parelaphostrongylus tenuis*. This parasite is hosted by deer who are less affected by it (Gibbs 1994). Denys (1908:382) says the moose in mid-seventeenth century Nova Scotia "are subject to fall from epilepsy." This remark clearly describes the symptoms of the infection, and

thus indicates that moose have been infested with the parasite in the Canadian Maritime Provinces for at least 350 years. We therefore assume that meningeal worm transmission from deer to moose has been common during the last 4,500 years in and near Maine. For these reasons we will not ascribe variations in moose-deer kill ratios over the last 5,000 years to the effects of this parasite.

Ethnographic Moose Hunting Accounts

According to Purchas (1906:282) the driving of moose on Mount Desert Island was accomplished "by making of severall fires, and setting the Countrey with people, to force them into the Sea, to which they are naturally addicted, and then there are the others that attend to them in their Boates with Boes and weapons of severall kinds, wherewith they slay and take at their pleasure."

Denys (1908), on the other hand, provides detailed descriptions of moose pursuit-hunting in Nova Scotia that should be applicable to the rest of the Maritime peninsula, including Maine. However, we suspect that deep snow conditions that Denys describes as providing snowshoe-clad hunters an opportunity to run moose down were rare prehistorically on North Haven Island and the rest of the islands of coastal Maine. Denys states that the techniques described apply to the period before 1640, before firearms commonly replaced aboriginal weapons in the Maritime Provinces.

First he (1908:426–9) describes a method of trailing and stalking moose used primarily during summer, but also during spring. The hunters would go to an area where they knew moose could be found, then search for a track. "Having found one they followed it, and they knew by the track, and even from the dung, whether it was male or female, and whether it was old or young. By its track they knew also whether they were near the beast..." Then they guessed where the moose was likely to be and circled downwind and "approached it very softly." They approached close enough for an arrow shot (less than 40 paces). The moose rarely fell to the first arrow, so it was necessary to follow the track again. Eventually the moose would slow down, allowing a second approach and arrow-shot. If the second arrow did not fell it, they followed again. If necessary, an overnight camp was made and the trail picked up the next morning. After the second arrow, an effort was made to get in front of the moose and "make it turn toward the camp,"presumably the main camp. They followed it until it fell dead, often working it up very close to camp. "They always found several together, but in summer they could never follow more than one." Thus, this type of hunting returned only one moose at a time .

During the fall rut, "hunting was done at night upon the rivers in a canoe. Counterfeiting the cry of the female, the Indians would take up some water, and let it fall into the water from a height" imitating a female calling and urinating. They could hear the bull approach through the woods. "They were all ready to draw upon him, and never missed him" (Denys 1908). Thus, this method procured bull moose only, one at a time.

Winter hunting was potentially even more successful. Deep snows could make travel difficult for moose, while the Indians could move quickly on snowshoes (Figure 5–1), especially on a late winter snowcrust. Such conditions occur commonly in the Maine interior, but less frequently on the coast today. In winter, hunters searched for areas that had been browsed. "Where they found the wood eaten, they met straightway with the animals, which were not far distant, and approach them easily, they being unable to travel swiftly. They then speared them with the lance (a long wooden shaft tipped with bone)" (Denys 1908). However, if there were several moose in the band, the Indians deliberately made them flee, when the moose would follow each other in file on a more or less circular track. There was always one Indian chasing them; the rest went to wait in ambush. Each time around the circuit one moose would be speared. "Their fall always five or six, and, when the snow would carry, the Dogs followed whatever ones were left. Not a single one would escape" (Denys 1908). Thus, late winter moose hunting in deep snow was capable of returning several moose from one hunt.

Figure 5-1. Penobscot snowshoes leaning against a woodpile. These are of mid-ninteenth century date, and were once owned by Brewer fur dealer Manly Hardy. Maine State Museum collection.

Denys (1908:430–431) mentions the use of dogs to hunt moose as an alternative method in spring, summer, or autumn, as well as in winter when the snow crust was strong enough to support the dog. The dogs would cast about for a track, then follow it "without giving tongue." If one overtook a moose, he got in front of it, jumping for its nose. Then the dog howled. "The moose amused himself, and wished to kick the dog in front." All the other dogs came to the cry and attacked it from all sides, trying to seize its nose or ears. "In the meantime the Indian arrives, and tries without being seen to approach within shot below the wind." If the moose detected the hunter he fled without regard to the dogs. Once shot, the moose became weaker. Sometimes the dogs dragged it to earth, and sometimes the Indian completed the kill. Note that this method lacks the advantage of turning the moose toward camp before it was killed.

In sum, moose were hunted using a variety of techniques. They were sometimes driven into the sea by groups of hunters using fire. During warm weather, individual moose were taken by hunters using bows and arrows. During the fall, individual bull moose were hunted from canoes. During periods of deep snow, moose, sometimes in multiples, were driven by hunters and dogs and killed with lances.

SEALS

Harbor Seal Behavior and Biology

The harbor seal (*Phoca vitulina*) is the common seal of the Maine coast today. This species is found from the arctic, where it lives in areas with year-round open water, down the east coast of the United States as far as North Carolina. Adults reach 60 inches in length and 90 kg (200 lbs) live weight (Mansfield 1967). Other measurements are "up to six feet" (Lockley 1966; King 1964), 110 kg (250 lbs) (King 1964), or 160 kg (350 lbs) (Lockley 1966). Newborn harbor seals weigh 10 kg (20–25 lbs) and they reach 25kg (55 lbs) during their first summer, remaining near this weight for the rest of their first year. Full-grown male harbor seals in eastern Canada average about 170 cm length and 96 kg (212 lbs), while the females average 159 cm and 81kg (179 lbs) (Boulva and McLaren 1979).

The following paragraphs on the biology of the harbor seal are summarized from Boulva and McLaren (1979), who summarize eastern Canadian data. The harbor seals of eastern Canada are found today in small, evidently isolated populations. Variations in the number of postcanine teeth between different areas in eastern Canada suggests that genetic mixing is limited between populations. However, there is a tendency for sub-adult animals to move from areas of relative over-population to less crowded areas. A total of approximately 900 harbor seals is reported for the Bay of Fundy and the Yarmouth, Nova Scotia area, although the population has been decimated by decades of bounty hunting. Approximately 2,800 seals live along the south coast of Nova Scotia, an area in length of coastline similar to the coast of Maine. This figure is about ½ to ⅓ that of 1949 population levels. A 1949 estimate of harbor seal population in the Maritimes was 10,000 to 15,000 individuals, down to about 5,500 by 1973. Population figures and the data collected during bounty hunting in eastern Canada until 1973 suggest that an average sustainable yield would be 1.5% of the seal population, if the animals are being taken at random with respect to age and sex. Harbor seals are generally considered to be animals of inlets, islets and rocky reefs. The number of pups harvested by bounty in Nova Scotia correlated closely with the number of small islands along the coast on a county by county basis, and thus may correlate with variations in local seal population density.

Harbor seals are regularly present along the Nova Scotia coast in winter, but they are loath to haul out during winter and they avoid areas of land-fast ice. With warming in April or May, harbor seals appear more often in bays and estuaries. Normally, in the southern part of the Maritime Provinces, whelping starts in early May. In Maine the whelping covers May and June, with most pups weaned in late June (Leslie Cowperthwaite, personal communication 1986). Harbor seals mate in July, after weaning.

During the summer and fall, harbor seals spend much of their time in small groups sleeping or sunning on rocks (or sandy beaches as on Sable Island in the Gulf of St. Lawrence). A map of modern harbor seal haul-out ledges in lower Penobscot Bay (Conkling 1995:106–7) shows only a few such ledges located in the thoroughfare between North Haven and Vinalhaven, within an easy paddle of the Turner Farm site. A large concentration of ledges can be found within a mile north of North Haven or around the islets fringing the southern half of Vinalhaven.

The molt starts by early July on Sable Island, and a few seals are still molting by the end of July. At this time, groups of 100 seals on one tidal ledge are not uncommon (Coperthwaite, personal communication 1986). The first seals to haul out during any summer and autumn day do so in the hour before sunrise, and sunning herds are usually near full size 1½ hours after sunrise. Occasionally, on warm days in winter and early spring, nearly 95% of the Sable Island population was hauled out on beaches. Apparently the individuals that spend their days ashore feed at night. Vision may not be essential to the harbor seal for successful feeding, since apparently healthy, wild, but blind individuals have been observed.

Herring was the most common food of harbor seals in the Sable Island area, followed by squid, flounder, alewife, and hake. The largest intact fish found in harbor seal stomachs were herring up to 30 cm long. Larger fish are sometimes brought to the surface, held in the foreflippers, and bitten into pieces. Blubber thickness is high in winter and early spring, variable and decreasing in later spring, and low from early summer to late autumn. The likely explanation for this variability is not a decrease in feeding frequency, for which there is no evidence, but rather a decrease in the food value of the fishes in the seal diet. The species making up most of the seal's diet all spawn from April through September, and are fat-poor after spawning. Thus, the fat content of the seal's food decreases during late spring and summer.

Harp Seal Behavior and Biology

The harp seal, gathers in large herds in February and March to pup and mate on the ice in the Gulf of St. Lawrence, or off the east coast of Newfoundland. During the spring and summer they swim northward along the Labrador coast and across Davis Strait to Greenland. Then in late fall they migrate southward down the Labrador coast toward the Gulf of St. Lawrence.

Harp seals are occasional visitors to the east coast of the United States as far south as New Jersey (Hall and Kelson 1959; McAlpine 1990). Their bones are uncommon in aboriginal shell middens along the Maine coast. The species is definitely identified in the basis of auditory bullae from the Grindle site in Blue Hill. The Loomis and Young collection at Amherst College, made before 1920 in the "shellheaps of Casco Bay," has at least one harp seal bulla, and there is one bulla from the Todd site in mid-coast Maine. A site in the Cranberry Isles, Hancock County, has also yielded a harp seal bone. As mentioned in a previous chapter, a harp seal tooth from the Seabrook Marsh site in New Hampshire, came from a juvenile individual killed in late fall or early winter. We assume that scattered individuals, mostly juveniles and adolescents, would wander along the Maine coast in late fall and early winter after going past the herd gathering area in the Gulf of St. Lawrence.

Grey Seal Behavior and Biology

The grey seals now number approximately 30,000 individuals in Canadian and United States waters (Mansfield 1966). Grey seals are large, males growing to 2.75 m (9 feet) in length, females to 2.20 m (7 feet) (King 1964; Lockley 1966). Adults weigh 140–280kg (300–600 lbs) (King 1964). Breeding grounds for the grey seal presently occur in the Gulf of Maine at Grand Manaan Island and on Cape Cod.

Cameron (1970) has reviewed the seasonal and diurnal movements of grey seals in Nova Scotia. In December, adult males and pregnant cows congregate on exposed rocks near their breeding grounds. At this time diurnal movements are random, with some seals always on the rocks and some in the sea usually within a mile of the rocks. In the last days of December or early January the seals occupy their breeding beach. Usually a pregnant cow is the first to haul out, but within the space of a week the entire herd is hauled out on the breeding area. For about two months the bulls remain on land. The cows go to sea twice daily, beginning about a week after giving birth to the pups. (This diurnal pattern may not necessarily apply in other parts of the breeding range.) Thus, from about January 1st until about March 1st, grey seals are extremely vulnerable to attack on their breeding beaches.

Timing of the molt and post-pupping season behavior are poorly known at present. British grey seal cows molt from January to March, while the males molt from February to April (Cameron 1970: 17). However, in Nova Scotia "nothing is known regarding the dispersal of the adult or pups at the close of the breeding season. It is known, however, that from mid-April until mid-June, large aggregations of adults... frequent the beaches of the breeding islands" (Cameron 1970). The molt in New England grey seals occurs from early March to late May, and is characterized by a second annual mass haul out (Valerie Schurman, personal communication). One New England grey seal female has been observed molting in late May (Schurman personal communication). Thus, grey seals exhibit a second period of concentration, and easy availability during all of late winter and early spring.

Ethnographic Accounts of Seal Hunting

William Wood (1865) states that Indians often sought seals sleeping on the rocks. Denys (1908:349) is a bit more detailed about Nova Scotian Indian seal use: "There are two species of them.... The second kind is much smaller, and they also bear their young on land at those islands, on the sand on the rocks, and whatsoever coves of sand occur, to which they resort." The Indians use the oil as "a relish at all the feasts they make" and also "to grease their hair." Denys states that there are places where two or three hundred seals land, but some always act as sentinels. However, at some places only two or three will haul out to sleep in the sun, "without a sentinel". "They are easily approached by a canoe. If they are mortally injured they fall into the water and thrash about, and there they are taken. But if they are killed instantly, they go to the bottom like a stone. ... They are often lost where there is too much water at the foot of the rock." Based on Denys' account, it appears that isolated sleeping groups of seals were easier to approach than the larger rookeries. His description evidently applies to hunting in summer when harbor seals have a low fat content and a relatively high specific gravity. Indeed, in summer most seals will sink when killed. "All the oil they can yield is about their bladder-full, and it is in this the Indians place it after having melted it. This oil is good to eat fresh, and for frying fish (Denys 1908:350)." Apparently seal fat was a

Figure 5-2. "Spearing a porpoise" as illustrated by Ward (1880:803) for offshore porpoise hunting along the downeast Maine coast. This illustration adequately conveys the skill required in handling a birchbark canoe and a spear or harpoon.

more highly prized product of the seal hunt than the meat, which Denys does not mention.

The Jesuit missionary Pierre Biard (Thwaites 1897 vol.3:79–83) states of Micmac Indians that in "January they have the seal hunting," a reference to hunting grey seals during their haul out/pupping time. He does not mention a spring hunt for grey seals, possibly indicating that the hunt was primarily for fat-rich winter seals.

PORPOISE AND WHALES

Denys (1908) mentions walrus, porpoise, beluga whale ("a white whale the size of a cow") and large whales in the Gulf of St. Lawrence off the coast of Nova Scotia. The three smaller species, and other small species of Cetacean, may have been occasionally available in the Gulf of Maine. Only the porpoise *(Phocaena)* seems to have been taken with any frequency, however, based upon archaeological fauna.

The only North Atlantic porpoise species is the harbor

porpoise *(Phocaena phocaena)* (Walker 1968:1129). These animals reach 1.2–1.8 m length and 50–75 kg (100–165 lbs). The largest-sized porpoises taken by Passamaquoddies in the 1870s weighed 135 kg (300 lbs), and their blubber yielded from six to seven gallons of oil (Ward 1880:803). Harbor porpoises travel in groups of two to several hundred, frequenting the coast and river mouths, sometimes ascending rivers. "The flesh of the porpoise, when cooked, is not unlike fresh pork," and was in great demand to vary a fish diet (Ward 1880:804). Denys (1908) says that during the seventeenth century porpoises traveled in large bands and were "found everywhere on the sea. They also go near the land following the bait (fish). They are good to eat." This species could have been found just offshore from the Turner Farm site, or scavenged as a washed-up carcass. Apparently boat-based seal hunting (at seasons of the year when seals were not hauled out to pup) occurred commonly during Occupation 4. Porpoises could easily have been taken incidentally when seal hunting.

In the late nineteenth and early twentieth centuries, porpoise hunting was a common summer and fall occupation of the Passamaquoddy along the eastern Maine coast. By 1880, the hunter often used a rifle to kill the porpoise, but a spear or harpoon was used to retrieve the animal, whether it had been shot first or not (Figure 5–2). Ward (1880) provides a vivid account of hunting porpoise from a birchbark canoe in moderate wind and waves between Passamaquoddy Bay and Grand Manan Island. A passage of at least 15 km from the protected inshore waters of Passamaquoddy Bay to Grand Manan was routine for the most skilled hunters, which provides a reasonable estimate of the offshore range of the birch bark canoe-borne hunters of Occupation 4.

Right and humpback whales move inshore near the coastline of New England on their annual migrations. These species average 30 tons as adults, but are slow and approachable. Denys (1908:403) says whales "frequently came ashore on the coast (of Nova Scotia), and on the blubber of which they made good cheer." Little and Andrews (1982) document the important part played by processing drift whales in the seventeenth-century Indian economy of Nantucket Island, in Massachusetts. Dead drift whales of several large species were apparently frequent enough there to be the subject of formalized customs for division and distribution, and of Indian-European treaty relations. However, as both the eastern coast of Nova Scotia and Nantucket are outside the Gulf of Maine, it is unclear whether dead drift whales would have been such a regular occurrence anywhere in the Gulf of Maine. The ethnographic hints in Rosier (below) of the technology and willingness to hunt large whales argues against the regular occurrence of dead drift whales along the shore inside the Gulf of Maine.

Large whales may have been accessible to intrepid hunters on the Maine coast. Rosier's account of Weymouth's voyage to the Maine Coast during the late spring and summer of 1605 (Quinn and Quinn 1983:303–304) specifically mentions that Maine Indians pursued large whales of unknown species:

> One especiall thing is their maner of killing the Whale, which they call Powdawe; and will describe his forme; how he bloweth up the water; and that he is 12 fathoms long; and that they go in company of their King with a multitude of their boats, and strike him with a bone made in fashion of a harping iron fastened to a rope, which they make great and strong of the barke of trees, which they veare out after him: then all their boats come about him, and as he riseth above water, with their arrowes they shoot him to

death; when they have killed him and dragged him to shore, they call all their chiefe lords together, and sing a song of joy: and those chiefe lords, whom they call Sagamos, divide the spoile, and give to every man a share, which pieces so distributed they hang up about their houses for provision: and when they boile them, they blow off the fat, and put to their peaze, maiz, and other pulse, which they eat.

This description applies specifically to the large species, although similar techniques could have been used on porpoise. We know that Indian arrows could mortally wound deer at a reasonable range (40 or more meters?), so that they must have had enough power to pass through the soft tissues of a whale and reach a vital spot. Unfortunately there is not enough ethnographic information to assess just how frequent whale-hunting was during the Late Ceramic period in the Gulf of Maine. The possibility must be considered that it played a significant part in subsistence.

BEAR

Biology and Behavior

Maine black bear biology has been reviewed by Spencer (1966) and Hugie (1974/5), whom we follow here. Bear cubs are born in mid-winter while the female is in her den. Cubs reach weights of 20–45 kg (45–95 lbs) by November or December of their first year. Yearlings weigh between 16 and 55 kg (37 and 121 lbs) between July and December of their second year. Trophy-sized male Maine bears weigh 140–160kg (300–350 lbs), with large females weighing 90–110kg (200–250 lbs). The state record is a 245 kg (540 lbs) male.

Bears are practically ubiquitous in distribution in Maine, avoiding only the urban areas of the southwestern portion of the state. They certainly inhabited the whole state before the nineteenth century. Maine's spring 1989 bear population was estimated at 20,500 individuals (Maine Department of Inland Fisheries and Wildlife 1990). A sustainable annual harvest is estimated at 1,500 to 2,500 individuals.

Winter den choices do not follow any particular pattern other than that they are hidden and sheltered. Apparently obesity or food supply regulates denning, rather than freezing weather or snow depth. Spencer (1966:12) believes that bears can be expected to den earlier in years of bountiful food supplies and to be abroad later in the fall during lean years. In 1953, when food supplies were plentiful, most bears had denned by early December, and reemerged in early April, 1954. Most recent radio-collared bear studies provide information that conflicts with this pattern, however. "Abundant fall foods (beechnut crop) allow bears to delay denning; radio-collared research bears in northern Maine delayed denning until late November (1989). When fall foods are scarce, bears usually enter their dens during October" (Maine Department of Inland Fisheries and Wildlife 1990:5). Apparently Spencer was reporting an unusually late fall denning with plentiful food in early December 1953.

Black bears are primarily herbivores in Maine, concentrating on nuts, fruits, and berries. Animal matter averages about 8% by volume of the diet annually, and is composed mostly of carrion and insects. Denys' (1908:109, 383) description of bear abundance and habits along the Maine and Nova Scotian coast makes it clear that bears were abundant and well-adapted to coastal habitat. "But to return to the River of Pentagoet (Penobscot). Quantities of bears occur, which subsist upon the acorns that are found there; their flesh is very delicate and white as that of veal....It has long claws and climbs trees, lives on acorns, eats little of carrion, but goes along the edge of the sea where it eats lobsters and other fish which the waves cast upon the coast." Apparently this coastal niche harbored a strong bear population until human population growth forced them away from the immediate shoreline.

Ethnographic Accounts of Bear Hunting

William Wood (1865:100) mentions that the same spring-pole snares used to catch deer also captured bear. We assume that black bears were also located and attacked in their winter dens. Although no detailed description of this hunting method exists for seventeenth-century New England, it was common practice across the subarctic and eastern woodlands. We would expect fall and early winter to be the prime bear season, as they are fattest at this time. The Turner Farm site data indicate that bears were also hunted after they emerged from hibernation in the spring.

MINK

Two species of mink, the extinct sea mink and the common mink, were present on the mid-coast of Maine until recently. Marginal records for the coastal range of *Mustela macrodon*, the sea mink, are from Campobello Island in Passamaquoddy Bay in the north to the Casco Bay Islands (Portland) in the south, essentially the coast of the present state of Maine. Denys' (1908:388) description of the mink present during the mid-seventeenth century on the Gulf of St. Lawrence coast of New Brunswick and Nova Scotia fits *Mustela vison*, the common or modern mink.

The widespread presence of the common mink in Maine today, and its presence on North Haven Island for the past 5,000 years, indicates that the range of these two species overlapped for that period of time at least. The question of differential distribution or niche differentiation becomes one of the scale of allopatry in the coastal and near-coastal environment.

As pointed out in Chapter 2, these two minks are separated by size and by marked cranial and post-cranial rugosity in sea mink, including markedly stronger hands and feet (Mead et. al. 2000). Evidently there was some niche differentiation, perhaps different prey in salt water and near-coastal freshwater, along the Maine coast where both species were present.

Common mink is a "predatory, semiaquatic mammal that is generally associated with stream and river banks, lake shores, fresh and salt water marshes, and marine shore habitats" (Allen 1983). The species exhibits considerable variation in diet according to season, prey availability, and habitat type. It feeds on aquatic prey (fish, crustaceans), waterfowl and semiaquatic mammals, and small terrestrial mammals (rabbits and rodents). Fish, shellfish and crustaceans were the major food of common mink inhabiting coastal Alaska and British Columbia (Allen 1983). Rockpool-inhabiting fish, shore crabs, and rabbits, supplemented by birds (often obtained as carrion), provide the diet of a coastal-living feral mink population in Scotland (Dunstone and Burks 1987).

Mink den sites are usually within a few dozen meters of slowly flowing or non-flowing surface water. Shrubby vegetation, rocks, and logs provide necessary cover (Allen 1983). Mink use several dens within a home range. After kits become mature dens are used briefly and irregularly. New dens tend to be 100 m to 500 m removed. Mink typically spend 50% of their time in a linear "core area" along 300 m or so of shoreline, where the core area represents roughly 10% of total range. Male movements to new den sites are longer than female movements, and males tend to have larger ranges.

The habits of the sea mink must have been similar to those of coast-living common mink. We hypothesize that sea mink held the niche of smallest carnivore of the immediate seashore and inter-tidal zone along the Maine seacoast. This habitat is now devoid of carnivores except for common mink, fox, and racoon, and habitat productivity of meat has been drastically reduced by over-fishing, lobstering and bird population reductions. In discussing the habits of the black bear in the mid-seventeenth century, Denys (1908:383) gives us a glimpse of this now-vanished habitat, where bears foraged along the edge of the sea for lobsters and fish cast up by waves. We guess that sea mink was a specialized predator of lobster, crab, seabirds, and a scavenger of cast up fish on the shore. Selection for larger size and greater rugosity would confer obvious advantages over common mink in dealing with the above-mentioned prey, especially shellfish, larger marine fish and larger colony-nesting shorebirds (gulls, terns and alcids). (common mink, perhaps, was freshwater oriented before the demise of the sea mink.)

Common mink are trapped today with steel traps, set near their aquatic habitat (Bierman 1975). We assume that similar patterns of trapping, perhaps using deadfalls, would have been successful in the past. Manly Hardy (1903:125, see also Mairs and Parks 1964:23) left the following account of Euro-American (nineteenth-century) hunting for sea mink along the Maine coast :

> They carried their dogs with them, and besides guns, shovels, pickaxes, and crowbars, took a good supply of pepper and brimstone. If they (the mink) took refuge in holes or cracks of the ledges, they were usually dislodged by working with shovels or crowbars, and the dogs caught them when they came out. If they were in the crevices of the rocks where they could not be got at, and their eyes could be seen to shine, they were shot and pulled out by means of an iron rod with a screw at the end. If they could not be seen they were usually driven out by firing in charges of pepper. If this failed, then they were smoked with brimstone, in which case, they either came out or were suffocated in their holes. Thus, in a short time, they were nearly or quite exterminated.

Prehistoric hunters may likewise have used specially trained dogs to procure sea mink.

BEAVER

Beaver are widespread in Maine today. At high population levels they dam any freshwater flowage small enough for their engineering abilities. Three-month-old beavers weigh 2–4kg (5–10 lbs), yearlings 8–11kg (17–25 lbs), and two-year-olds 11–16kg (25–35 lbs). Adult beaver weigh 14–18kg (30–40 lbs). Their large size, high fat content, sedentary (predictable) location, and ubiquitous distribution in small groups make them an excellent source of food and fur.

Statewide annual beaver trapping harvests have ranged from 11,000 to 13,000 individuals from 1984–5 until 1987–8, when a drop in fur prices caused a decrease in trapping effort (Maine Department of Inland Fisheries and Wildlife 1990). Apparently this harvest level (0.4 per square mile) is a long-term sustainable yield under modern conditions of partial suburban and agricultural development. Since beaver accept moderate human development (some beaver damming wetlands adjacent to the Maine Turnpike) the prehistoric population may have been only marginally higher.

The Indian hunting methods reported below may frequently have resulted in the destruction of a whole beaver family and abandonment of a dam for several years. Modern research (Maine Department of Inland Fisheries and Wildlife 1990: 13) indicates that such a hunting strategy would actually increase the productivity of interior wetlands, especially for waterfowl. To maintain productivity, interior wetlands need to "drain periodically and recycle. Recycling occurs naturally as old beaver dams wash out, new vegetation grows in the drained pond site," and eventually a new family of beavers recolonizes the location to reflood the pond site. Most of the vegetation growing in the drained ponds is grassy meadow, providing increased white-tailed deer seasonal forage for a few years (Spiess, personal observation). Thus, appropriate levels of beaver harvest actually increase interior carrying capacity for humans.

The amount of beaver habitat available on North Haven and Vinalhaven Island prehistorically is unknown. A survey of stream miles available for beaver habitation and recommended beaver population limits (Hodgdon and Hunt 1966: 88) indicates no suitable stream miles and a nil limit on beaver population for North Haven, Vinalhaven, and similarly-sized Isle au Haut. Bourque (1995:219) is of the opinion that "limited suitable habitat exists [today] around the islands freshwater ponds." At lower relative sea levels during Late Archaic occupation of the Turner Farm site, there would certainly have been more extensive freshwater wetlands (Belknap 1995), and presumably beaver habitat. The presence of suitable freshwater wetlands for turtle habitat on North Haven and/or Vinalhaven is indicated for the entire span of human use of the Turner Farm site, since it is unlikely that human hunters would have consistently brought snapping turtles to the islands from the mainland. The dramatic increase in beaver bone counts relative to other large mammals (Table 3–33) between the Late Archaic occupations and the Occupation 4 strata makes it seem likely that beaver hunting on the mainland would have been necessary to supplement the relatively small populations available from the islands.

Denys (1908:429–432) describes both summer and winter beaver hunting. During the summer, beaver were shot with arrows in the woods, or in "lakes or ponds, where the Indians placed themselves in canoes at a proper spot to watch until they came to the surface of the water to take the air." But the "commonest and most certain" method was to break their dam. "Then the beavers found themselves without water, and did not know any more where to go." The Indians then took as many as they wished with arrows or spears. Winter beaver hunting was a complex matter involving a group of hunters. Denys account explicitly states that there was no selectivity for age during winter hunting, and does not indicate selectivity by age or sex during the summer hunt either.

Denys makes oblique reference to a taboo about feeding beaver bones to the dogs, or putting beaver bones in the fire. He is speaking of the practice of not feeding any bones to the dogs for fear of dulling their teeth: "not even those of the beaver. If they should eat of that, it would keep the Indians from killing any, and the same if one were to burn them."

LeClercq (1910:226) states that giving beaver bones to the dogs would cause them to "lose the senses needed for hunting of the beavers." Throwing beaver bones in the water, he claimed, would allow the spirit of the bones to carry the news to other beavers who would then leave in fear of being killed, too.

SMALL FURBEARERS

Red Fox and Grey Fox

The red fox *(Vulpes vulpes)* is a ubiquitous and common resident of Maine. Until recently, there has been dispute concerning the taxonomic status of red fox in North America,

its relationship with European red fox, and its antiquity in North America. Hall and Kelson (1959:855) label it *Vulpes fulva* and question whether the species was introduced from Europe after European contact. Recently the red fox has been reclassified as *V. vulpes* (Hamilton and Whitaker 1979), the same species as European red fox. Archaeological data, including those presented herein, demonstrate thousands of years of antiquity for the species in eastern North America.

In fact, the Fox Islands in Penobscot Bay, including North Haven where the Turner Farm site is located, were so named by Martin Pring in 1603: "One of them we named Foxe Iland, because we found those kind of beasts thereon". (Quinn and Quinn 1983:217). The Quinns thought that these might have been grey fox, but the archaeological evidence suggests that they were more likely red fox. Adult red foxes average 1 meter in body length (excluding tail) and 3.5–6 kg (8–14 lbs) in weight. The species occupies a diverse range of terrestrial habitats, preferring broken woodlands, marshes and meadows over unbroken woodland. The red fox is omnivorous, eating birds, small mammals, reptiles, amphibians, large insects, carrion, berries, and even grasses (Hamilton and Whitaker 1979).

Red foxes live in dens, usually excavated into the ground. They may mate for life. Litters of four to ten kits are born usually in late March or April. In the fall, the family disbands and the young disperse to find a new hunting territory. Between 4,000 to 5,000 foxes were taken by trapping and hunting annually in Maine between 1984/5 and 1987/8.

The present-day northern range limit of the grey fox *(Urocyon cinereoargenteus)* occurs in southern and western Maine (Hall and Kelson 1959, Palmer 1956). Northern grey foxes are slightly larger than conspecifics further south. Individuals of 6 kg (13 lbs) or more have been recorded in Massachusetts and New York (Hamilton and Whitaker 1979:270). The grey fox is more arboreal than the red fox, preferring mature woodlands with deciduous trees over open country or coniferous woodland. The species is an adept climber, climbing as do bears or using its stout nails similarly to a cat.

Usually three to five kits are born in March or April. The grey fox may eat more birds than the red fox (Hamilton and Whitaker 1979). It also feeds on small mammals, amphibians and reptiles, beechnuts, corn, and fruit. The number of grey fox in Maine presently is unclear.

There is little ethnographic information about specific techniques of hunting or trapping these species, or of their use as food and for pelts. They were, of course, the focus of later commercial trapping activity.

Porcupine

The porcupine *(Erethizon dorsatum)* is a slow-moving rodent weighing 8 to 15 kg (15 to 30 lbs), whose dorsal surface is covered with quills. The porcupine is a deliberate but accomplished climber, whose preferred food is the cambium layer of certain gymnosperms (pine, fir). This species will also eat birds, forbs, twigs, and evergreen needles. Except during the mating season they are solitary. One offspring is born in the spring, with the exact month of birth dependent on latitude (Hall and Kelson 1959:780–781). The porcupine does not hibernate. The animals are slow and easily shot or clubbed when located. Denys (1908:384) says: "Being singed, well roasted, washed, and placed on a spit it is as good as suckling pig." Denys also says the Indians place it on the fire "to be grilled like a pig."

Muskrat

The muskrat *(Ondatra zibethicus)* is a large microtine rodent up to 45 cm (1½ feet) long including the tail with a widespread range. The muskrat is fecund, raising one or two litters, averaging six or seven young per litter, per year. In Maine it is found along both estuaries and freshwater whether flowing or not. The muskrat is well adapted to a partially aquatic life with a laterally compressed tail and swimming fringes on enlarged hind feet. Muskrats either build small houses of sticks, twigs, grass, and mud similar to beaver houses, or dig dens into the muddy banks of a river.

The animals weigh only 0.5–1.5 kg (1–3 lbs), but the pelt is luxurious. The carcasses are consumed for food by many arctic and subarctic groups, and are also sold commercially as "marsh rabbit."

There is little ethnographic information from the seventeenth century about specific techniques of hunting or trapping muskrat and the other furbearing species described below, or about their use as food and for pelts. Many were, of course, the focus of later commercial trapping activity.

River Otter

The river otter *(Lutra canadensis)* is a large, aquatic Mustelid. The average weight of adults is from 6–8 kg (12–16 lbs),

with length ranging from 75–125 cm (30–55 inches). The fur is a dense dark-brown or black. Females bear from one to four young after a variable gestation period (Blanchard 1966). Old beaver lodges, stream banks, hollow logs, brush piles, or upturned tree roots serve as denning sites.

Otters are highly aquatic, being able to stay underwater for up to four minutes. In winter they spend much of their time underwater, breathing air trapped in pockets under the ice. Otters feed on fish, primarily "rough fish" such as chubs and suckers, which may be slower than other species and thus easier to catch. Otters generally have a home range of a circular route, often traveled in a regular sequence. In Maine part of the route may be over land from one watershed to another. Some routes are up to 40 miles in circumference. The size of the home range varies with seasonal and other conditions.

Some otters are presently caught in baited mink traps. Unbaited traps set near where otters leave or enter water are also effective. During winter, otter can be caught in baited traps set under the ice. Approximately 1,000 otter per year were trapped in Maine from 1984/5 through 1987/8 (Maine Department of Inland Fisheries and Wildlife 1990).

Fisher

The fisher *(Martes pennanti)* is characterized by strong sexual dimorphism. Adult males may measure up to one meter in length, and weigh between 3–9 kg (6–20 lbs), while females weigh between 2–3 kg (5–7 lbs). Males reach weights of 3–4 kg by their first winter. Fisher skeletal dimorphism has been described by Leach (1977). The fur of the smaller female is finer than that of the male, and is preferred in modern markets.

Fisher biology in Maine has been reviewed by Coulter (1974). Fishers are solitary predators and scavengers of mixed and coniferous forests. At present they are doing very well in Maine, including coastal terrain. Fishers travel the forest hoping to find prey (small rodents, rabbits, birds, porcupines), carrion, and occasionally mast food (acorns). Even predation upon frogs has been recorded. Fishers prefer to travel ridges, crossing streams perpendicularly to high ground on the other bank. Thus, they are not aquatically oriented, in contrast to the mink and otter. Fisher are active predators all winter long. Three or four young are born in March or April, and are cared for in a nest or hollow tree for several months. Between 4,000 and

9,000 fishers per year were trapped in Maine between 1984/5 and 1987/8 (Maine Department of Inland Fisheries and Wildlife 1990).

Lynx

The lynx *(Lynx canadensis)* is a specialized predator of the boreal forest, eating squirrels, grouse and lemmings, but primarily dependent on the snowshoe hare *(Lepus americanus)*. The size of the lynx population is directly dependent on the size of the snowshoe hare population; and lynx will not remain in areas lacking snowshoe hare (Hall and Kelson 1959:967; Hunt 1974). Adult lynx weigh between 7 and 14 kg (15–30 lbs). This species breeds in March, and one to four young are born in May.

Denys (1908:383) presents some information on seventeenth century Indian use of lynx: "the flesh is white and very good to eat. ... (I)f the Indians meet them and they or their Dogs pursue them, this animal mounts into a tree where it is easily killed, whilst the Dogs are terrifying it with their barkings (Denys 1908:434)." Thus, the lynx is a forest animal which would be occasionally taken. Denys does not mention intentional trapping of this species.

Bobcat

Bobcat *(Lynx rufus)* average 65 to 80 cm (26 to 31 in) in length, and 7 to 16 kg (15 to 35 lbs) in weight. The species is ubiquitous south of lynx range, overlapping with lynx in the mixed hardwood-softwood forest and southern subarctic (including Maine). Usually a nocturnal hunter, in the winter it sometimes hunts during the day (Guggesberg 1975:59–63). Male bobcat territories range up to 170 square km, while female hunting and home ranges are smaller than 15 square km. Bobcat prey primarily on small mammals, and will kill deer in winter when they are in poor condition and cannot escape. Bobcat trapping and hunting harvests have ranged from about 100 to about 300 animals per year from 1984/5 to 1987/8 (Maine Department of Inland Fisheries and Wildlife 1990). We suspect that bobcat would have been utilized similarly to lynx.

Raccoon

The raccoon *(Procyon lotor)* is a nocturnal omnivore of modest size 5–15 kg (11–33 lbs), usually found near water. Raccoons breed in late winter and bear a litter of one to six young in the spring (Hall and Kelson 1959:884). The family often stays together as a foraging and social unit.

Raccoons today are often attracted to garbage concentrations or food caches left by human beings. It is interesting to speculate that such behavior might have been part of a commensal relationship with Maine's prehistoric inhabitants as well. As in the case of lynx, dogs may have been important in hunting this species. Raccoon hunting and trapping harvests have ranged from 18,000 to 22,000 animals from 1984/5 to 1987/8 (Maine Department of Inland Fisheries and Wildlife 1990).

Striped Skunk,

The stripped skunk *(Mephitis mephitis)* is a small, primarily nocturnal omnivore and insectivore. In summer it is primarily insectivorous, but in winter it feeds on small mammals and carrion. Skunks live in burrows in woodland, and under buildings in developed areas. They are not particularly attracted to or adverse to wet environments. Four to seven young are born during the spring (Hall and Kelson 1959:934).

BIRDS

After brief review of the biology of bird taxa represented at the Turner Farm site, we present information on species that are conspicuous by their absence. Bird weight data taken from Sibley 2000 and Bellrose 1976.

Ducks

Various duck species *(Anatidae)* provided the mainstay of the bird hunting for Turner Farm site inhabitants. Data on duck behavior is taken from Palmer (1949:75–132).

The common or American eider *(Somateria mollissima)* is essentially a bird of the marine coast, present year-round, nesting on coastal islands. Flocks of 200–1,000 have been recorded. Males weigh about 2 kg (4.38 lbs), females about 1.5 kg (3.38 lbs). The white-winged scoter *(Melanitta fusca),* weighing 1.7 kg (3.7 lbs), is not quite as marine as the eider, staying closer inshore and spending more time on freshwater. This species is abundant in spring and fall along the coast, is a common winter and uncommon (non-breeding) summer coastal resident. Migration from interior freshwater, where it breeds, to the coast begins in September and continues into early November.

The great scaup *(Aythya marila)*, weighing 1.05 kg, (2.3 lbs) and lesser scaup *(Aythya affinis)*, weighing .83 kg (1.8

lbs), commonly associate with each other, often forming large flocks or "rafts." However, lesser scaup are less common than greater scaup. Both species arrive on the coast in the last half of October or the first half of November and become common to abundant members of the wintering coastal avifauna. Both species depart for their breeding grounds in March and April. Thus, if found in any numbers in an archaeological sample, their presence indicates hunting between October and April.

The black duck (*Anas rubripes*), weighing 1.2 kg (2.6 lbs), is common to numerous throughout the state as a summer and winter resident, and an abundant fall migrant. The teals (green-winged, *Anas carolinensis*; blue-winged, *A. discors*), weighing 0.4 kg (.75 lbs), are common to numerous spring and fall migrants, and occasional summer residents. The bufflehead (*Bucephala albeola*), weighing 0.4 kg (.75 lbs), is a common or numerous winter resident, and spring or fall migrant. It is a rare coastal summer resident. The harlequin duck (*Histrionicus histrionicus*), weighing 0.6 kg (1.3 lbs), is a common winter resident and occasional spring and fall transient on salt water. It departs in March, and is not present in summer. On balance, the small ducks (teals, bufflehead, harlequin) as a skeletally identifiable group do not constitute a definitive seasonality marker based upon presence or absence, although many more individuals are present along the coast during winter than in other seasons. Thus, a large number of small ducks in an assemblage indicates late fall or winter seasonality.

Canada Goose

There are several subspecies of Canada goose. Herein we refer to the "Atlantic" Canada goose, (*Branta canadensis*), weighing 2.7–4. 5 kg (6–10 lbs). Uncommon summer and winter residents on salt water, Canada geese are most abundant during spring and fall migrations. Their highest concentration occurs during March and April. Fewer birds appear along the coast during the fall migration, which lasts from October into December in some years (Palmer 1949:64–68). An immature goose bone from Occupation 4 at the Turner Farm site indicates a summer breeding residence of this species on the Maine coast in the past as well as in the present.

Other Geese

Other species of geese (*Anserinae*) are either uncommon spring or fall migrants, or very rare non-breeding summer residents (Palmer 1949:68–75). An exception to the general rarity of smaller goose species on the coast of Maine may be the brant (*Branta bernicula*), weighing 1.4 kg (3.1lbs), which concentrates on some offshore islands along the coast in late winter/early spring. Flocks appear occasionally on inshore estuaries such as Merrymeeting Bay. The large numbers of this species using the Maine coast were not suspected until the late 1980s (Susan Woodward, personal communication 1988).

Loons

The common loon (*Gavia immer*) is a year-round resident of Maine, but the vast majority of birds spend their summers on interior freshwater. During summer a few non-breeding individuals, as well as rare breeding pairs, occur on salt water. Common loons are numerous to common transients on salt water in spring (late April and early May) and fall (October and early November). This bird is a common winter resident on salt water, scattered in inshore waters and sometimes about outer islands. Common loons average 4.1 kg (9 lbs), but may weigh up to 6 kg (13.5 lbs). Identification of high numbers of common loons in the bird bone sample indicates inshore marine bird hunting sometime from October through April, inclusive. The red-throated loon (*Gavia stellata*), weighing 1.4 kg (3.1 lbs), is mainly an inshore marine bird found in small flocks of uncommon frequency during the winter. It is a common spring and fall transient, and an occasional salt water non-breeding summer resident (Palmer 1949:23–24).

Cormorants

The European cormorant (*Phalacrocrax carbo*), weighing 3.3 kg (7.2 lbs), is a common to numerous winter resident along the coast and common to numerous spring and fall transient. It is an uncommon summer resident, most of the birds moving northward. Those that remain during summer often share roosts with the northern double-crested cormorant (*P. auritus*), weighing 1.7 kg (3.7 lbs). Double-crested cormorants are numerous to very abundant summer residents, spring and fall transients. They are rare during the winter, being replaced by *P. carbo*. Double-crested cormorant eggs are laid in late May. Young reach flying age by the middle or end of August (6 weeks of age). Cormorants generally fish in less than 30 feet of water, and closely follow the coastline in their flights to and from feeding areas, rarely crossing points of land (Palmer 1949:41–47). These species are alternate season indicators, but unfortunately are difficult to separate skeletally. The only breeding species (with medullary bone and immature bones) should be *P. auritus.*

Great Blue Heron

The great blue heron *(Ardea herodias),* weighing 2.4 kg (5.3 lbs), is an occasional to numerous summer resident, and common spring (April) and fall (October to November) migrant. Rarely, individuals of this species winter in Maine, usually along the southwestern Maine coast. This species breeds mostly in colonies, often in trees on the mainland shore or large islands. Young are hatched in early June, and fledging occurs in about 50 days (late July/early August). Herons feed on fish, amphibians and reptiles along the shores of bays, islands, coves, flats, and marshes (Palmer 1949: 48–50).

Medium and Small-Sized Ardeids

American egret *(Ardea alba),* weighing .87 kg (1.9 lbs), is a rare or uncommon spring, summer and fall visitor. This species frequents salt marshes and tidal flats, and is seen most often in August (Palmer 1949:50–52). The snowy egret *(Egretta thula),* weighing .36 kg (.75 lbs), is an occasional summer coastal resident (Spiess, personal observation). The northern little blue heron *(Egretta caerulea),* weighing .34 kg (.75 lbs) is a rare spring and uncommon summer and early fall visitor. Most are the immature white birds of this species (Palmer 1949:52–53). The black-crowned night-heron *(Nycticorax nycticorax),* weighing .87 kg (1.9 lbs), is a common coastal spring (April to May) and fall (August to September) transient and summer resident. Young of this species fledge in early August. This species nests in small colonies in conifers near the shoreline (Palmer 1949:55–57). The American bittern *(Botaurus lentiginosus),* weighing .7 kg (1.51 lbs), is an uncommon spring and fall transient, and summer resident (Palmer 1949:57–58). An immature longbone of a medium-sized ardeid was recovered from Occupation 4 at the Turner Farm site. It indicates July through September coastal bird hunting, although no species identification was possible.

Great Auk

The flightless great auk *(Pinguinus impennis)* is now extinct. Rosier (Quinn and Quinn 1983:306) mentions "penguins" as an economic resource of the broad area. Palmer (1949:279,

280, apparently based on Rosier) mentions that the bird probably was resident in Maine, but that the only historic records note its presence in late spring.

The great auk is a significant part (7–15%) of the identified avifauna at the Turner Farm site. It is possible that it was a winter as well as summer resident, and that it bred locally on inshore and offshore islands during the summer. Recovery of two immature great auk bones, including one with an unfused distal epiphysis, may be evidence for the proximity of a breeding colony, although we do not know how far fledgling birds might have migrated before their growth was complete. However, the total sample of fragmented great auk bones was examined for medullary bone deposits and none were discovered, so the Turner Farm site hunters probably did not have direct access to a breeding colony.

Most reviews of great auk biology focus on the distribution and extinction of the species (Grieve 1885, Jordan and Olson 1982, Bengston 1984, Meldgaard 1988). By the time naturalists were recording its behavior, the great auk had been reduced to breeding on Funk Island, Newfoundland and islands around the margins of the North Atlantic, from the Hebrides to Iceland and Newfoundland (Grieve 1885). Evidence from southwest Greenland indicates a small breeding population surviving there into the end of the eighteenth century (Meldgaard 1988:157). However, most great auk sightings in Greenland were in late fall and early winter, September through January. These birds were probably migrants from Iceland and/or Newfoundland. Reconstruction of great auk behavior include long-distance population movements by "swimming," in large groups and in a manner similar to some species of Antarctic penguins (Meldgaard 1988: 163).

Great auks fed on small fish caught by "flying" underwater, in a manner similar to flighted alcids, at depths of less than 75 m (Meldgaard 1988:161–2). They nested in colonies on rock islets with relatively low, shelving access to the sea, not on the sheer cliff faces used by flighted alcid colonies. Females laid only one egg per year. There was some variability in the timing of egg laying between colonies. Great auks in Newfoundland and Iceland produced fully fledged young by mid-July. There is one record of a fledgling in southwest Greenland as late as August (Meldgaard 1988:157). Based upon comparisons with smaller alcids, and simple regression with other birds of large size, Meldgaard (1988:152) calculates that the great auk reached full skeletal maturity between 5 months and 1 year of age.

There is some evidence of geographic variation in size, which might indicate several distinct breeding great auk populations within northwest Europe (Hufthammer in Meldgaard 1988:164).

The great auk was a large bird, weighing roughly 5 kg (11 lbs) live (Bengston 1984). Grieve (1885) states that it yielded more meat than a goose. Use of the great auk for its meat, fat, oil, skins (for garment bags and amulets), and its windpipe as a dart float have been recorded (Meldgaard 1988:165) for traditional Inuit culture in West Greenland.

Medium-sized Alcids

The razor-billed auk *(Alca torda)*, weighing .72 kg (1.6 lbs), maintains breeding colonies in the Bay of Fundy today. It is a rare summer resident along the Maine coast, but an uncommon to common spring/fall transient and winter resident. The number seen along the Maine coast in winter varies considerably, indicating that the Fundy population is occasionally augmented by migrants from further away. Except during the breeding season, this is a bird of offshore waters, although not pelagic (Palmer 1949:283–284).

The Atlantic murre *(Uria aalge)*, weighing .99 kg (2.2 lbs), is a rare offshore winter resident (Palmer 1949:285). Brunnick's murre *(Uria lomvia)*, weighing .97 kg (2.1 lbs), is a fairly common offshore spring/fall transient and winter resident. It is uncommon in inshore waters, but it is often driven ashore by storms. This species arrives in Maine in November and early December, and departs in February and early March (Palmer 1949:286).

Skeletal growth in the medium-sized alcids is completed by 2½ months of age (Meldgaard 1988:152). There is no evidence of local breeding in the form of medullary bone or immature skeletal elements in the Turner Farm site assemblage. Unless the Maine coast supported breeding populations in the past, the presence of medium-sized alcids represents late fall or winter offshore birding.

Small Alcids

The dovekie *(Plautus alle)*, weighing .16 kg (.375 lbs), is a fall/spring transient and winter resident offshore, where it can be numerous in any given year. Occasionally, storms drive substantial numbers inshore. This species arrives in November-December and departs in early March. The species is gregarious in winter, and typically an offshore plankton feed-

er (Palmer 1949:287–288). The Atlantic Puffin *(Fratercula arctica)*, weighing .38 kg (.75 lbs), is a year-round resident of the Maine coast, maintaining breeding colonies at isolated places. A single egg, laid in a hole in a rock, usually hatches on or about July 1st. The birds are fledged by mid- to late August. This species spends the winter in offshore and outer inshore waters. It is gregarious at all seasons (Palmer 1949:287–288).

The black guillemot *(Cepphus grylle)*, weighing .43 kg (.94 lbs), is a fairly common to numerous resident year-round. Mature birds of this species congregate at their breeding places in April and disperse again in August, after the young begin to float and swim. Eggs are laid in rocky crevices near the tide-line. Clutches are complete by mid-June, with hatching in mid-July. The young are fledged by mid-August. The guillemots spend winter dispersed in the vicinity of outer shores and shoals (Palmer 1949:288–290).

The incomplete calcified longbone of a young small alcid from Occupation 4 (1GF) at the Turner Farm site is evidence of July/August raids on nesting areas of one or more of these species.

Grebes

The pied-billed grebe *(Podilymbus podiceps)*, weighing 0.45 kg (1 lb), is a common spring and fall transient and summer resident. This species is found among the vegetation of freshwater ponds, marshes and lake coves, rarely in open water. Eggs are laid in late May, and a second clutch is sometimes laid. The fledging period is unknown (Palmer 1949:27–28).

The horned grebe *(Colymbus auritus)*, weighing .45 kg (1 lb), is a common spring to fall transient and winter resident, especially along the coast. It does not breed in Maine, but can be a rare non-breeding summer resident. This species appears in numbers along the coast in October, and departs in April (Palmer 1949:26–27). Both grebe species are represented in very low frequency in the Turner Farm site sample. Immature bones must represent young *Podilymbus*, taken in late summer in freshwater marshy situations, or upper estuaries.

Hawks and Eagles

Various species of hawks (genus *Buteo*) are uncommon to common spring to fall transients, and summer residents. Some are rare coastal winter residents. The rough-legged hawk *(Buteo lagopus)*, weighing 0.99 kg (2.2 lbs), is a normal winter resident (Palmer 1949:138–143). The bald eagle *(Haliatus leucocephalus)*, weighing 4.3 kg (9.5 lbs), is a year-round resident. The golden eagle *(Aquila chrysaetos)*, weighing 4.6 kg (10 lbs), also occurs throughout most of the year (Palmer 1949:144, 146).

Procellariid

A single bone identifiable to this family, probably the sooty shearwater *(Puffinus griseus)*, weighing .78 kg (1.7 lbs), was recovered from the Occupation 4 deposits. This bird breeds in the southern hemisphere in November and December. It is a non-breeding (biologically wintering) resident from late spring to fall. It is fairly common off-shore, and occasionally strays into the outer fringes of islands (Palmer 1949:29).

Rallid/Scolopacid

The king rail *(Rallus elegans)*, weighing .36 kg (.81 lbs), is a rare summer and fall visitor. The clapper rail *(R. longirostris)*, weighing .29 kg (.625 lbs), seems to be a rare fall and winter visitor to southern Maine. The coot *(Fulica americana)*, weighing .65 kg (1.4 lbs), is a rare, year-round transient, especially near the coast. It is slightly more common in fall than at other times, and a few of the summer sightings may have been breeding residents (Palmer 1949:183–190).

The Eskimo curlew *(Numenius borealis)* is nearly extinct, or extinct. It was formerly an abundant fall transient across the Gulf of Maine, common along the coast. The flight usually passed between about August 27th and September 11th. This species only came inshore in numbers as a result of heavy weather during their migration (Palmer 1949:206). The osprey and other birds described below are conspicuous by their absence in the Turner Farm site sample.

Osprey

Ospreys *(Pandion halaietus)*, weighing 1.6 kg (3.5 lbs), are common summer residents today. Skeletally, they are easily distinguishable from the eagles and hawks. Although the sample of bird-of-prey bones is small in the Turner Farm site assemblage, we would expect more ospreys than hawks/eagles based on the relative modern frequency of the species.

Swan

No swan bone has been identified from the Turner Farm site. However, this is the largest-bodied species of bird that could have been present in the area. The tundra swan *(Cygnus columbianus)*, sometimes called whistling swan, weighing 6.6 kg (14.4 lbs), is an uncommon spring and fall transient. The Eastern population of tundra swans winters on the Atlantic coast principally from New Jersey south, but rarely as far north as Massachusetts and casually in Maine (Limpert and Earnst 1994). Seventeenth-century records indicate that it was a common to uncommon transient during early historic times (Palmer 1949:61–62). The current "Eastern" population of tundra swan breeds along the arctic coast of Canada and north coast of Alaska, migrates through the upper Midwest (Minnesota and North Dakota), to the Chesapeake Bay region. Staging areas on the northward migration are the Susquehanna River valley and southwest Ontario (Limpert and Earnst 1994). This migration pattern means swans would rarely appear in Maine. However, Lumsden (1984, cited in Limpert and Earnst 1994) postulates an extinct breeding population in Labrador. We suspect that such a population would have migrated south through Maine.

Grouse Family

No bones of the *Tetraonidae* family were identified, although ruffed grouse or "partridge" *(Bonasa umbellus)* may have been present on the large inshore islands. These birds are strictly terrestrial, found in deep woods and brush. Most bird hunting at the Turner Farm site seems to have been a marine coastal and inshore activity.

Turkey

In colonial times, the turkey *(Meleagris gallopavo)* was resident only in extreme southwestern Maine (Palmer 1949). It is a bird of the mast-bearing hardwood forest and scrub; consequently it is not surprising that it did not occur at the Turner Farm site. However, there is one report (dated 1880) of a turkey tarsus from a shellheap on the east side of Mt. Desert Island (Palmer 1949:180). Turkey bones are common in shellheaps in southern New England, so its absence indicates that this species was not hunted by the Turner Farm site occupants locally.

Gulls

Bones of Gulls *(Larridae)* are quite distinctive, even while fragmentary. Several species are common to abundant along the inshore coast of Maine, and some species winter over.

Given the general inshore marine orientation of bird hunting by Turner Farm site residents, it is surprising that gull bones do not appear in the Turner Farm site sample. Perhaps there existed a cultural prejudice on the part of the site's inhabitants against eating these species.

Passenger Pigeon

The passanger pigeon *(Ectopistes migratorius)* seems to have been terrestrially oriented, and a migratory spring-fall visitor in New England. Pigeon bones are distinctive, and none were identified in the sample.

Bird Economic Use — Hunting and Capture

Denys' account contains several references to Indian use of birds. Speaking of the wild goose he says (1908:370): "Its plumage is gray-brown after the fashion of that of a [domestic] goose.... The Indians make robes of it." Denys (1908:435) provides the following description of inshore duck and goose hunting, which might account for the high proportion of duck remains at the Turner Farm site:

> In certain closed coves which are under cover from the wind, the Wild Geese, the Brant, and the Ducks go to sleep out upon the surface, for on land they would not be safe because of the Foxes. To those places the Indians went, two or three in a canoe, with torches which they made of Birch bark; these burn more brightly than torches of wax. Reaching the place where all these birds are, they laid down in the canoe, which they allowed to drift without their being seen. The current carried them right into the midst of all these birds, which had no fear of them, supposing them to be logs of wood which the sea was carrying from one place to another, something that often happens, which makes them accustomed to it. When the Indians were in their midst they lighted their torches all at once. This surprised the birds and obliged them all at the same moment to rise into the air. The darkness of the night makes this light very conspicuous, so that they suppose it is the sun or other [such] thing. They all proceeded to wheel in confusion around the torches which an Indian held, always approaching the fire, so close that the Indians, with sticks they held, knocked them down as they passed. Besides, by virtue of much wheeling about, these birds became dizzy so that they fell as if dead; then the Indians took them and wrung their necks. As a result in a single night they filled their canoe.

Nets were also used to take inshore birds. "Davis account in the History of Wareham, Massachusetts (tells) of how Indians got Penguins (great auks) by trapping them in a weir across an inlet, then killing them with clubs after the tide had receded" (Palmer 1949:283). Palmer also mentions accounts of Europeans taking great auks with clubs on islands.

The capture of cliff-nesting seabirds, and the collection of eggs from their nests by means of a rope used to scale the cliffs is a common practice in North Atlantic islands. Williamson (1948:156–157) describes a twentieth century method of trapping guillemots and razorbill auks at sea. Large boards (7 feet by 3–4 feet wide) are covered with 50 or more small loops of braided horsehair, a stuffed bird of the species sought is affixed to one end, and the board is set adrift in a place where many of the birds congregate. The alcids are attracted to the board by the stuffed bird and become ensnared. One boat often set 10 such boards in a day, and harvests of 500 to 600 birds are recorded. Some similar trap could easily have been used on great auk and other gregarious species.

Cormorant roosts were raided by stealth, at night, with the hunter often filling his canoe. Josselyn (1988:73) describes the method as an approach in a drifting canoe at night, with the Indian seizing the lone cormorant "watchman" by the neck. The Indian then climbed out softly on the rock, and took as many cormorants by the neck as he wished. Whatever the exact techniques used, the avian sample at the Turner Farm site could have been all taken from the shoreline of North Haven and Vinalhaven Islands, or on the water within one or two miles.

One final aspect of Indian bird use to be considered is egg collecting. The presence of immature duck, guillemot, goose, and heron bones in the Turner Farm site sample makes it probable that the nesting areas of these species were raided during the summer. Late spring visits to the same areas would have produced eggs. Williamson (1948:156–157) includes egg collecting in his account of preying upon cliff-nesting birds. Rosier (Quinn and Quinn 1983:262) reports finding an Indian campfire littered with shells of eggs "bigger than goose eggs" (along with fish bones and the "bones of some beast"). These eggs could have been swan, heron, or great awk eggs.

FISH BEHAVIOR AND SEASONAL AVAILABILITY

Next we summarize the general ecological conditions of the Gulf of Maine that affect fish feeding, movements and seasonal availability. The three largest fish contributors to the faunal sample (cod, sturgeon, and swordfish) are each discussed separately. These sections are followed by a review of other large, medium-sized, and small fish species.

Gulf of Maine Ecology

The movements of fish that live in the Gulf of Maine or visit it seasonally are determined by a complex of inter-related factors such as temperature, salinity, prior reproductive success, available foods, and predator populations. Here we discuss the range of variables governing fish appearance and availability as a background to the fish faunal sample recovered from the Turner Farm site.

Penobscot Bay generally, and the Fox Islands in particular, are located just west of a nutrient-rich upwelling from the Gulf of Maine floor which extends southwestward from the mouth of the Bay of Fundy and the southern and western periphery of Nova Scotia to just south of Penobscot Bay (Apollonio 1979). The strong tidal action that characterizes the Gulf of Maine, the bottom flow of oceanic waters along Northeast Channel, prevailing westerly winds, and the seasonal influx of cool, low salinity surface water around the southern shore of Nova Scotia that originates in the Gulf of St. Lawrence all contribute to a counter-clockwise current or gyre in the Gulf of Maine. This gyre is strongest in spring when cool, fresh snow-melt run-off mainly from the St. Lawrence watershed (and to a far lesser extent in the St. John and Penobscot watersheds) flows over the denser/warmer masses of oceanic water (Apollonio 1979:35–36). Spring phytoplanktonic blooms reach their peak, providing abundant food for zooplanktonic organisms and, in turn, for plankton feeding fish such as herring, alewife, shad, and menhaden. The plankton bloom generally declines in mid-summer.

The anadromous species of the herring family (mainly alewife and shad) arrive beginning in April in Maine, when they can take advantage of the spring run-off to ascend water-courses ranging from large rivers to streamlets. Close behind them are the anadromous salmon, which begin their runs in May. The herring arrive in late June in the vicinity of the Fox Islands and may be followed by mackerel if the water temperature warms sufficiently (above 46°F.), and lastly by menhaden at temperatures above 50°F in years when the supply of diatomic zooplankton are high enough (Bigelow and Schroeder 1953:117).

The arrival of these transients brings larger predator species ranging from inshore varieties, such as striped bass, to large oceanic species, including swordfish, tuna, common dolphin, and common bonito. These latter species rarely appear before water temperatures exceed 50°F, and sometimes do not appear at all. Interspersed are the medium and smaller size predators, including the spiney dogfish, the bluefish, butterfish, weakfish, and scup which pursue their prey into rivers and tidal estuaries. The spiney dogfish, bluefish and butterfish are hardy to the generally cool waters of the Gulf of Maine around the Fox Islands and eastward. Weakfish and scup, however, prefer warmer waters and rarely appear north of Casco Bay.

The activity of the warmer water predators rapidly tapers off with the return of cool weather in September and, by the end of October, they are gone completely. The larger cod move closer inshore again in fall, paralleling local movements of winter founder from deeper bottoms to tidewater areas. By November resident fish populations are reestablished in their winter ranges.

There are a number of incompletely understood variables that affect the scenario described above. The occasional failure of the westerlies (particularly during periods of intense storm activity), and/or drought conditions (particularly in the St. Lawrence watershed) may reduce the strength of the spring gyre. In 1934, during the severe drought in the Great Plains, the volume of cool low-salt water flowing around Nova Scotia was apparently reduced to such an extent that plankton growth in the Gulf of Maine increased during the summer rather than going into normal precipitous decline. This unusual variation led to the suggestion that the phytoplankton decline in normal years resulted mainly from the plankton being caught in the outflow of warmer waters over the outer banks of the Gulf of Maine (see Conkling 1995). We presently lack data to assess the effect of the warmer water conditions produced by this anomaly on the fish populations, but it seems likely that larger warm-water prey species such as swordfish or tuna would be more abundant inshore during such drought years. Warmer conditions during the Late Archaic might have been analogous. Other variables might include reproductive failures in the transient schooling fish (herring family) that attract the larger predators. We now turn to a discussion of specific major species behavior and harvest strategies.

Cod

Cod (*Gadus morhua*) are a so-called "ground fish," usually lying within a fathom of rocky or pebbly bottom where they hunt for prey among seaweed, although they will chase certain prey, such as herring, to the surface (Bigelow and Schroeder 1953:184). Cod can be found in water temperatures between 32° F and 55° F, which includes all but the warmest summer surface layers of the Gulf of Maine. Small cod are more tolerant of high water temperature than large cod, hence smaller and younger age schools are found in shallow water less than 2 fathoms (4 m) deep during summer. Generally the larger fish are deeper than 7 fathoms (12 m) in summer. During spawning runs, large cod are often found in outer estuaries at depths of 3–5 fathoms (6–10 m) (Bigelow and Schroeder 1953:184–189).

Cod spawn at a limited number of "grounds" within the Gulf of Maine. Several spawning grounds are found within 20 km of land between Casco Bay and Mount Desert Island, including the mouth of Penobscot Bay. Cod in the Gulf of Maine are considered to be one population or "stock", in fisheries managment terms). Sub-stocks, or local populations, within the gulf often exhibit homing behavior and return to ancestral spawning grounds (Perkins et al. 1997). Many adults disperse from the spawning grounds throughout the Gulf of Maine. However, the majority of small (immature) cod shift little from season to season (Bigelow and Schroeder 1953:190–191; Carlson 1986:168).

Within the Gulf of Maine, spawning is seasonally variable from sub-stock to sub-stock, generally occurring between November and February in those that spawn offshore (Bigelow and Schroeder 1953:193–194). A recent study (Perkins et al. 1997; preliminary data cited in Carlson 1986:167) reports spawning of the Sheepscot Bay sub-stock on the central Maine coast from May through July. Tagging studies of fish captured in the mouth of Sheepscot Bay estuary show that mature cod entered Sheepscot Bay in late April and remained at least until mid-July. Sheepscot Bay mature cod are, therefore, available in inshore waters at the mouth of the estuary, often in less than 20 m of water, from May through July at least. The same recapture study shows

availability of mature cod in the mouth of Penobscot Bay (including North Haven, Vinalhaven and Monhegan Islands areas) in May through July or August.

Carlson (1986:120–122) uses these data to differentiate two seasonal patterns of codfishing in the Sheepscot Bay area. An inshore fishery for adult cod would be seasonally restricted, although the seasonality might vary from one spawning ground to another. Juvenile cod are available in shallower water year-round. Carlson uses an age of four years, visible archaeologically as a caudal vertebral diameter of 1.1 cm, as an approximate divider between adult and juvenile cod. In fact, roughly 80% of the cod vertebra from all occupations at the Turner Farm site exceed this diameter (Chapter 3). Hence, it is the adult cod, and their availability to Native American fishermen inshore in late spring and early summer, that will help us reconstruct major economic activities at the Turner Farm site.

There are no early ethnohistoric accounts with specific references to the seasonality of Native American codfishing. While Weymouth's ship was anchored at Monhegan "about a league from shore" on May 18, 1605 "our men aboord with a few hours got about thirty great Cods and Haddocks, which gaue vs a taste of the great plenty of fish which we found afterward where so ever we went upon the coast" (Quinn and Quinn 1983:260). On the 19th, the ship anchored between Allen, Benner and Burnt Islands, "the other islands more adjoining to the Maine" (Quinn and Quinn 1983:263). On May 20th, the ship's boat "went about a mile from our ship, and in small time with two or three hours was fished sufficiently for our whole company three days worth great cod, haddocke and thornbache" (Quinn and Quinn 1983:263). Rozier's account could not be clearer: very large cod were extremely plentiful within easy canoeing distance from land in late May.

The Jesuit Pierre Biard wrote an account of aboriginal subsistence in the eastern Gulf of Maine in 1616. Although the account is non-specific geographically, it applies to the area between Penobscot Bay and the Bay of Fundy. Biard says, "from May to the middle of September they are free from all anxiety about their food; for the cod are upon the coast" (Thwaites 1897:3:81). It is clear from these accounts that from late spring through summer large cod were easily available inshore, although perhaps not in the warmer waters of mid- or upper estuaries.

Seventeenth-century European commercial fishing along the Maine coast, pursued from shore stations in small boats inshore, was a multi-seasonal or nearly year-round activity (Faulkner 1985:60–66). The best fishing was in January and February, but spring and summer fishing was also pursued. Small boat fishermen worked within 5 to 8km of their shorebase, about a 2–3 hour row or sail, using pairs of lines with baited hooks fished just above the bottom.

This pattern of multi-seasonal inshore fishing from small open boats continued as an opportunity for young fishermen just "starting out" into the early twentieth century (Clifford 1974:48–9,55). Distances of "½ mile off Damariscove Harbor" and "1–2 miles offshore" are noted for cod fishing using trawls of baited hooks set on the bottom and recovered a day or so later. Cod fishing in March, "summer" and "winter" is specifically mentioned. It appears that the seasonality of the inshore fishery, easily accessible from small boats, was more a matter of when a person could go fishing than when the cod were present. The definition of "inshore" is important here.

Swordfish

Swordfish *(Xiphias gladius)* are pelagic predators with a preference for warm water (Tibbo et. al. 1961). Today most swordfishing is carried on at the edge of the Gulf Stream from June through September, some 250 km southeast of the central Maine coast. Approximately 10% of the swordfishing locations reported by Tibbo, et. al. are inside the Gulf of Maine within 100 km of the Central Maine coast.

In the nineteenth century, the species was apparently more abundant closer to shore. Gibson (1981:40) is of the opinion that swordfish tend to be solitary and thus that at higher population levels more individuals would have come well into the Gulf of Maine. He specifically mentions Jeffrey's Ledge, about 100 km south of North Haven Island, as well as "close inshore grounds" stretching as far east as Mount Desert Island. During the nineteenth century it included the waters surrounding the outermost islands of the Maine coast some 20 to 30 km offshore. Rich (1947:58) states that the swordfish arrived early in July and that "inside Jeffrey's Ledge, about Boon Island, alongshore to Mount Desert ...were profitable fishing spots". Clarke (1884, quoted in Rich 1947:58–9) says that "In August the best grounds were Inner Jeffreys, and 12–15 miles offshore from Boon Island, and Wood Island, Me., some within 3 or 4 miles of land". During the Late Archaic period, however, there were villages at the inland heads of major bays, such as the Waterside site in Frenchman's Bay (Rowe 1940), which

accumulated large amounts of postcrania. Therefore, we suspect that swordfish swam well into large bays such as Penobscot Bay during the Late Archaic.

Ross and Biagi (1990) summarize the recent data on swordfishing up to 1990. The average dressed weight of fish caught on Georges Bank in June is 70 kg (150 lbs), while those caught on the Grand Banks of Newfoundland in August average 140 kg (300 lbs). Until recently, swordfishing has beena surface-water activity, but stomach contents and an occasional fish taken on a trawl-line demonstrate that swordfish feen at depths of 60 to 150 fathoms (120 to 300 m). The majority of the catch is made along the edge of the continental shelf when surface water temperatures range between 61 and 64°F. Very few fish are found in surface waters of less than 60°F and none occur in water below 55°F (13°C). Swordfish apparently come to the surface only during daylight, when they either lie quietly of swim lazily about. This behavior may be an attempt to rest or warm up in order to increase digestive rate after successful feeding in colder water at greater depth (Gibson 1981:38). Such swordfish are often easy to approach, and often contain full stomachs. Swordfish prey primarily on squid, on schooling smaller fish (mackerel, herring family species, and squid) and some deep sea fish. Based upon the frequency of cut and mutilated fish in swordfish stomachs, fishermen believe that swordfish use their sword to slash side-to-side through dense schools of prey fish, then pick up the dead and disabled. Other stomachs show no evidence of slashing.

Swordfish are often taken today by harpooning with a long, iron-tipped lance thrust from the bow of a medium-sized boat. The harpoon is tied to a (150 m) rope and floats. After being harpooned, tired fish are killed with a lance that cuts into the gills and causes it to bleed to death (Tibbo et. al. 1961). Another modern method includes long-lining, setting a series of baited hooks at considerable depth. Swordfishing methods must be described as a special case because there are no ethnohistoric accounts of aboriginal swordfishing in the Northeast. However, the modern harpoon and float technology seems a most logical model for the Late Archaic fishery.

Modern swordfishing in the Northeast is commonly done out in the edge of the Gulf Stream during summer from medium-sized motor boats equipped with harpooner's platform on a bowsprit and masthead observers platform, often aided by spotter aircraft (Cornell 1982). These activities often take place at the edge of the Northeast Channel into the Gulf of Maine, some 240–320km (150–200 miles) off-shore from the central Maine coast. However, swordfish are found in much lesser frequency inside the Gulf of Maine during August in some years (Bigelow and Schroeder 1953). During the early twentieth century, swordfishing in the Gulf of Maine was done from non-motorized sailing schooners (Clifford 1974:23–45). The advantage of visibility from the mast-top allowed these vessels to harpoon and recover up to 15 swordfish in an exceptional day of light breezes. The recovery of the fish was usually handled by dories put over by a mother ship, even though the fish was "ironed" from the bowsprit of the schooner. On flat calm days, all hunting was done from rowing dories. "Then we set up a small pulpit in the stern of each dory and row off, two men to a bo't, one pullin', one pushin'. You can't see so well in from the top of the mast, but you have the advantage of a flat sea. Both men are watchin'. Whey they spot a fin, they row up to him. The stern oarsman steps into the pulpit and heaves the harpoon into his broadside. When the fight is done, you roll him over the scale of the bo't, remove the dart..." and look for the next one (Clifford 1974: 28).

Swordfish are pugnacious once struck, and the hazard they pose to small boats is well known:

> The frequency of the records suggest that this is a very common occurrence... and occurs most often after the fish has been harpooned. (On our trip in) 1959, two swordfish punched holes through the bottoms of dories. One of the fish rammed its sword more than a foot through the planks and remained stuck until the protruding section of sword was sawed off and the stump driven out with an axe. The crewman who hauled the fish said that he felt the line go slack just before the fish hit the boat. This seemed to be a deliberate attack... (Tibbo et. al. 1961:13–14).

Multiple anecdotal accounts of swordfish attacks on dories are provided by Rich (1953:50–52; see also Gudger 1940).

Maine fisherman Charlie York also tells about swordfish attacking dories:

> My Uncle Bill had a close shave. We was out in the dory, see a fish, got up close to him, and I ironed him. He zoomed right around in a circle on his side and druv his sword through the side of the dory to his head. It seemed to go right into Bill and come out his shirt front he clutched his side and yelled.

This fish gave a big slat and pulled free. Did he git ye, Bill? I shouted. He took his hands down; use wa'n't hurt a mite. That sword had come up through his clothes but hadn't broke the skin. Just the least change of angle and it would of gone into his chest (Clifford 1974:29).

The earliest known record of such an attack was made by John Josselyn (1988:11) somewhere on the coast of the Canadian Maritime Provinces:

> ...in the afternoon we saw a great fish called the vehuella or Sword fish, having a long, strong and sharp finn like a Sword-blade on the top of his head, with which he pierced our Ship, and broke it off with striving to get loose, one of our sailors dived and brought it aboard.

Nicholas Denys (1908:356–7) provides a long account of two swordfish attacking one large whale with their swords, apparently to drive the whale away possibly from food fish. Such attacks on whales have been confirmed by modern observations (Peers and Karlsson 1976).

The best ethnographic accounts of swordfish hunting in north temperate conditions derive from the Ainu of northern Japan. There, swordfish hunting was a summer, offshore fishery, often out-of-sight of land. "(T)he fish swam round in groups of several near the surface. The fishermen chased them in dugouts with broadened sides, and pierced them with harpoons" (Watanabe 1972:146). This type of technology certainly was available to the Occupation 1 and 2 inhabitants of the Turner Farm site.

Based upon a variety of paleoecological indicators, we (Spiess et. al. 1983) believe that the inshore surface waters of the Gulf of Maine were warmer circa 4,000–5,000 B.P., and that the cold upwelling current in the eastern Gulf of Maine was less powerful than it is today. Under these conditions, swordfish would have followed their prey fish schools commonly into inshore waters along the central coast of Maine. Under such conditions, there would be no need for 100 km trips offshore. However, a sturdy-hulled vessel such as a dugout, rather than a birch bark canoe, would have been necessary for any kind of systematic swordfish hunting.

Sturgeon

Sturgeon are an anadramous fish requiring suitable riverine and estuarine waters for reproductive success (Smith 1985). In the Gulf of Maine they mature at around 20 years, and exhibit a long inter-spawning period of 2–5 years. Thus, they are highly sensitive to environmental change and very slow to recover from environmental insult. Chiefly because of dam building across their spawning rivers during the late nineteenth century, today's sturgeon populations are radically depleted from aboriginal levels.

Sturgeon spawn in brackish upper estuaries and in lower freshwater portions of rivers, in running waters over rock or rubble bottoms and in pools below waterfalls (Smith 1985:65–66). Calcined scutes from numerous Maine sites demonstrate that sturgeon ascended over low falls. The timing of spawning runs is regulated by temperature; adult sturgeon move into Maine rivers in May and June. Young fish inhabit lower freshwater rivers. Juveniles usually remain within the riverine system for 1–6 years before moving along the coast and onto the continental shelf where they reach maturity; large juveniles weigh up to 10 kg (22 lbs). Adults and juveniles alike rest along the bottom, sucking in bottom sediments that include various invertebrates such as insect larvae, worms, small bivalve and univalve mollusks, and dead animal material.

Non-spawning adults normally participate in spawning runs but do not feed. Adults have been aged up to 60 years, and lengths of 4.3–5.3 m (131–162 in) were not infrequently reported in the past. Average commercially caught females in South Carolina are 188 cm, 72kg (165lbs), and 16 years of age. The males average slightly smaller. Weight in kilograms approximates the third power of length in meters in this species, thus fish over 150kg were not rare.

All modern studies of sturgeon (references in Smith 1985; Lazzari et al. 1986) focus on the riverine portion of the life cycle. Perhaps their much reduced population status makes them nearly invisible in coastal waters. However, tagging studies have shown that adult sturgeon move north and south along the coast and among the islands of the Northeast, away from their spawning rivers (Lewis Flagg, Maine Department of Marine Resources, personal communication 1994).

Writing about 1630, Wood (1865:37) says "the best catching of them be on the shoals of Cape Codde and in the Rivers of Merrimacke." His comment that sturgeon were common inshore in shallow salt water is confirmed by sturgeon dorsal scutes recovered from several Maine shell middens including the Turner Farm site itself which is located miles from the nearest river that is large enough for an adult spawning sturgeon to swim in, let alone support a spawning population. We infer that large adult sturgeon were part of the shallow water (perhaps tidal flat) fish fauna, probably during the late spring, summer and fall when water temperatures were elevated.

Wood (1634:100) describes night fishing for sturgeon (see Figure 5–3), but the most detailed description of that activity appears in an account by Nicholas Denys (1672/2):

> The fishery is made in the night. Two Indians place themselves in a canoe; the one in front is upright, with a harpoon in his hand, the other is behind to steer, and he holds a torch of birch bark, and allows the canoe to float with the current of the tide. When the sturgeon perceives the fire, he comes and circles all around, turning from one side to the other. So soon as the harpooner sees his belly, he spears it below the scales. The fish, feeling himself struck, swims with great fury. The line is attached to the bow of the canoe, which he drags along with the spead of an arrow. It is necessary that the one in the stern shall steer exactly as the sturgeon goes, or otherwise it will overturn the canoe, as sometimes happens. It can swim well, but with all its strength it does not go with fury more than a hundred and fifty or two hundred paces. The (ride) being over, the line is drawn in, and it is brought dead against the side of the canoe. They then pass a cord with a slipknot over the tail, and they draw it thus to land, not be(ing) able to take it into a canoe because it is too heavy...

Massachusetts' Indians made "very strong Sturgeon nets with which they catch Sturgeons of 12, 14, and 16, some 18 foote long in the daytime....Their cordage is so even, soft, and smooth, that it looks more like silke than hempe; their Sturgeon nets be not deepe, not above 30 or 40 foote long, which in ebbing low waters they stake fast to the ground, where they are sure the Sturgeon will come, never looking more at it, till the next low water" (Wood 1885:100). The earliest direct evidence of perishable netting in eastern North America dates approximately 9,500–9,300 B.P. (Petersen et al. 1984). Stone objects possibly identifiable as net sinkers are present as early as 8,000–7,000 B.P. in the Northeast. Thus, the technology needed for producing net-

Figure 5-3. "Spearing salmon by night on the Restigouche," from Grant 1882:781, depicts Maliseets night fishing for salmon in New Brunswick. Note the a leister and birchbark torch to attract the fish.

based or weir-plus-netting-based fisheries has been available in eastern North America since long before the beginning of the Turner Farm site stratigraphic sequence. Speck (1997:86–87) mentions two Penobscot net forms but does not indicate the circumstances of their use. Kwa'phigan refers to a dipnet, a hoop netted of basswood cord on a handle about 10 feet long. Ala'pi refers to a rectangular net used for fishing. The shuttle used in making the net was the same as that found throughout the Montagnais and Cree area and is called lapiki'gan, "net tool," made of hardwood about 9 inches long by 2 inches wide.

There is one report of Iroquois on the Hudson River cutting summer-caught sturgeon into strips and drying it specifically for winter consumption (Benson 1937). Whether coastal Maine Indians applied the same food storage technique is unknown.

We now turn to reviews of the fish species of lesser importance at the Turner Farm site.

Large Fish — over 9 kg (20 lbs)

Striped Bass, Pollock, Halibut, and Salmon

Seven of 10 large edible fish that frequent the Gulf of Maine are represented by at least one positively identified bone from the Turner Farm site. These include, in the order of frequency found: cod, Atlantic sturgeon, swordfish, striped bass, pollock, halibut, and salmon. The first three are discussed above. Three large fish (tuna, dolphin and goosefish or angler) have not been identified. The remaining four identified large fish species (striped bass, pollock, halibut, and salmon) are only occasionally represented, frequencies parallel with their relative modern scarcity in the Fox Islands area. Striped bass rarely stray more than a mile or two off-shore (Bigelow and

Schroeder 1953). Pollock, abundant in the southern half of the Gulf of Maine, appear erratically north of Casco Bay. Halibut, a deep water fish, is present on shoal bottoms not far off the Fox Islands in July and August (Rich 1930) but is rare during the remainder of the year. Early European cod fishermen using long handlines looked upon halibut as a pest that seized the cod bait, entangled their lines and occupied a disproportionate amount of their time and energy in trying to bring them over the side (see Denys 1908). Bigelow and Schroeder (1953:257) indicate that before intensive fishing for halibut began in the nineteenth century the species could be caught in waters as shallow as 7–10 fathoms. However, the relative scarcity of halibut bone in the Turner Farm site sample suggests that long lines with baited hooks for bottom fishing were limited to shallower depths.

The near absence of salmon speaks for itself. There are no large streams on North Haven Island where spawning runs of salmon might be expected. The few salmon vertebrae recovered may represent an occasional fish hooked or gaffed while pursuing herring (Bigelow and Schroeder 1953:123–124), or caught in a shore-set weir or net, as it moved along the coast.

Medium-Size Fish — 2–9 kg (5–20 lbs)

Dogfish, Pollock, Haddock, White Hake, Cusk, Bluefish, Weakfish, Wolffish

Of eight medium-size species of edible fish found in the Gulf of Maine, six are represented at the Turner Farm site. The Spiney Dogfish, considered a food fish when fresh in Northwest European markets, is regarded as a destructive pest by American fishermen. Visits of the dogfish to the Gulf of Maine are seasonal, from the end of May through December (Clifford 1974:125). Their schools penetrate to all parts of the Gulf in the pursuit of mackerel, herring, cod, and haddock and all other species smaller than themselves. Dogfish are well represented among the Turner Farm site remains; and their frequency indicates their probable consumption as food, though capture may well have been incidental to fishing for other species upon which the dogfish prey.

Haddock, cusk and white hake belong to the cod family and are bottom feeders. Haddock and cusk prefer a depth greater than 30 fathoms. Both are represented by very few bones. White hake tolerates warmer water temperatures and can be found in tidal estuaries, yet the species is

apparently absent in the Turner Farm site sample. Weakfish, now rare in the Gulf of Maine, may have been present prehistorically at times (circa 4,000–5,000 B.P) when water temperatures were warmer. Unlike the bluefish, also a warm-water species, weakfish school close inshore in shallow water. Bluefish schools wander indifferently from oceanic depths to shallow estuaries, tearing their way through schools of mackerel, menhaden, herring, and alewives. This species is present inshore along the Maine coast only during late summer when water temperatures are warmest. The wolffish, by contrast, is a solitary year-round resident, living close to bottom among seaweed or rocks in cool to cold waters ranging from 1 to 80 fathoms or more in depth. It feeds exclusively on hard-shelled mollusks, crustaceans, and echinoderms. The occasional bluefish bones and conical wolffish teeth that appear in the Turner Farm site sample suggest that they were taken infrequently.

Smaller Fish — .23–2 kg (0.5 to 5 lbs)

Herring, Alewife, Blueback, Shad, Menhaden, Sea Trout, Capelin, Smelt, Silver Hake, Tomcod, White and Squirrel or Red Hake, American Dab, Yellowtail Flounder, Butterfish, Scup, Rosefish, Hooked-eared Sculpin, Long-horned Sculpin, Short-horn Sculpin, Sea Raven, Cunner, Tautog, and Ocean Pout

Only 12 of the 28 smaller edible fish species available in the Gulf of Maine were definitely identified in the Turner Farm site faunal sample, and several of these are represented by a single bone element only. This scarcity can be attributed to the incomplete comparative osteological sample available to us, to the small size of the bones which makes archaeological retrieval more difficult, and to poorer preservation for the same reason. All these factors make it more difficult to determine whether the absence of some species should be attributed to: a) absence of the species from the Fox Islands; b) unavailability of the species for aboriginal technical reasons; c) lack of aboriginal interest in the species; or d) technical problems in retrieval and identification from archaeological context.

Of the four possibilities, the first is most probable for scup and tautog, both of which prefer warmer waters than are now characteristic of the Fox Islands. (The presence of these species near the Fox Islands during Occupation 2, when there are indications of warmer water temperatures, cannot be ruled out.) At the other temperature extreme is capelin, a boreal (cold water) schooling species that appears only rarely in the waters of the Gulf of Maine today and has not been reported as far south as the Fox Islands.

The absence of certain fish that prefer deep waters, such as rosefish, witch flounder and ocean pout, might be attributed to limited fishing technology. (Though on rare occasions, such as during winter for the rosefish, they may be found in shallow waters). The absence of silver, white and squirrel or red hake, butterfish and sea raven can be attributed to the last two possibilities—a lack of interest in fishing for them or a failure in the archaeological retrieval and identification process.

The bones of the smaller schooling fish such as herring, alewife, blueback, smelt, shad, menhaden, and mackerel are tiny for the most part. However, the absolute scarcity of any vertebrae of herring size suggests that they were not brought to the site except, perhaps, as an accident or by-product of the pursuit of larger fish that preyed on them. One stream suitable for alewife spawning runs existed not far from the Turner Farm site and this might explain the single alewife vertebra recovered.

All of the remaining fish in this group, including the various flounders (with the exception of witch flounder and yellowtail flounder, which frequent deeper waters), the sculpins (with the exception of the hooked-eared sculpin, which prefers cooler waters), the tomcod and the cunner are characteristic of the inshore or coastal waters of the Gulf of Maine, particularly the cool waters in the vicinity of the Fox Islands where they are found year-round. The flounders are easily speared, and the flounders, sculpins, tomcod, and cunner bite a baited hook readily.

Tomcod in spawning condition are presently caught in smelt nets in the Kennebec River in January. Thus, winter-caught tomcod at the Turner Farm site may have been obtained in the estuaries of small drainages. Winter flounder is a brackish water spawner that moves in some numbers into brackish water along the central Maine coast in March, before ice-out. Winter flounder are not hard to catch with a movable stop net set across a shallow tidal channel, but the use of permanent weirs to catch these fish at this time of year would have been difficult because of moving ice. If weirs were used they probably would have been very lightly constructed or otherwise "expedient."

General Fishing Methods

A traditional method (Speck 1997) of taking mackerel, pollock and other schooling species was to jig for them with a fairly large-sized hook, or mogi'kan, weighted with a stone, without bait and attached to a long line of braided basswood fibre. The hook was made from a crotch of willow about four or five inches long, its point hardened by charring. To the back of this point, a long thin stone was lashed...." "The line...is of a fourply braid of basswood inner bark. Armed with this jigging outfit, they went among the fish and snagged them in the stomach by jerking the hook up and down in the water.

"...Gluskabe (the Penobscot culture hero) instructed man to take a bird's breast bone (furcula), rub one end upon a stone to sharpen it, and attach it to a line of wi'kobi, basswood, and this to a pole of hardwood..." Speck also mentions two forms of "gullet hooks' used by the Penobscot. One consisted of a sharpened bone set obliquely in a split wooden shank baited with a minnow; the other was a "toggle of bone splinter." It is unclear whether any of Speck's informants had tried these "old" methods, or were simply passing on hearsay.

Speck seems to have been describing other fishing methods from actual observation. He (1997:85) notes that among the Penobscot the fish spear or leister was in general use for getting "pollack and eels," following "the usual method of spearing from a canoe" (see Figure 5–3). Flounders were speared. "When they are down the bay or river and want flounders, the Indians find some cove where they can see the fish. Then they go ashore, cut and trim a few long spruce poles. The ends are next sharpened and a notch cut in. From the canoes they stick these crude spears into the flounders and pull them up. Turtles are obtained the same way...". Speck goes on to state:

> For not only large bay fish but also river fish- salmon, shad and others — the harpoon, si'gowan, with a toggle-head was used. This implement consisted of a ten-foot pole with a rectangular cavity in the end wrapped with an eelskin throng. Into this aperture was mortised the spearhead, fastened loosely to the main shaft by a double strip of rawhide. This was a shank with a single lateral barb, detachable from the main shaft under a little resistance. The shank or foreshaft and head are all in one, about a foot long, made of hardwood charred in a fire to

make it harder, with a barb an inch long on one side. The tying is ingenious, a doubled rawhide passed through a hold in the shaft and one in the shank of the spearhead, and tied with a double wrapped knot... (Ibid :87).

Speaking of the 1660s, Josselyn (1988:100) describes spearing of lobster, flouke (flounder), and lumps (sculpin?) with a self-pointed wooden spear, "a staff two or three yards long, made small and sharpened at one end, and nicked with deep nickes to take hold." This tool was used from a brich canoe in two fathoms of water on calm days. He also confirms the method of night fishing for sturgeon described by Denys.

> The *Bass* and *Blew-fiush* they take in harbours, and at the mouth of barr'd rivers being in their *canows*, striking them with a fisgig, a kind of dart or staff, to the lower end whereof they fasten a sharp jagged bone ... with a string fastened to it, as soon as the fish is struck they pull away the staff, leaving the bony head in the fishes body and fasten the other end of the string to the canow: Thus they will hale after them to shore half a dozen or half a score great fishes: this way they take sturgeion; and in dark evenings when they are upon the fishing ground near a bar of sand (where the sturgeon feeds upon small fishes (like Eals) that are called Lances ... The Indian lights a piece of dry birchbark which breaks out into flame & holds it over the side of his canow, the sturgeion seeing this glaring light mounts the surface of the water where he is slain and taken with a fisgig. (Josselyn 1988:110).

Josselyn also mentions taking alewives with "nets like a purse net put upon a round hooped stick with a handle."

Intertidal fish-trapping technology is at least as old as the Late Archaic period. Willoughby and S. J. Guernsey excavated a portion of a stake-and-wattle weir below 30 feet of recent sediment on Boylston Street in Boston's Back Bay during construction of the subway in 1913 (Willoughby 1935:6–10). The largest preserved upright stakes are 2½ inches in diameter. This arrangement recalls Wood's description of sturgeon nets staked to the ground during ebb tide, although the weir need not have been used specifically for sturgeon. The stakes recovered by Willoughby have since been radiocarbon dated to the Late Archaic period, and the weir is currently undergoing extensive modern restudy. Johnson (1942: 197ff.) summarizes the form and function of fishweirs on the Maine and Nova Scotian coast. He comments on the Boylston Street fishweir, which was constructed and reconstructed of large stakes with some space between them, as follows: (1) reconstruction of the weir indicates that the fishweir was the focus of Indian activity over a substantial period of time; (2) the construction of the weir indicates that it was either used for large species of fish, or it was strung with nets if used to catch small fish. The recent discovery of a wooden-stake fishweir complex in a lake in central Maine (Petersen et al. 1994), with radiocarbon dates ranging from ca. 6000 to 1700 B.P., and with associated stone construction tools and birchbark container fragments, provides a great opportunity to study weir forms that might also have been used in shallow salt water. Finally, Diereville (1933:113) describes, from seventeenth-century Nova Scotia, the use of weirs to catch flounder by both Micmacs and Acadian settlers.

SHELLFISH

Josselyn (1988:100) describes spearing lobsters with the same, two-meter long self-pointed wooden spear used on flounder: "When they spye the *lobster* crawling upon the sand in two fathom water, more or less, they stick him towards the head and bring him up. I have known thirty *Lobsters* thaken by an *Indian* lad in an hour and a half ...."

The two major species of bivalve mollusk collected by Turner Farm site inhabitants, soft-shelled clam and blue mussel, are intertidal species that do not move during their adult life cycle. Clams prefer a sandy, muddy, or clay bottom into which they burrow, leaving a small hole in the surface of the mud for the "siphon" feeding apparatus. Mussels form colonies of individuals by attaching themselves to each other or to a rock on gravel substrate.

Given the ubiquitous shell middens that dot the Maine coast, it is surprising that there are so few seventeenth century accounts of shellfish harvesting there. On the western Maine coast, according to Josselyn (1998:100), "Clams they dig out of the clambanks upon the flats and in creeks when it is low water, where they are bedded sometimes a yard deep one upon the other, the beds a quarter of a mile in length, and less...", but he gives no information on seasonality. Champlain (1922, vol. 3:308) implies that on the eastern Maine coast mollusks ("coquillage") were eaten during the winter when a lack of snow made hunting unproductive. As late as 1709, winter remained "the usual Season of visiting their Clam-banks..." (Penhallow 1973:60).

Spiess and Hedden (1983), Barber (1982) and Chase (in Sanger 1987:81) have all reported that the clams from prehistoric sites are much larger, on average, than modern clams. (However, small clams are found at some sites [Spiess et al. 1990].) Today soft-shelled clams are usually harvested with a metal fork or "rake" that turns over clumps of inter-tidal sediment. Sanger (1987:80–83) has suggested two factors that may explain the size variability. The first is that shell middens were intermittently occupied, thus allowing clam populations to recover from periods harvesting. Second, as aboriginal inhabitants did not have a digging tool capable of turning over large hunks of sticky inter-tidal sediments and breaking it up efficiently, hand-recovery of clams may have focussed on the lower portions of the intertidal zone, where sediment particle size is smaller and the matrix in which the clam grows is in fact a soft muddy ooze (on most flats). In this soft ooze, it is possible to "pick" clams by squeezing one's fingers together, forcing them down the siphon hole until encountering the clam, then grasping it and pulling the whole organism out of the mud. Sanger reasons the muddy lower inter-tidal zone is much lower in total area than the inter-tidal zone as a whole, but the clams can grow faster because they have access to food for more hours during a tidal cycle. It is possible for the harvester to guess the size of the clam from the size of the siphon hole, so selectivity for large size is one possible harvesting strategy. After a certain amount of harvest pressure, measured in days to months depending on the harvesting intensity, the harvesters would be subject to diminishing returns as they begin to pick smaller and smaller clams, on average. At that time a move to another location might have been advantageous.

There is scanty ethnohistoric evidence for shellfish storage in the Northeast (Black and Whitehead 1988). Because most shellfish seasonality evidence from the Maine and Maritime coast points toward late winter and early spring harvesting (Spiess and Hedden 1983; Chapter 3 herein), when other food is scarce, we assume that most shellfish were consumed expediently. Hence we assume that the collecting and processing of shellfish was done in small batches similar to the proverbial "basketload" of clams.

6

The Turner Farm Fauna Synthesis:
Human Subsistance and Environmental Change

Introduction

In this summary chapter we use the faunal data, known animal behavior patterns, and ethnograpically documented hunting techniques presented in earlier chapters to produce qualitative reconstructions of subsistence patterns for each occupation. These reconstructions are presented as seasonal cycles specific to the Turner Farm site. A picture of the range of economic variability among contemperanious communities over the central Maine coast region must await future studies. A section on the faunal content of features and on horizontal distribution patterns summarizes data presented in detail elsewhere (Spiess and Lewis 1995), and provides further background for understanding the human behavior that created the faunal record. Seasonal subsistence calendars for each occupation allow visual interpretation of annual resource use patterns as well as changes in resource emphasis over time.

We also address the interpretation of data on two taxa in particular: swordfish and large whales. Both are poorly understood, and each represents the major "wild card" in economic reconstruction of a particular period of time. If our understanding of the meager data on these two species is weak, then our economic reconstructions for the Moorehead phase and the Late Ceramic period become tenuous.

Finally, we examine diachronic (time-dependent) change in the faunal record and compare it with an outline of environmental change. Our purpose is to explore the relative roles of human choice and "adaptation" versus environmental change in Gulf of Maine prehistory. Again, our analysis is exploratory. Greater rigor must await future increases in data samples, and especially comparison with other sites.

SHELL MIDDEN FAUNAS IN NEW ENGLAND AND THE MARITIME PROVINCES

Although it is not the only modern faunal analysis of a shell midden in New England and the Maritime Provinces, ours may be the most detailed and rigorous, and we hope that it will serve as a basis for compiling regional reconstructions. The review of other sites that follows is organized geographically, first looking at Penobscot Bay then at the central coast of Maine eastward from Penobscot Bay into the Maritime Provinces, and finally westward from Penobscot Bay to southern New England. The amount of data cited from unpublished sources is greater nearer to Penobscot Bay because of the authors' geographic and research experience. For other New England faunas with greater time depth and interior geographic location, mostly based on calcined bone assemblages, the reader is referred to Spiess 1992.

Penobscot Bay to the Maritime Provinces

The Kidder Point site at the head of Penobscot Bay (see map, Figure 6–1) has been the only other detailed, fully published faunal analysis from the coast of Maine (Spiess and Hedden 1983). Kidder Point was a single-component Early to Middle Ceramic period spring and summer occupation. Season of occupation was investigated using bird medullary bone, tooth eruption, tooth sectioning, and shell sectioning techniques (Spiess and Hedden 1983:197–206). A minimum of 32,000 clams contributed to the shell in one area of the occupation. However, Bourque has sampled some 40 additional shell middens in Penobscot Bay for which the faunal analysis is underway or not yet begun.

These data will eventually allow the reconstruction of seasonal settlement patterns for Penobscot Bay from the Susquehanna tradition onward.

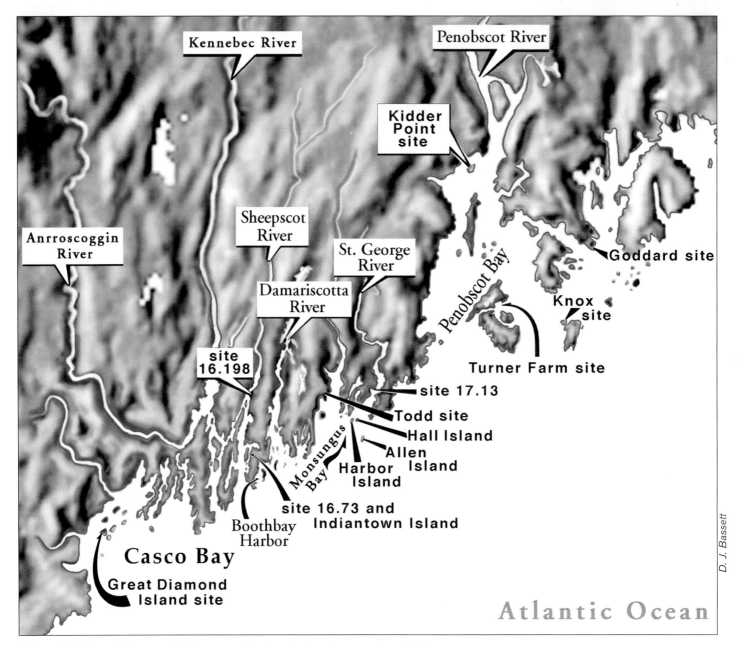

Figure 6-1. Map of the central Maine coast showing site locations mentioned in the text.

On the western fringes of Penobscot Bay, Bourque (unpublished 1993), Eldridge (1990), and Spiess (unpublished) have sampled a number of shell middens from the St. George estuary and offshore islands, and larger shell middens on the mainland (e.g., site 17.13, Spiess and Eldridge 1985). Faunal materials from these sites are undergoing analysis under protocols used in this study, so the data will be comparable. In Muscongus Bay, just west of the St. George, several sites have been tested by Kellogg (1984, 1985) and Spiess (1984a). It is evident from this work that the outer islands of the St. George and Muscongus Bay region (e.g., Allen, Harbor, and Hall Islands) were used during the Ceramic period as summer camps for fishing, fowling, and trapping the now-extinct sea mink. The Todd site, excavated by David Sanger, has produced a large and well-stratified faunal sample beginning with the Susquehanna tradition. This site has been the subject of thesis work (Mack 1994, Skinas 1987, and others), and the fauna have been partially identified but remain unpublished. When the larger faunal collections from the Todd site, site 17.13, and Allen's Island (site 17.76) have been fully reported using the techniques and attributes such as those used for the Turner Farm assemblage, an outline of settlement patterns in the St. George estuary and Muscongus Bay will be possible.

Just east of Penobscot Bay, Bourque (1992) , Cox (1983, 1992) and Kopec (Cox and Kopec 1988) have sampled several shell middens, with their faunal remains variously reported. Bourque (1992: Appendix 8) contains numbers of identified specimen counts for three of these sites. Cox's reports (Cox and Kopec 1988:42, identification by Spiess) contain some summary faunal counts, and reports of rare identifications such as caribou teeth. The Goddard site, a non-shell midden coastal site, has yielded a large Ceramic period faunal collection providing evidence of an economic focus on summer seal hunting. A much smaller, calcined Moorehead phase faunal sample from the Goddard site records swordfish and deer hunting similar to the Turner Farm Occupation 2 sample (Cox in prep., Spiess 1990b).

The faunal sample from the Nevin site (Byers 1979), on Blue Hill Bay, is undergoing reanalysis (Hamilton and Crader, personal communication 1996). Swordfish are present in the Late Archaic levels at the Nevin site. Faunal remains from the Richards site, a nearby Ceramic period shell midden, are also being analyzed.

Faunal remains from a series of early and middle Ceramic period house pits at the Knox site, again just east of Penobscot Bay, have been summarily reported (Belcher 1988, 1989a, 1989b). In this case, attempts at reconstructing season of occupation are based on species presence or absence, without benefit of tooth sectioning. Subsistence remains from the Early Ceramic period assemblage (n=685) are dominated by fish, primarily sculpin and cod, with sea mink, deer and bird bone also present. Seasonality of the occupation is estimated on the basis of scoters (a duck, *Melanitta*), said to be present from late summer to late fall, and sculpin, thought to be present in late fall and early spring. Actually, scoters are abundant in spring and fall, common during winter and uncommon (non-breeding) during summer (e.g., Pierson and Pierson 1981). The middle Ceramic period faunal assemblage (n=3108) is dominated by fish, primarily cod and sculpin, plus bird, sea mink and deer. A predominance of Cod plus the presence of scoters again is used to deduce a spring, summer and fall occupation. Shell sectioning (n=68) revealed a "growth season" (i.e., May through December) harvest. In fact, these assemblages could reflect merely a late spring and summer occupation if the scoters are spring migrants or summer non-breeding residents.

Further east, in the Roque Island area (see map, Figure 6–2), Sanger has tested several sites, finding large numbers of sea mink and other furbearers, plus seal, moose and deer.

Although the work has not been published in detail, Sanger and Chase (1983) report MNI and NISP of various species, along with several observations of interest, such as the fact that most of the mammal material from house floors is cranial, while much of the material from shell midden dump areas is postcranial. They infer winter occupation is inferred on the basis of marker species (e.g., scaup, and tomcod). Test excavation of a small site on Cobscook Bay yielded a faunal collection including shellfish, a variety of terrestrial and marine mammals, birds, and fish. Spiess et. al. (1990) present NISP and skeletal element counts, and infer a February through July season-of-occupation estimate is inferred from tooth eruption data.

Shell midden excavations and faunal analyses on sites from the New Brunswick side of Passamaquoddy Bay include summary publications (Bonnichsen and Sanger 1977; Davis 1978; Sanger 1987), a thesis (McCormick 1980) and unpublished reports (Burns 1970, Stewart 1974). These studies overlap in reporting faunal data from four sites: Davis (1978) summarizes Teacher's Cove, Sanger (1987) summarizes the Carson site, Stewart (1974) reports primary data from the Carson site, and Burns (1970) reports primary data from Teacher's Cove, Sand Point, and Minister's Island. McCormick (1980) provides an MNI analysis for various features from all four sites based on bone element counts. A mixed maritime, littoral, and terrestrial economy is indicated, with clams, beaver, deer, caribou, moose, seals, and various bird and fish species comprising most of the faunal remains. Seasonality estimates, where made, are primarily based upon species (mostly bird) presence/absence. At the Carson site, for example, Stewart (Sanger 1987:69) infers a cold-season occupation (fall through early spring), although she (Stewart 1974:31–360) notes a few bones of summer resident species. Stewart (1974:35–37) also uses eruption and age criteria of loose beaver teeth to examine the season-of-death of young beaver. She states that beaver in New Brunswick are born in April and May, and reports two teeth from one or more individuals killed at 9 to 9.5 months, and a mandible at 5 to 5.5 months age. Although Stewart assigns the latter to December to May (apparently a math error), it could represent a kill between September and November. Stewart's study of Carson site seasonality is the most detailed of these seasonality studies, none of which include annual growth increment analysis. Burns (1970) used primarily bird species presence/absence to infer a winter occupation to Sand Point and Teacher's Cove, and a multi-seasonal occupation to Minister's Island. One interesting conclusion emerged from McCormick's MNI analysis: 29 moose bones were recovered from three of the four houses at Sand Point. Based upon bone elements recovered, a minimum of one moose was represented

(McCormick 1980: 97), leading McCormick to infer the sharing of a single carcass among the three houses. This MNI analysis did not, however, take epiphyseal fusion or bone measurements into consideration, which could have been used to further test these hypotheses.

David Black (1983, 1985, 1992) has published several detailed faunal analyses of several Ceramic period sites in the Bliss Islands on the New Brunswick portion of Passamaquoddy Bay, and inferred a mixed multi-seasonal economy based upon shellfish collecting, seal and land mammal hunting, fishing and bird hunting. Subsistence practices at each site were relatively specialized (contra Sanger 1985a), focussing on shellfish and marine resources (Black 1992:117). Black's work includes shell midden quantification using column samples, and seasonality determination using shell sectioning and tooth sectioning. Much of Black's seasonality work included consultation with Spiess (personal communication to David Black, January 1988), who did tooth sectioning analysis, so that his results should be comparable with ours. Some theoretical considerations, especially with respect to shellfish preservation and storage, have also come from this work (Black and Whitehead 1988).

Stewart (1986; see Spiess 1989) has published one other major shell midden faunal analysis from a site at Delorey Island in northeast Nova Scotia (Stewart 1986; see Spiess 1989). The collection numbers 1,400 vertebrate specimens, including fish, land and sea mammals, and birds dating from the "Late Woodland" period. The occupation was multi-seasonal. The faunal data reported are mostly NISP, MNI and element counts, with little in the way of additional attributes (e.g., tooth wear, epiphyseal fusion). Seasonality information is based mainly on foetal cervid bones, lack of bird medullary bone, and in part on limited tooth sectioning by Spiess, who also contributed some comments on faunal identifications, so the data are comparable with some from the Maine coast and the Bliss Islands.

A detailed study by Rojo (1990) of fish bone from a "Woodland" period shell midden near Halifax, Nova Scotia, includes MNI, element counts, size and weight regressions, and seasonality information from species presence/absence and vertebral growth rings. The fishing was a warm-season through late fall activity, although the author states that it was impossible to differentiate end-of-growth from possible early beginning-of-new-growth on some vertebrae. Unfortunately this detailed report only examined the fish remains from the site.

Western Maine to Southern New England

Returning to Maine, and moving west from the central coastal Penobscot Bay region, David Sanger has led a multidisciplinary investigation of the paleoecology and human ecology of the Boothbay Harbor area (Damariscotta and Sheepscot River estuaries), including faunal samples from several dozen shell midden sites. Detailed multi-site faunal sample analyses have been presented in several theses, including one concentrating on the mammals and shellfish (Chase 1986), and the other (Carlson 1986) on fish. These analyses included faunal remains collected from screens as well as from laboratory-analyzed column samples; faunal counts and attributes are presented in detail. Season-of-occupation estimates were made for many sites by both authors using annual layers (teeth and shellfish in one, fish vertebrae in another), and by using fish species presence/absence based upon modern inshore fisheries census data. Despite the depth and breadth of these two analyses, the seasonality conclusions for certain sites appear to contradict each other. For example, the fish data for site 16.73, on Fort Island are interpreted as summer/early fall occupation, while the shellfish and mammal data are interpreted as winter and spring. And at site 16.198 at Parson's Creek, the fish data are interpreted as winter occupation, while the shellfish and mammals indicate late winter and spring (into May and June). These collections deserve a detailed reanalysis because the multi-site sample has the potential for elucidating a Ceramic period seasonal settlement pattern in the two estuaries involved. Either the seasonality interpretations are flawed or many of the sites are multi-seasonal in occupation, each including a series of seasonally different economies. And although the studies are more than a decade old, the data they include still represents the largest localized sample yet reported from coastal New England or the Maritimes.

Integration of these Boothbay-region faunal data might ultimately compliment an intensive faunal analysis of stratified Ceramic period faunal assemblages excavated from the Indiantown Island site near Boothbay under the direction of Deborah Wilson in 1995 and 1996. A half-dozen archaeologists with faunal expertise (including the authors) have formed an informal working group to provide a detailed faunal analysis of this collection. Techniques will be comparable with this study, but much more detail will be provided on such aspects of the faunal assemblage as taphonomy, and bone tool production.

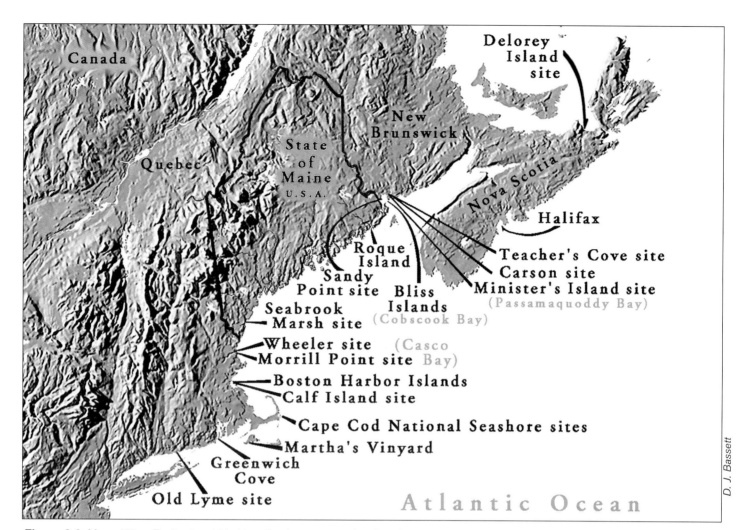

Figure 6-2. Map of New England and Maritime Provinces coast showing site locations mentioned in the text.

There has been a great deal of site testing and faunal analysis of shell middens in Casco Bay, including some summary publications (Yesner 1980a, 1980b), and unpublished reports (Hamilton 1992). One site on Great Diamond Island yielded bones from very large cod and other fish apparently from storage or garbage pits, along with a mixed terrestrial and inshore marine vertebrate and invertebrate fauna (Hamilton 1985). Hamilton used tooth sectioning, epiphyseal fusion, and tooth eruption to develop seasonality information following the techniques used in the Turner Farm site analysis. Hamilton (1985:390–493) presented the data in detail, including MNI counts and attributes comparable with our data. Faunal work on other Casco Bay sites, such as the Basin site, with its assemblage of calcined Late Archaic fauna, is ongoing and unpublished.

The Seabrook Marsh site is the only coastal New Hampshire faunal sample to be well-analyzed and reported (Robinson 1985). This assemblage comes from a site that is submerged

by coastal subsidence and covered by a tidal marsh; it is unclear whether it once was a shell midden. The faunal remains date from the Small Stemmed Point (Late Archaic) tradition, roughly contemporary with Occupation 1 at the Turner Farm. They record active swordfish hunting, as well as other salt-water fishing. The faunal data are presented as counts and percentages, with some text comments on attributes such as size.

Waters (1962) provided a faunal list from several sites on Martha's Vineyard, Massachusetts. In northeastern Massachusetts, the small sample from the Wheeler site remains the best-reported (Barber 1982). Barber (1983) also tested other nearby sites. The ceramic assemblage at the Wheeler site indicates multi-component middle and late Ceramic period occupations. Barber interprets a large number of small hearths and associated post molds as drying racks, where a surplus of food harvested during the fall was processed for winter use. Barber (1982:60) estimates that 117,000 soft-shelled clams contributed to the clam shell in the area excavated. Season of clam harvest was investigated by sectioning and reading annual layers in a small sample (n=19), with season of harvest ranging from June to November with a peak in September (Barber 1982:76). The metric data used to make these determinations are not reported. A sample of 24 gadid (cod family) fish scales were also read for seasonality, for which the period of rapid growth was assumed to be April through November (see Chapter 2 and 5 for a discussion of gadid behavior and annular growth). Barber (1982:79) reports fishing in September and October, but his data may indicate cod fishing in late July and August primarily. Two male deer skulls were found with antlers still attached (late summer to fall). Deer teeth were sectioned (by Spiess), but only one was found to be readable; it showed an annulus forming, indicating death in winter or early spring. Barber summarized the Wheeler site as a late fall (clam and cod?) processing station, to provide a surplus of food for winter use. This conclusion is based on the assignment of gadid seasonality one or two months later in the fall than supportable, ignoring the wide range of summer and fall shell collection data, and emphasized the only sectioned readable deer tooth. Evidently the site actually represents spring through fall occupation, instead of late fall.

Barber (1983) excavated in three other sites near the Wheeler's site (Morrill Point, Whittall, and Sweet Apple Tree), but only the Morrill Point site yielded a significant faunal assemblage, reported only as "percentage of total flesh weight", lacking numbers of identified specimens (Barber 1983:118).

Shell midden faunal samples have been recovered from some sites on the Boston Harbor Islands, but are reported in summary only. For the Calf Island site, MNI counts are reported, and season of occupation is deduced from species presence-absence (Luedtke 1980). Extensive shell midden testing has occurred on Cape Cod as part of a study in the National Seashore. Some of the data from this work have been reported (McManamon 1984). The unpublished faunal study (Spiess 1984b) contains detailed seasonality and faunal attribute information comparable with this study. Further shell midden faunal analysis is ongoing for sites on Cape Cod (Bradley and Spiess 1994). Shaw (1994) reports on excavations at the Willowbend site on the south shore of Cape Cod, but the faunal sample remains unpublished. South of Cape Cod, of course, Ritchie's landmark study of Martha's Vineyard (Ritchie 1969) includes faunal identification counts. More recently, theses by Carlson (1990) and others have reported on faunal studies focused on seasonality.

David Bernstein's (1988, 1993) faunal analysis of the Ceramic period (Early and Middle Woodland) Greenwich Cove site on Potowomut Neck, Rhode Island (Bernstein 1988, 1993) provides one of the more detailed studies so far published for any part of the New England coast. The study includes numbers of identified specimens, minimum numbers of individuals, and seasonality information from vertebrate and invertebrate growth increments. The vertebrate sample is small (n=3,047) and attributes such as tooth eruption, epiphyseal fusion and measured size are rarely given, so the data are only partially compatible with this study. Bernstein's (1993:92-93) discussion of the difficult and controversial differentiation between red and gray fox fails to mention the skeletal elements identified. Throughout the occupation sequence, mammals, primarily white-tailed deer, provided the majority of the faunal sample, although the resource base included shellfish and a few reptile and bird species. Despite the small sample size, Bernstein (1993:102) detects an increase in the number of taxa harvested (i.e., the intensity and breadth of the faunal resource base through time)

Much work has apparently been done on Potowomut Neck, than has been fully published. Kerber (1984, 1984/5) partially reports faunal work at four shell middens including shell density, shell species counts (quahog, oyster, and soft-shelled clam), and some vertebrate bone identifications. Seasonality inferences are based upon a small sample (n=30?) of sectioned quahog shells, and "juvenile deer" jaws. In the case of the latter, Kerber (1984/5:109) does not mention which teeth are in what state of eruption, so that even the assessment of a summer/early fall kill cannot be judged independently. A fifth site, the Lambert Farm site, also contains quahog shell. Although a summary report is now available (Kerber 1997a), a detailed report on a dog burial from the site (Kerber et al. 1989) makes it evident that much more faunal data exist in these sites than has been reported. Lambert Farm season-of-death information is reported in summary fashion for quahogs, deer and moose (Kerber 1997a:60–61). Moose hunting during the winter is inferred at these sites based on ethno-historic analogy.

Amarosi (1991) has reanalized vertebrate fauna excavated in 1939 and 1940 from a shell midden in Old Lyme, Connecticut. The site has components ranging from Late Archaic to Late Woodland (i.e. late Ceramic period in our terminology), with the whole assemblage treated as a unit because of weak stratigraphic provenience. The data are presented as detailed NISP and element counts, with measurements of several taxa following von den Driesch (1976). Thus, the measurements presented are comparable in this regard with those for the Turner Farm site. However, Amorosi does not present epiphyseal fusion or tooth eruption data, and his spring and fall seasonality estimates (Amorosi 1991:97) represent little more than estimates based on goose species presence and "numerous remains of adult deer." However, this report does represent a very useful summary of prehistoric archaeofaunas from the Northeast. In sum, while the potential certainly exists for multisite comparative studies and reconstructions of regional coastal economies, much work remains to be done to realize this potential.

SUMMARY OF ECONOMIC FOCUS AND HUNTING METHODS AT THE TURNER FARM

The faunal analyses reviewed above provide a background for evaluating the faunal data from the Turner Farm site. We now turn to a summary of those data and a consideration of their significance to interpretations of the site's periods of occupation in a regional context. White-tailed deer hunting was pursued multi-seasonally during all occupations, although there appears to have been a summer hiatus in deer hunting during Occupation 2. Hunting was non-selective with respect to age and sex for the most part. There is no positive evidence from the archaeological record for the use of large drives. However, the island setting is well suited for small-scale drives ending in water. Moreover, a wide variety of ethnographically-attested techniques such as stalking and the use of decoys and traps, could have been used to take individual deer. The attention paid to dogs in Occupation 2, as indicated by burials (see Bourque 1995:86), especially means that trained dogs must have contributed to finding or driving deer. Whole deer carcasses were delivered to the Turner Farm site for butchery. Deer carcass butchery is quite uniform over time; variability focussed on the final stages of carcass processing, perhaps reflecting differing efforts to extract more fat.

During Occupation 2 deer hunting occurred seasonally from October or November through April or May. Possibly a few deer were taken in June or July. Evidence from Occupation 3 and 4 indicate year-round hunting. The sample from the plow zone is small, but suggests that deer hunting occurred at least during the summer and early fall during the late Ceramic period.

Deer demographic data indicate an increase in proportion of younger (< 5 years) deer killed after Occupation 2. The Occupations 3, 4, and plow zone samples share similar deer demographic statistics. Deer postcranial measurements demonstrate a shift toward smaller mean size after Occupation 3. Although this effect is partially due to demographics of the kill, with younger (3-year-old) deer being recorded as smaller deer, Occupation 4 still does preserve evidence of large bucks, equivalent in size to those in the Occupation 2 sample. We suggest that the environmental conditions controlling or selecting for deer growth did not change radically, so that large deer body size was still biologically attainable. Rather, we suggest that more deer were killed before reaching large size, and that proportionately fewer bucks survived to reach full maturity during Occupation 4. Moreover, the proportion of deer killed to other large vertebrates drops significantly after Occupation 2. At the same time the seasonality of deer hunting spreads from fall-winter-spring to include the whole year. These data suggest increased relative pressure on the deer herd, i.e. more hunting kills as a proportion of total deer herd size. The data do not, however, necessarily reflect an increased total annual kill since the deer herd itself may have been decreasing, or the human population increasing, or both.

The long-term sustainable yield of the large islands in Penobscot Bay was probably between 1 and 3 deer per square mile per year. Total land area for the islands of North Haven, Vinalhaven and nearby islands approximates 30 square miles. We conclude that full use of the island deer herd, between 30 and 90 individuals killed per year, was the rule during the Ceramic period if not before.

Moose definitely increased in importance throughout the Turner Farm site occupation sequence, approaching an order-of-magnitude relative to deer between Occupations 2 and 4. Even during the Ceramic period they were probably hunted on the large islands in Penobscot Bay singly or small groups of 2–3 individuals. Early European accounts indicate that moose were plentiful in Penobscot Bay. However, snowfalls probably never approached the critical depth where hunters on snowshoes could be assured of killing all of a group of wintering moose. Again, dogs may have contributed substantially to hunting moose. Moose carcasses were evidently partially butchered where they fell, and were brought to the site as butchered "packages" of meat.

The Occupation 2 population paid less attention to seals than did any later group. During Occupation 3, tooth sectioning of grey and harbor seal teeth confirm seal hunting during seal pupping and mating season. Based upon the fact that Occupation 3 was less maritime oriented than other occupations at the Turner Farm, we conclude that Occupation 3 seal hunting involved attacks upon rookeries. Seal hunting during the Ceramic period diversified seasonally and intensified dramatically. The demographic distribution of the seal kill can be coupled with seasonality reconstructions as follows. Studies of ringed seal *(Phoca hispida)* in the high arctic have shown that Eskimo hunting of seals on the spring ice, at pupping and mating time, takes a sample composed of adult females and foetal or newborn pups (Smith 1973). We expect this situation to be analogous to attacks on pupping and breeding colonies in Penobscot Bay (with the different seasons of pupping for harbor and grey seals). Seal hunters in Labrador (both Eskimo and settler) have commented to Spiess that open-water hunting takes a disproportionately high number of adolescent seals, which seem to be relatively inexperienced at avoiding boat-based hunters compared with older seals. We therefore surmise that a variety of open-water seal hunting techniques with some sort of harpoon technology, as well as raids on rookeries, were involved. We use these observations to interpret the Turner Farm site data.

In Occupation 3, the demographic data (5 specimens) represent only foetal and adult seals, consistent with raids on pupping and breeding colonies in season. During the Ceramic period, as the seasonality of seal hunting diversifies so did the seal kill demography to include foetal-newborn, adult and immature seals. The seasonality data still indicate a focus on attacking concentrations of seals at pupping time. However, immature seals form nearly 40% of the sample, indicating some open-water hunting. Finally, the latest Ceramic period, represented by the plow zone material, shows a further increase in the proportion of immature seals (60% in a modest sample). Thus, as the seasonality of hunting both grey and harbor seals became more diversified, seals apparently also became a primary source of meat and fat. For these reasons we interpret at least the latest Ceramic period seal hunting as a very competent, multi-seasonal, open-water boat-based activity.

Bears were hunted most often in late fall, winter, or early spring, perhaps involving a variety of hunting techniques such as locating bears in their winter dens, possibly using dogs. Bears were undoubtedly also killed with spear or bow and arrow when encountered during the rest of the year.

The prevalence of furbearers in the Turner Farm sample indicate a highly developed trapping technology, as well as specialized hunting techniques for some species. Sea mink were a focus of special trapping or hunting efforts, perhaps aided by dogs. The seasonality evidence indicates a late winter/early spring focus on sea mink procurement, but this reconstruction is provisional because no modern analog is available for this extinct species.

A few beaver might have been available locally on the large islands in Penobscot Bay, since freshwater marshes and small streams are present. Winter hunting is confirmed for the Ceramic period. Relatively little beaver hunting or trapping occurred during Occupation 2, and what did occur was basically subsistence-oriented. Later in time, the use of beaver pelts apparently increased, probably for use as clothing. Beaver pelts may also have become important as trade items. During the Ceramic period as well, there was a parallel increase in the attention paid to a wide variety of fur-bearing species, reinforcing the idea that peltries became economically important well before European contact.

Bird hunting included raids on colonies of alcids (guillemots, puffins), and other colonial nesting species such as great blue herons. Other water birds, particularly ducks and geese, were killed in great numbers. Ethnographic accounts of nets and night ambushes using torches provide probable explanations for the faunal evidence. Duck hunting in particular was both a cold-season and warm-season activity, although the species involved differed with the season. Other bird species, birds-of-prey for example, must have been individual targets perhaps taken for a specific reason, such as use of particular feathers.

Bird hunting was of relatively little importance during Occupation 2, compared with later times. More attention was paid, proportionately, to the great auk than to other birds; awks may have been taken incidentally at sea when fishing. Generalized inshore bird hunting, for geese, cormorants, ducks, and small alcids, possibly occurred year-round. Herons were definitely hunted during the summer, loons and medium-sized alcids during the late fall to winter. During Occupation 3, bird hunting was relatively twice as important as during Occupation 2, but the pattern did not change greatly except for less emphasis on the great auk. During the Ceramic period, late fall to winter bird hunting for loons and scaup (inshore wintering species) increased, as all bird hunting became much more important. Spring and summer bird hunting took geese, ducks, small alcids, great auk, herons, and grebe. We infer that more effort was expended on bird hunting during fall migrations than previously. This pattern of bird hunting continues during the late Ceramic period (plow zone).

Cod were a strong focus of summer fishing during Occupation 2, consistently taking very large fish. Based upon the large fishhooks recovered from Occupation 2 deposits (Bourque 1995:77), we suspect a sophisticated hook-and-line method was used. Whether it involved mollusc-baited hooks or simple jigging is unknown. Flounder, sculpin and sturgeon were taken inshore during Occupation 3 and the Ceramic period. Brush weirs set on tidal flats, and nets, were the likely methods employed, as well as small baited hooks (Bourque 1995:193) and leisters. Harpoons may have aided in landing huge sturgeon (Bourque 1995:71–72). A variety of species of lesser importance could also have been taken with hook-and-line. The seasonality of fishing for (several) flounder species, sculpin and sturgeon, and many minor fish species, is difficult to reconstruct because of a paucity of modern baseline biological data.

Occupation 2 is decidedly specialized in its fishing, concentrating on cod and swordfish, two species that can reach huge size. During Occupation 3, the importance of cod and swordfish drop dramatically. As pointed out above, swordfish was apparently not hunted at all during Occupation 3, and the codfishing season seems to have shifted toward fall rather than summer. Sturgeon use also drops. Flounder, and possibly sculpin, become a year-round resource but one of minor importance.

Exploitation of many diverse fish species began with Occupation 4. Sturgeon must have been the most important fish resource, judging from its relative frequency and size. Flounder and sculpin fishing became important, and increased in importance throughout Occupation 4. These species are joined by an impressive diversity of other fish species (especially dogfish) as minor resources. The fishing seems to have had an "in shore" focus based upon sturgeon and flounder. The increased importance of seal and bird hunting may be a corollary of inshore marine activity.

Soft-shelled clams provided the focus of shellfish harvesting, which occurred mostly during winter and early spring. Large numbers of soft-shelled clams were harvested in late winter and early spring by Occupation 2 and all subsequent residents. There is no evidence of size selectivity in clam harvest, although some very large individuals were harvested; nor does the average size or seasonality change over time. Apparently clams provided a major stable resource during a time of scarce food supply. By analogy with many ethnographically known populations, shellfish harvesting was probably pursued by most of the population not involved with hunting or fishing when other food was scarce.

Approximately 1 million clams were deposited in the excavated area by Occupation 2 and 800,000 by Occupation 3. Shellfish were also collected by Occupation I residents, but the small sample size precludes quantification. However, the relative contribution to the diet of clams versus vertebrates decreased by a factor of two from Occupation 2 to the Late Ceramic occupation, i.e., clams became relatively less important. They could, nonetheless, have remained important as emergency or "lean season" food.

We hypothesize that the method of "picking" clams, by inserting fingers in their siphon holes at low tide and pulling them from the mud, stayed in use over time. Because this method selects for large individuals, the picking method apparently helped maintain the constant average size. In this case, increasing human pressure on the clam resource would not be reflected by a decrease in average size over time.

FEATURE CONTENTS AND HORIZONTAL PATTERNING: A SUMMARY

This section summarizes horizontal distribution data and data on the faunal content of features, which are presented in greater detail in Spiess and Lewis 1995. These data provide additional insight into site formation processes and, in some cases, methods of hunting or use patterns.

Occupation 2

Three kinds of features occur in Occupation 2: hearths, pits, and dog burials. Faunal samples from the hearths are too small to be informative. Faunal suites associated with the dog burials are small, but they are unusual. For example, Feature 22-1973 is a cache pit apparently associated with a dog burial containing two Cervid distal tarsal bones (*naviculo-cuboid*), one each from a deer and a moose, as well as a sea mink skull. Moose are rare in Occupation 2, and inclusion of the same moose skeletal element with one of deer, the only Cervid bones in the feature, must have had some symbolic significance.

The Occupation 2 pits contain relatively small identifiable bone samples. Some contain both winter and warm-season catch remains. If these pits contain fill generated by one occupancy (rather than, say, material accumulated over a few years, swept up and dumped in one episode), then there often is good evidence for multi-seasonal use of the site within each annual cycle. The only detectable difference in faunal content between hearths and pits is a significantly different distribution of deer axial (e.g., skull, vertebra, pelvis, ribs) versus appendicular (e.g., limb) elements. Although neither appendicular nor axial body parts are exclusively distributed in either category, axial body parts tend to be found in hearth debris, while pit debris tends to contain more appendicular elements. Material deposited in hearths may have been the first discard from the use of a carcass, while the pits accumulated refuse processed further or curated longer.

In the case of fish and birds there is horizontal patterning on a scale smaller than the 5-ft^2 provenience unit. This patterning is evidenced by high concentrations of bone limited to areas within one unit, with much lower or no distribution outside it. These concentrations may represent highly localized processing or discard events, such as dumping the contents of a soup pot.

Further examination of horizontal distribution patterns shows three areas of high bone frequency associated with feature groups. Discrete groups of features correspond with the three faunal concentrations. The congruence of feature groups with bone concentrations, and the low density of bone between each concentration, allows definition of three activity areas (see Spiess and Lewis 1995:Figure A8.3). Area 1 consists of a dense group of features, including hearths, associated with a dense bone scatter on the south-central portion of the site. The highest bone density is immediately shoreward (south) of the features, suggesting a refuse dumping area peripheral to the hearth activity area.

Area 2 consists of a group of pits roughly congruent with a moderately dense scatter of bone. Area 2 is immediately adjacent to Area 1, but further inland. Area 3 is comprised of features, including hearths, and a moderate density of faunal remains among the features. If there is an area of high bone density adjacent to and associated with Activity Area 3, it exists in the unexcavated portion of the site shoreward, and may be mostly eroded away. The attributes of Areas 1 and 3 appear similar, exhibiting hearth presence, high cod bone count, low seal bone count, high bird bone count, and low isolated deer tooth count.

We hypothesize that the hearth and feature portion of Area 1 represents a focus of domestic activity (centered on the hearths), and that the heavy bone concentration extending seaward represents a dump that was shoreward of the domestic area. This pattern implies some sort of structure associated with the hearth-feature complex, although the only evidence for one is the boundedness of the rear (northern) limit of the bone distribution. Area 3 is similar to Area 1 in many respects.

Area 2 clearly contrasts with Area 1 in its lack of hearths, a scatter of pits, less intense bone concentration, low cod and bird bone proportion, high seal bone count (especially postcrania), and high count of isolated deer teeth. There is no focus of obvious human activity in Area 2. The pits tend to be shallow and irregularly spaced.

The suite of bones from Area 2 includes a low proportion of fish and bird bone and a high proportion of seal bone, especially postcrania. The Occupation 2 population made much of their dogs, according them special treatment upon death. In arctic and sub-arctic cultures, working dogs, are often tied up adjacent to human living quarters. While whole fish can be fed to dogs, other evidence suggests that human dependence on cod was high during Occupation 2, and that humans often discarded leftovers in discrete piles in the dump of Area 1. Because fish bone (especially the size of cod bone) and bird bone, as well, are notorious for choking dogs, most owners of working dogs would avoid feeding them defleshed fish "racks" or bird carcasses. In the arctic, pinniped meat is often used preferentially to cervid meat for dog food, because it has a lower human preference value. Since seals were not often taken during Occupation 2, it is even more likely that such less preferred meat went to the dogs. Moreover, many of the seal bones from this site (Occupation 2 and elsewhere) exhibit ragged epiphyseal ends, a classic mark of dog-chewing. We would expect seal skull fragments to end up in the dump of Area 1, and most of the postcrania to end up as dog food, as the data indicate. The high proportion of isolated deer teeth in Area 2 possibly results from human discard of the jaws, followed by Canid chewing which destroys the bone holding the teeth, leaving isolated teeth. Thus it is possible that Areas 1 (human) and 2 (dog) represent a human/dog relationship of some kind.

Occupation 3

Three types of features that contain bone are found in Occupation 3: pits, cobble hearths and floors, and graves. The hearths tend to be extensive cobble or boulder structures that merge with cobble pavements to form hearth/floor complexes (e.g., Bourque 1995:98–9, 134). The graves contain cremated, non-cremated secondary burial, and non-cremated articulated human remains. In many cases the grave pits contain cremated (calcined) animal bone, and some fresh animal bone. For detailed descriptions see Bourque (1995:97–167) and Spiess and Lewis (1995).

By far the largest faunal sample from an Occupation 3 feature comes from Feature 19–1972, a hearth complex. It is dominated by deer bone from a minimum of eight individuals. Faunal remains represent all seasons of the year, with the possible exception of March through May. The collections from Occupation 3 pits are generally small and unremarkable. For example, Feature 35–1974, a pit with shell in the fill, contains a variety of furbearers, a seal, and probably one tomcod which was a late fall or winter catch.

Two major associations between groups of hearths and pits can be postulated on the basis of contiguity or proximity. Together these features form a functional complex exhibiting multiple faunal seasonality, greatly strengthening the hypothesis that year-round habitation of the site occurred during Occupation 3. The alternative hypothesis, a series of short occupations at random with respect to season, is seemingly contradicted by the clustering of these features within one activity complex.

Collections of non-human faunal remains from Occupation 3 burials are dominated by calcined bone fragments. Unburned bone is also included within these features, as is some burned bone. (Burned [carbonized black] bone has been in a fire, but not heated enough for calcination.) The presence of a few pieces of burned faunal bone indicates incomplete or partial combustion of some faunal inclusions. Since the human bone included calcined, burned and unburned bone, we assume that faunal material (as food for the deceased perhaps) might also include all three types of bone. Some unburned bone could have been mixed with the feature fill as grave pits were dug in pre-existing midden matrix, but generally there is little shell mixed with the grave fill, indicating little midden admixture. Therefore, we can only state with certainty that the calcined and burned faunal material was included in the grave fill with the human interment. Unburned bone may or may not be deliberate inclusions in the grave fill.

Looking primarily at data derived from the calcined bone inclusions, certain inclusion patterns emerge. The volume of calcined faunal bone in these features varies tremendously, from nil in several cases to approximately 800 fragments and 1kg mass in the case of Feature 24–1975 (Bourque 1995:153). The largest volumes are primarily dependent upon the amount of identified deer bone and large mammal (probable deer) bone in the feature. There is no standard set of faunal inclu-

sions such as might be expected of a deer or bear cult. However, the faunal sample from each feature may be dominated by the bones of one taxon, and usually the minimum number of individuals represented by that taxon is one or two. The most common dominant species inclusion is deer. In several cases deer antler and jaw fragments are present along with postcrania, so that we can reasonably conclude that whole deer, or large portions thereof, were cremated. In one feature beaver bone, apparently from one individual, is dominant. In addition to whole deer and beaver, or deer and/or moose parts, there are other common inclusions. Canids, sometimes identifiable by size as probable domestic dogs, but including one probable wolf (Feature 9–1975; Bourque 1995:158), are commonly represented by skull parts. The most commonly identifiable bird inclusions are wing bones of large geese, presumably Canada goose. Furbearers, such as bobcat, mink (species indeterminant) and fox are represented by a few bones, as are one or more seal species.

A substantial amount of horizontal patterning of Occupation 3 faunal remains exists at a scale below the size of the 5 ft² excavation unit. This scale of patterning manifests itself as units with high bone concentration adjacent to ones almost devoid of bone. Thus, even apart from recognized features, there are faunal-deposition episodes which covered very small areas of the site. The horizontal distribution of faunal remains has been divided into six different activity areas (Spiess and Lewis 1995:357–360), but the relatively clear functional hypotheses available for Occupation 2 activity areas do not seem to be applicable.

Occupation 4 (subdivisions defined in Table 4–1)

It is possible that up to five activity areas are represented by the faunal remains in B2GF although each was sampled by only one or two excavation units. Most taxa and all deer element categories appear to be distributed at random with respect to the rest of the bone sample, exceptions being duck bone, unidentified bird bone, and flounder. Ducks and unidentified bird bone represents 10–21% of the bone sample in some squares, but are absent from others.

A concentration of features was encounted at the eastern end of 2GF in the excavated area. Four of these have yielded identifiable faunal samples. The collection from Feature 16–1974 is notable for its Cervid composition, including two adult deer and parts of a moose. Also notable is a house floor, Feature 8–1973, which contained a proximal rib end from a whale, probably Eubalaena (right whale).

Bone distribution allowed us to divide the 2GF deposits into two activity areas. There are no differences in deer body part distribution between the two areas. Distributions of mink and bear, however, seem heavily weighted toward Area 2. In the case of mink, both cranial and postcranial fragments are involved. The skewed distribution favoring Area 2 is even more marked for birds and fishes. All bird taxa are almost exclusively confined to Area 2. A partial exception is loon, with four of 31 bones in Area 1; these four are appendicular longbone elements from a minimum of one individual. Moreover, three bird species exhibit localized distributions within Area 2. Fishbone exhibits is confined almost exclusively to Area 2 as well. Flounder occurs in two localized patches within Area 2, a pattern congruent with sculpin. Sturgeon, however, occur only in one patch in Area 2. The most obvious hypothesis to test is that Areas 1 and 2 represent different seasons of habitation. Area 2, which essentially lacks features and has a great diversity of fauna, contains evidence of multiple seasonal use. Area 1 has many features, but contains almost solely deer, moose, bear, and seal bones. Unfortunately, there are no tooth sectioning or tooth eruption data, nor any immature seal bones which might indicate seasonality for Area 1. Thus, we lack comparative seasonality data from these two areas to test the hypothesis.

The CCS strata essentially cover the entire excavated area of the site. It is impossible to delimit activity areas of internally uniform faunal content larger than a few contiguous excavation units in this palimpsest of overlapping faunal distribution patterns. However, as in 2GF, there is an area in the northeast corner of the main excavation area that contains primarily deer and seal bone, while those taxa are joined by the majority of bird and fishbone in the south-central and southwest portions of the main excavation. A horizontal plot of deer teeth analyzed for season of death shows no apparant seasonal patterning within the Coarse-Crushed Shell unit.

As with the underlying strata, deposits assigned to 1GF are widespread. Two features associated with it have yielded identifiable faunal remains. Both contain a variety of taxa. Feature 2–1975 is of at least summer seasonality, while Feature 3–1974 is of at least summer and early fall seasonality. Deer postcrania and tooth distribution closely parallel those of seal, moose and beaver. Bear bones and mink crania and postcrania concentrate in the south-central/southwest areas of the main excavation. Most fishbone (flounder, sturgeon, and sculpin) is concentrated at the western edge of the excavation. There is an additional concentration of 100 flounder bones in excavation unit S100W20. Striped bass and swordfish show distributions independent of this pattern. (Swordfish is regarded as mixed upward from Occupation 2 by some pit or other disturbance.) Bird bones, best represented by ducks, concentrate in the south-central and southwestern portions of the excavation. Again, concrete season-of-death information does not correlate with these species distribution patterns.

Deposits assignable to the MCS stratum are widespread across the site, but with large lacunae. For the first time, however, there is a disparity between the distribution of deer teeth/cranial parts and deer postcrania, teeth being much less frequent in the western and southern areas of the excavation. Moose, seal and beaver distribution patterns concentrate with deer postcrania. Also, for the first time, there is a recognizable contrast between the distributions of mink crania and postcrania. The cranial parts concentrate in the north and south-central corners of the excavation while the postcrania concentrate in the south-central and southwest corners. Bird bones of all taxa concentrate in the northeast and south-central areas of the excavation, but are virtually absent from the western edges. Flounder bones concentrate in the northeast corner of the excavation, with a small concentration in section S80W50. Cod, sturgeon, sculpin, and striped bass also follow this pattern. Again, we are at a loss to explain these large-scale distribution patterns.

Deposits assignable to the NGF stratum are concentrated in the northeast corner of the excavation. Because of the small bone sample size and limited horizontal distribution, little can be said about horizontal distribution within the NGF.

The scale of horizontal faunal patterning seems to change between the Archaic occupations (2 and 3) and Occupation 4. Part of the difficulty in interpreting these changes may be the paucity of features in Occupation 4 with which to associate the faunal distributions. However, the whole site seems differentiable into only two or three major faunal deposition areas in each of the Occupation 4 strata. While it seems most likely that we are looking at major seasonal differences in use of the large area involved, we cannot prove it despite a plethora of seasonality data. The best we can say is that the nature of faunal processing and deposition at the site changed significantly between the Archaic and Ceramic period occupations.

SEASONAL ECONOMIC CYCLES

The Turner Farm site provides an excellent record of subsistence patterns on Fox Islands for about 5,000 years. The record is good enough to detect the major features of the annual cycle of subsistence activities for each occupation. During the various occupations there may have been longer or shorter excursions to other sites in the Penobscot Bay area by some or all of the people living at the site. In fact, ethnographic accounts of maritime hunter-gatherers (Yesner 1980b, 1984), foraging theory (Winterhalder and Smith 1981), and archaeological evidence for seasonal use of some other sites in Penobscot Bay, virtually demand such a settlement model. However, during the site's periods of occupation (measured in years or decades) these shorter (seasonal) absences of either part or all of the population are not readily detectable in the archaeological record. Thus, we are constructing a summary account of what most of the site's population did for most of the time.

For our purposes, the relative significance of the quest for different taxa, and the amount of procurement effort invested, cannot be based strictly on quantitative counts of identified faunal remains, for these in turn must be heavily dependent upon an assessment of the changing pattern of faunal counts over time, assumptions about butchery and discard practices based on modern behavioral analogues, and some knowledge of the vicissitudes of archaeological recovery and preservation. Thus, the most detailed division of resource importance and relative frequency that we will attempt herein is a division into "primary", "secondary" and "tertiary" resources.

We define a primary resource as a major source of protein or calories, without which there would have been dietary hardship. Deer, moose and seals fill this role at various seasons during various occupations. There will only be a few taxa identified as primary resources for any given season. We define secondary resource as an alternative to protein or calories making a substantial contribution to the diet, or capable of ameliorating the scarcity of a primary resource. Clams must have filled this role during the late winter during Occupations 2 and 3. We hesitate to rank them as a primary resource because of the relatively small amount of protein and especially fat represented by a few bushels of clams, and because isotope data indicate the greater importance of other marine species (Bourque 1995:140). A tertiary resource is defined as supplying a minor source of protein or calories, or as a resource that supplies dietary diversity (perhaps scarce minerals or vitamins) or a non-food material.

Figures 6–3 and 6–7 summarize our hypothesis of the seasonal economic cycle for five periods of occupation at the Turner Farm site. Major features of the Occupation 2 seasonal cycle included primary dependency on deer from December, or perhaps slightly earlier, into May, supplemented with shellfish in late winter.

Subsistence during June, July, August, and possibly September was focussed primarily on cod fishing and swordfish hunting. Assuming that the swordfish retreated southward as the surface waters of the Gulf of Maine cooled in early October, there may not be a primary subsistence base for late October and November, between the diminishment of swordfishing and increasing importance in deer hunting. It is possible that stored fish (cod or swordfish) provided subsistence during the fall, and likely given isotope data showing the importance of marine species. However, September and October is the height of catadramous eel runs downstream on smaller streams on the mainland, so some occupants may have left the site during this season. Late winter clam collecting supplemented the food supply as stored fish and deer meat supplies were exhausted. There also was an hiatus or low level of site occupation in the late spring (May and June), coincidentally with runs of anadramous fish (alewife, shad, sturgeon, and salmon, in that order) on the upper estuaries and lower rivers along the mainland coast. This alternative hypothesis, which will have to be evaluated using data from other sites, is a spring population movement to advantageous fishing locations either westward into the St. George River, upstream on the Penobscot, or northeastward to the Union River.

During Occupation 3 we can identify only one primary resource: deer. Seal hunting (in season), codfishing in the fall, and shellfish collecting in late winter and spring seem to have been secondary. Based on limited evidence, codfishing occurred later in the fall in Occupation 3 than in Occupation 2. There is clear evidence for year-round use of the site without substantial seasonal breaks.

The earlier episodes of Occupation 4 placed primary reliance on moose and deer from late fall through winter, as well as on a winter grey seal hunt. Primary summer subsistence was based on harbor seal, supplemented by sturgeon, flounder and sculpin. Birds, in aggregate, probably provided a year-round secondary resource. Later Occupation 4 episodes represented by MCS and NGF show the same pattern, but with an increased reliance on sturgeon, flounder, and sculpin during summer. The intensification of furbearer trapping or hunting through Occupation 4 is, we suspect, evidence of a prehistoric fur trade which may have preadapted people in this region to the European fur trade (Spiess et. al. 1983). It should be noted that this multiplication of primary resources over those of the Late Archaic is the basis for our thinking that the variety of food sources exploited increased with time. The episodes of Occupation 4, represented by the plow zone, reflect intense fall through winter use of moose, and year-round use of seals

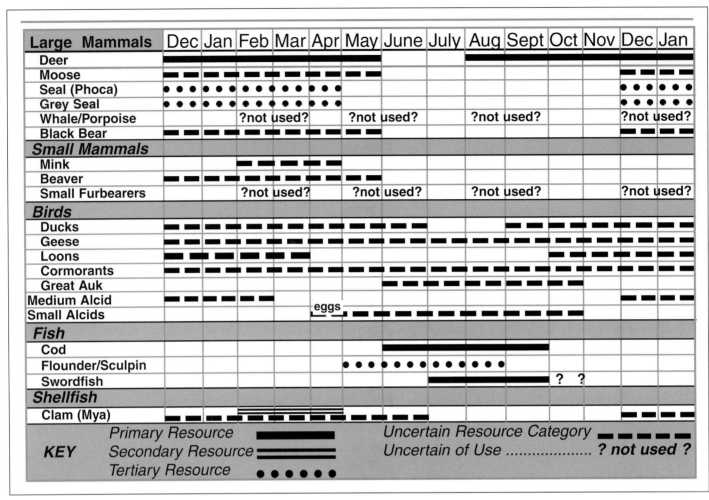

Large Mammals	Dec	Jan	Feb	Mar	Apr	May	June	July	Aug	Sept	Oct	Nov	Dec	Jan
Deer														
Moose														
Seal (Phoca)														
Grey Seal														
Whale/Porpoise			?not used?		?not used?			?not used?			?not used?			
Black Bear														
Small Mammals														
Mink														
Beaver														
Small Furbearers			?not used?		?not used?			?not used?			?not used?			
Birds														
Ducks														
Geese														
Loons														
Cormorants														
Great Auk														
Medium Alcid														
Small Alcids						eggs								
Fish														
Cod														
Flounder/Sculpin														
Swordfish											?	?		
Shellfish														
Clam (Mya)														

KEY
Primary Resource ▬▬▬▬
Secondary Resource ≡≡≡≡
Tertiary Resource ● ● ● ● ● ●
Uncertain Resource Category ▬ ▬ ▬ ▬
Uncertain of Use .... ? not used ?

Figure 6-3. Reconstruction of seasonal faunal use during Occupation 2 (Moorehead phase) at the Turner Farm site. See text for definitions of primary, secondary and tertiary resources.

as primary resources. This primary subsistence focus is supplemented by a wide variety of secondary and tertiary resources.

Thus, there is abundant evidence from Occupations 2 through the plow zone for multi-seasonal use of each occupation. Two alternative behavioral analogues could account for the observed seasonality pattern. One hypothesis is that the occupations reflect groups of people who were year-round residents, or nearly so; or that a portion of the population remained resident at the site if some left it for task-specific or short-seasonal occupations elsewhere. A second hypothosis is that the occupation levels were built by shorter seasonal occupations without seasonal preference. Put in other terms, perhaps there was seasonal randomness of use of the site in short-term episodes as suggested by David Sanger (personal communication to Spiess). We argue that the data presented in Chapters 3 and 4 tend to support the former hypothosis: that occupation at the site was relatively long-term and multi-seasonal, if not year-round. For example, for Occupation 2 our ability to separate the horizontal

distribution into three discrete activity areas argues against random, short-term re-occupation of the site, unless some factor acted to exactly superimpose each successive occupation over its predecessor. In Occupation 3, the multi-seasonal nature of the Feature 19–1972 hearth complex is unquestionable. Thus it seems parsimonious to argue that this single feature complex or structure floor was not re-occupied many times at random with respect to seasonality, but instead that it was used (for a limited number of years) on a multi-seasonal basis.

SWORDFISH AND WHALES

Here we address the interpretation of faunal data on two taxa, swordfish and large whales, each of which, because of body size and the likelihood of incomplete return of skeletal elements to the shell midden (taphonomy), represents a major uncertainty in the economic reconstructions presented.

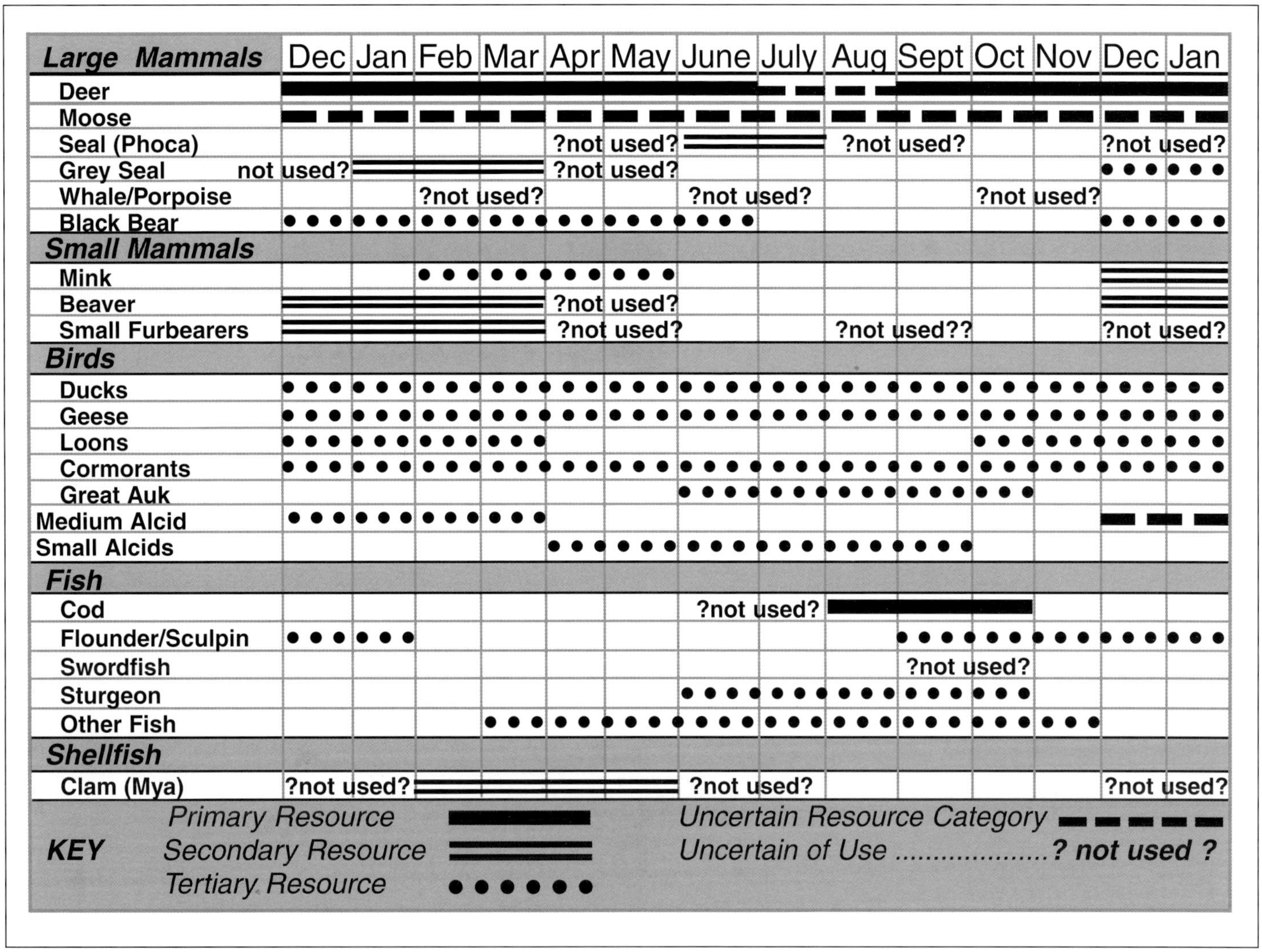

Large Mammals	Dec	Jan	Feb	Mar	Apr	May	June	July	Aug	Sept	Oct	Nov	Dec	Jan
Deer														
Moose														
Seal (Phoca)					?not used?				?not used?				?not used?	
Grey Seal	not used?				?not used?									
Whale/Porpoise			?not used?				?not used?			?not used?				
Black Bear														
Small Mammals														
Mink														
Beaver					?not used?									
Small Furbearers					?not used?				?not used??				?not used?	
Birds														
Ducks														
Geese														
Loons														
Cormorants														
Great Auk														
Medium Alcid														
Small Alcids														
Fish														
Cod							?not used?							
Flounder/Sculpin														
Swordfish										?not used?				
Sturgeon														
Other Fish														
Shellfish														
Clam (Mya)	?not used?						?not used?						?not used?	

KEY
- Primary Resource — (solid bar)
- Secondary Resource — (double line)
- Tertiary Resource — (dotted)
- Uncertain Resource Category — (dashed bar)
- Uncertain of Use .... ? not used ?

Figure 6-4. Reconstruction of seasonal faunal use during Occupation 3 (Sesquehanna tradition) at the Turner Farm site. See text for definitions of primary, secondary and tertiary resources.

Swordfish

Approximately 65% of all swordfish bone (excluding rostrum fragments), and approximately 80% by count (91% by weight) of all swordfish rostrum from the site was found in Occupation 2. Some of the swordfish material found in later strata was mixed upward after deposition, as shown by refitting pieces (see discussion in Chapter 3). However, the difference in body parts frequency between swordfish in Occupation 2 and Occupation 3 indicates that upward mixture was not entirely random.

Swordfish sword was a valued raw material during Occupation 2 times. Strauss (1989:66) uses an earlier estimate (not derived from our work) of a minimum of 25 swordfish to account for the number of rostrum fragments in

the Turner Farm, a reasonable estimate in our view. Strauss uses an average meat weight of 250 lbs per fish to calculate that these fish represent 6,050 lbs (2,800kg) of meat. But how important were swordfish in terms of overall subsistence? We have noted the probability that butchery and off-site disposal practices may have caused under-representation of swordfish bone at the site compared with some other taxa. There are several lines of evidence suggesting that swordfish were indeed important in the subsistence economy during Occupation 2. First, we have reconstructed this economy as relying primarily on deer from December through April, with no major food source other than maritime fishing from sometime during June through September. We reconstruct cod as the most heavily used resource during June through early August, with swordfish as the likely focus of subsistence as water temperatures peaked during late

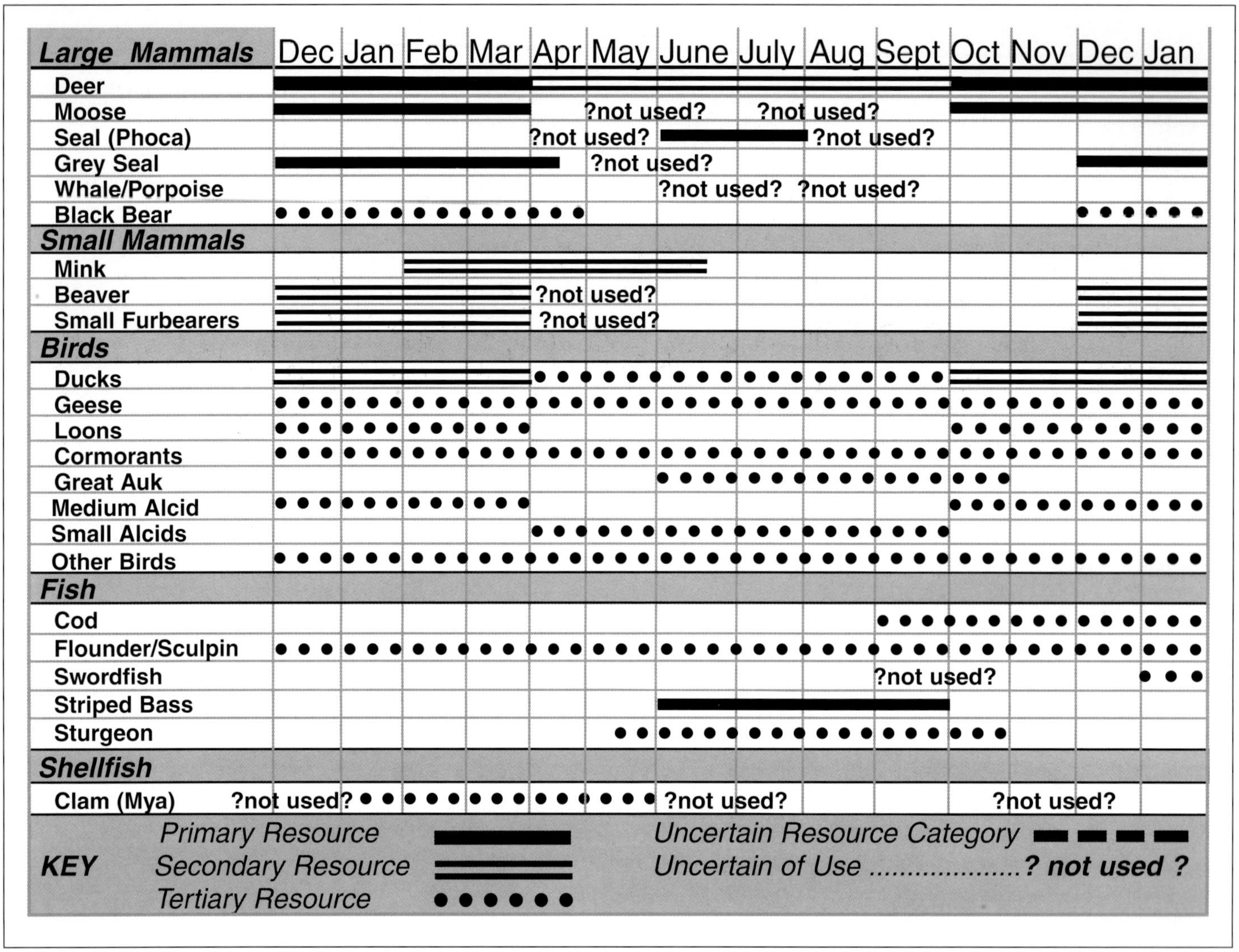

Large Mammals

Species	Dec	Jan	Feb	Mar	Apr	May	June	July	Aug	Sept	Oct	Nov	Dec	Jan
Deer	▬	▬	▬	▬	═	═	═	═	═	═	▬	▬	▬	▬
Moose	▬	▬	▬	▬	?not used?	?not used?		?not used?	?not used?		▬	▬	▬	▬
Seal (Phoca)					?not used?	?not used?	▬	▬	?not used?	?not used?				
Grey Seal	▬	▬	▬	▬	?not used?	?not used?						▬	▬	▬
Whale/Porpoise						?not used?	?not used?	?not used?	?not used?					
Black Bear	•	•	•	•	•	•	•					•	•	•

Small Mammals

Species	Dec	Jan	Feb	Mar	Apr	May	June	July	Aug	Sept	Oct	Nov	Dec	Jan
Mink			═	═	═	═	═	═						
Beaver	═	═	═	═	?not used?	?not used?							═	═
Small Furbearers	═	═	═	═	?not used?	?not used?							═	═

Birds

Species	Dec	Jan	Feb	Mar	Apr	May	June	July	Aug	Sept	Oct	Nov	Dec	Jan
Ducks	═	═	═	═	═	•	•	•	•	•	•	═	═	═
Geese	•	•	•	•	•	•	•	•	•	•	•	•	•	•
Loons	•	•	•	•	•						•	•	•	•
Cormorants	•	•	•	•	•	•	•	•	•	•	•	•	•	•
Great Auk							•	•	•	•	•			
Medium Alcid	•	•	•	•	•						•	•	•	•
Small Alcids					•	•	•	•	•	•	•			
Other Birds	•	•	•	•	•	•	•	•	•	•	•	•	•	•

Fish

Species	Dec	Jan	Feb	Mar	Apr	May	June	July	Aug	Sept	Oct	Nov	Dec	Jan
Cod										•	•	•	•	•
Flounder/Sculpin	•	•	•	•	•	•	•	•	•	•	•	•	•	•
Swordfish										?not used?			•	•
Striped Bass						▬	▬	▬	▬					
Sturgeon						•	•	•	•	•	•	•		

Shellfish

Species	Dec	Jan	Feb	Mar	Apr	May	June	July	Aug	Sept	Oct	Nov	Dec	Jan
Clam (Mya)	?not used?	•	•	•	•	•	•	•	?not used?			?not used?		

KEY
- Primary Resource: ▬▬▬ (solid bar)
- Secondary Resource: ═══ (double line)
- Tertiary Resource: • • • • • •
- Uncertain Resource Category: ▬ ▬ ▬ ▬ (dashed bar)
- Uncertain of Use: ....? not used?

Figure 6-5. Reconstruction of seasonal faunal use by Middle Ceramic occupants at the Turner Farm site (2nd gravel floor, Coarse-crushed shell, 1st gravel floor). See text for definitions of primary, secondary and tertiary resources.

summer and early fall.

Strauss (1989) also proposes a theory, based mainly upon ethnographic analogy from Ainu swordfish hunting, that swordfish hunting during the Moorehead phase was responsible for a mortuary and social system that paid great attention to status associated with the hunting of this dangerous fish. His hypothesis connects offshore swordfish hunting with the need for large dugout canoes and a highly trained crew, led by a boat captain with considerable personal fortitude, organizational skill, and supernatural power. Offshore swordfish hunting in Maine during the Moorehead phase, according to Strauss, was followed by butchery of the kill on offshore islands, and transport of only the most desirable portions of the animal back to sites further up the bay.

There are, however, strong arguments against the offshore butchering hypothesis as stated. Swordfish remains are present in the Seabrook Marsh site in New Hampshire, which predates the Moorehead phase and which lacks its mortuary elaboration (Robinson 1985, 1996a). Moreover, many data (counts of swordfish rostra versus postcranial parts) presented in favor of Straus' argument are incorrect. Recent collections analysis has shown that there are many more swordfish postcrania (ribs, vertebrae) than previously reported at the Nevin (n=342, MNI >25, Nathan Hamilton, personal communication 1993) and Waterside sites (Harbour Mitchell 3, personal communicaton 1991). Both of these sites are found toward the heads of large bays, on mainland shores, and some of the Nevin strata predate the Moorehead phase. On Monhegan Island, an offshore island about 50 km to the southwest of North Haven, Ron Stanley encountered a feature filled with swordfish rostra at

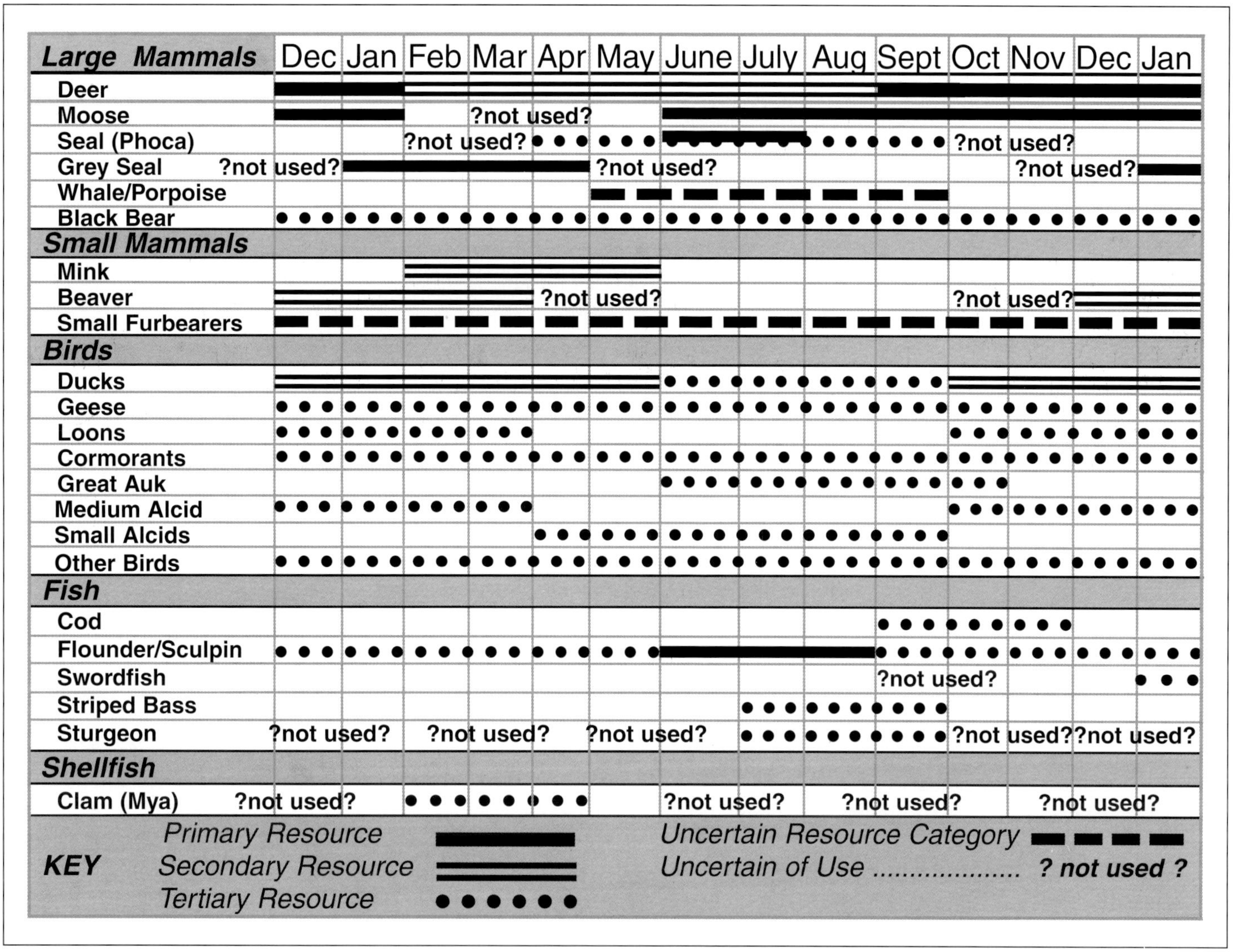

Large Mammals — Dec Jan Feb Mar Apr May June July Aug Sept Oct Nov Dec Jan

Large Mammals	Dec	Jan	Feb	Mar	Apr	May	June	July	Aug	Sept	Oct	Nov	Dec	Jan
Deer														
Moose			?not used?											
Seal (Phoca)			?not used?							?not used?				
Grey Seal	?not used?					?not used?						?not used?		
Whale/Porpoise														
Black Bear														
Small Mammals														
Mink														
Beaver						?not used?					?not used?			
Small Furbearers														
Birds														
Ducks														
Geese														
Loons														
Cormorants														
Great Auk														
Medium Alcid														
Small Alcids														
Other Birds														
Fish														
Cod														
Flounder/Sculpin														
Swordfish										?not used?				
Striped Bass														
Sturgeon		?not used?		?not used?		?not used?				?not used?		?not used?		
Shellfish														
Clam (Mya)		?not used?					?not used?		?not used?			?not used?		

KEY
- Primary Resource ▬▬▬▬▬
- Secondary Resource ═══════
- Tertiary Resource • • • • • •
- Uncertain Resource Category ▬ ▬ ▬ ▬
- Uncertain of Use .... ? not used ?

Figure 6-6. Reconstruction of seasonal faunal use by Late Ceramic occupants at the Turner Farm site (Medium-crushed shell and New Gravel Floor levels). See text for definitions of primary, secondary and tertiary resources.

the Stanley site (17.43). The extant faunal collections from the site are mostly swordfish vertebrae, and recent testing there by Stuart Eldridge (Stuart Eldridge, personal communication 1995) encountered swordfish vertebrae and fin ray fragments securely associated.

Thus, the argument for exclusive offshore butchering of this large prey species is countered by the faunal data, and it seems likely, therefore, that swordfish swam in among or close to the Penobscot Bay islands during Moorehead phase times. If this was the case, the risk of offshore voyaging could have been avoided, although swordfish hunting would still have been a dangerous activity due to the propensity of the species to attack small boats. Moreover, the presence of plentiful swordfish bone in one site\ predating the Moorehead phase means that we must rexamine Strauss' hypothesis of late Moorehead phase mortuary efflo-

rescence being associated with the social organization needed for swordfish hunting. The factors involved with Archaic mortuary elaboration around the Gulf of Maine may be multi-causal and complex. Still, it seems that swordfish were a regular and predictable subsistence resource for the Moorehead phase occupants of the central Maine coast, both those living on offshore islands and further toward the heads of coastal embayments.

Whales

The importance of whales to Occupation 4 subsistence is also questionable. We have Rosier's account (quoted above) as evidence for the hunting of large baleen whales in the Ceramic period which, although not an eye witness one, gives enough detail to seem factual. Moreover, aside from the few pieces of worked whalebone (large baleen whale ribs) found at the

Large Mammals	Dec	Jan	Feb	Mar	Apr	May	June	July	Aug	Sept	Oct	Nov	Dec	Jan
Deer		?not used?		?not used?		?not used?			● ● ●	● ● ●	● ● ●	● ● ●	?not used?	
Moose	(primary)				(secondary)				(primary)					
Seal (Phoca)	(secondary)													
Grey Seal	(secondary)													
Whale/Porpoise						■	■	■	■	■	■			
Black Bear	● ● ● ● ● ●	● ● ●											● ● ●	● ● ●
Small Mammals														
Mink			(secondary)											
Beaver	(secondary)				?not used?				?not used?		?not used?		(secondary)	
Small Furbearers	▬ ▬ ▬	▬ ▬	▬	▬	▬	▬	▬	▬	▬	▬	▬	▬	▬	▬
Birds														
Ducks		(secondary)				● ● ●	● ● ●	● ● ●	● ● ●	● ● ●				
Geese	● ● ●	● ● ●	● ● ●	● ● ●	● ●	● ● ●	● ● ●	● ●	● ● ●	● ● ●	● ● ●	● ● ●	● ● ●	● ● ●
Loons	● ● ●	● ● ●	● ● ●	● ●						● ● ●	● ● ●	● ● ●	● ● ●	● ● ●
Cormorants	● ● ●	● ● ●	● ● ●	● ●	● ● ●	● ● ●	● ● ●	● ●	● ● ●	● ● ●	● ● ●	● ● ●	● ● ●	● ● ●
Great Auk						● ● ●	● ● ●	● ● ●	● ● ●	● ● ●				
Medium Alcid	● ● ●	● ● ●	● ● ●	●						● ● ●	● ● ●	● ● ●	● ● ●	● ● ●
Small Alcids					● ● ●	● ● ●	● ● ●	● ●	● ● ●	● ● ●				
Other Birds	● ● ●	● ● ●	● ● ●	● ●	● ● ●	● ● ●	● ● ●	● ●	● ● ●	● ● ●	● ● ●	● ● ●	● ● ●	● ● ●
Fish														
Cod									● ● ●	● ● ●	● ● ●	● ●		
Flounder/Sculpin	● ● ●	● ● ●	● ● ●	● ●	● ● ●	● ● ●	● ● ●	● ●	● ● ●	● ● ●	● ● ●	● ● ●	● ●	● ● ●
Swordfish										?not used?			● ● ●	
Sturgeon	?not used?		?not used?		?not used?	● ● ●	● ● ●	● ●	● ● ●	● ● ●	?not used?		?not used?	
Shellfish														
Clam (Mya)	?not used?		● ● ●	● ● ●	● ● ●	● ● ●	?not used?		?not used?			?not used?		

KEY			
Primary Resource ▬▬▬		Uncertain Resource Category ▬ ▬ ▬ ▬	
Secondary Resource =		Uncertain of Use .... ? not used ?	
Tertiary Resource ● ● ● ● ● ●			

Figure 6-7. Reconstruction of seasonal faunal use by the Late Ceramic and Contact Period occupants at the Turner Farm site, represented by material in the plow zone. Definitions of primary, secondary and tertiary resources as in Figure 6-3.

Turner Farm site, whalebone has also been reported for a Ceramic period component at site 61.7 in the Roque Islands, Washington County, Maine (William Belcher, personal communication 1987), and a large whalebone harpoon point, undated but probably of Ceramic period provenience was recovered from the Taft Point site near Bar Harbor.

We propose two hypotheses for Late Ceramic period whale use: (1) either whales were a regularly used and therefore an important or primary source of meat and fat (at 30 tons live weight per animal); or (2) their use was sporadic in temporal and geographic distribution. In comparative terms, one whale at 60,000 lbs would have made a substantial addition to the larder of a local group. During the Ceramic period we calculated (in Chapter 3) an estimate of 56,500 lbs live weight of 14 moose, 92 seal and 9 bear for every 100 deer killed. One whale would thus equal other mammal produc-

tion, over whatever time span is represented by the kill of 100 deer. For the plow zone, we calculate 100 deer killed associated with 21 moose, 225 seal and 15 bear, for a total of 103,700 lbs live weight. One whale approximately equals half this production.

Rosier's account, however, indicates that the proceeds of one whale kill was possibly distributed among several bands, since at least several sagamores (chiefs) participated in the distribution. Little and Andrews (1982) discuss the effect of frequent redistribution of portions of dead drift whales among the Indian inhabitants of Nantucket: the redistribution effort seems to have been a major function of the Sachems. Rosier's account indicates a similar effect in Maine at historic contact. Every man got a piece for his household, and since the chief lords had to be called together, distribution was evidently across more than one or two residential groups. We think it conceivable that during the late Ceramic period, one or two whales were killed annually in the central Maine coast region and redistributed to regional resident groups.

ECOLOGICAL CHANGE

Seals, inshore fish and birds were definitely minor resources for Occupation 2. They later came to dominate subsistence, while swordfish disappeared from the faunal list and cod declined. Moreover, the ratio of moose to deer kills increased dramatically from Occupation 2 to Late Occupation 4. Explanations of these changes might be found in the nature of the Gulf of Maine environment subsequent to 5000 B.P. Spiess et al. (1983) developed a model of coastal ecology before 4500 B.P. based on a reconstruction of the Gulf of Maine as warmer and less tidal than today. Our model includes the following points: Warmer summer surface waters in the Gulf, at a minimum, would be necessary to allow the presence of swordfish inshore in any quantity. The less tidal aspect of the Gulf is presumed to be responsible for low inshore productivity, which, in conjunction with the warmer temperatures, meant smaller populations of flounder, sculpin and other shallow-water fish. The resident grey or harbor seal populations of the Gulf of Maine are in part dependent on these shallow-water fish populations, meaning that they would have been correspondingly lower during Occupation 2 times as well. We suspect that as intertidal and inshore productivity increased coastal waterfowl populations, especially ducks and geese would have increased as well. Progressive cooling of the Gulf of Maine due to increased tidal mixing eliminated swordfish as a near-shore migrant. It also increased the dominance of spruce over hardwood along the Maine coast, which we suspect favored an increase in moose population relative to deer. In sum, we hypothesize measurable change in coastal ecology within the last 5,000 years in Penobscot Bay. We now review the information available from other disciplines that supports this model.

Descriptions of Maine coastal geomorphology (Kelley 1987), coupled with subbottom profiling, coring, and radiocarbon dates (e.g., Belknap 1995; Belknap et al. 1987; Young et al. 1992) indicate transgression (relative sea level rise and/or land subsidence) throughout the Holocene, but relatively minor change in the overall geomorphological character of various regions along the Maine coast. As the sea has transgressed, it has eroded soft sediment from upper estuarine shorelines and outer coastal headlands and recycled it into beaches and mid-estuarine

mudflats; coastal environments have progressed inland and up-estuary. Some shoreline locations have remained consistently attractive to prehistoric settlement as relative sea level has risen and the shoreline has moved inland. Young et al. 1992 have called these chronologically shingled settlement areas. The Turner Farm site is one such location. Thus, we expect relatively minor geomorphological change in the region of the Fox Islands around the Turner Farm site over the last 5,000 years, although local geomorphological change at the site itself has apparently altered it from a wetland orientation at 4500 B.P. to a beach front orientation today (Belknap 1995).

Grant (1970) proposed that after ca. 4000 B.P. sea level rise led to increasing tidal amplitudes in the Gulf of Maine. Sanger (1975:72) argued that these changes led to "... upwelling and water mixing, followed by a cooling of surface water, and finally by affecting marine organisms, especially warm water fauna such as swordfish and cold water adapted soft shell clams." Rapid early Holocene relative sea level rise reached -15m by 6300 B.P., and continued to rise at a decreasing rate until the recent past (Belknap 1995). A relative sea level curve for the Maine coast (Belknap et al. 1989, Geherls et al. 1995) shows changes in rates of shore subsidence (coastal transgression): rapid before 5000 B.P., slightly slower 5000 to 2500 B.P., and relatively slow after 2500 B.P. A relative sea level curve for the Maine coast (Belknap et al. 1989) shows similar changes in rates of inshore subsidence.

This recent information raises questions about the timing of the proposed tidal amplitude increase. Between 8600 and 6300 B.P. the Minas Basin (part of the Bay of Fundy, and therefore an eastern extension of the Gulf of Maine) was non-tidal (Amos 1978). Amos concluded that the tidal amplitude has been increasing linearly since 6300 B.P. A mathematical model of the Gulf of Maine, coupled with sea level curve data, allows more detailed models of tidal amplitude change, which is controlled by basin shape and relative sea level in the Gulf of Maine (Geherls et al. 1995; Scott and Greenberg 1983), although the timing of most rapid change varies between these models. Primary control of tidal amplitude in the Gulf of Maine has been controlled by the subsidence of offshore shallows on Georges Bank. Scott and Greenberg (1983) indicate that the change in tidal amplitude has not been constant during the mid- and late Holocene. Rates of tidal amplitude increased rapidly between 7000 and 4000 B.P., slightly more slowly between 4000 and 2500 B.P., and quite slowly after 2500 B.P. According to Scott and Greenberg (1983) tidal amplitude at 2500 B.P. was about 95% of what it is at present. According to the most recent and detailed (3-dimensional) model (Geherls et al. 1995) tidal amplitude at 7000 B.P. was 54–59% of present values; thus, with a modern tidal range of roughly 3 meters along mid-coast Maine, the tides at 7000 B.P. were a maximum of 1 to 1.8 meters. By 4000 B.P. the tidal amplitude was 78% of present values (e.g., 2.4 meters in our example). By 2000 B.P., it was approximately 94% of the present value, and 98% at 1000 B.P. (Geherls et al. 1995; slightly different emphasis in Bourque 1995: 243–4).

It seems to be currently unknown at what point tidally-driven mixing (upwelling) of subsurface waters would have been widespread in the central Gulf of Maine. Once underway, however, such mixing would have increased in intensity, although not in a linear fashion. The upwelling subsurface waters are derived from a deep current flowing from the Gulf of St. Lawrence, which in part is fed by the cold Labrador current (Apollonio 1979).

Today water is upwelled along a vertical eddy that parallels the Maine coast from Matinicus Island to Jonesport, producing a surface cooling effect (Apollonio 1979: 38–39). The upwelling is driven in part by amplitude of tidal mixing. As tidal amplitude has increased, presumably the volume of upwelling has also increased. When cold (Labrador current) water became available along the bottom of the Gulf of Maine, the upwelling began to produce cooling effects which have increased with tidal amplitude. Foraminifera in Gulf of St. Lawrence cores (Bartlett and Molinsky 1972) reveal a complex, tripartite alternation over the last 6000 years between relatively brackish water (more freshwater outflow from the Great Lakes), warm subtropical water derived from the Gulf Stream, and colder arctic water. Many of these marine fluctuations are not recorded in nearby terrestrial sediments. Thus, the exact nature of the water flowing into and along the bottom of the Gulf of Maine that was available for upwelling may have had a dominant component from any one of the three types of water in the Gulf of St. Lawrence.

Beginning about 6000 B.P. the diatom flora of the Wilkinson Basin, in the southwestern Gulf of Maine, approached a near-modern composition (Schnitker and Jorgensen 1990), indicating a biological response to the increasing tidal amplitude, with increasing productivity and evidence of cooling since 6000 B.P.

Notwithstanding the exact timing of increases in tidal amplitude, upwelling and the availability of cold water for

the upwelling, there remains convincing evidence at the Turner Farm site for decreasing water temperature in Penobscot Bay by ca. 3800 B.P. in the disappearance of quahog from the sequence, and the apparent cessation of swordfish capture. Thus, some time between 7000 B.P. and 4000 B.P. the Gulf of Maine neared 75% of its current capacity for tidal mixing, and it neared 95% of that capacity, or more, about 2500 B.P. Meanwhile, the Gulf of St. Lawrence, which contributes to Gulf of Maine water via southwesterly current flow, was sometime dominated by arctic water (Labrador current), subtropical water (Gulf Stream), or neither (more brackish water) (Bartlett and Molinsky 1972). We presume that subtropical Gulf Stream water influence in the Gulf of Maine would have varied as well. The general trend toward increasing cold water upwelling may thus have been interrupted, or made more episodic than the model based on unidirectional tidal increase alone would predict.

Local environmental changes were taking place against the backdrop of region-wide Holocene environmental change in eastern North America and the North Atlantic. Greenland ice cores (Dansgaard et al. 1982; Zielinski et al. 1994) show an early to mid-Holocene climatic warm period, followed by oscillating climate ending in recent cooling. In the mountains of New England, white pine and hemlock grew 300 m or more above present altitudinal limits from 9000 to roughly 5000 B.P., which has been explained by a minimum 2°C average higher temperature than today (Davis et al. 1980). Spruce, generally favored by cooler temperatures, did not become frequent at any elevation until 2000 B.P. In the Milford area of central Maine, roughly 100 km north of the Turner Farm site and at the northern limit of Maine seaboard lowlands, the interior forest was characterized by alternations between pine and hemlock domination from 7500 until about 5000 B.P., when hemlock was decimated by a pathogen and a birch-beech dominated forest developed, sustained by cooler climate until a spruce-fir dominance developed with continued cooling after 2000 B.P.(Almquist-Jacobson and Sanger 1995).

The changes in surface water temperature in the Gulf of Maine produced localized effects on the coastal terrestrial ecology. Today dense spruce forest dominates Maine coastal peninsulas and islands from the New Brunswick border as far west as the eastern margin of Casco Bay, although this vegetation cover does not extend far inland. Only in Casco Bay and southward is there a hardwood-dominated mixed forest along the immediate coast. This zone has a cooler and wetter microclimate than contiguous areas of interior Maine

(Baron et al. 1980). This coastal spruce forest zone has spread inland in eastern Maine and westward along the coast over the last few thousand years. For example, a pollen core from Moulton Pond (20 km inland from the head of Penobscot Bay and about 50 km north of the Turner Farm) shows an increase in spruce pollen within the last 1,000 years (Davis et. al. 1975). At Ross Pond (Kellogg 1991) on the Pemaquid Peninsula west of Penobscot Bay, spruce pollen begins an increase at 1500 B.P. to a value higher than any since the late Pleistocene.

The intensification of spruce forest cover correlates with the increased ratio of moose to deer kills in archaeological sites. The increase from 2½ to 21 moose killed per 100 deer at the site over 4,000 years reflects the effects of this ecological change at one location. Using the same method of comparing certain moose and deer foot bone frequencies to estimated moose/deer kill ratios from more-or-less contemporaneous Middle Ceramic period sites in Casco Bay (Yesner, personal communication 1980) and Passamaquoddy Bay (Sanger 1987; McCormick 1980), we have demonstrated a striking west-to-east trend in increasing moose to deer ratios: 5 per 100 in Casco Bay, 11 per 100 at the Turner Farm, and 42 per 100 in Passamaquoddy Bay.

In sum, there was an increase in tidal amplitude over time within the Gulf of Maine, although the rate of increase has slowed most substantially over the last 2,500 years. At some point, increasing tidal amplitude would have forced upwelling and substantial tidal mixing within the Gulf. In the absence of substantial upwelling and mixing, surface waters in the Gulf could have warmed appreciably during the summer, and invited Gulf Stream fish into inshore waters. Elimination of the warm surface and inshore water conditions conducive to swordfish and quahogs would require both enough tidal amplitude to mix bottom water upward to the surface, and cold water in the subsurface flow into the Gulf.

The change could have been very rapid if substantial tidal mixing developed slowly while relatively warm water was flowing into the Gulf, then the inflow changed rapidly to colder water. The disappearance of swordfish could, therefore, have been relatively rapid. Increasing tidal amplitude, increasing inshore productivity, and decreasing surface water temperature (especially during summer along the central and eastern Maine coasts) could also account for what appear to be several general trends in faunal change during the Ceramic period.

ECOLOGY AND CULTURE CHANGE

In this section we wish to explore the relationship of culture change to ecological change. This is, as many realize, a proverbial "chicken and egg" dilemma. The Turner Farm site sequence, as described by Bourque (1995), seems to be characterized by relative continuity in culture and economy between Occupation 1 and Occupation 2 over nearly a millennium. There is a dramatic change in culture between Occupation 2 (Moorehead phase) and Occupation 3 (Susquehanna tradition), including a rapid change in stone and bone tool and decorative styles, mortuary behavior, intra-site settlement patterns, and other aspects of culture. Radiocarbon dates at other sites in Maine and the Maritime Provinces suggest that the latest Moorehead phase and earliest Susquehanna occupations may have been either contemporary or seperated by only a century or two. There is certainly a major economic change between the two cultures. The Moorehead phase occupants of the Turner Farm site had distinctly separate seasonal subsistence patterns: terrestrial and tidal zone hunting and collecting in winter and a summer near-shore or offshore fishing season. People may not even have been present on the coast during spring fish runs. The Susquehanna occupants, on the other hand, were primarily terrestrial and tidal zone hunters, collectors and year-round fishermen.

The conclusion, based upon faunal data, that the Susquehanna tradition occupants of the Turner Farm were less maritime-oriented than their predecessors of the Moorehead phase is supported by isotope fractionation studies (Bourque 1995:140; Bourque and Kreuger 1994). In these two references, the Turner Farm skeletal population is composed exclusively of Susquehanna tradition individuals. The Nevin site population is Moorehead phase in origin, and the Crocker site skeletal population dates to the late Middle Ceramic period (1000 to 1200 B.P.). The Nevin site is located in Blue Hill Bay, approximately 40 km northeast of the Turner Farm. The Crocker site is located a few kilometers west of the Turner Farm site, and could well contain the skeletal remains of some of the people who left the Coarse Crushed Shell deposits at the Turner Farm site. Although there is greater isotope ratio variability within the Susquehanna skeletal population than any other population measured, it has a much weaker marine dietary signal than either the Nevin (Moorehead phase) or Crocker site populations.

The transition from the Moorehead phase to the Susquehanna tradition bears further examination. The two cultures were clearly exploiting different economic niches at the Turner Farm site. This difference is also evident in the incomplete congruence in site locations elsewhere in Maine. Both cultural and ecological explanations for this difference are possible, and depend heavily on the unresolved issue of partial contemporanteity or cultural succession. If these cultures were successive and non-overlapping in time, (a model favored by Bourque 1995), then a rapid and dramatic ecological change, such as a major introduction of cold water into Gulf of Maine upwelling, could have caused the Moorehead summer fishery to collapse. Disruption of the summer swordfish fishery may have caused the Moorehead phase occupants either to leave or to radically alter their way of life (Sanger 1975:70–1; Bourque 1995:244–5). Under this scenario, culture change, either population replacement or cultural assimilation, would have followed. Alternatively, perhaps the Susquehanna tradition and Moorehead phase cultures were both present along the coast of the Gulf of Maine for a century or so. Economic differences would have tended to cause niche differentiation, slightly differing settlement patterns, and to constrain the ability of both groups to use the geographic area of coastal and near-coastal areas for a limited time. Such an arrangement would certainly have been unstable, both culturally and ecologically. In sum, while various scenarios of ecological change or cultural competition might account for the disappearance of Moorehead phase culture, it appears that when Susquehanna tradition people occupied the Turner Farm site, there apparently was no great economic (and ecological) incentive for them to adopt any of the distinctive Moorehead phase economic patterns.

Radiocarbon dates of less than 3700 B.P. have recently been obtained on carbonized plum pits from Occupation 3 Feature 18 (Bourque 1995:225; Robinson 1996b: 39). Being annual products, fruit seeds produce dates that are free from uncertainties of those on charcoal, which may include wood of significantly different ages. Moreover, recent dates on Moorehead phase burials at the Nevin site of about 3800 B.P. (Robinson 1996a: 122–124) confirm virtually contemporaneous Moorehead phase occupation of the Turner Farm area. Therefore, Bourque (1995:243–254) feels that the difference in economy between the Moorehead phase and Susquehanna tradition is the result of population replacement and niche differentiation between cultures in contact and rejects the possibility that the period between about 3700 and 3800 B.P. is a node of rapid change in a course of punctuated equilibrium.

A diversity of opinion currently exists in Maine concerning the later half of the fourth millennium (3500 to 3000 B.P.).

Certainly there is a major change in material culture, especially the organization of production of broadspear stone bifaces between the first and second half of the millennium. Moreover, the number of recognizable components in Maine decreased dramatically after the broadspear technology disappears. In southern New England the Susquehanna tradition undergoes a clear subsequent evolution (Dincauze 1968, 1972, 1975) einding with the Orient phase-like material (Ritchie 1980). Bourque (1995:253–254) sees an end to the Susquehanna tradition in Maine about 3400 B.P. Spiess and others (Petersen 1995), however, prefer to consider the Susquehanna tradition as continuing to about 3000 B.P., recognizing some continuation of material culture influence in the face of an admittedly drastic decline in the number of recognized components.

In a sense, this is mostly a semantic disagreement. Recent years of archaeological survey in Maine have discovered three sites with components associated with radiocarbon dates of 3200 or 3100 B.P.: Smith site (Petersen 1991, 1995:221), Little Ossipee North site (Will et al. 1996), and Fort Halifax (Spiess, unpublished). In fact, the Turner Farm also contains some material from this late fourth millennium period, associated with charcoal dates of 3185+65 (SI 4244) and 3280+150 (SI 4243) obtained from the Below Second Gravel Floor stratum (Bourque 1995:263). Perhaps in keeping with the sparse evidence of occupation for this period elsewhere in Maine, this portion of the Turner Farm stratigraphy is least differentiated. In any case, the economy of Turner Farm Occupation 3 inhabitants starts a seemingly directional change back toward a more maritime economy during Occupation 4, but an economy focusing much more upon inshore fish and a greater diversity of species than during Occupation 2.

There were evidently no sudden changes in technology, and only gradual change in social organization and general economy within the Ceramic period in Maine until just before the arrival of Europeans. Most of the economic (faunal) trends in the Occupation 4 sequence fit a two-fold hypothesis: 1) environmental change, primarily increasing tidal amplitude and cooling, increasing fish, seal and bird biomass in the intertidal and near-shore zone, and changes in the near-shore forest; 2) while at the same time, human population grew and put increasing pressure on the available resources. This pressure includes some increase in economic breadth, adding a few species of fish and furbearers to the list of prey. But primarily the increasing pressure fell on major species already being exploited, for example broadening the seasonality of seal hunting. Perhaps in conjunction was a gradual change from habitats favoring deer to those favoring moose, thus increasing demographic pressure on the deer herd. The only change we see during the Occupation 4 sequence that seems to be culturally driven, i.e., without a proximate ecological cause, is an intensification of trapping or hunting of a few species of furbearers, primarily the sea mink. Butchery patterns indicate that these animals were sought for their pelts, and they may have been a valued trade item with a geographically limited source area. The cause of this intesification may be an increase in regional trade involving furs and other commodities, many of which are not preserved archaeologically. Such a trend toward increasing trade would have had consequences for social organization which are best discussed using data from other sites, for example the Goddard site (Bourque and Cox 1981; Spiess et al. 1983).

As is so often the case, major new archaeological data open new avenues of inquiry without being able to take us far along them. The Turner Farm fauna have given us a whole new perspective on Late Archaic and Ceramic period coastal economy. Other types of data, as well as faunal remains from other sites, must now be examined to broaden the horizons of inquiry.

References

Aikens, C. Melvin, Kenneth M. Ames, and David Sanger 1986. Affluent Collectors at the Edges of Eurasia and North America: Some Comparisons and Observations on the Evolution of Society among North-Temperate Coastal Hunter-Gatherers. In *Prehistoric Hunter-Gatherers in Japan: New Research Method*, edited by Takeru Akazawa and C. Melvin Aikens, pp. 3-26. University of Tokyo Press.

Alexander, Maurice M. 1960. Dentition as an Aid in Understanding Age Composition of Muskrat Populations. *Journal of Mammalogy* 41:336-342.

Allen, Arthur W. 1983. Habitat suitability index models: mink. Department of the Interior, Fish and Wildlife Service. FWS/OBS- 821/10.61. Washington, D.C.

Almquist-Jacobson, Heather, and David Sanger 1995. Holocene Climate and Vegetation in the Milford Drainage Basin, Maine, U.S.A., and Their Implications for Human History. *Vegetation History and Archaeobotany* 4:211-222.

Amorosi, Thomas 1991. The vertebrate archaeofauna from the Old Lyme shell heap site: biogeographical/subsistence model for Late Woodland coastal southern New England. In *The Archaeology and Ethnohistory of the Lower Hudson Valley and Neighboring Regions: Essays in Honor of Louis A. Brennan*, edited by Herbert C. Kraft, pp. 95-123. *Occasional Publications in Northeastern Anthropology* 11, Archaeological Services, Bethlehem, Connecticut.

Amos, Carl Leonetto 1978. The postglacial evolution of the Minas basin, Nova Scotia: a sedimentological interpretation. *Journal of Sedimentary Petrology* 1978:965-981.

Anonymous 1622. A Relation or Journal of the Beginning and Proceedings of the English Plantation settled at Plimouth in New England. Redex Microprint Corporation, 1966.

Appelget, J. and L. L. Smith, Jr. 1950. The determination of age and rate of growth from vertebrae of the channel catfish. *American Fisheries Society Transaction* 80:119-139.

Apollonio, Spencer 1979. *The Gulf of Maine.* Courier of Maine, Rockland.

Armstrong, Joe C. W. 1987. *Champlain.* McMillan of Canada, Toronto, Ontario.

Bagenal, T. B., editor 1974. *Ageing of Fish.* Unwin Brothers, Ltd. Surry, England.

Banasiak, Chester F. 1961. *Deer in Maine.* Game Division Bulletin No. 6. Maine Department of Inland Fisheries & Game, Augusta.

Barber, Russel J. 1982. *The Wheeler's Site: A Specialized Shellfish Processing Station on the Merrimack River.* Peabody Museum Monographs No 7., Harvard University, Cambridge.

Barber, Russel J. 1983. Diversity in shell middens: The view from Morrill Point. *Man in the Northeast* 25:109-125.

Bardack, J. E. 1955. The opercular bone of the yellow perch Perca flavescens as a tool for age and growth studies. *Copeia* 55:91- 98.

Baron, W. R., D. C. Smith, H. W. Borns, Jr., J. Pastook, and A. E. Bridges 1980. *Long-term Series Temperature and Precipitation Records for Maine, 1808-1978.* Life Sciences and Agriculture Experiment Station Bulletin 771, University of Maine at Orono.

Bartlett, Grant A. and Linda Molinsky 1972. Foraminifera and the Holocene history of the Gulf of St. Lawrence. *Canadian Journal of Earth Sciences* 9:1204-1215.

Behrend, Donald F. 1967-8. The deer's year. *Maine Fish and Wildlife*, Augusta.

Belcher, William R. 1988. Archaeological Investigations at the Knox Site (30-21), East Penobscot Bay, Maine. Master of Science Thesis, University of Maine at Orono.

Belcher, William R. 1989a. The Archaeology of the Knox Site, East Penobscot Bay, Maine. *The Maine Archaeological Society Bulletin* 29:1:33-46.

Belcher, William R. 1989b. Prehistoric Fish Exploitation in East Penobscot Bay, Maine: The Knox Site and Sea-Level Rise. *Archaeology of Eastern North America* 17:175-191.

Belknap, Daniel. 1995. Geoarchaeology in Central Coastal Maine. Appendix 5, pp. 275-296 in *Diversity and Complexity in Prehistoric Maritime Societies: A Gulf of Maine Perspective*, by Bruce J. Bourque. Plenum Press, New York.

Belknap, Daniel F., Joseph T. Kelley, and R. Craig Shipp 1987. Quaternary stratigraphy of representative Maine estuaries; initial examination by high-resolution seismic reflection profiling. In *Glaciated Coasts*, edited by Duncan M. Fitzgerald and Peter S. Rosen, pp. 117-207. Academic Press, San Diego.

Belknap, Daniel F, R. Craig Shipp, Robert Stuckenrath, Joseph T. Kelley, and Harold W. Borns, Jr. 1989. Holocene sea-level change in coastal Maine. In *Neotechtonics of Maine: Studies in Seismicity, Crustal Warping, and Sea Level Change*, edited by Walter A. Anderson and Harold W. Borns, Jr. Maine Geological Survey, Augusta.

Bellrose, Frank C. 1976. *Ducks, Geese and Swans of North America.* The Stackpole Co., Harrisburg, Pa., & Wildlife Management Institute, Washington, D.C.

Benn, D. W. 1974. Annuli in the dental cementum of white-tailed deer from archaeological context. *Wisconsin Archaeologist* 55:91-98.

Bengtson, Sven-Axel 1984. Breeding Ecology and Extinction of the Great Auk *(Pinguinus impennis)*: Anecdotal Evidence and Conjectures. *The Auk* 101:1-12.

Benson, Adolph 1937. *Peter Kalm's Travels in North America (The English Version of 1770)*. Wilson-Erickson, Inc., New York.

Bernstein, David J. 1988. *Prehistoric Subsistence at Greenwich Cove, Rhode Island.* Ph.D. dissertation, Department of Anthropology, State University of New York, Binghamton.

Bernstein, David J. 1993. *Prehistoric Subsistence on the Southern New England Coast: The Record from Narragansett Bay.* Academic Press, San Diego.

Bierman, Donald G. 1975. *Expert Mink and Coon Trapping.* Revised Second edition. Copyright by the author.

Bigelow, Henry B. and William C. Schroeder 1953. *Fishes of the Gulf of Maine.* Fishery Bulletin of the U. S. Fish and Wildlife Service, Volume 53.

Binford, Lewis R. 1978. *Nunamiut Ethnoarchaeology.* Academic Press, New York.

Black, David W. 1983. What Images Return: A Study of the Stratigraphy and Seasonality of a Small Shell Midden in the West Isles of New Brunswick. M.A. Thesis, Department of Anthropology, McMaster University.

Black, David W. 1985. *Living in Bliss: An Introduction to the Archaeology of the Bliss Islands Group, Charlotte County, New Brunswick.* Manuscript in Archaeology 8, New Brunswick Department of Tourism, Recreation and Heritage, Fredericton.

Black, David W. 1986. What Images Return: A Study of Stratigraphy and Seasonality of a Shell Midden in the Insular Quoddy Region of New Brunswick. Unpublished Manuscript, Department of Tourism, Recreation and Heritage, Fredericton, New Brunswick.

Black, David W. 1992. *Living Close to the Ledge: Prehistoric Human Ecology of the Bliss Islands, Quoddy Region, New Brunswick, Canada. Occasional Papers in Northeastern Archaeology No. 6.* Copetown Press, Dundas, Ontario.

Black, David W. and Ruth Holmes Whitehead 1988. Prehistoric shellfish preservation and storage on the Northeast Coast. *North American Archaeologist* 9:17- 30.

Blalock, Herbert M. 1960. *Social Statistics.* McGraw Hill, London and New York.

Blanchard, Harold M. 1966. The river otter. *Maine Fish and Game* Winter, 1965/66.

Bloom, William, Margaret A. Bloom, and Franklin C. McLean 1941. Calcification and ossification: medullary bone changes in the reproductive cycle of female pigeons. *The Anatomical Record* 81:443-466.

Boise, C. M. 1975. Skull measurements as criteria for ageing fishers. *New York Fish and Game Journal* 22:32-37.

Bonner, W. N. 1971. An aged grey seal *(Halichoerus grypus). Notes from the Mammal Society* 22:261-262.

Bonnichsen, Robson and David Sanger 1977. Integrating faunal analysis. *Canadian Journal of Archaeology* 1:109-133.

Boulva, J. and I. A. McLaren 1979. *Biology of the Harbor Seal, Phoca vitulina in eastern Canada.* Fisheries Research Board of Canada Bulletin 200.

Bourque, Bruce J. 1975. Comments on the Late Archaic Populations of Central Maine. *Arctic Anthropology* 12(2):35-45.

Bourque, Bruce J. 1976. The Turner Farm Site: A Preliminary Report. *Man in the Northeast* 11:21-30.

Bourque, Bruce J. 1992. *Prehistory of the Central Maine Coast.* Garland Publications, New York.

Bourque, Bruce J. 1995. *Diversity and Complexity in Prehistoric Maritime Societies: A Gulf of Maine Perspective.* Plenum Press, New York.

Bourque, Bruce J. 1996. On misguided methodology: A response to Dincauze. *The Review of Archaeology.* 17:1:50-54. (Published 1997.)

Bourque, Bruce J. and Steven Cox 1981 Maine State Museum investigation of the Goddard site, 1979. *Man in the Northeast* 22:3-27.

Bourque, Bruce J. and Harold W. Kreuger 1994. Dietary reconstruction from human bone isotopes for five coastal New England populations. In *Paleonutrition: The Diet and Health of Prehistoric Americans,* edited by Kristin D. Sobolik, pp.125-209. Center for Archaeological Investigations, Occasional Paper No. 22. Southern Illinois University, Carbondale.

Bourque, Bruce J., Kenneth Morris, and Arthur Spiess 1978. Determining the season of death of mammal teeth from archaeological sites: a new sectioning technique. *Science* 199:530-531.

Bourque, Bruce J. and Arthur E. Spiess 1980. Final Report to the National Science Foundation: Fox Islands Archaeological Project, Analysis of Faunal Remains. Manuscript on file, Maine Historic Preservation Commission, Augusta.

Bradford, William. 1953. *Of Plymouth Plantation 1620-1647.* Alfred A. Knopf, New York.

Bradley, James W. and Arthur E. Spiess 1994. Two Shell Middens on Indian Neck, Wellfleet, Massachusetts: The Excavations of Fred A. Luce. *Bulletin of the Massachusetts Archaeological Society* 55:2:45-59.

Burns, James A. 1970. Accounts of Faunal Material from Three Shell Midden Sites near St. Andrew's, New Brunswick. Manuscript report on file, Archaeological Survey of Canada, National Museum of Canada.

Byers, Douglas S. 1979. *The Nevin Shellheap: Burials and Observations.* Papers of the Robert S. Peabody Foundation for Archaeology 9. Andover, Massachusetts.

Cameron, Austin W. 1970. Seasonal movements and diurnal activity rhythms of the Grey seal *(Halichoerus grypus). Journal of Zoology* 161:15-23. London.

Cannon, Debbi Yee 1987. *Marine Fish Osteology: a Manual for Archaeologists.* Publication no. 18, Department of Archaeology. Archaeology Press, Simon Fraser University, Burnaby, British Columbia

Carlson, Catherine 1986. Maritime Catchment Areas: An Analysis of Prehistoric Fishing Strategies in the Boothbay Region of Maine. Masters of Science Thesis, Quaternary Studies, University of Maine at Orono.

Carlson, Catherine 1988. An evaluation of fish growth annuli for the determination of seasonality in archaeological sites. In R. Esmee Webb, ed. *Recent Developments in Environmental Analysis in Old and New World Archaeology.* BAR International Series 416:67-78.

Carlson, Catherine 1990. Seasonality of Fish Remains from Locus Q-6 of the Quidnet Site, Nantucket Island, Massachusetts. *Mass-achusetts Archaeological Society Bulletin* 51:2-14.

Casselman, John M. 1974. Analysis of hard tissue of pike (Esox lucius L.) with special reference to age and growth. In T. B. Bagenal (ed.). *Ageing of Fish*, pp. 13-27. Unwin Brothers, Ltd. Surry, England.

Casteel, Richard 1972a. Some biases in the recovery of archaeological faunal remains. *Proceedings of the Prehistoric Society* 38:382- 388.

Casteel, Richard 1972b. Some Archaeological Uses of Fish Remains. *American Antiquity* 37:404-419.

Casteel, Richard 1974A. Method for Estimation of Live Weight of Fish from the Size of Skeletal Elements. *American Antiquity* 39:94-98.

Champlain, Samuel de 1929. *The Works of Samuel de Champlain,* edited by H. P. Biggar. The Champlain Society, Toronto. {1603-1632}

Chase,Thomas H. P. 1986. Shell Midden Seasonality Using Multiple Faunal Indicators: Applications to the Archaeology of Boothbay, Maine. Masters of Science Thesis, Quaternary Studies, University of Maine at Orono.

CHOMAP Members 1988. Climatic changes of the last 18,000 years: observations and model simulations. *Science* 241:1043-1052.

Claasen, Cheryl 1988. Shellfishing seasons in the prehistoric southeastern United States. *American Antiquity* 51:21-37.

Claasen, Cheryl 1990. The Shell Seasonality Technique in the Eastern United States: A Reply to Lightfoot and Cerrato. *Archaeology of Eastern North America* 18:75-87.

Clifford, Harold B. 1974. Charlie York: *Maine Coast Fisherman.* International Marine Publishing Company, Camden, Maine.

Conkling, Philip W. 1995. *From Cape Cod to the Bay of Fundy: An Environmental Atlas of the Gulf of Maine.* The MIT Press, Cambridge, Massachusetts.

Cole, Sarah 1993. Terrestrial Mammal Survey of Isle au Haut, Maine. *Maine Naturalist* 1:161-168

Cornell, Chris 1982.Harpooning swordfish on George's Banks. *National Fisherman* January, 1982: 12 ff.

Coulter, Malcolm W. 1974. Maine's black cat. *Maine Fish and Game* Summer, 1974.

Cox, Steven L. 1983. Blue Hill Bay Survey. *The Maine Archaeological Society Bulletin* 25(2):21-30.

Cox, Steven L. 1991. Site 95.20 and the Vergennes Phase in Maine. *Archaeology of Eastern North America* 19:135-162.

Cox, Steven L. 1992. Report on the 1992 Site 95.18 Survey. Report on file, Maine Historic Preservation Commission, Augusta.

Cox, Steven L., and Diane Kopec 1988. Archaeological Investigation of the Watson Site, Frenchman Bay. *The Maine Archaeological Society Bulletin* 28(1):38-45.

Dansgaard, W., H. B. Clausen, N. Gundestrup, C. U. Hammer, S. F. Johnsen, P. M. Kristinsdottir, and N. Reeh 1982. A New Greenland Deep Ice Core. *Science* 218:1273-1277.

Dasmann, William. 1971. *If Deer Are to Survive.* Stackpole Books, Harrisburg, Pennsylvania.

Davis, Margaret B., Ray W. Spear, and Linda C. K. Shane 1980. Holocene Climate of New England. *Quaternary Research* 14:240-250.

Davis, Ronald B., Theodore Bradstreet, Robert Stuckenrath, Jr., and Harold W. Borns, Jr. 1975. Vegetation and associated environments during the past 14,000 years near Moulton Pond, Maine. *Quaternary Research* 5:435-465.

Davis, Stephen A. 1978. *Teacher's Cove: A Prehistoric Site on Passamaquoddy Bay.* New Brunswick Archaeology, Series 1, Number 1. Historical Resources Administration, Fredericton.

Denys, Nicholas 1908. *The Description and Natural History of the Coasts of North America (Acadia).* Translated and edited by William F. Ganong. The Champlain Society, Toronto. [1672].

Dincauze, Dena F. 1968. *Cremation Cemeteries in Eastern Massachusetts.* Papers of the Peabody Museum of Archaeology and Ethnology 59:2. Harvard University, Cambridge, Massachusetts.

Dincauze, Dena F. 1972. The Atlantic Phase: A Late Archaic culture in Massachusetts. *Archaeology of Eastern North America* 4:40- 61.

Dincauze, Dena F. 1975. The Late Archaic period in southern New England. *Arctic Anthropology* 12(2):23-34.

Dincauze, Dena F. 1996. Deconstructing shell middens in New England. *The Review of Archaeology.* 17:1:45-50. (Published 1997.)

Dodds, D. G. 1974. Distribution, habitat and status of moose in the Atlantic Provinces of Canada and Northeastern United States. *Naturaliste Canadien* 101:51-65.

Drolet, Charles A. 1976. Distribution and movements of white-tailed deer in southern New Brunswick in relation to environmental factors. *Canadian Field Naturalist* 90:123-136.

Dunstone, N. and J. D. S. Burks 1987.The feeding ecology of mink *(Mustela vison)* in coastal habitat. *Journal of Zoology* 212:69-83. London.

Elder, William H. 1965. Primeval deer hunting pressures revealed by remains from American Indian middens. *Journal of Wildlife Management* 29:366-370.

Eldridge, Stuart A. 1990. Ceramic Period Occupation of the Central Maine Coast: Hunter-Gatherer Estuarine Adaptations in the St. George River Drainage. Ph.D. dissertation, Department of Anthropology, University of Pennsylvania.

Errington, Pual. 1963. *Muskrat Populations.* The Iowa University Press. Ames, Iowa.

Faulkner, Alaric 1985. Archaeology of the cod fishery: Damariscove Island. *Historical Archaeology* 19:2:58-86.

Galtsoff, P. 1952. Staining of growth rings in the vertebrae of tuna. *Copeia* 1952:103-5.

Gehrels, W. Roland, Daniel F. Belknap, Bryan R. Pearce, and Bin Gong 1995. Modeling the contribution of M2 tidal amplification to the Holocene rise of mean high water in the Gulf of Maine and the Bay of Fundy. *Marine Geology* 124:71-85.

Gibbs, Harold C. 1994. Meningeal Worm Infection in Deer and Moose. *Maine Naturalist* 2:71-80.

Gibson, Charles Dana. 1981. History of the Swordfishery of the Northwestern Atlantic. *The American Neptune* January 1981:36-65. Peabody Museum, Salem, Massachusetts.

Gifford, Diane P. and Diana C. Crader 1977A. Computer Coding System for Archaeological Faunal Remains. *American Antiquity* 42:225-238.

Gilbert, Frederick. 1969. The life of the white-tail. *Maine Fish and Game* Augusta, Summer, 1969.

Gramly, Richard Michael 1977. Deerskins and hunting territories: competition for a scarce resource of the Northeastern Woodlands. *American Antiquity* 42:601-605.

Grant, D. R. 1970. Recent coastal submergence of the Maritimes provinces, Canada. *Canadian Journal of Earth Sciences* 7:676-689.

Grant, George Monro 1882. *Picuresque Canada: The Country as It Was and Is*. Volume II. Belden Brothers, Toronto.

Grayson, Donald K. 1984. *Quantitative Zooarchaeology: Topics in the Analysis of Archaeological Faunas*. Academic Press, Orlando.

Grieve, Symington 1885. *The Great Auk or Garefowl (Alca impennis L.): Its History, Archaeology, and Remains*. Thomas C. Jack, London.

Grue, Helen and Birger Jensen 1979. Review of the formation of incremental lines in tooth cementum of terrestrial mammals. *Danish Review of Game Biology* 11:3, 48 pp. Ronde, Denmark.

Gudger, Eugene Willis 1940. The alleged pugnacity of the swordfish and the spearfishes as shown by their attacks on vessels. (A study of their behavior and the structures which make possible these attacks). Royal Asiatic Society of Bengal, Calcutta. Memoirs of the Royal Asiatic Society of Bengal. Vol. 12, no. 2.

Guggesberg, C. A. W. 1975. *Wild Cats of the World*. Taplinger Publishing, New York.

Hall, Eugene R. and Keith R. Kelson 1959. *The Mammals of North America*. Ronald Press, New York.

Hamilton, Nathan D. 1985. Maritime Adaptation in Western Maine; The Great Diamond Island Site. Ph.D. dissertation, Department of Anthropology, University of Pittsburgh.

Hamilton, Nathan D. 1992. Final Report for Northeast Casco Bay and Casco Bay Intensive Site Survey: 1988 and 1989. Report on file, Maine Historic Preservation Commission, Augusta.

Hamilton, William J., Jr., and John O. Whitaker, Jr. 1979. *Mammals of the Eastern United States*, Second Edition. Cornell University Press, Ithaca, New York.

Hardy, Manly 1903. The extinct mink from the Maine shell heaps. *Forest and Stream* 61:125.

Hawkins, E. and D. Klimstra 1970A. preliminary study of the social organization of white-tailed deer. *Journal of Wildlife Management* 34:2.

Hilson, Simon 1986. *Teeth*, Cambridge University Press, New York.

Hinckley, Horace 1969. Mystery of the Hinckley Deer. *Outdoor Life* August, 1969: 44ff.

Hodgdon, Kenneth W. And John H. Hunt 1966. *Beaver Management in Maine*. Department of Inland Fisheries and Wildlife, Augusta, Maine. Final Report of Federal Aid to Wildlife Restoration Project 9-R.

Horton, D. R. 1984. Minimum numbers: a consideration. *Journal of Archaeological Science* 11:255-271.

Howley, James P. 1915. *The Beothucks or Red Indians: The Aboriginal Inhabitants of Newfoundland*. Cambridge University Press, Cambridge.

Hugie, Roy D. 1974/5. Black bear. *Maine Fish and Wildlife* Winter, 1974/5.

Hunt, John H. 1974. The little-known lynx. *Maine Fish and Game* Spring, 1974.

Jackson, Lawrence 1974. The carrying capacity of the deer range in the town of Malone. *New York Fish and Game Journal* 21:47-57.

Johnson, Frederick 1942. *The Boylston Street Fishweir*. Papers of the Robert S. Peabody Foundation for Archaeology. Number Two. Andover, Massachusetts.

Jordan, Richard and Storrs L. Olson 1982. First record of the Great Auk *(Pinguinus impennis)* from Labrador. *Auk* 99:167-168.

Josselyn, John. 1998. *An Account of Two Voyages to New England*. University of New England, Hanover and London (1674).

Kay, Marvin. 1974. Dental annuli age determination on white-tailed deer from archaeological sites. *Plains Anthropologist* 19:224.

Keene, Fred W. 1929. "Clarence H. Clark of Lubec is possessor of only known specimen of extinct sea mink." *Portland Sunday Telegram* May 26, 1929.

Kelley, Joseph T. 1987. An inventory of coastal environments and classification of Maine's glaciated shoreline. In *Glaciated Coasts*, edited by Duncan M. Fitzgerald and Peter S. Rosen, pp. 151-176. Academic Press, San Diego.

Kellogg, Douglas C. 1984. Site Survey and Settlement Pattern Analysis of the Muscongus/St. George Region of the Maine Coast. Report on file, Maine Historic Preservation Commission, Augusta.

Kellogg, Douglas C. 1985. 1984 Survey, Testing and Shore Studies in Western Muscongus Bay. Report on file, Maine Historic Preservation Commission, Augusta.

Kellogg, Douglas C. 1991. *Prehistoric Landscapes, Paleoenvironments, and Archaeology of Western Muscongus Bay, Maine*. Ph.D. dissertation, University of Maine, Orono.

Kelsall, John P. and William Prescott 1971. *Moose and deer behavior in snow*. Canadian Wildlife Service Report Series #15.

Kent, Brett 1988. *Making Dead Oysters Talk.* Maryland Historical Trust, Historical Saint Mary's City.

Kerber, Jordan E. 1984. Prehistoric Human Occupation and Changing Environment of Potowomut Neck, Warwick, Rhode Island: An Interdisciplinary Approach. Ph.D. dissertation, Department of Anthropology, Brown University.

Kerber, Jordan E. 1984/5. Digging for Clams: Shell Midden Analysis in New England. *North American Archaeologist* 6(2):97-113.

Kerber, Jordan E. 1997a. *Lambert Farm: Public Archaeology and Canine Burials Along Narragansett Bay.* Harcourt, Brace and Company, Orlando, Florida.

Kerber, Jordan E. 1997b. Native American Treatment of Dogs in Northeastern North America: Archaeological and Ethnohistorical Perspectives. *Archaeology of Eastern North America* 25:81-96.

Kerber, Jordan E., Alan D. Leveillee, and Ruth L. Greenspan 1989. An Unusual Dog Burial Feature at the Lambert Farm site, Warwick, Rhode Island: Preliminary Observations. *Archaeology of Eastern North America* 17:165-174.

King, Judith 1964. *Seals of the World.* British Museum of Natural History, London.

Klein, Richard G. and Katheryn Cruz-Uribe 1984. *The Analysis of Animal Bones from Archaeological Sites.* University of Chicago Press, Chicago.

Klein, Richard G., Cornelia Wolf, Leslie G. Freeman, and Katheryn Allwarder 1981. The use of dental crown heights from constructing age profiles of red deer and similar species in archaeological samples. *Journal of Archaeological Science* 8:1-31.

Knight, Ora Willis 1908. *The Birds of Maine.* Charles H. Glass Company, Bangor.

Koike, Hiroko 1980. *Seasonal dating by growth-line counting of the clam, Merectrix lusoria: toward a reconstruction of prehistoric shell collecting activities in Japan.* The University Museum, University of Tokyo Bulletin 18. 104 pp.

Koike, Hiroko and Noriyuki Ohtaishi 1985. Prehistoric hunting pressure estimated by the age composition of excavated Sika deer (Cervus nippon) using the annual layer of tooth cement. *Journal of Archaeological Science* 14:251-269.

Koike, Hiroko and Noriyuki Ohtaishi 1987. Estimation of prehistoric hunting rates based on the age composition of Sika deer *(Cervus nippon). Journal of Archaeological Science* 14:251-269.

Lazzari, Mark, John O'Herron II, and Robert Hastings 1986. Occurrence of juvenile Atlantic Sturgeon, *Acipenser oxyrhynchus,* in the upper tidal Delaware River. *Estuaries* 9:356-361.

Leach, B. Foss 1979. Maximizing minimum numbers: avian remains from the Workpool Midden site. In Atholl Anderson, ed. *Birds of a Feather.* New Zealand Archaeological Association Monograph II.

Leach, Douglass 1977. The descriptive and comparative postcranial osteology of marten *(Martes americana Turton)* and fisher *(Martes pennanti Erxleben)*: the appendicular skeleton. *Canadian Journal of Zoology* 55:199-214.

LeClercq, Chrestien 1910. *New Relation of Gaspesia: With the Customs and Religion of the Gaspesian Indians.* Translated and edited by William F. Ganong. The Champlain Society, Toronto.

Lewall, E. F. and I. McT. Cowan 1963. Age Determination in blacktail deer by degree of ossification of the epiphyseal plate in the longbones. *Canadian Journal of Zoology* 41:629-636.

Lewis, Robert A. 1990. Site 95.20, The Narrows: Faunal Report on a Vergennes Phase Site. Manuscript on file, Maine State Museum, Augusta.

Lieberman, Daniel 1993. Life History Variables Preserved in Dental Cementum Microstructure. *Science* 261:1162-1164.

Limpert, R. J. and S. L. Earnst 1994. Tundra Swan. In *The Birds of North America* 89. Edited by A. Poole and F. Gill. The Academy of Natural Sciences, Philadelphia

Little, Elizabeth A. and J. Clinton Andrews. 1982. Drift Whales at Nantucket: the Kindness of Mosup. *Man in the Northeast* 23:17-38.

Lockley, R. M. 1966. *Grey Seal, Common Seal.* Octoberhouse, New York.

Lockwood, G. R. 1972. Further studies of dental annuli for aging white-tailed deer. *Journal of Wildlife Management* 36:46-55.

Loomis, F. B. 1911. A new mink from the shell heaps of Maine. *American Journal of Science* 34:227-229.

Luedtke, Barbara E. 1980. The Calf Island site and the late prehistoric period in Boston Harbor. *Man in the Northeast* 20:25-76.

Lumsden, H. G. 1984. The pre-settlement breeding distribution of Trumpeter, *Cygnus buccinator*, and Tundra swans, *C. columbianus*, in eastern Canada. *Canadian Field Naturalist* 98:415-424.

Lutz, Richard A. and Donald C. Rhoads 1980. Growth patterns within the molluscan shell. Chapter 6, In *Skeletal Growth of Aquatic Organisms*, edited by Rhoads and Lutz, pp. 203-254. Plenum Publishing.

MacDonald, B. A. and M. L. H. Thomas 1980. Age determination of the soft-shelled clam *Mya arenaria* using shell internal growth lines. *Marine Biology* 58:105-109.

Mack, Karen E. 1994. *Archaeological Investigations at the Todd Site (17-11), Muscongus Bay, Maine.* Master of Science thesis, Institute for Quaternary Studies, University of Maine, Orono.

Maine Department of Inland Fisheries and Wildlife 1990. *Wildlife Division, Research and Management Report 1989.* Augusta, Maine. 49pp.

Mairs, Donald F. and Richard B. Parks 1964. Once common...now gone. *Maine Fish and Game* Spring, 1964:22-24.

Mansfield, Arthur W. 1966. The grey seal in Eastern Canadian waters. *Canadian Audubon Magazine* November-December 1966:159-166.

Mansfield, Arthur W. 1967. *Seals of the arctic and Eastern Canada.* Fisheries Research Board of Canada Bulletin 137.

Marchinton, R. Larry and David H. Hirth 1984. Behavior. In *White-Tailed Deer: Ecology and Management*, edited by Lowell K. Halls, pp. 203-254. Wildlife Management Institute, Washington, D. C.

Marion, M. D. 1949. The use of bones, other than otoliths, in determining the age and growth rate of fishes. *Journal de la Conseil International d'Exploration de la Mer* 16:311-335.

Marzoff, R. C. 1955. Use of pectoral spines and vertebrae for determining age and rate of growth of channel catfish. *Journal of Wildlife Management* 19:243-9.

Mattfield, George F. 1984. Eastern Hardwood and Spruce/Fir Forests. In *White-Tailed Deer: Ecology and Management*, edited by Lowell K. Halls, pp. 305-330. Wildlife Management Institute, Washington, D. C.

McAlpine, Donald 1990. Extralimital records of the Harp Seal. *Maine Mammal Science* 6:248-252.

McCabe, Richard E. and Thomas R. McCabe 1984. Of Slings and Arrows: An Historical Retrospection. In *White-Tailed Deer: Ecology and Management*, edited by Lowell K. Halls, pp. 19-72. Wildlife Management Institute, Washington, D. C.

McCartney, Alan P. and James M. Savelle 1985. Thule Eskimo whaling in the central Canadian arctic. *Arctic Anthropology* 22:37-58.

McCormick James S. 1980. Criteria in archaeological faunal analysis: four Passamaquoddy Bay cases. Unpublished M.S. thesis, University of Maine at Orono.

McKern, W. C. 1939. The Midwestern taxonomic method as an aid to archaeological culture study. *American Antiquity* 4:301-313.

McManamon, Francis P. 1984. *Chapters in the Archaeology of Cape Cod*, I. Cultural Resources Management Study No. 8. North Atlantic Regional Office, National Park Service, Boston.

Mead, Jim I., Arthur Spiess, and Kristin Sobolik 2000. Skeleton of Extinct North American Sea Mink (*Mustela macrodon*). *Quaternary Research* 53: 247-262.

Meister, Waldemar 1951. Changes in histological structure of the long bones of birds during the molt. *The Anatomical Record* 111:1- 14.

Meldgaard, Morten 1988. The great auk, *Pinguinus impennis* (L.) in Greenland. *Historical Biology* 1:145-178.

Monks, Gregory G. 1981. Seasonality studies. In *Advances in Archaeological Method and Theory*: 4th edition by Michael Schiffer, pp. 177-240. Academic Press, New York.

Morse, David 1975. Ecological perspective of coastal Maine: an ethnozoological analysis of the Turner Farm site. Unpublished M.A. Dissertation, Department of Anthropology, Ball State University.

Munson, Patrick 1984. Teeth of juvenile woodchucks as seasonal indicators on archaeological sites. *Journal of Archaeological Science* 11:395-403.

Munyer, Edward 1964. Growth of the appendicular skeleton of the muskrat, *Ondatra zibethecus zibethecus* (Linnaeus). *Transactions of the Illinois State Academy of Sciences* 57(4):243-252.

Nelson, Charles M. n.d. Understanding prehistoric subsistence in New England: the exemplary soft shell clam. In Final report on the archaeological and paleobotanical resources of twelve islands in Boston Harbor, Barbara Luedtke. Unpublished report to the Massachusetts Metropolitan District Commission (circa 1975).

Newall, Carter R. 1983. Growth rates and patterns in the soft-shelled clam (*Mya arenaria*). M.S. dissertation, University of Maine at Orono.

Olson, Storrs L. 1974. A great auk, *Pinguinis,* from the Pliocene of North Carolina (Aves: Alcidae). *Proceedings Biological Society of Washington* 90:690-697.

Palmer, Ralph Simon 1949. *Maine Birds*. Bulletin of the Museum of Comparative Zoology, Harvard University, No. 102. Cambridge, Massachusetts.

Palmer, Ralph Simon 1956. Gray fox in the northeast. *Maine Field Naturalist* 12:3:62-70.

Panella, Giorgio 1971. Fish otoliths: daily growth layers and periodical patterns. *Science* 173:1124-1127.

Payne, S. 1972. Partial recovery and sample bias: the results of some sieving experiments. In Papers in Economic Prehistory, edited by E. S. Higgs, pp 49-64. Cambridge University Press.

Peek, J. M. 1974. A review of moose food habit studies in North America. *Naturaliste Canadien* 101:195-215.

Peers, Barry, and Karl Karlsson 1976. Recovery of a swordfish (*Xiphias gladius*) sword from a fin whale (*Balaenoptera physalis*) killed off the west coast of Iceland. *The Canadian Field Naturalist* 90:492-493.

Penhallow, Samuel 1973. *The History of the Wars of New England with the Eastern Indians.* Corner House Publishers, Williamstown, Massachusetts. {1724}

Perkins, Herbert C., Stanley B. Chenoweth, and Richard W. Langton 1997. The Gulf of Maine Atlatnic Cod Complex: Patterns of Distribtuion and Movement of the Sheepscot Bay Substock. *Bulletin of the National Research Institute of Aquaculture (Japan)*. (In press, spring 1997).

Petersen, James B. 1991. *Archaeological Investigations in the Central Kennebec River Drainage: Phase III Data Recovery at the Smith and Smith's Landing Sites, Somerset County, Maine.* University of Maine at Farmington Archaeology Research Center. Report on file, Maine Historic Preservation Commission, Augusta.

Petersen, James B. 1995. Preceramic Archaeological Manifestations in the Far Northeast: A Review of Recent Research. *Archaeology of Eastern North America* 23:207-230.

Petersen, James B., Nathan D. Hamilton, J. M. Adovasio, and Alan L. McPherron 1984. Netting technology and the antiquity of fish exploitation in Eastern North America. *Mid-Continental Journal of Archaeology* 9:199-225.

Petersen, James B. , Brian S. Robinson, Daniel F. Belknap, James Stark, and Lawrence K. Kaplan 1994. An Archaic and Woodland Period Fishweir Complex in Central Maine. *Archaeology of Eastern North America* 22:197-222.

Peterson, Randolph L. 1955. *North American Moose.* University of Toronto Press.

Peterson, Rolf O., Charles Schwartz and Warren B. Ballard 1983. Eruption patterns of selected teeth in three North American moose populations. *Journal of Wildlife Management* 47:884-888.

Pierard, Jean 1971. Osteology and myology of the Weddell seal *Leptonychotes weddelli*. From William Burt, editor, *Antarctic Pinnepedia*. American Geophysical Union.

Pierson, Elizabeth Cary and Jan Eric Pierson 1981. *A Birder's Guide to the Coast of Maine*. Down East Books, Camden, Maine.

Prentiss, Daniel Webster 1903. Description of an extinct mink from the shell-heaps of the Maine coast. *Proceedings of the U. S. National Museum* 26:887-888.

Purchas, Samuel 1906. English Discoveries and Plantations in New England and Newfoundland. *Hakluytus Posthumus or Purchas His Pilgrimes,* Vol. 19.269-284. James MacLehose and Sons, Glasgow. {1622}

Purdue, James R. 1983. Methods of determining sex and body size in prehistoric samples of white-tailed deer (*Odocoileus virginianus*). *Transactions of the Illinois State Academy of Science* 76:3-4:351-357.

Purdue, James R. 1986. The size of white-tailed deer (*Odocoileus virginianus*) during the Archaic period in central Illinois. In *Foraging, Collecting and Harvesting*, edited by Sarah W. Neusius, pp. 65-66. Southern Illinois University, Center for Archaeological Investigations, Occasional Paper 6. Carbondale.

Quinn, David B. and Alison M. Quinn 1983. *The English New England Voyages 1602-1608*. The Hakluyt Society, London.

Rasmussen, Gerald P., James Powers and Stephen H. Clarke 1982. Relation of mandible length to age and its reliability as a criterion of sex in white-tailed deer. *New York Fish and Game Journal* 29:142-151.

Rice, Leslie A. 1980. Influences of irregular dental cementum layers on ageing deer incisors. *Journal of Wildlife Management* 44:266-268.

Rich, Walter H. 1930. *Fishing Grounds of the Gulf of Maine*. Report U. S. Commissioner of Fisheries for 1929. App. 3, pp. 51-117, 5 maps.

Rich, Walter H. 1947. *The Swordfish and Swordfishery of New England*. Proceedings of the Portland Society of Natural History, vol. 4, pt. 2, 102 pp., 1 chart., Portland, Maine.

Rick, Anne. 1975. Bird medullary bone: a seasonal dating technique. *Canadian Archaeological Association Bulletin* 7:183-190.

Ritchie, William A. 1969. *The Archaeology of Martha's Vineyard*. Natural History Press, Garden City.

Ritchie, William A. 1980. *The Archaeology of New York State*. Harbor Hill Books, Harrision, New York.

Robertson, Ralph A. and Albert R. Shadle 1954. Osteological criteria of age in beavers. *Journal of Mammalogy*, 35:197-203.

Robinson, Brian 1985. *The Nelson Island and Seabrook Marsh Sites*. Occasional Publications in Northeastern Anthropology, No. 9. Franklin Pierce College, Rindge, New Hampshire.

Robinson, Brian 1996a. A Regional Analysis of the Moorehead Burial Tradition: 8500-3700 B.P. *Archaeology of Eastern North America* 24:95-148.

Robinson, Brian 1996b. Archaic Period Burial Patterning in Northeastern North America. *The Review of Archaeology* 17(1):33-44.

Rojo, Alfonso 1986. Live Length and Weight of Cod (*Gadus morhua*) Estimated from Various Skeletal Elements. *North American Archaeologist* 7:329-351.

Rojo, Alfonso 1987. Excavated Fish Vertebrae as Predictors in Bioarchaeological Research. *North American Archaeologist* 8:209-225.

Rojo, Alfonso 1990. Faunal Analysis of Fish Remains from Cellar's Cove, Nova Scotia. *Archaeology of Eastern North America* 18:89-108.

Ross, Michael R. 1990. Swordfish. In *Recreation Fisheries of Coastal New England*, by Michael R. Ross and Robert C. Biagi, pp. 228-232. University of Massachusetts Press, Andover.

Rowe, John Howland 1940. *Excavations in the Waterside Shell Heap, Frenchman's Bay, Maine*. Papers of the Excavator's Club 1(3), Harvard University, Cambridge, Massachusetts.

Sanger, David 1975. Cultural change as an adaptive process in the Maine-Maritimes Region. *Arctic Anthropology* 12(2):60-75.

Sanger, David 1981. Unscrambling messages in the midden. *Archaeology of Eastern North America* 9:37-42.

Sanger, David 1985a. Cultural Ecology in Passamaquoddy Bay. *The Maine Archaeological Society Bulletin* 25(1):10-16.

Sanger, David 1987. *The Carson Site and the Late Ceramic Period in Passamaquoddy Bay, New Brunswick*. Archaeological Survey of Canada Paper No. 135, Mercury Series. Canadian Museum of Civilization.

Sanger, David and Thomas Chase 1983. An Introduction to the Archaeology of the Roque Island Group, Maine. Paper presented to the Canadian Archaeological Association.

Sauer, Peggy R. 1973. Seasonal Variation in Physiology of White-tailed Deer in Relation to Cementum Annulus Formation. Ph. D. dissertation, State University of New York at Albany.

Sauer, Peggy R. 1984. Physical Characteristics. In *White-Tailed Deer: Ecology and Management*, edited by Lowell K. Halls, pp. 73-90. Wildlife Management Institute, Washington, D. C.

Schemnitz, Sanford 1975. Maine island-mainland movements of white-tailed deer. *Journal of Mammalogy* 56:535-537.

Schnitker, Detmar and Julie B. Jorgensen 1990. Late glacial and holocene diatom successions in the Gulf of Maine: response to climatologic and oceanographic change. In *Evolutionary Biogeography of the Marine Algae of the North Atlantic,* edited by D. J. Garbary and G. R. South, pp. 35-53. Springer-Verlag, Heidelberg.

Scott, David B. and David A. Greenberg 1983. Relative sea-level rise and tidal development in the Fundy tidal system. *Canadian Journal of Earth Science* 20: 1554-1564.

Severinghaus, C. W. 1949. Tooth development and wear as criteria of age in white-tailed deer. *Journal of Wildlife Management* 13:195-216.

Shaw, Leslie C. 1994. Improved Documentation in Shell Midden Excavations: An Example from the South Shore of Cape Cod. In *Cultural Resource Manaagement: Archaeological Research, Preservation Planning, and Public Education in the Northeastern United States*, edited by Jordan E. Kerber, pp. 115-138. Bergin and Garvey, Westport, Connecticut.

Sibley, David Allen 2000. *National Audubon Society The Sibley Guide to Birds.* Alfred A. Knopf, Inc. , New York.

Sieur de Diereville. 1933. *Relation of the Voyage to Port Royal in Acadia or New France (1699-1700).* The Champlain Society, Toronto. [1703]

Skinas, David C. 1987. The Todd Site: A Case Study of Shell Midden Formation. Master of Science thesis, Institute for Quaternary Studies, University of Maine at Orono.

Smith, Theodore I. J. 1985. The fishery, biology and management of Atlantic Sturgeon, *Acipenser oxyrhynchus*, in *North America. Environmental Biology of Fishes* 14:61-72.

Smith, Thomas G. 1973. Population Dynamics of the Ringed Seal in the Eastern Canadian Arctic. Fisheries Research Board of Canada Bulletin 181.

Smith, Thomas G. 1987. *The Ringed Seal, Phoca hispida, of the Canadian Western Arctic.* Canadian Bulletin of Fisheries and Aquatic Sciences 216.

Sobolik, Kristin, and D. Gentry Steele 1996. *A Turtle Atlas to Facilitate Archaeological Identifications.* Mammoth Site of Hot Springs, South Dakota.

Speck, Frank G. 1997. *Penobscot Man: The Life History of a Forest Tribe in Maine.* University of Maine Press, Orono.

Spencer, Howard E., Jr. 1966. *The black bear and its status in Maine.* Maine Department of Inland Fisheries and Wildlife, Game Division Bulletin 4.

Spiess, Arthur E. 1976a. Determining season of death of archaeological fauna by analysis of teeth. *Arctic*, 29:53-55.

Spiess, Arthur E. 1976b. Labrador grizzly *(Ursus arctos L.)*: first skeletal evidence. *Journal of Mammalogy* 57:787-790.

Spiess, Arthur E. 1978. Zooarchaeological evidence bearing on the Nain area Middle Dorset subsistence-settlement cycle. *Arctic Anthropology* 15:2.

Spiess, Arthur E. 1979. *Reindeer and Caribou Hunters: An Archaeological Study.* Academic Press, New York. 305 pp.

Spiess, Arthur E. 1984a. Faunal Analysis. In Site Survey and Settlement Pattern Analysis of the Muscongus/St. George Region of the Maine Coast, by Douglas C. Kellogg, pp. 134-150. Report on file, Maine Historic Preservation Commission, Augusta.

Spiess, Arthur E. 1984b. Cape Cod National Seashore Archaeological Survey Faunal Analysis. Manuscript report, on file with Northeast Regional Office, National Park Service, and Maine Historic Preservation Commission, Augusta.

Spiess, Arthur E. 1988. On New England shell middens: response to Sanger's cautionary tale. *American Antiquity* 53:174-177.

Spiess, Arthur E. 1989. Review of Mi'kmaq: Economics and Evolution, Ronald J. Nash and Faunal Remains from the Delorey Island Site (BjCj-9) of Nova Scotia, Frances L. Stewart. *Man in the Northeast* 38:105-108.

Spiess, Arthur E. 1990a. Deer tooth sectioning, eruption, and seasonality of deer hunting in prehistoric Maine. *Man in the Northeast* 39:29-44.

Spiess, Arthur E. 1990b. Summer at Naskeag: Faunal Analysis of the Goddard Assemblage. Revised 1993. Report on file Maine Historic Preservation Commission and the Maine State Museum, Augusta.

Spiess, Arthur E. 1992. Archaic Period Subsistence in New England and the Atlantic Provinces. In *Early Holocene Occupation in Northern New England*, edited by Brian Robinson, James B. Petersen, and Ann K. Robinson, pp. 163-185. Occasional Publications in Maine Archaeology 9, Augusta.

Spiess, Arthur E., Bruce J. Bourque and Steven L. Cox 1983. Cultural Complexity in Maritime Cultures: Evidence from Penobscot Bay, Maine. In *The Evolution of Maritime Cultures on the Northeast and Northwest Coasts of North America*, edited by Ronald J. Nash, pp. 91-108. Publication No. 11, Department of Archaeology, Simon Fraser University.

Spiess, Arthur E. and Steven L. Cox 1976. Discovery of the skull of a grizzly bear in Labrador. *Arctic* 29:194-200.

Spiess, Arthur E. and Stuart A. Eldridge 1985. Cushing/St. George Archaeological Survey 1985. Manuscript report on file, Maine Historic Preservation Commission, Augusta.

Spiess, Arthur E. and Mark H. Hedden 1983. *Kidder Point and Sears Island in Prehistory.* Occasional Publications in Maine Archaeology Number 3. Maine Historic Preservation Commission, Augusta. 103 pp.

Spiess, Arthur E. and Robert A. Lewis 1995. Features and activity areas: the spatial analysis of faunal remains. Appendix 8 in *Diversity and Complexity in Prehistoric Maritime Societies: A Gulf of Maine Perspective*, by Bruce J. Bourque, pp. 337-373. Plenum Press, New York and London.

Spiess, Arthur E. and Kristin D. Sobolik 1997. Blanding's Turtle Specimens from the Turner Farm Archaeological site, North Haven, Maine. *Herpetological Review* 28 (1): 24-25.

Spiess, Arthur E. Spiess, Elizabeth Trautman and Timothy Kupferschmid 1990. Prehistoric Occupation at Reversing Falls. Report on File, Maine Historic Preservation Commission, Augusta.

Stanton, Don C. 1963. *A History of the White-Tailed Deer in Maine.* Game Division Bulletin No. 8. Maine Department of Inland Fisheries and Wildlife, Augusta.

Stewart, Frances L. 1974. Faunal Remains from the Carson Site (BgDr-5) of New Brunswick. Manuscript report on file, Archaeological Survey of Canada, National Museum of Canada.

Stewart, Frances L. 1986. *Faunal Remains from the Delorey Island Site (BjCj-9) of Nova Scotia.* Curatorial Report Number 57, Nova Scotia Museum, Halifax.

Strauss, Alan Edward 1989. A study of prehistoric swordfishing by members of the Moorehead Burial Tradition between 4500 and 3700 B.P.: the exploitation of a dangerous resource and its effects on social status and religion. Master of Arts Thesis, Department of Anthropology, State University of New York at Binghamton.

Strickland, Marjorie, Carman Douglas, Mark Brown, and Gary Parsons 1982. Determining the age of fisher from cementum annuli of the teeth. *New York Fish and Game Journal* 29:1:90-94.

Sumner-Smith, G, P. W. Pennock, and K. Ronald 1972. The Harp seal, *Phagophilus groenlandicus*, (Erxleben, 1777): XVI Epiphyseal Fusion. *Journal of Wildlife Diseases* 8:29-32.

Taylor, T. G. 1970. How an eggshell is made. *Scientific American* 222:2:88-95.

Thwaites, Reuben Gold 1897. *The Jesuit Relations and Allied Documents: Travels and Exploits of the Jesuit Missionaries in New France 1610-1791*. The Burrows Brothers Company, Cleveland.

Tibbo, S. N., L. R. Day and W. Doucet 1961. *The Swordfish (Xiphias gladius L.): Life History and Economic Importance*. Fisheries Research Board of Canada Bulletin 130.

Treganza, A. E. and S. F. Cook 1947/8. The Quantitative investigation of aboriginal sites: complete excavation with physical and archaeological analysis of a single mound. *American Antiquity* 13:287-297.

Trigger, Bruce G. 1981. Webster Versus Champlain. *American Antiquity* 46:520-421.

van Nostrand, F. C. and A. B. Stephanson 1964. Age determination for beavers by tooth development. *Journal of Wildlife Management* 28:3:430-434.

van Soest, R. W. M. and W. L. van Utrecht 1971. The layered structure of bones of birds as a possible indicator of age. *Bijdragen tot de Dierkunde* 41:1:61- 66.

Verme, Louis J. and Duane E. Ullrey 1984. Physiology and Nutrition. In *White-Tailed Deer: Ecology and Management*, edited by Lowell K. Halls, pp. 91-118. Wildlife Management Institute, Washington, D. C.

von den Driesch 1976. *A guide to the measurement of animal bones from archaeological sites*. Peabody Museum Bulletin 1, Cambridge, Massachusetts.

de Vos, Anton 1958. Summer observations on moose behavior in Ontario. *Journal of Mammalogy* 39:128-139.

Walker, Ernest P. 1968. *Mammals of the World*, Second Edition, 2 Vols. Johns Hopkins Press, Baltimore.

Ward, Charles C. 1880. Porpoise-shooting. *Scribner's Monthly* 20:6:801-811.

Waselkov, Gregory A. 1978. Evolution of deer hunting in the eastern Woodlands. *Mid-Continental Journal of Archaeology* 3:15-34.

Wasserman, Maurice Marc 1954. The American Indians as Seen by the Seventeenth Century Chroniclers. Ph.D. dissertation, Department of English Literature, University of Pennsylvania.

Watanabe, H. 1972. *The Ainu Ecosystem*. University of Washington Press, Seattle.

Waters, Joseph H. 1962. Some animals used as food by successive cultural groups in New England. *Bulletin of the Archaeological Society of Connecticut* 31:32-46.

Weber, Andrzej, Olga I. Goriunova, and Aleksandr K. Konopatskii 1993. Prehistoric Seal Hunting on Lake Baikal: Methodology and Preliminary Results of the Analysis of Canine Sections. *Journal of Archaeological Science* 20:629-644.

Webster, Gary S. 1979. Deer hides and tribal confederacies: an appraisal of Gramly's hypothesis. *American Antiquity* 44:816-820.

Webster, Gary S. 1981. Reply to Trigger. *American Antiquity* 46:421-422.

Will, Richard, James Clark, and Edward Moore 1996. Phase III Archaeological Data Recovery at the Little Ossipee North Site (7.7), Bonny Eagle Project (FERC #2529), Cumberland County, Maine. Report on file, Maine Historic Preservation Commission, Augusta.

Williams, Roger 1827. *A Key into the Language of America.* Collection of the Rhode Island Historical Society, Vol. 1. John Miller, Providence. {1643}

Williams, T. and B. C. Bedford 1974. The use of otoliths for age determination. In *The Aging of Fish*, edited by T. B. Bagenal, pp 114-123. Unwin Brothers, England.

Williamson, Kenneth 1948. *The Atlantic Islands: A Study of the Faroe Life and Scene*. Collins, London.

Willoughby, Charles C. 1935. *Antiquities of the New England Indians*. Peabody Museum, Cambridge, Massachusetts.

Winterhalder, Bruce and Eric Alden Smith 1981. *Hunter-gatherer Foraging Strategies*. University of Chicago Press.

Wood, A. J., I. McT. Cowan, and H. C. Norden 1962. Periodicity of growth in ungulates as shown by deer of the genus *Odocoileus*. *Canadian Journal of Zoology* 40:593-603.

Wood, William 1865. *Wood's New England's Prospect*. The Prince Society, Boston. [1634]

Yesner, David 1978. Animal bones and human behavior. *Reviews in Anthropology* Summer, 1978:333-355.

Yesner, David 1980a. Archaeology of Casco Bay: A Preliminary Report. *Maine Archaeological Society Bulletin* 20(1):60-74.

Yesner, David 1980b. Maritime Hunter-Gatherers: Ecology and Prehistory. *Current Anthropology* 21(6):60-74.

Yesner, David 1984. Population pressure in coastal environments: an archaeological test. *World Archaeology* 16:108-127.

Young, Robert S., Daniel F. Belknap, and David A. Sanger 1992. Geoarchaeology of John's Bay, Maine. *Geoarchaeology* 7:209-249.

Zielinski, G. A., P. A. Mayewski, L. D. Meeker, S. Whitlow, M. S. Twickler, M. Morrisson, D. A. Meese, A. J. Gow, and R. B. Alley 1994. Record of vulcanism since 7000 B.C. from the DISP2 Greenland ice core and implications for the volcano-climate system. *Science* 264:948-952.

Index